MW01073507

"From a scholar who sits at the foretront of Bonhoeffer ~~
this book by Peter Frick is an amazing anthology of thought. In
this text, readers encounter a behind-the-scenes look at the work of
translating Bonhoeffer, a thoughtful analysis of the underpinnings
of Bonhoeffer's theology, as well as a constructive extension of
Bonhoeffer's work in recent conversations. An important text for
any student of Bonhoeffer's theology."

> —**REGGIE WILLIAMS**, *Associate Professor of Christian
> Ethics, McCormick Theological Seminary*

"Frick demonstrates how Bonhoeffer's theology affords important
orientations and perspectives that allow us to frame these pressing
penultimate questions Christianly and—precisely thereby—to
approach them humanely."

> —**PHILIP ZIEGLER**, *Chair in Christian Dogmatics,
> University of Aberdeen*

"One of the stellar interpreters of Bonhoeffer's life and work in
our time, Peter Frick's breadth of theological and philosophical
expertise positions him to read Bonhoeffer in an integrative
manner that the field has lacked for too long. These essays are
rigorous, clearly written, and well documented. An excellent
introduction to understanding Bonhoeffer from a scholar who
captures Bonhoeffer's diverse interests and commitments."

> —**MICHAEL PASQUARELLO**, *author of* Dietrich:
> Bonhoeffer and the Theology of a Preaching Life

Peter Frick

Understanding Bonhoeffer

BAYLOR UNIVERSITY PRESS

Originally published as *Understanding Bonhoeffer* by Peter Frick (Mohr Siebeck GmbH & Co. KG Tübingen, 2017) with the ISBN 978-3-16-154723-2. © 2017 Mohr Siebeck Tübingen. www.mohr.de

The ISBN for this 2018 Baylor University Press paperback is 978-1-4813-0900-4.

Cover art by Rachel Sanders
Cover design by Jordan Wannemacher

PETER FRICK, born 1961. Professor of Religious Studies and Academic Dean at St. Paul's University College, University of Waterloo, Canada.

To

Moni

our delightful friend

loving and kind
contemplative and resilient
joyful and spirited
grateful and blessed

Preface

This monograph is a collection of sixteen essays on Dietrich Bonhoeffer (1906–1945) that I wrote between 2007 and 2014. During that time I was a member of the Editorial Board that was responsible for the translation and publication of the German critical edition *Dietrich Bonhoeffer Werke* (*DBW*) into the English standard edition *Dietrich Bonhoeffer Works English* (*DBWE*). This project was carried out under the auspices of the International Bonhoeffer Society in cooperation with Fortress Press. As part of the work of the Editorial Board I became passionately fascinated with the life, ideas and theology of Bonhoeffer. I worked my way methodically through every page of the 16 volumes of *DBW*. Not only did I diligently underline every page as I progressed, I also kept many notes on Bonhoeffer's life and thought. More and more, these notes morphed into a deepening understanding of who Bonhoeffer was and why he developed the unique theology that he did during the difficult years of the Nazi regime. The time commitment, intellectual perseverance and labour necessary to work my way through nearly 10.000 pages of text was daunting – but in the end all worthwhile. I think it is a fair conclusion to say that without encountering Bonhoeffer's thought and life I would not have been able to clarify my own theology and life journey.

Initially, my approach was simply to let his works take hold of my own theological mind, reflect on his ideas, attempt to sort them out and, most of all, arrive at an *understanding* of where he was coming from and what the significance of his theological ideas may be for us contemporary readers. The answers to the question "where did Bonhoeffer come from" are reflected in the section "Backgrounding Bonhoeffer." Similarly, the question of contemporary significance is explored in the section "Foregrounding Bonhoeffer." The bridge between both of these sections is always the either explicit (as in the first three essays) or on the implicit focus on making intelligible Bonhoeffer's thinking.

When I use the term *understanding*, I do so in view of Wilhelm Dilthey's distinction between explanation, to explain a thing (*erklären*) and understanding, to understand a larger context (*verstehen*).[1] This distinction, interestingly, is not the invention of the philosopher Dilthey, but has precursors in both the

---

[1] Cf. Wilhelm Dilthey, "Die Entstehung der Hermeneutik," in Gesammelte Schriften. Stuttgart: B. G. Teubner 1964, vol. 5, 332–336.

Puritan and Pietistic traditions.[2] Explanation and understanding are not necessarily juxtaposed or mutually exclusive ways of approaching a subject matter, in our case, Dietrich Bonhoeffer. They rather point to a hermeneutical dynamic, namely the correlation between particular insights and details within a larger matrix of sense-making and understanding. As I said elsewhere,[3] understanding always implies more than just understanding an author or a text. Precisely by understanding an author and his or her text does the reader encounter a new and deeper level in his or her own self-understanding. In my own case, by wanting to understand the thought of Bonhoeffer I encountered the freshness of his theology to the extent that it impacted my own self-understanding as a person and as a theologian. There is no doubt that the sustained encounter with Bonhoeffer's legendary life and dynamic theology has substantially shaped my own way of thinking and being. Something has happened in that encounter that is irreversible. And this is a good thing.

Given the fact that these essays were all published in various journals and books and followed dissimilar editorial, stylistic and bibliographic conventions, here all of these matters are standardized. Perhaps the most significant change is that all essays are updated to the critical text of the *DBWE*. When I wrote the first essays, many of the *DBWE* volumes were not yet published. In some cases I translated the German text of the *DBW* volumes myself into English, sometimes I used the German text without translation and sometimes I provided the reference to the *DBW* volumes in footnotes. All essays have now been updated and use the text of the *DBWE*. For scholars and readers interested in locating the German text in *DBW* it is quite possible to do so as the *DBWE* volumes have the page number of the corresponding *DBW* volume printed in the margin of each page. Cross-referencing between *DBWE* and *DBW* is thus quite user-friendly.

For the most part, the essays have been slightly revised, stylistically as necessary and at times in terms of content. Since scholarship is dynamic and does not stand still, I could have updated and added bibliographic material in a rather substantive manner. Nevertheless, both in view of keeping to the substance and form of the original essays, I decided to update the essays only sparingly in terms of bibliographic additions. These updates are simply added in the footnotes.

As I was preparing this book and worked my way through the various essays, I realized that there is much overlap between some of the essays. In fact, there is too much overlap for my own liking. However, rather than cutting material that overlaps, I accept that the reason for the overlap has to do with the original

---

[2] Cf. Jens Zimmermann, *Recovering Theological Hermeneutics. An Incarnational-Trinitarian Theory of Interpretation*. Grand Rapids: Baker Academic 2004, 104–107.

[3] Cf. the essay below: "Understanding Bonhoeffer: from Default to Hermeneutic Reading."

occasion of each essay. In other words, all essays have a context-specific history, a *Sitz im Leben*, in the academy and church. Some essays were written out of my early academic interest, others for journals. Yet most were written for particular occasions or invitations to contribute a chapter to a book, conference participation, or requests to present a lecture on Bonhoeffer with a given theme and focus. In some essays language is strictly academic, but in other essays language is deliberately non-academic in view of the audience.

In a sense these essays are like light houses along the sometimes foggy shores of Bonhoeffer's life and theology. The topics studied in these essays tell only a small part of Bonhoeffer's life and theology, but they were important questions to me in my journey through the vast corpus of his oeuvre and secondary literature. These studies helped me to situate Bonhoeffer in my quest for understanding. They do not tell the whole story and make no claims otherwise. I am quite aware of the fact that there is a great deal more of Bonhoeffer's thinking that I have not yet adequately examined and understood. Still, I trust that the reader will be encouraged to find his or her own enthusiasm in encountering Bonhoeffer by reading these essays. If they are of help in this regard, I am more than pleased.

Finally, I would like to thank all the original publishers for the permission to publish these essays again in slightly revised form. My gratitude also to Dr. Henning Ziebritzki, Klaus Hermannstädter, Philipp Henkys and Susanne Mang, Mohr Siebeck, Tübingen, for accepting these essays for publication and for their exemplary support throughout the entire production process. I would also like to thank Carmen Celestini for her work on the indices and her careful reviewing of the manuscript.

Last but not least, my wife and I would like to dedicate these pages with deepest affection to our friend Moni, whom we have known for more than half our lives.

Peter Frick   Waterloo, 29 June 2016

Content

Abbreviations

The Anti-Christ	Nietzsche, Friedrich. *The Anti-Christ, Ecce Homo, Twilight of the Idols, and Other Writings.* Translated by Judith Norman. Edited by Judith Norman and Aaron Ridley. Cambridge: Cambridge University Press, 2005.
Beyond Good Good and Evil	Friedrich Nietzsche. *Beyond Good and Evil.* Translated by Judith Norman. Cambridge: Cambridge University Press, 2002.
CCDB	*The Cambridge Companion to Dietrich Bonhoeffer.* Edited by John de Gruchy. Cambridge: Cambridge University Press 1999.
CCFS	*The Cambridge Companion to Friedrich Schleiermacher.* Edited by Jacqueline Mariña. Cambridge: Cambridge University Press 2006.
CCH	*The Cambridge Companion to Heidegger.* Edited by Charles B. Guignon. Cambridge: Cambridge University Press, second edition 2007.
Daybreak	Nietzsche, Friedrich. *Daybreak. Thoughts on the Prejudices of Morality.* Translated by R.J. Hollingdale. Cambridge: Cambridge University Press 1982.
DBW	*Dietrich Bonhoeffer Werke*, 17 volumes. Chr. Kaiser/Gütersloher Verlagshaus, 1986–1999. See Bibliography for individual volumes.
DBWE	*Dietrich Bonhoeffer Works English*, 17 volumes. Fortress Press, 1996–2014. See Bibliography for individual volumes.
Genealogy	Nietzsche, Friedrich. *On the Genealogy of Morality.* Translated by Carol Diethe. Edited by Keith Ansell-Pearson. Cambridge: Cambridge University Press, 2007.
Human, All too Human	Nietzsche, Friedrich. Human, *All too Human.* Translated by R.J. Hollingdale. Cambridge: Cambridge University Press, 1996.
KSA	Nietzsche, Friedrich. *Kritische Studienausgabe*, 15 volumes. Edited by Giorgio Colli and Mazzino Montinari. Munich: dtv 1980.
PTMS	Princeton Theological Monograph Series.
RGG	*Die Religion in Geschichte und Gegenwart*, fourth edition. Tübingen 2000–2005.
TRE	*Theologische Realenzyklopädie.* Berlin/New York 1977–2004.
WCA	Ronald Gregor Smith (ed). World Come of Age. Philadelphia: Fortress Press 1967.
Zarathustra	Nietzsche, Friedrich. *Thus Spoke Zarathustra.* Translated by Adrian del Caro. Edited by Adrian del Caro and Robert B. Pippin. Cambridge: Cambridge University Press, 2006.
ZNW	*Zeitschrift für die neutestamentliche Wissenschaft.*
ZThK	*Zeitschrift für Theolgie und Kirche.*

Understanding Bonhoeffer

1. Dietrich Bonhoeffer:
Engaging Intellect – Legendary Life

Introduction

Dietrich Bonhoeffer leads the list among the theologians of the 20th century known outside the theological world – ahead of even such eminent thinkers as Karl Barth, Rudolf Bultmann, Paul Tillich, Jürgen Moltmann and Hans Küng. This is not to claim that the general public, or even the Christian public, knows much of Bonhoeffer's theological ideas. For those who have heard of him, Bonhoeffer is known for the fact that he was somehow connected to a circle of conspirators who planned to kill Hitler. But when that plan failed, he and others among the conspirators were murdered in a concentration camp at the end of World War II. In other words, Bonhoeffer is not principally known for his theological insights, but for his resistance to the evil Nazi regime and his death as a martyr. Given such civil courage, more his legacy than his theology made him into a kind of Christian saint or phenomenon.[1]

Nonetheless, the minimalist "knowledge" of Bonhoeffer as a conspirator and martyr amounts to a one-sided and ultimately deficient portrayal of his thought and life. Hence, the objective of this study is to present Bonhoeffer's thought, life and legacy in a succinct, even-handed and responsible manner. In order to achieve this objective, I will proceed as follows: first, I will sketch out the important lines of Bonhoeffer's biography in order to exemplify the dynamic correlation between his theology and actions; second, I will examine the decisive milestones of his theological thinking and development; and third, I will briefly comment on his legacy.

---

[1] Stephen Haynes, *The Bonhoeffer Phenomenon: Portraits of a Protestant Saint.* Minneapolis: Fortress Press 2004.

Bonhoeffer's Life: A Biographical Sketch

Given the vast corpus of secondary literature on Bonhoeffer, a comment on available biographies is in order. The most authoritative biography on Bonhoeffer is that of Eberhard Bethge,[2] Bonhoeffer's closest friend and brother-in-law. As it is written "from within" the Bonhoeffer family circle, this biography is the oldest (originally published in 1967) and most comprehensive biography, regarded by many scholars as the classic work on Bonhoeffer. The recent more popular work by Eric Metaxas,[3] although written in an appealing style, claims Bonhoeffer for a conservative American audience. A good middle-ground between Bethge in terms of length and Metaxas in terms of impartiality are the works of Josef Ackermann[4] and Ferdinand Schlingensiepen.[5] Solid introductions to Bonhoeffer are also the works of Plant[6] and Clements.[7]

The Bonhoeffer Family

Dietrich Bonhoeffer was born in Breslau, then Germany, on 4 February 1906, as the sixth of eight children. In 1912 the family moved to Berlin when his father, Karl Bonhoeffer, was appointed to the prestigious position of psychiatry at the University of Berlin and also as the head of the university hospital Charité. With a quiet but strong personality the father left a deep impression on his children. One of the things Dietrich Bonhoeffer remembers from his father was his distaste for the "phraseological" in favour of the "real." Karl Bonhoeffer's mother, Julie Bonhoeffer, lived with the Bonhoeffer family in the same household. It is said that when the Nazis declared an official boycott of Jewish stores in 1933, the 91 year old woman walked past the SS guards into the Jewish department store *Kaufhaus des Westens* "to demonstrate against this injustice."[8] Paula Bonhoeffer, Dietrich's mother, came from a noble family that was shaped to some degree by

---

[2] Eberhard Bethge, *Dietrich Bonhoeffer. Theologian, Christian, Man of his Time. A Biography*, translated and revised by Victoria Barnett. Minnesota: Fortress Press 2000.

[3] Eric Metaxas, *Bonhoeffer: Pastor, Martyr, Prophet, Spy*. Nashville: Thomas Nelson 2010.

[4] Josef Ackermann, *Dietrich Bonhoeffer – Freiheit hat offene Augen. Eine Biografie.* Gütersloh: Gütersloher Verlag 2006.

[5] Ferdinand Schlingensiepen, *Dietrich Bonhoeffer 1906–1945. Martyr, Thinker, Man of Resistance*, translated by Isabel Best. London/New York: T & T Clark 2010.

[6] Stephen Plant, *Bonhoeffer*. New York: Continuum 2004.

[7] Keith Clements, *Bonhoeffer*. London: SPCK Publishing 2010.

[8] Schlingensiepen, *Bonhoeffer*, 8.

Lutheran pietism. Her father, Dietrich's grandfather, was a chaplain at the court of Emperor Wilhelm II. But when he protested against the Emperor's description of the proletariat as "rabble," he promptly lost his job. Evidently, the young Bonhoeffer had ample opportunity to witness the stories of civil courage modeled by his grand-parents, a trait that he himself was called to emulate in his own life.

On the whole, the Bonhoeffer family was at best nominally Christian; they observed the Christian rituals of baptism and confirmation and celebrated the high holidays. Paula Bonhoeffer attended church, but none of the men in the family. The ideals of the family did not stem from their Christian heritage as they were humanistic, bourgeois and intellectual. This meant that respect for human beings, their rights and dignity were assumed in the household. Similarly, culture – including literature, music, art – was very important to the family, as was education. Indeed, all the Bonhoeffer children studied at university and all the men earned doctorates, as did the brothers-in-law that joined the family.

University of Berlin

For the Bonhoeffers' the intellectual fountain was the University of Berlin. Today historians of science suggest that in the 1920s and 1930s, the University of Berlin was the scientific center of the world. By the mid-1930s, Berlin had 28 Nobel Laureates (at that time, Harvard University had three). From the father to almost all the children, the family was connected to the university during this glorious period. For example, Karl Friedrich, the oldest Bonhoeffer son, worked with Walther Nernst as his doctoral supervisor when the latter became a Nobel laureate in chemistry. As a post-doctoral researcher, Karl Friedrich worked with Fritz Haber who received the Nobel Prize in chemistry in 1918 and who was one of the best friends of Albert Einstein – who still taught at Berlin when Dietrich Bonhoeffer matriculated – himself Nobel laureate in physics in 1921.

The young Bonhoeffer was brilliant himself: he finished his doctoral dissertation at the age of 21, with a work entitled *Sanctorum Communio* (*DBWE* 1) that he had written on the side of his regular studies! Even by Berlin standards, he had achieved much at an early age. Nonetheless, Bonhoeffer's career began with a surprise when as a mere 14 years old he announced to the family that he was going to become "a minister and theologian," and apparently "he never seems to have wavered in this ambition."[9]

---

[9] Bethge, *Dietrich Bonhoeffer*, 36.

This decision was more tolerated than supported by the family. Especially his father would have preferred that the youngest son follow in the footsteps of his brothers and study physics or law, at any rate, a scientific discipline.

Barcelona, New York, Berlin, London

In 1928, Bonhoeffer went for a year to Barcelona as an assistant pastor to serve a German Lutheran congregation. On his way there he visited a mass in Paris that was attended by prostitutes and marginalized persons. This experience left "an enormously impressive picture" on the young pastor as "these burdened people are [close] to the heart of the gospel."[10] These words bear witness to one of the earliest expressions of Bonhoeffer's growing social conscience. From now on, the number of burdened people in his life was to increase. More and more, Bonhoeffer's eyes were opened to a reality that he called the "social question."[11] In one of his sermons of the time he proclaims: "Christians are people of the present in the most profound sense. Be it political and economic problems, moral and religious decline, concern for the present generation of young people – everywhere the point is to enter into the problems of the present."[12] When he returned to Berlin, he wrote a second dissertation, *Act and Being (DBWE* 2), in which he took on a host of German philosophers, including Kant, Hegel, Heidegger and others. This dissertation (*Habilitation*) qualified him to become a university professor.

In 1930–1931 Bonhoeffer studied in New York, at Union Theological Seminary. While there, we observe a subtle yet noteworthy terminological change in his classification of social realities. Whereas in Barcelona he had spoken broadly of the "social question," now in New York, he speaks more narrowly of the "social problem."[13] For the first time Bonhoeffer witnessed that racism and poverty stem from injustice and inevitably lead to social inequity and evil. Now he saw that social problems bring about terrific existential hardship, distress, discrimination, dysfunction, and all kind of

---

[10] *DBWE* 10, 59.

[11] *DBWE* 10, 62 and 69. The social question emerged as Bonhoeffer witnessed both the extravagance of the German business community (cf. *DBWE* 10, 69 and 78), human hardship (cf. *DBWE* 10, 78: financial difficulties) and social marginality (cf. *DBWE* 10, 110. He encountered globetrotters, vagrants, escaped criminals, hired killers, legionnaires, circus performers, dancers).

[12] *DBWE* 10, 529.

[13] *DBWE* 10, 307.

attacks on life. At stake was not academic theology or neutral social realities, but human lives; hence, Bonhoeffer realized that theology must address social problems in a way that facilitates social transformations.

While Bonhoeffer's theology gains new perspectives at Union, he was himself transformed as a person. In 1936, Bonhoeffer wrote a rather atypical letter to Elisabeth Zinn about his own path from theology to becoming a Christian. Looking back at the years 1929–31 – in other words, at the time in Barcelona, Berlin and New York – Bonhoeffer acknowledges that "something happened, something that has changed and transformed my life to the present day. For the first time I discovered the Bible ... I had often preached, I had seen a great deal of the church, spoken and preached about it – but I had not yet become a Christian."[14]

When Bonhoeffer visited America in 1930, slavery had been abolished for over six decades. Nonetheless, the issue of racism was still a palpable social evil, blatantly evident to the young German visitor. At Union, Bonhoeffer befriended Franklin Fisher, an African American student from Alabama. This friendship became crucial not only for his first-hand experience of the racist reality encountered by the African American community, but also for his own ability to unmask anti-Semitism in Nazi Germany. Fisher introduced Bonhoeffer to the Abyssinian Baptist Church in Harlem and arranged that the German friend could teach Sunday school, offer Bible studies for women and help out in "weekday school." As an active participant he was welcomed into many African American homes and even introduced to the leaders of the black movement at Howard College.[15] On 8 January 1931 he wrote home: "The separation of whites from blacks in the southern states really does make a rather shameful impression ... The way the southerners talk about the Negroes is simply repugnant, and in this regard the pastors are no better than the others ... It is a bit unnerving that in a country with so inordinately many slogans about brotherhood, peace, and so on, such things still continue completely uncorrected."[16]

Back in Berlin in 1931, something happened that from then on shaped the direction of his life forever: the rise to power by Hitler in January 1933. The entire Bonhoeffer family was of one accord: Hitler meant no good news for Germany! On 1 February 1933 – two days after Hitler came to power – the young Dietrich Bonhoeffer, 3 days short of his twenty-seventh birthday, gave a public radio broadcast in which he warned the young

---

[14] Bethge, *Dietrich Bonhoeffer*, 205.
[15] Cf. Bethge, *Dietrich Bonhoeffer*, 205.
[16] *DBWE* 10, 269.

generation of the danger that the leader could become the misleader! Almost immediately, Hitler showed his true colours in April 1933 with the so-called Aryan Paragraph, a policy that was to restrict non-Aryans from holding the office of civil servant. This measure included professors and pastors and hence his brother-in-law, Gerhard Leibholz, who was a professor of law, and his best friend, Franz Hildebrandt, a Christian pastor with Jewish roots. Bonhoeffer instantly saw through this first act of "ethnic cleansing" and responded by issuing a clear condemnation.[17] He reminded those in the church that "here the most intelligent people have totally lost both their heads and their Bible."[18] As a protest and corrective, he wrote the essay "The Church and the Jewish Question." If the state fails "to create law and order" and attacks the Jewish people, he argued, then one of the possibilities for "the church" is to destroy the wheel of that machine.[19]

In retrospect, Bonhoeffer's writings are the earliest documents of the German church struggle. But others as well, for example Martin Niemoeller, a pastor in Berlin, realized early on that the "German Christians" would not resist Hitler. Therefore, he and Bonhoeffer and others formed what is known as the Pastors' Emergency League. Initially, 3000 of the 18000 pastors in Germany joined this association in protest against the German Christians, the National church controlled by Nazi ideology. The Pastors' Emergency League, increasingly known as the Confessing Church, drafted under the leadership of Karl Barth the earliest memorandum against the German Christians. In this document, known as "The Barmen Declaration" of May 1934, the Confessing Church set itself distinctly apart from the German Christians by declaring allegiance only to Jesus Christ and his word.

As the church struggle intensified, Bonhoeffer left Berlin and went to London (1933–1935) to serve as the pastor for a German Lutheran congregation. There he met Bishop George Bell, who became a life-long friend and confidant. Through him Bonhoeffer was connected to the world-wide ecumenical councils and later, during his activity as a conspirator, kept the allies informed of the activity of the resistance groups within Germany.

---

[17] Cf. *DBWE* 12, 425–432.
[18] *DBWE* 12, 101.
[19] *DBWE* 12, 361–370.

Underground Seminary and Continued Church Struggle

While Bonhoeffer was in London, the Confessing Church established its own seminaries, an act that was illegal by Nazi law. In 1935 Bonhoeffer agreed to become the director of the seminary, first in Zingst then in Finkenwalde, on the coast of the Baltic Sea. In retrospect he notes that the time with the students during these two years was perhaps the most fulfilling time of his adult life. The basic objective of the seminary was to prepare students – who had for the most part already studied theology at a Nazi controlled faculty of theology – for the pastorate in congregations that belonged to the Confessing Church. For the students this meant the highest kind of sacrifice: first, to study theology at an underground seminary run by the Confessing Church was a crime; and second, it implied an uncertain economic future because the pastors of the Confessing Church had forfeited their status and salary as civil servants.

As the director of the seminary, Bonhoeffer was the chief architect of the theological curriculum. Solid and disciplined academic work was the norm. But equally significant was for Bonhoeffer the practice of Christian community. It was one thing to be a good theologian, but quite another to have a firm spiritual foundation. Hence, spiritual formation and theological education went hand in hand. The two classic books, *Discipleship* (*DBWE* 4) and *Life Together* (*DBWE* 5) have their origin in this community of seminarians.

At the seminary, Bonhoeffer met Eberhard Bethge who became his closest friend, brother-in-law and – posthumously – the redactor of his writings. It is questionable how much the world would know of Bonhoeffer's life and thought without Bethge. He not only wrote a monumental biography[20] but also initiated the publication of the critical edition of Bonhoeffer's writings, the 17-volume *Dietrich Bonhoeffer Werke*, a series now completed in its English translation, the *Dietrich Bonhoeffer Works English*.

After the Nazis had closed the seminary in 1937, Bonhoeffer visited New York a second time in 1939 in order to escape his immanent conscription into Hitler's armies. In New York he realized that he had escaped from family, church and country when he was needed the most in times of extreme national upheaval. He returned to Germany with the last ocean liner in July 1939, fully aware of what would await him: war.

---

[20] Cf. note 2.

Conspiracy and Imprisonment

Bonhoeffer was well informed by his brother-in-law Hans von Dohnanyi, who was a lawyer in the Counter Intelligence Office in Berlin (the *Abwehr*), of the ever-increasing acts of brutality by the Nazi regime against Jewish people and other regime critics. Almost from the beginning, Dohnanyi secretly compiled a "chronicle of shame" in which he listed Nazi atrocities against Jews as they became known to him in his office. He did this in view of the needed post-war evidence against the Nazi regime. Through Dohnanyi's clandestine initiative, the Bonhoeffer family was informed of what was actually happening in Nazi Germany. Dohnanyi persuaded a small cluster of people to take action against the regime – and this meant against Hitler. After many discussions – many of which took place in the Bonhoeffer House – the group saw the only solution to overcome the evil of Nazism in a carefully planned coup on Hitler's life. The circle of conspirators recruited by Dohnanyi included Dietrich, his brother Klaus, their brother-in-law Rüdiger Schleicher and a number of high military and intelligence officials who worked closely together with Dohnanyi.

When Bonhoeffer joined the circle of conspirators he had in all practical terms become a double agent. On the one hand, it looked now as if he actually worked for the Nazis, since he was associated with the counter intelligence offices in Berlin and Munich. On the other hand, the real purpose of his assignment was the very opposite: to inform the allied nations of the plans of the conspirators and to negotiate their cooperation after the defeat of the Nazi regime. The key international contact in this regard was Bishop George Bell. Following a meeting with Bonhoeffer in Sweden, Bell was not successful in securing understanding and support for the conspirators from the British government. Neither Anthony Eden, British foreign minister, nor Winston Churchill were inclined to concede anything to Germany but unconditional surrender. This was a severe and bitter blow to the conspirators!

When Bonhoeffer was not traveling in Europe for the Counter Intelligence Office, he was preoccupied with a project of an entirely different nature. From November 1940 until February 1941, Bonhoeffer lived at the Benedictine Monastery in Ettal, south of Munich. Why was he there? For two reasons: to be in close proximity to the Munich office and to write a book on ethics. Given the context of the tyranny of the state and the inability of the Confessing Church to critique it publicly and effectively, the issue of ethical responsibility became perhaps the most demanding concern for him. Urged on by these unusual times Bonhoeffer wrote a book on ethics, posthumously published as *Ethics* (*DBWE* 6). For Bonhoeffer, who had over the years become a pacifist and supporter of nonviolent resolutions of international conflicts, the involvement in tyrannicide posed a particularly serious ethical predicament. Those who think of Bonhoeffer as a great Christian example are somehow able to reconcile his involvement in the conspiracy with the rest of his faith and actions; for others, this very involvement becomes the cornerstone of suspicion toward Bonhoeffer, if not a flat-out rejection of him. How he ethically justified his participation in tyrannicide we will discuss below.

On 5 April 1943, Bonhoeffer – now engaged to Maria von Wedemeyer, nearly 20 years younger than him – was arrested by the Gestapo in his parents' retirement home in Berlin. Up to that moment he had been working on the manuscript for Ethics. The reason for his arrest was not directly related to his involvement in the conspiracy. Dohnanyi's office was scrutinized for inconsistencies in official documents, foreign currency transactions and other such matters. After Dohnanyi was arrested, the documents in his office led to Bonhoeffer who was arrested the same afternoon and incarcerated in Tegel Prison. Against what Bonhoeffer had hoped for, he was not released after a short while. As time went on, he befriended a guard who smuggled letters in and out of prison. At one point there was even an escape plan; but Bonhoeffer gave it up when his brother Klaus and brother-in-law Rüdiger Schleicher were also arrested.

Bonhoeffer's experience in prison is recorded in the now famous *Letters and Papers from Prison* (*DBWE* 8). In these pages – mostly an exchange of personal and theological letters with his friend Eberhard Bethge – Bonhoeffer reflects on his life and imagines the future. His reflections may be broadly divided into two categories: one was his personal life (family, marriage) and the other was his theological reflections. His overarching question was how Jesus Christ can be proclaimed in a secular and autonomous world (*mündige Welt*); does theology have to learn a new language, one that proclaims biblical concepts in "religionless" terminology?

It was not meant to be for him to regain his freedom, his family and a wife. In October 1944 Bonhoeffer was brought to a Gestapo prison in Berlin, then moved to Buchenwald Concentration Camp and finally transferred to Flossenbürg Concentration Camp. There, after a mock trial the night before, Bonhoeffer was hung early in the morning on 9 April 1945, a month before World War II was over.

Why this biographical sketch? Although it is tautological to say that all theology is contextual, in the case of Bonhoeffer such insight is paramount. Given the extraordinary difficult circumstances of his adult life, his thought was inextricably bound to emerge, develop and mature in the midst of the church struggle and the attempt to see the Nazi regime come to its end.

Bonhoeffer's Intellectual Formation

Theology, Philosophy, Ethics and Homiletics

I will now present the main intellectual presuppositions that undergird and shape Bonhoeffer's thought in its complexity and entirety – his theology, his philosophy, ethics and homiletics. It is crucial to understand that these presuppositions are not to be correlated sequentially but concurrently. In other words, Bonhoeffer did not begin studying one discipline or formulate these presuppositions and then move to the next, and so on; rather, he engaged all of these disciplines and thus articulated these presuppositions in view of gaining a comprehensive theological understanding as an educator and pastor.

Basic Theological Presupposition: Christuswirklichkeit

Many scholars hold the position that Bonhoeffer's most basic theological presupposition is the concept of reality or, in his own term, *Wirklichkeit*, or stated even more precisely, the concept *Christuswirklichkeit*, the reality of Christ. This presupposition cements and shapes all of Bonhoeffer's thought: his philosophy, theology, ethics and homiletics. As early as in his doctoral dissertation *Sanctorum Communio*, Bonhoeffer argued that "one can never arrive at the reality of the other by means of epistemology and metaphysics. Reality is simply not deducible, but given – to be acknowledged or rejected. It can never be explained theoretically; likewise it is only given for the whole person as an ethical being."[21] Even though Bonhoeffer speaks here of the reality of the human being, his conception of reality as "given" suggests that he assigned reality an overarching basic ontological structure[22] that defies both construction and deconstruction. Elsewhere he describes reality as "ultimate reality" and even identifies that ultimate real-

---

[21] *DBWE* 1, 53 note 68; Cf. *DBWE* 2, 66.

[22] Jürgen Moltmann, *Herrschaft Christi und soziale Wirklichkeit nach Dietrich Bonhoeffer*. Munich: Chr. Kaiser 1959, 5, speaks correctly of a "theological ontology" in Bonhoeffer's early writings.

ity with God: "God alone is the ultimate reality."[23] This identification he explains in these terms: "That God alone is ultimate reality, is, however, not an idea meant to sublimate the actual world, nor is it the religious perfection of a profane worldview. It is rather a faithful Yes to God's self-witness, God's revelation."[24] In other words, for Bonhoeffer God's self-disclosure in the world is inextricably bound to the incarnation of Jesus. For him this means that "for a disciple of Jesus, 'God-given realities' exist only through Jesus Christ."[25] In addition, "only insofar as the ultimate reality is revelation, that is, the self-witness of the living God, is its claim to ultimacy fulfilled. But then the decision about the whole of life depends on our relation to God's revelation."[26]

Put differently, Bonhoeffer's basic theological presupposition is that all reality is constituted, centered and completed in Jesus Christ. From this presupposition follows for Bonhoeffer the conclusion that there exists no reality outside or apart from the one divine reality revealed in Christ. "The world has no reality of its own independent of God's revelation in Christ."[27] All reality, whether primordial, ancient, modern or postmodern, is constituted by the one Christ-reality. In Bonhoeffer's scheme of ultimate reality as constituted by Christ, the question is not how Christ or Christianity fit into our contemporary reality but rather how the reality of our contemporary world measures up vis-à-vis the ultimate reality of God in Christ. Similarly, the question is not how the Christian faith should be made contemporary in the context of our postmodern lives, but how the postmodern person may be able to embrace the actuality of *Christuswirklichkeit*. For Bonhoeffer the logic of the relationship is this: the contemporary, postmodern subject must justify him/herself vis-à-vis *Christuswirklichkeit* and not the reverse. The sequence is such that the path of the human being must always lead to *Christuswirklichkeit*. There is, however, for Bonhoeffer no direct insight or path to the ultimate reality and knowledge of Christ. This brings us now to Bonhoeffer's understanding of philosophy.

---

[23] *DBWE* 6, 48.
[24] *DBWE* 6, 48.
[25] *DBWE* 4, 95.
[26] *DBWE* 6, 48–49.
[27] *DBWE* 6, 58.

Basic Philosophical Presuppositions

Until recently, Bonhoeffer research has with few exceptions focussed on examining Bonhoeffer's theology. While the first six decades of research were characterized by an interest in Bonhoeffer's theology, it is only in recent years that due recognition is given to the philosophical influences that shaped Bonhoeffer's intellectual formation.[28] Indeed, as a student of theology in Tübingen, Bonhoeffer himself concentrated on the study of philosophy. He studied the history of philosophy, history of logic, formal logic and Kant's *Critique of Pure Reason*. We also know that he read Nietzsche's work, much of Hegel, Dilthey and many other philosophers. The significance of Bonhoeffer's life-long interest in philosophy is in its correlation with theology. To articulate his basic philosophical presupposition is now our next task.

The Limited Self

Bonhoeffer's basic ontological category – that all reality is constituted and "given" by God in Jesus Christ – corresponds to a further ontological distinction with epistemological implications. In *Act and Being*, Bonhoeffer argues that the one overarching reality includes the fact that no human being is "untouched by sin."[29] "Being in Adam" he says explicitly is an ontological designation for being a sinner. But being a sinner includes not only *cor curvum in se* (a heart turned in upon itself) but more significantly precludes the epistemological possibility "that human beings could place themselves into the truth."[30] In the end, the fact that the power of sin disfigures human life radically and on all levels of being makes null a person's ability to overcome the dilemma of life. The power of sin makes it impossible for a person to repair the broken relationship between God and humanity as sin makes it impossible even to perceive itself as sin. Why this epistemological impasse?

"Philosophical thinking," Bonhoeffer remarks, "attempts to be free from premises (if that is possible at all); Christian thinking has to be con-

---

[28] Cf. Peter Frick (ed), *Bonhoeffer's Intellectual Formation. Theology and Philosophy in His Thought*. Religion in Philosophy and Theology 29. Tübingen: Mohr Siebeck 2008 and Brian Gregor and Jens Zimmermann (eds), *Bonhoeffer and Continental Thought: Cruciform Philosophy*. Bloomington/Indianapolis: Indiana University Press 2009.

[29] *DBWE* 2, 136.

[30] *DBWE* 2, 136.

scious of its particular premise, that is, of the premise of the reality of God, before and beyond all thinking. In the protection of this presupposition, theological thinking convicts philosophical thinking of being bound also to a presupposition, namely, that thinking in itself can give truth. But philosophical truth always remains truth which is given only within the category of possibility.[31] Philosophical thinking never can extend beyond this category – it can never be a thinking in reality. It can form a conception of reality, but conceived reality is not reality any longer. The reason for this is that thinking is in itself a closed circle, with the ego as the center."[32] Elsewhere he says in a similar vein that in philosophical discourse, "the I, now thinking itself, simply becomes the point of departure instead of the limit-point of philosophy. But thinking cannot do this without losing two very different things, reality and transcendence, that is, the one through the other. Philosophy, thinking, the I, all come under the power of themselves, rather than transcendence … Thinking languishes in itself; precisely where it is free from the transcendent, from reality, there it is imprisoned in itself."[33]

Here Bonhoeffer discerns a decisive difference between basic philosophical and theological presuppositions. Theology is predicated on "the reality of God, before and beyond all thinking" while philosophy is falsely predicated on assuming "that thinking in itself can give truth." Unlike philosophy, theology reckons with truth in an ontological sense. Philosophy's weakness is that it wants to establish, if not truth itself, then at least minimally the parameter for truth to demonstrate itself. For Bonhoeffer such an attempt is in utter vain because philosophical truth is self-limited. "Godless thought – even when it is ethical – remains self-enclosed. Even a critical philosophy cannot place one into the truth, because its crisis emerges from within itself, and its apparent reality is still subservient to the claims of the *cor curvum in se* that have lost the power to claim anyone. Revelation gives itself without precondition and is alone able to place one into reality. Theological thought goes from God to reality, not from reality to God."[34] Precisely here lies for Bonhoeffer the hermeneutical dilemma in philosophy's claim: philosophical thinking is entrapped in the circle of sin and therefore

---

[31] Bonhoeffer vehemently rejects the category of possibility for theology. For its Heideggerian origin and Bonhoeffer's rejection of the category; cf. *DBWE* 2, 136; *DBWE* 1, 143 and *DBWE* 10, 403. See also my essay in this volume, "Bonhoeffer and Philosophy," especially the section on Heidegger.

[32] *DBWE* 10, 442.

[33] *DBWE* 2, 39.

[34] *DBWE* 2, 89.

tied to a self-limiting rationality. In his own words, "although theology accepts these results of philosophical inquiry, it interprets them in its own fashion as the thinking of the *cor curvum in se*. The I does indeed remain self-enclosed; this, however, is not its credit but is its guilt."[35] In short, Bonhoeffer's basic philosophical presupposition amounts to the position that the one overarching Christ-reality of the world includes a self that is limited because of the reality of sin.

Theological Epistemology

What is the ramification of Bonhoeffer's position that there is no genuine philosophical epistemology because of a self limited by sin, because of the human heart turned upon itself? For him the insight of the limited self is drawn from philosophy but becomes concrete in theology. His philosophical position that the I cannot come to itself – because of its self-confining ratio – is a decisive insight that in one way or another shapes all of his theology.[36] Consistent with his theological premise, Bonhoeffer maintains logically that if it were really a philosophical "possibility for persons themselves to know that they are sinners apart from revelation, neither 'being in Adam' nor 'being in Christ' would be existential designations of their being. For it would mean that human beings could place themselves into the truth."[37] But since for Bonhoeffer human sinfulness is a matter of our human reality, the understanding of this ultimately life-destroying reality is given to humanity by means of God's revelation and appropriated in faith. For this reason he upholds the Lutheran saying *sola fide credendum est nos esse peccatores* (only by faith can we believe that we are sinners). Given the epistemological constraint of the I, such a confession is only possible as a declaration of faith. Philosophy cannot have an adequate comprehension of its own epistemological limit because it can never place a person into the reality of sin. The very nature of sin is its impossibility to know itself as sin. As Bonhoeffer suggests, sin cannot be seen in its own darkness, but only in the light of revelation. If thinking undistorted by sin were a possibility, then sin would not really be an epistemologically enslaving power and, consequently, the salvific and redemptive work of Jesus Christ would

---

[35] *DBWE* 10, 399–400,

[36] Cf. *DBWE* 10, 461; "No religion, no ethics, no metaphysical knowledge may serve man to approach God" and *DBWE* 1, 45: "there is no purely cognitive way to know God."

[37] *DBWE* 2, 136.

be rendered futile. In other words, the I, the self, cannot come to itself because its ontological reality and hence epistemological possibility is distorted by the power of sin.

Basic Ethical Presupposition: Creation of Values

As early as his year in Barcelona the young Bonhoeffer proclaims: "Christians create their own standards for good and evil; only Christians themselves provide the justification for their acts, just as they alone bear responsibility for them. Christians create new tables, new decalogues, as Nietzsche said of the Overman [*Übermensch*]. Nietzsche's Overman is not, as he imagined, the opposite of the Christian; without realizing it, Nietzsche imbued the Overman with many of the features of the free Christian as described and conceived by both Paul and Luther."[38] Quite unexpectedly, these lines strongly agree with one of Nietzsche's main ideas. Like the philosopher, Bonhoeffer proposes that the responsibility of ethics is the creation – or in Nietzschean terms, the revaluation (*Umwertung*) – of (new) values, but he does so for reasons that are different from Nietzsche. With typical Nietzschean flair Bonhoeffer claims: "The knowledge of good and evil seems to be the goal of all ethical reflection. The first task of Christian ethics is to supersede that knowledge." For Bonhoeffer, the traditional Christian distinction of "the mere possibility of knowing about good and evil is already a falling away from the origin [*Ursprung*]."[39] In other words, humanity's quest to decide what is good and evil is a mere reminder of the fall and the reality of our impaired rational selves; we are unable to decide the question of good and evil.

Bonhoeffer's starting point for constructing a Christian ethic corresponds to his conception of the reality of God in Jesus Christ: In Ethics he expresses his ideas succinctly: "The source of a Christian ethic is not the reality of one's own self, not the reality of the world, nor is it the reality of norms and values. It is the reality of God that is revealed in Jesus Christ." A few lines further, he says even more sharply: "The subject matter of a Christian ethic is God's reality revealed in Christ becoming real [*wirklichwerden*] among God's creatures."[40] When the focus is no longer on the possibility of the self as the criterion for ethics, "the question of the good becomes the question of participating in God's reality revealed in Christ.

---

[38] *DBWE* 10, 366–367.
[39] *DBWE* 6, 300.
[40] *DBWE* 6, 49.

Good is no longer an evaluation of what exists, for instance my essence, my moral orientation [*Gesinnung*], my actions, or of a state of affairs in the world. It is no longer a predicate that one can apply to something that exists of itself. Good is the real itself [*das Wirkliche*], that is, not the abstractly real that is separated from the reality of God, but the real that has its reality only in God. Good is never without this reality. It is no general formula."[41]

Bonhoeffer's basic ethical premise – that Christians must create their own values and make responsible decisions – stems from his basic theological premise that there is only the one reality of God revealed in the world. Given further his philosophical premise – that the self is limited and incapable because of sin to come to itself – his prescription for ethical behaviour is simply the discernment of the will of God in a given situation. His own personal test case, so to speak, was the ethical dilemma of whether or not he should participate in the conspiracy on Hitler's life.

Responsible Action

The "ethical test case" for Bonhoeffer was his involvement in the conspiracy to kill Hitler. For a theologian who was a pacifist and advocate of non-violent international conflict resolution, one's active contribution to tyrannicide posed a momentous ethical predicament. How could Bonhoeffer reconcile his involvement in the conspiracy with his faith and ethics? Why did he decide to join the conspiracy on Hitler's life? There is no uncomplicated answer. Every answer is the attempt to make intelligible perhaps the most complex aspect of his life. At the risk of oversimplification, I would advance the following explanation, in four steps:

The One Reality of Jesus Christ

As we noted above, Bonhoeffer's basic theological assumption was that there is only one reality. He rejected the Lutheran Doctrine of the Two Kingdoms, one sacred and the other profane. Instead he argued that all reality is a unity and encompasses every aspect of life – good and evil. In his own words: "There are not two realities, but only one reality, and that is God's reality revealed in Christ in the reality of the world ... The world has no reality of its own independent of God's revelation in Christ."[42] "As reality is one in Christ, so the person who belongs to this Christ-reality is

---

[41] *DBWE* 6, 50.
[42] *DBWE* 6, 58.

also a whole. Worldliness does not separate one from Christ, and being Christian does not separate one from the world. Belonging completely to Christ, one stands at the same time completely in the world."[43] Hence, the reality of Nazi atrocities was also part of the one reality of the world, marred as it is by the destructive power of sin and calculated evil.

Ethical Responsibility

Because of the Christian's standing and living in the reality of this world, "to act responsibly means to include in the formation of action human reality as it has been taken on by God in Christ."[44] "The task is not to turn the world upside down but in a given place to do what, from the perspective of reality, is necessary objectively [*sachlich*] and to really carry it out."[45] Bonhoeffer says it most eloquently in one of his poems from prison. In a stanza entitled 'Action,' he proclaims: "Hover not over the possible, but boldly reach for the real. / Not in escaping to thought, in action alone is found freedom."[46] Hence, the evil times of Nazi crimes in which Bonhoeffer lived charged him with responsible action.

Ethical Borderline Situations

On rare occasions, ethical situations are such that they "cannot be captured by any law and can never become laws themselves. They appeal directly to the free responsibility of the one who acts, a responsibility not bound by any law. They create an extraordinary situation, and are in essence borderline cases (*Grenzsituation*)."[47] Bonhoeffer joined the conspiracy, I propose, because Hitler's Nazism constituted an unprecedented "ethical boundary case" that could not be overcome by negotiation but demanded uncompromising "free responsible action." Given the bleakness to end the evil boundary situation of Nazism by reasonable means, for Bonhoeffer responsible action was to participate in tyrannicide.

Leaving Judgement in God's Hand

In an ethical boundary situation, responsible action can even be an act of sin! Bonhoeffer knew that his involvement in the conspiracy was an action that went directly against the explicit commandment of God "not to kill." Therefore, judgement of that act must be utterly suspended and left entire-

---

[43] *DBWE* 6, 62.
[44] *DBWE* 6, 224.
[45] *DBWE* 6, 225.
[46] *DBWE* 8, 513.
[47] *DBWE* 6, 273.

ly up to the mercy of God. "Because it was God who became human, responsible action ... must completely surrender to God both the judgement on this action and its consequence ... responsible action renounces any knowledge about its ultimate justification. The deed that is done ... is completely surrendered to God the moment it is carried out. Ultimate ignorance of one's own goodness or evil, together with dependence upon grace, is an essential characteristic of responsible historical action."[48]

In other words, given the unique historical circumstance of Nazi atrocities – a boundary case par excellence – Bonhoeffer's participation in tyrannicide cannot be used as a model for current ethical decisions. Bonhoeffer cannot be used to legitimate contemporary ethical decisions that involve violence and the destruction of life.

Basic Homiletical Presupposition

Theological, philosophical and ethical presuppositions have a bearing also on Bonhoeffer's homiletics. All intellectual roads, so to speak, lead for him to the Word of God, expressed in the sermon. Bonhoeffer's overarching hermeneutical presupposition is that the Christian message, concretely the sermon, is the locus and reality where the self, entrapped by sin, is addressed by the power of the revealed Word of God and places the hearer into truth and freedom. The aim of contemporizing the sermon "is not a justification of Christianity to the present but a *justification of the present to the Christian message*."[49] How can this be accomplished? The Christian message cannot be justified by the rhetorical giftedness of the preacher or a homiletical technique; indeed, in the strictest theological sense, for Bonhoeffer any justification of the Christian message as such is impossible. For Bonhoeffer the contemporary relevance of the Christian message is guaranteed in the uniqueness that God's Word is its own self-effective and relevant power. In his own words: "Whenever God is present in the divine word, there one has the present; there God posits the present. The *subject of the present* is the Holy Spirit, not we ourselves, and that is also why the subject of *contemporization* is the Holy Spirit itself... [For this reason,] Christ speaks to us through Christ's Holy Spirit... this takes place not outside or alongside but only and exclusively *through the word* of Scripture."[50] In a nutshell, Bonhoeffer asserts that "the *concretissimum* of the Christian

---

[48] *DBWE* 6, 225.
[49] *DBWE* 14, 416; original emphasis.
[50] *DBWE* 14, 417.

message and textual exposition is not a human act of contemporizing but rather always God, the Holy Spirit."[51] Expressed in the words of the young theology student Bonhoeffer, "I will never be able to convert through the power of my sermon unless the Spirit comes and makes my word into the Spirit's word."[52]

Why does the Word of God, revealed in scripture and proclaimed in the sermon, have such a fundamental place in Bonhoeffer's hermeneutic? What is it about God's Word that permits Bonhoeffer to assign it such theological weight? The answer is unambiguous: God's Word is self-effective [*selbstwirksam*].[53] Bonhoeffer made perhaps his first encounter with this idea during his teenage years when he received at confirmation the Bible verse, Romans 1:16, in Greek: Οὐ γὰρ ἐπαισχύνομαι τὸ εὐαγγέλιον, δύναμις γὰρ θεοῦ ἐστιν εἰς σωτηρίαν παντὶ τῷ πιστεύοντι (For I am not ashamed of the gospel because it is the power of God to bring about salvation for everyone who believes)! This verse expresses for him the non-negotiable hermeneutic of his preaching, namely τὸ εὐαγγέλιον, δύναμις γὰρ θεοῦ, that the gospel is the power (δύναμις) of God for a person's salvation. The "Word of God is power, victory, overcoming. It still works and bears fruit; it creates new life out of nothing,"[54] he explains. In his first sermon in London, he says it well: "Not our word, but God's Word: yet even so, God's Word speaking through ours. This is what makes a sermon something unique in all the world, so completely different from any kind of speech. When a preacher opens his Bible and interprets the Word of God, a mystery takes place, a miracle."[55] The proclamation of a mystery, indeed; but an act that is predicated on nothing less but the intellectual effort to work out one's philosophical, theological, ethical, exegetical and homiletical presuppositions.

---

[51] *DBWE* 14, 417.

[52] *DBWE* 9, 363. Cf. *DBWE* 14, 422: "The *concretissimum* of the sermon is not the *application I provide* but the Holy Spirit itself speaking through the text of the Bible."

[53] Peter Zimmerling, *Bonhoeffer als praktischer Theologe*, Göttingen: Vandenhoeck & Ruprecht 2006, 87: "Bonhoeffer geht von der Selbstwirksamkeit des Wortes Gottes, seiner Eigenbewegung aus." Cf. also 89, where he speaks correctly of the "Selbstmächtigkeit" and "Selbstwirksamkeit" of God's Word.

[54] *DBWE* 16, 498; cf. also *DBWE* 16, 501 and *DBWE* 15, 511 where Bonhoeffer speaks of the power of God's Word [*Macht des Wortes Gottes*].

[55] *DBWE* 13, 323.

Bonhoeffer's Legacy

Given both the complexity of Bonhoeffer's thought as a whole and the precarious context of his life under the Nazi regime, any interpretation of his life in terms of his legacy will necessarily remain a hermeneutically subjective and fragmentary task. Even though, the fact that he courageously resisted the Nazi regime to the point of a violent death is in itself admirable and heroic. But Bonhoeffer did not want to be a hero; he wanted to live a life that was faithful to his own intellectual convictions and to the dire circumstances of his own life and those around him. Perhaps it was Bonhoeffer's ability to find an existential balance in the midst of life's challenges, disappointments, failures, fragments and so on. With clarity and calmness he was able to accept the polarities of life without setting up false dichotomies or looking for easy escapes. For Bonhoeffer, ultimately, life was constituted by polarities: spiritual – secular; intellectual – emotional; joy – suffering; freedom – imprisonment; life – death. But none of these pairs was absolute; there was in him the ability to accept these polarities and tensions as belonging to the whole of life. It is fitting to give him the last word in this regard.

On 21 July 1944 – one day after the failed attempt on Hitler's life – Bonhoeffer writes a letter from prison to his friend Eberhard Bethge. It is more than a letter, perhaps we should think of it as a testament, or as a way of discerning how he would want to be remembered: "In the last few years I have come to know and understand more and more of the profound this-worldliness of Christianity. The Christian is not a *homo religiosus* but simply a human being, in the same way that Jesus was a human being ... one throws oneself completely into the arms of God, and this is what I call this-worldliness [*Diesseitigkeit*]: living fully in the midst of life's tasks, questions, successes and failures, experiences and perplexities – then one takes seriously no longer one's own sufferings but rather the sufferings of God in the world. Then one stays awake with Christ in Gethsemane. And I think this is faith; this is μετάνοια [repentance]. And this is how one becomes a human being, a Christian."[56]

---

[56] *DBWE* 8, 485–486.

Reading Bonhoeffer

2. Understanding Bonhoeffer: from Default to Hermeneutic Reading

Die Seele der Hermeneutik
besteht darin, daß der andere recht haben kann.
Jean Grondin on Gadamer[1]

Introduction

The ability to read is one of the marks of the educated person and the beginning of civility. Those who are able to read usually do so without giving any thought to their underlying "perspective," "approach" or "interpretive method." Reading happens nearly automatically. The reader's eyes glance at the words and lines of a specific text, and with little effort, the meaning of the text forms in our minds. We have found the information we were looking for, or we have gained a certain understanding or answer regarding a specific question. There are, of course, various levels of reading which involve distinct degrees of interest and intellectual alertness. It is one thing to leaf superficially through a newspaper or glance at a flyer advertising groceries but quite another thing to read a philosophical discourse, such as Anselm's *Prologion*, Aquinas' *Summa* or Heidegger's *Being and Time*. There is also a marked difference in reading an author in his or her original language of composition or in translation.

In other words, reading – and correspondingly understanding – are decisively hermeneutical tasks. But as even a glance at the vast corpus of secondary literature on Bonhoeffer makes apparent, when it comes to reading and understanding his writings hermeneutically – and correctly – there seems to be much inconsistency and confusion. Is it even reasonable, permissible and politically correct to assume that one reading is hermeneutically more self-conscious and sophisticated and therefore more "correct"

---

[1] Jean Grondin, *Einführung zu Gadamer*, UTB 2139. Tübingen: Mohr Siebeck 2000, 187.

than another reading of the same text? Let us demonstrate this dynamic of complex questions with two, at the moment seemingly unrelated, examples.

One case in point is Bonhoeffer's now classic *Letters and Papers from Prison*.[2] As Martin E. Marty's recent work, *Dietrich Bonhoeffer's Letters and Papers from Prison. A Biography*[3] demonstrates, the readings and the various and contradictory meanings imputed on just this one work are simply unfathomable. How can it be that one and the same work can be claimed by former East German Marxists, by socialists, by God-is-Dead secularists, by mainline Protestants, by Catholics and by Evangelicals? Are the hermeneutical assumptions brought to the interpretation by each reader really on the same level? Are they really equally legitimate tools for interpretation? And who is to decide on the legitimacy of each reading and if so by what standard? Who is the judge between interpretation and misinterpretation?

A second example is an autobiographical reflection by Paul Tillich. Decades after he was forced to leave his chair at the University of Frankfurt and started teaching in the United States of America, he wrote an essay with the curious title "Überwindung des Provinzialismus in der Theologie (Overcoming of Provincialism in Theology)."[4] He notes that he wrote to a friend that "everywhere in the world there are sky, air and ocean." He continues to make clear that he did not write that "everywhere I can continue with my theological and philosophical work." The rationale for these words, he says, was because he did not initially think that his work could be continued anywhere else but in Germany. He goes on to admit that his thinking was incorrectly dominated by the idea that all great post-Enlightenment philosophy and theology happened predominantly in Germany. He terms such an attitude "theological provincialism." Once he lived and taught in various places of academia in the United States, he realized that his initial ideas were simply false. At the risk of oversimplifying, it may be said that his entire work can be characterized as a hermeneutical attempt to correlate the fields of theology and philosophy, in the widest sense of these terms, with the worlds across the ocean and even further away. At the end of this essay we will return to both Marty and Tillich and integrate these two examples into our hermeneutic journey with Bonhoeffer.

---

[2] Cf. *DBWE* 8.

[3] Cf. Martin E. Marty's recent work, *Dietrich Bonhoeffer's Letters and Papers from Prison. A Biography*. Princeton: Princeton University Press 2011.

[4] Cf. Paul Tillich, *Offenbarung und Glaube*, Gesammelte Werke 8. Stuttgart: Evangelisches Verlagswerk 1970, 13–16.

The objective of this essay is to trace the hermeneutical circle of reading and understanding the works of Bonhoeffer. Since the hermeneutical task is dynamic rather than static, it follows that any knowledge of a great person such as Bonhoeffer comes in stages and phases. No reader is able to interpret and understand Bonhoeffer by perusing his writings once. This is to claim that any understanding of Bonhoeffer follows certain stages and specific protocols of engagement and hermeneutical self-reflection. The task of this essay is to examine hermeneutical milestones in the contemporary reader's encounter with Bonhoeffer's texts. I will begin with a discussion of author and text, followed by sections on interpretation, hermeneutical presuppositions and the limit of understanding author and text.

Bonhoeffer the (Dead) Author

For a person interested in Dietrich Bonhoeffer in the twenty-first century, the encounter with "Bonhoeffer" cannot be a face-to-face encounter. For us, the person "Dietrich Bonhoeffer" does not exist anymore as a living, flesh-and-blood human being. Any knowledge – however shallow or profound – is a mediated knowledge that comes to us not from the living person "Bonhoeffer." For a very small circle of persons, it may be the case that they gain knowledge of Bonhoeffer from an "eyewitness" or someone who was close to his family. This kind of knowledge will be a rare exception and sooner than later virtually impossible. For the vast majority of people interested in Bonhoeffer, their acquaintance with his life and thought will come through texts (see below) and the study of secondary sources that share the same function of making his life and thought intelligible.

Given that a text is a composition of words and that words require a person to express them, it follows that a text presupposes an author. In our case, my main thesis is thus straightforward: our knowledge of Bonhoeffer comes by way of his texts and these come by way of his authorship. Although, at first glance, such a thesis seems nearly self-evident, it is arguably a controversial one. Indeed, given the development in modern literary theory known as "the death of the author," most poignantly expressed by Roland Barthes,[5] it is possible to postulate the antithesis, namely that we

---

[5] Cf. Roland Barthes, "The Death of the Author," in his *Image, Music Text*. Glasgow: Fontana 1977, 142–148.

can come to know Bonhoeffer only and precisely by abandoning the very idea that he is the author whom we seek to discover.[6]

To set in sharp relief my thesis that Bonhoeffer must be understood as the author behind his writings, I will begin by illustrating the dynamic of authorship, and the corresponding death of authorship, by recourse to a recent example in the field of Pauline studies. I am thinking of the interpretation of the apostle Paul by the French philosopher Alain Badiou (born 1937). Like Giorgio Agamben, Slavoj Žižek, Gianni Vattimo and other Continental philosophers, Badiou is engaged in a philosophical critique of what is often termed "the empire," namely a philosophical critique of political and economic systems build on oppressive power structures. As a philosopher with strong Marxist leanings, Badiou is fascinated by the thought of the apostle Paul. But his appeal is anything but a fascination with the theology of Paul. Quite to the contrary, Badiou says in the preface to his work on Paul: "For me, truth be told, Paul is not an apostle or a saint. I care nothing for the Good News he declares, or the cult dedicated to him."[7] From the outset, before Badiou pens the first lines about what he thinks the message of Paul is all about, he makes no bones about his aversion to the good news Paul was called to proclaim, the message that became the core of Christian theology. Badiou remarks, almost proudly, I dare say, that he is "irreligious by heredity" and has "never really connected Paul with religion. It is not according to this register, or to bear witness to any sort of faith, or even antifaith, that I have been for a long time, been interested in him."[8]

What is at stake with Badiou's interest and interpretation of Paul? What does Badiou's hermeneutical stance on Paul's message do to Paul as a person, an author and the authorial intent of his letters? These are the key questions. There can be no doubt that Badiou's disposition, his open disavowal of the core of the Pauline message – namely that Jesus is the risen Messiah for the salvation of both Jews and non-Jews – has severely disfigured the person of Paul and virtually killed him as an author. For Badiou, Paul is not the apostle to the Gentiles but merely "a poet-thinker of the event"[9] whose universalist message may function even today as the revolu-

---

[6] Cf. the essay by Markus Franz, "Inside and Beyond the 'Bonhoeffer-Archive' – Foucaultian Reflections on the Discourse of Bonhoeffer's Life and Theology," in Peter Frick (ed), *Bonhoeffer and Interpretive Theory. Essays on Methods and Understanding.* International Bonhoeffer Interpretations 6. Frankfurt: Peter Lang 2013, 27–51.

[7] Alain Badiou, *Saint Paul. The Foundation of Universalism.* Stanford: Stanford University Press 2003 (French original, 1997), 1.

[8] Badiou, *Saint Paul,* 1.

[9] Badiou, *Saint Paul,* 2. Cf. Badiou's observation that "I am not the first to risk the

tionary potential to bring about the demise of (evil) empires. To read Paul as if his message was merely a template for political or revolutionary action does, however, violence to Paul the human being. Ironically, such (distorted) reading is contrary to the postmodern claim that calls for the unconditional acceptance[10] of the "other." In Badiou's hermeneutical scheme, Paul "the other" has been erased in spite of the fact that Badiou is somehow fascinated with the Pauline idea of "subject" and "subjectivity."[11]

Let me be clear: I am not employing Badiou as a straw argument to expose him and denounce him. Badiou is a respected philosopher in his own terms. I have learned much from his reading of Paul and have many sympathies for his philosophical critique of empire and capitalism. I point to him as an example in order to illustrate how hermeneutical assumptions – however noble, well-intended or virtuous they may seem – will have inextricable consequences on how the author's intent expressed in a text will be (mis)treated and possible even "murdered." In other words, every reader's hermeneutical presuppositions for reading Bonhoeffer texts will have implications for how he fairs as human being and as author.

Here, then is the crux of the matter for me. Inadvertently but nonetheless ironically, the death of the author, the suspension of author may lead in the extreme to the "murdering" of a person. Erasing the author is nothing else but taking hostage the self of the author-person.[12] In the words of Emmanuel Levinas: the grandeur of modern antihumanism (his term) "consists in making a clear space for the hostage-subjectivity by sweeping away the notion of the person."[13] The irony lies precisely in the fact that Continental philosophy is at the vanguard of creating a significant space for "the

---

comparison that makes of him [Paul] a Lenin for whom Christ will have been the equivocal Marx."

[10] One of the most insightful points in Bonhoeffer's account of Christian community is precisely "that I must release others from all attempts to control, coerce, and dominate them with my love. In their freedom from me, other persons want to be loved for who they are, as those for whom Christ became a human being, died, and rose again ... This is the meaning of the claim that we can encounter others only through the mediation of Christ. Self-centered love constructs its own image of other persons, about what they are and what they should become" (*DBWE* 5, 44).

[11] Cf. Badiou, *Saith Paul*, 55–64, 110.

[12] Cf. Seán Burke, *The Death and Return of the Author. Criticism and Subjectivity in Barthes, Foucault and Derrida*. Edinburgh: Edinburgh University Press, third edition 2008.

[13] Emmanuel Levinas, *God, Death and Time*, translated by Bettina Bergo. Stanford: Stanford University Press 2000, 182. For an excellent discussion of Levinas from the point of philosophical hermeneutics, cf. Jens Zimmermann, *Recovering Theological Hermeneutics. An Incarnational-Trinitarian Theory of Interpretation*. Grand Rapids: Baker Academics 2004, 187–229.

other." There can be no doubt that Barthes and Foucault wanted to open up new and hitherto unexplored spaces for "the other" precisely by suspending the idea of author. It seems to me that the very space that postmodern thinkers want to open up, namely more freedom, recognition and space for being "the other" is vitiated by the death of the author as it turns out to be also the death of "the other." For how is it possible to suspend the notion of author without not also suspending the notion of the other? The retrieval of alterity hinges precisely on the fact that the "other" is permitted and free to live – to speak and to be heard – as the "other" person. There is no such thing as a "dead other." Is it not that for both Levinas and Bonhoeffer the author is always and necessarily the other?

Let us return to Bonhoeffer. As the example of Badiou's interpretation of Paul indicates, it is not possible to hold on to the Paul as other and at the same time suspend him as an author without doing violence to his otherness and his texts. Just as Levinas has made a convincing case that the other comes to me in the face-to-face encounter,[14] so similarly Bonhoeffer's entire theology of sociality and Christian community is predicated on the unconditional acceptance of the other on the basis of ἀγάπη. Levinas explicitly speaks of "the death of the other" and remarks that death "implicates me and puts me in question as if, by this death that is invisible to the other who is thereby exposed, I became the accomplice by way of my indifference." The other "summons me, asks for me, lays claim to me."[15] Similar to Levinas, Bonhoeffer insists already in his doctoral dissertation that the I "exists only in relation to an 'other'" and is indeed formed "only through the claim of the You."[16] Later in Life Together Bonhoeffer explicates in much more detail what the relationship between I and You entails. It means "that I must release others from all attempts to control, coerce, and dominate them with my love. In their freedom from me, other persons want to be loved for who they are, as those for whom Christ became a human being, died, and rose again... This is the meaning of the claim that we can encounter others only through the mediation of Christ. Self-centered love constructs its own image of other persons, about what they are and what they should become."[17]

Our insistence on the necessity of the concept of author is thus deeply embedded to reading Bonhoeffer who himself stakes out the framework

---

[14] Emmanuel Levinas, *Of God Who Comes to Mind*, translated by Bettina Bergo. Stanford: Stanford University Press 1998, 161–162.

[15] Levinas, *Of God Who Comes to Mind*, 162.

[16] *DBWE* 1, 51.

[17] *DBWE* 5, 44.

for such a concept. The author has not merely a narratological function. The author is not merely a narrator of an event or idea that is as such foreign to the author as person. In fact, Bonhoeffer says explicitly that the concept of the "other" in its core "refers to another human being."[18]

Bonhoeffer's Texts

For Roland Barthes, the suspension of the author inextricably impinges on the meaning of text: "The removal of the Author ... is not merely an [sic] historical fact or an act of writing; it utterly transforms the modern text (... the text is ... read in such a way that at all its levels the author is absent)."[19] Because there is no author, there can also be no book. In Barthes' words: "the modern scriptor ... is not the subject with the book as predicate."[20] The term "scriptor" designates the person who employs words and casts those into a text, but it is best to avoid the use of literature and speak merely of writing. Writing itself has no longer the purpose to create texts or literature, but it is basically a function of "enunciation." The scriptor enunciates ideas or events but has completely vanished into the background. For Barthes it follows that "once the author is removed, the claim to decipher a text becomes quite futile. To give a text an Author is to impose a limit on that text, to furnish it with a final signified, to close the writing."[21] Moreover, "by refusing to assign a 'secret', an ultimate meaning, to the text (and to the world as text), liberates what may be called an anti-theological activity, an activity that is truly revolutionary since to refuse to fix meaning is, in the end, to refuse God and his hypostases – reason, science, law."[22] Barthes' proposal to suspend author, and with it text or meta-narrative, leaves the scriptor only with his or her enunciations. But meaning is not to be found in these enunciations, at least not in the sense that the author intended meaning. Meaning must come from elsewhere, but not from texts.

To illustrate what happens when the reader approaches a text in the way Barthes suggests, let us look once again at Alain Badiou. How does Badiou read Paul's texts? These are his presuppositions: "I have always read the

---

[18] Barthes, "The Death of the Author," 145.
[19] Barthes, "The Death of the Author," 145.
[20] Barthes, "The Death of the Author," 145. Even Roland Barthes as a scriptor created a text (he would call it a writing) in order to demonstrate that there is no such thing as an author or text. Hence his "enunciation" did have an implied purpose. The writing of mere "enunciations" seems to vitiate against the very presupposition it advocates.
[21] Barthes, "The Death of the Author," 147.
[22] Barthes, "The Death of the Author," 147.

epistles the way one returns to those classic texts with which one is particularly familiar; their paths well worn, their details abolished, their power preserved. No transcendence, nothing sacred, perfect equality of this work with every other."[23] How does Badiou use the Pauline texts? In this instance, Badiou is also clear: "we may draw upon them freely, without devotion or repulsion."[24] In other words, when the author is suspended (although Badiou does not make this claim), his or her text is open to any meaning. For Badiou, in effect, the Pauline texts have become a mere foil for his own philosophical and ideological speculations. The meaning is not in the texts, but in the person who reads an enunciation and constructs the meaning – and in this very process becomes himself another author!

As we said at the beginning, the person interested in Bonhoeffer will encounter Bonhoeffer in his writings; this is our reality. Although an author can create works of art, literature etc., in the case of Bonhoeffer, the creation of the author is that of the text. Or, to put it differently, the retrieval of Bonhoeffer is the retrieval of the texts he authored. Against Barthes, we must therefore uphold that Bonhoeffer did not merely wish to offer us his neutral enunciations about his theological ideas or the evil of Nazi crimes. For Bonhoeffer, Nazi crimes were precisely not to be neutrally enunciated, but needed to be condemned by the author. Woltersdorff puts this matter in these terms: "My view is that interpretation at bottom is nothing done to an artifact but engagement with a person, albeit a mode of engagement mediated by the artifact; if the artifact in question is a text, it's a mode of engagement with the authorizer of the text, be it author or editor."[25]

That interpretation is "engagement with a person" recalls our reflections on Levinas and Bonhoeffer. The "other" will always encounter us as a person even though the mode of encounter may be distinct. For Levinas, we meet the other in an encounter, ideally a face-to-face encounter (*visage*). The encounter with the text of the author seems to me one such space where the other is not suspended, but where dialogue opens up space for genuine human understanding. In that sense, for the contemporary reader of Bonhoeffer, since a face-to-face encounter is no longer possible, we participate in a text-to-face encounter. It is precisely Bonhoeffer's text that we encounter "in our face," that is to say, in our being; retrieval of the text is

---

[23] Badiou, *Saint Paul*, 1.
[24] Badiou, *Saint Paul*, 1.
[25] Nicholas Woltersdorff, "Resuscitating the Author," in Kevin J. Vanhoozer, James K. A. Smith and Bruce Ellis Benson (eds), *Hermeneutics at the Crossroads*. Bloomington: Indiana University Press 2006, 35–50, here 36.

thus the retrieval of the author, indeed the person Bonhoeffer who puts claims to us mediated by his text.[26]

It is, moreover, noteworthy to call to mind that Bonhoeffer himself lived a life that can only be understood as a prime example of a hermeneutical life. He ordered his life utterly and comprehensively around making intelligible for himself and others the meaning of a text – the texts of the Bible. His assumption was the hermeneutical unity between the authority and meaning of the text (Scripture) and the full affirmation of its author (multiple writers inspired by God's Spirit). Hence, as a theologian and pastor, he was engaged on the level of textual hermeneutics. But this level of textual engagement was simply the foundation for the larger structure of his life as a whole. Interpreting and understanding the meaning of the texts of scripture was the solid ground under his feet.

A convincing argument in favour of the unity between person and text is expressed in a remark that Marty made in his assessment of *Letters and Papers from Prison:* "No publisher would have seen a potentially attractive book in the letters or his other various jottings, musings, and poems written in prison."[27] This point is unambiguous: the attractiveness of *Letters and Papers* from Prison is due to the fact that it was Bonhoeffer – the person – who wrote them. Were these musings written by a "normal" prisoner of war, what publisher and reader would have found them of any interest?

Interpretation and Understanding

I agree with Gadamer (following Schleiermacher) that the objective of interpretation is the art of understanding (*Verstehen*).[28] It is not enough, as Barthes and Foucault maintain, to enunciate a thought, idea etc. Indeed, it is precisely the overcoming of a mere enunciation that constitutes the heart of the hermeneutical circle.[29] Gadamer maintains that understanding happens exactly in the relation between two human beings and thereby touch-

---

[26] The primary Bonhoeffer texts are the German (*Dietrich Bonhoeffer Werke; DBW*) and English (*Dietrich Bonhoeffer Works English; DBWE*) standard editions. There are nearly 10000 pages of primary text, supplemented by a myriad of secondary literature.

[27] Marty, *Dietrich Bonhoeffer's Letters and Papers from Prison*, 3.

[28] Hans-Georg Gadamer. *Wahrheit und Methode. Grundzüge einer philosophischen Hermeneutik*. Tübingen: Mohr Siebeck, seventh edition 2010, 183–185. On Gadamer, cf. Jens Zimmermann, *Recovering Theological Hermeneutics*, 160–186.

[29] Relevant to this discussion is also Dilthey's distinction between *explanation* and *understanding*. Cf. Wilhelm Dilthey, *Einleitung in die Geisteswissenschaften*, Gesammelte Schriften 1. Stuttgart: B.G. Teubner Verlagsgesellschaft, ninth edition, 1995, 5.

es them in their very being (*in allem Wesentlichen*).[30] The key element is indeed the fact that understanding is a basic anthropological disposition. It is interesting in this connection that very early in his academic writings Bonhoeffer likewise pointed to the relation between being and thought (understanding). Following Heidegger, he reverses, correctly in my view, the Cartesian maxim cogito ergo sum into its contrary sum cogito ergo. In his own words, "It had been the basic mistake of Descartes and all his followers that, in explicating the cogito sum, they neglected to put the question of being to the sum. But this question cannot be raised unless there 'is something like an understanding of being'."[31] Bonhoeffer therefore assigns priority "to the question of being over that of thought."[32] In view of the hermeneutical circle, this implies that interpretation and understanding grow out of the more basic anthropological category of being. Bonhoeffer re-scripts Descartes in this manner: because we are human beings, therefore we are able to think, interpret and understand. Bonhoeffer agrees with Heidegger that the "scandal of philosophy" is not that the proof for *Dasein* has apparently not yet been given, but "that such proofs are expected and attempted again and again" while "the decisive point is, however, that it [*Dasein*] already is in every instance."[33] This, I propose, is the hermeneutical baseline in Bonhoeffer.

When Bonhoeffer assumes ontological priority of being over thinking, he also assumes a teleological direction of all being. In other words, human existence as such seeks purpose and meaning. It is our most basic human constituency that we desire to find a purpose and meaning for our lives. For the person interested in Bonhoeffer, this means that on the most basic level we encounter Bonhoeffer as a human being, as a person. Even though Bonhoeffer is now a dead, white male and we cannot meet him in a face-to-face encounter, we nonetheless encounter him as a human being. In this sense, Bonhoeffer simply is. His personhood is the foundation for his being an author and, in turn, his being an author is the foundation of his texts. We therefore encounter the person-author Bonhoeffer in his texts. Our task, therefore, is the art of interpreting these texts and seeking their understanding.

Concretely, it seems to me, the person interested in Bonhoeffer is not satisfied merely with explaining his life, but is engaging to understand it. Explaining, describing and understanding are different things. As Zimmer-

---

[30] Gadamer, *Wahrheit und Methode*, 184.
[31] *DBWE* 2, 70.
[32] *DBWE* 2, 70.
[33] *DBWE* 2, 70.

mann suggests, Gadamer has recovered "the universality of hermeneutics," and it is therefore appropriate to speak of "the hermeneutical nature of human existence."[34] The mediating link between being and meaning is language. Gadamer expresses this idea in a terse sentence at the end of *Truth and Method*. He notes that "Sein, das verstanden werden kann, ist Sprache (Being that can be understood is language)."[35] In a later essay Gadamer clarifies that he intended to demonstrate that language is the "hermeneutical dimension"[36] in which being appears; such an appearing is, however, never complete and always remains fragmentary. It is interesting for our purposes to note that Gadamer explicitly speaks of a "Sein zum Texte." In other words, the language of a text is the hermeneutic dimension in which we encounter an aspect of being – the being of the author-person and also our own being. For the contemporary reader of Bonhoeffer, the hermeneutical dimension of language, recorded as text, is thus the gateway to encounter being, engage in interpretation and arrive at understanding.

Hermeneutical Presuppositions

As mentioned at the beginning of this essay, when we read we engage our minds in a nearly automatic process that procures a "default" understanding of a text. This was true for Bonhoeffer himself as much as it is the case today for those who are reading his writings. Bonhoeffer himself brought hermeneutical presuppositions to his reading of texts in the same way that each of us brings his or her own presuppositions to Bonhoeffer. We will comment briefly on both aspects in relation to the hermeneutical circle.

Bonhoeffer's Hermeneutical Presuppositions

Bonhoeffer's most basic hermeneutical presupposition was the fact that he was male.[37] Bonhoeffer was born into a society of privilege that was patriarchal on both the macro and micro levels. His thought and behaviour as a whole were deeply embedded in a world constructed, shaped and con-

---

[34] Zimmermann, *Recovering Theological Hermeneutics*, 163–164.

[35] Gadamer, *Wahrheit und Methode*, 478.

[36] Hans-Georg Gadamer, "Text und Interpretation," in *Wahrheit und Methode. Ergänzungen, Register.* Tübingen: J.C.B. Mohr (Paul Siebeck) 1986, 334–335.

[37] On the question of gender in Bonhoeffer, see Lisa E. Dahill, "'There's Some Contradiction Here': Gender and the Relation of *Above* and *Below* in Bonhoeffer," in Peter Frick (ed), *Bonhoeffer and Interpretive Theory*, 53–84.

trolled by the ideas and power of men; indeed, some scholars have detected elements of chauvinism in his writings. As far as we know, all his professors were male, as were all the students at the Finkenwalde underground seminary and most of his friends, although some of the students attending his lectures at the University of Berlin were female.[38] His language, as it was typical for his time, was non-inclusive. As the use of pronouns demonstrates, he preferred masculine ones even when the referent may be feminine. In addition to the predominantly patriarchal structure as his *Sitz im Leben*, Bonhoeffer was also embedded in a bourgeois world of privilege, wealth and power. As is well known, the Bonhoeffers' belonged to a world of Berlin's social elite, were at home in the intellectual circles of the city and the university, and enjoyed an economic status of luxurious suburban living. As his life unfolded, Bonhoeffer increasingly lost these privileges which, in turn, changed the hermeneutical markers of his life.

The fact that Bonhoeffer had a positive, appreciative attitude toward women (grandmother, mother, sisters, Maria, Ruth von Kleist and others) should not minimize the fact that he inhabited a male world and was conditioned to relate to women from the perspective of that male world. To be clear: I am not faulting Bonhoeffer for being a male. However, the fact of his being a man is beyond dispute a decisive hermeneutical marker. It raises one crucial, albeit hypothetical question. What would Bonhoeffer's life and theology have looked like had he been a woman? Would his thinking, writing, actions etc. have had the same shape as we know it today? These reflections merely point out that Bonhoeffer's life was thoroughly determined by male perspectives. The questions of life and thought themselves were formulated by males and the answers provided were also, more or less, articulated by males. This is not only the case for Bonhoeffer's encounter with theology, but equally true in church and politics. The reality of Bonhoeffer's own hermeneutical presuppositions is one that Denise Ackermann characterizes as "malesteam theology,"[39] namely a theology that is blind to the question of gender and power. In postmodern hermeneutics, such questions are for good reasons at the forefront.

---

[38] Bonhoeffer had an untypically open relationship with Elisabeth Zinn. In an astonishingly transparent letter to her he relates how his life unfolded from being a theologian and pastor to becoming a Christian; cf. *DBWE* 14, 134.

[39] Cited in H. Russel Botman, "Is Bonhoeffer Still of Any Use in South Africa?" in John W. de Gruchy (ed), *Bonhoeffer for a New Day. Theology in a Time of Transition*. Grand Rapids/Cambridge: William B. Eerdmans 1997, 367.

Contemporary Reader Presuppositions

Bonhoeffer the person-author composed his texts on the basis of his own hermeneutical presuppositions. As contemporary readers we can only become cognizant of these. Equally important, however, is our own admission that we too, without exception, bring our own hermeneutical presuppositions to reading Bonhoeffer. Our reading of Bonhoeffer – that is to say our interpretation, description, assessment and ultimately our understanding – are so thoroughly coloured by our own unique hermeneutical presuppositions that they will yield an almost predicable result. Each reader is so deeply indebted to his or her hermeneutical markers that it is impossible to understand Bonhoeffer apart from those. In other words, a person's hermeneutical *Sitz im Leben* will inevitably lead to an understanding of Bonhoeffer that is congruent with one's own presuppositions. As is the case with Bonhoeffer, so too for us hermeneutical markers must be understood in the broadest possible sense to include our social, intellectual, gender, religious, economic, psychological and other determining factors. Taken together, these markers will yield what we may call a default understanding.

Initially there is no problem with a default reading as it comes about for every person as a result of his or her hermeneutical presuppositions. The task that now ensues from a default reading is how exactly one can progress to examine and evaluate one's default reading. This next step is in a sense the moment of hermeneutic enlightenment, or the gaining of a hermeneutically self-conscious reading.

Hermeneutical Self-Consciousness

As we just concluded, a default reading is a person's first understanding of author and text and is predicated on a person's hermeneutic horizon. The search for meaning and understanding is thus part of our basic humanity. Once we have arrived at a certain understanding – in our case of Bonhoeffer – we are faced with the crucial next step of becoming aware of our hermeneutic presuppositions. Up to this point, I have used the terms presupposition and marker as if they were neutral terms. This is not the case. Gadamer has persuasively demonstrated that each person's presuppositions or markers are in fact nothing else but prejudices (*Vorurteile*).[40] In

---

[40] Cf. Gadamer, *Wahrheit und Methode*, 274–275, 494.

other words, our presuppositions are essentially our prejudices that we bring to both author and text. As these are unique to every person they are never neutral – hence prejudice. A prejudice as such is not the real difficulty for hermeneutics; as they are simply belonging to human nature, prejudices partially form the identity of every person. From the hermeneutic point of view, the task is to become self-conscious of our prejudices, to discern how they position us within the hermeneutical circle and to be open of how they manipulate us in arriving at a hermeneutic understanding of a person-author.

To return to Alain Badiou once more: even though we may disagree with how he understands the Apostle Paul and how he interprets his texts, to be fair, however, it is to his credit that he is unambiguous in his hermeneutical self-consciousness. Badiou is "easy" to read to the extent that he does admit to clearly defined prejudices and that he articulates these candidly. We have now reached the critical point in our reflections on reading Bonhoeffer. For the contemporary reader of Bonhoeffer, the task is to move from a mere default reading to one that is hermeneutically self-aware. In short, hermeneutical self-consciousness consists in coming to terms with the presuppositions and markers that each person brings to the exercise of reading and ultimately understanding Bonhoeffer. Following Gadamer, we must seek to unmask these presuppositions for what they are, namely the inescapable prejudices that inform and determine our understanding. The first hermeneutical step is to admit to our prejudices, to name them and to make them intelligible in their functionality vis-à-vis our reading of Bonhoeffer. In my own case, I am trying to be aware of what these prejudices are and how they function in my understanding of Bonhoeffer. There are certain fixed presuppositions and markers that I cannot change: I am a white European male who lives a life of privilege, at least to a large degree. But there are also, in every person's life, a number of presuppositions and prejudices that can be changed and arguably must on occasion be modified. It is, indeed, possible to read against and in revision of my prejudices. In my case, hermeneutical self-consciousness means to be cognizant of the lens through which I read: whiteness implies privilege (not on the basis of a natural right or gift but because of historically and racially constructed modes of inequality), male implies dominance (not on the basis of nature, but a stolen and (sometimes) violent dominance); hence white males read from the perspective of privileged dominance. I am by no means saying that this is how I read Bonhoeffer or that all males are by nature dominating the "other;" I am however saying that each reader must scrutinize the particular prejudices that he or she brings to the hermeneutical circle. Without exception, each of the essays that follow below has a specific and unique set of hermeneutical presuppositions and prejudices.

The Limits of Understanding

One of my prejudices, significantly obvious in this essay, is that I do not think that the death of the author is a tenable presupposition. I have put forth some arguments above of why I think so. Nonetheless, hermeneutic sincerity entails, to speak with Gadamer, the openness that the other can be right in his or her understanding. In this sense, I do grant that Barthes and Foucault wanted to achieve something that hitherto had not been achieved in traditional, textual-oriented hermeneutics. In short, it was to elevate the person – who created his or her meaning from a text – above the author and text itself. Surprisingly, perhaps, there is a sentiment in Gadamer that the author in fact always remains behind the text. In his own words: "Nicht nur gelegentlich, sondern immer übertrifft der Sinn eines Textes seinen Autor (the meaning of a text goes beyond its author not only occasionally but always)."[41] In other words, while I agree with Barthes and Gadamer in that the meaning of a text – hermeneutically extracted – does go beyond the not always apparent authorial intent, I disagree with Barthes that therefore the author has to be suspended. I do think that in this way we do justice to the openness of the hermeneutic self-conscious task while holding on to the fact that the "other" is a person, namely an author.

In spite of what we have said so far, it would be utterly misleading to think of the hermeneutic path toward understanding as a straight or always successful one. Even if we grant a hermeneutic openness toward multiple interpretations of the same author, even if we uphold the disjunction between author, text and reader, we will still always approach the limit of understanding. We are somehow limited to engage in what Paul Riceour called "the hermeneutics of testimony."[42] Since the text itself is the limit for our understanding, the appropriate approach to the text is that of witness. Riceour says that "the witness is the author."[43] I would like to re-script this

---

[41] Gadamer, *Wahrheit und Methode*, 301.

[42] Paul Ricoeur, "The Hermeneutics of Testimony," in *Essays on Biblical Interpretation*, edited by Lewis S. Mudge. Philadelphia: Fortress Press 1980, 119–154. On Bonhoeffer's influence on Ricoeur's thought, see now Brian Gregor, "The Critique of Religion and Post-Metaphysical Faith: Bonhoeffer's Influence on Ricoeur's Hermeneutic of Religion," in Matthew D. Kirkpatrick (ed), *Engaging Bonhoeffer: The Impact and Influence of Bonhoeffer's Life and Thought*. Minneapolis: Fortress Press 2016, 259–282.

[43] Ricoeur, "The Hermeneutics of Testimony," 123.

statement as "the witness becomes the author." The curiosity of the hermeneutic undertaking is essentially thus that the reader bears witness to the testimony of an author, via the text, and attempts to decipher both for meaning. Reading Bonhoeffer is thus our witnessing him in our contemporary context, without falling into the trap of anachronism.

Finally, the limits of understanding are bound up with our humanity. It has perplexed many philosophers that Gadamer ends his *Truth and Method* with a discussion of the universality of hermeneutics. The universal aspect of hermeneutics is its finiteness (*Endlichkeit, Sterblichkeit*).[44] Hermeneutics is at the root thinking within the finiteness of language, meaning and understanding.[45] To express it differently, the hermeneutic circle is never fully closed; there is always an opening somewhere, a place where meaning can emerge, change and disappear. In the end this entails that the hermeneutic process is as fragmentary as life itself. Just as Bonhoeffer spoke of the fragmentary nature of life in its polyphony, we may similarly speak of a fragmentary hermeneutic within the polyphony of hermeneutic openness. The finiteness of language and thought – and to speak with Bonhoeffer: the finiteness of our self – constitutes a limit that no author, no text and no witness can overcome.

Conclusion

At the beginning of this study we referred to Martin Marty and Paul Tillich. Marty's book on *Letter and Papers from Prison* is a hermeneutical study of the reception of Bonhoeffer's prison writings. As we noted, it is staggering that East German Marxists, socialists, God-is-Dead theologians, Catholic and mainline and conservative Protestants all purport to have discovered the meaning of Bonhoeffer's last writing. Can all these readings, and with it the implicit claim to be one of "us," really be hermeneutically defended? Is the reason for such diverse interpretations not that the "author" Bonhoeffer was forfeited, or nearly so, in favour of a preferential ideology? Is it not that the death of his authorship made it possible that these conflicting understandings resulted in the first place? To what extent were these interpreters conscious of their prejudices? Are there not parallels with Badiou's reading of Paul? Would Paul not reject Badiou's reading

---

[44] Gadamer, *Wahrheit und Methode*, 479. Gadamer speaks of "the hermeneutic phenomenon" and says of it: "dessen alles bestimmender Grund aber ist die *Endlichkeit unserer geschichtlichen Erfahrung.*"

[45] Cf. Jean Grondin, *Einführung zu Gadamer*, 236.

of him as an author and his epistles as a blueprint for Marxist philosophy in the same way Bonhoeffer would no doubt reject many of the interpretations of his *Letter and Papers from Prison*?

Tillich demonstrated a nobler path. He became aware of his "theological provincialism" at a time when he could still correct it. The question that every contemporary reader, and therefore every interpreter, of Bonhoeffer's texts must face is the extent of his or her hermeneutic provincialism. Marty in his monograph showed the danger of hermeneutical provincialism; Tillich detected his own provincialism and overcame it. For us who read Bonhoeffer the task is the same: to break the circle of our sometimes un-reflected default reading and begin a path of hermeneutical self-conscious *Verstehen*.

Each of the essays in this volume has precisely the purpose of discussing how the hermeneutical circle and its underlying assumptions, prejudices, interpretive lenses, theoretical approaches and methods bears on the reading and ultimately the understanding of Bonhoeffer. Since the authors come from a diverse social, intellectual, geographic, ecclesial and personal location, the emphasis and arguments in each essay are distinct from each other. Although each of the authors shares in the common objective to demonstrate how a specific hermeneutic reading yields a distinct interpretation of Bonhoeffer, the path of that demonstration is as diverse as the *Sitz im Leben* of the authors. Shared prejudices and conceptual agreements notwithstanding, each essay has its own unique stamp, even implied disagreements with some of the other essays. It is the aim of this collection that the person interested in understanding Bonhoeffer will find here significant milestones in discovering his or her own prejudicial assumptions and in so doing will be encouraged to read Bonhoeffer with greater hermeneutical self-awareness.

3. *Interpretatio quaerens intellectum* – 'Translation Seeking Understanding': The Hermeneutics of Translating Bonhoeffer[*]

Introduction

This essay is a personal reflection on my experience as a translator and series editor for Greek and Hebrew in the now almost finished translation project *Dietrich Bonhoeffer Works English (DBWE)*. The purpose of these reflections is not so much to examine the details of the often painstaking work and dedication required for all the translators and editors of the project. Rather – as a scholar eminently interested in the intersection of theology, philosophy and biblical studies – I am attempting to make intelligible my experience of translating Bonhoeffer as a distinctly hermeneutic engagement – a hermeneutical journey as it were – and this in three distinct but interrelated levels. First, the translation of words; second, the translation of ideas, concepts, paragraphs, sections and so on; and third – and most important to me – the translation of the author as a person.

Translation as Hermeneutics

The deepest insight from my participation in the *DBWE* project is that translation is foremost a hermeneutical task. Indeed, the Greek word that means "to translate" is nothing else but the verb ἑρμενεύειν, based on the stem from which we derive the word "hermeneutics." There are several instances in the New Testament in which ἑρμενεύειν[1] or its cognate μεθερμενεύειν[2] are used in the sense of "translating" and this always means

---

[*] An abbreviated summary of these reflections was presented at Union Theological Seminary, New York, in November 2011 and a first version of this essay at the Annual Meeting of the International Bonhoeffer Society, American Academy of Religion, San Francisco, November 2011.

[1] John 1:42; 9:7; Hebrews 7:2.

[2] Matthew 1:23; Mark 5:41; 15:22, 34; John 1:38; Acts 4:36; 13:8.

to clarify specific words or phrases. Already in the New Testament, we find a strong correlation between the task of translation and that of hermeneutics. Indeed, to repeat, translation is essentially a hermeneutical task.[3]

Translation of Words

The beginning of my hermeneutical journey with Bonhoeffer started before I became one of the translators of his work. As a student of theology in Tübingen I had all too often heard of Bonhoeffer, but had not in any way started to study his thought. In order to fill this gap in my theological education I started reading Bonhoeffer in German – in order to *understand* his theology and life. In other words, given the compelling witness of his life, I was open-minded toward the possibility that this encounter would actually lead to intellectual clarification and existential shifts that may leave irrevocable traces in my own life. In retrospect, this proved to be the case.

The start of this journey was marked by my rather innocent review of *DBWE* volume 5 (*Life Together*), volume 2 (*Act and Being*) and volume 4 (*Discipleship*). When I pointed out dozens of morphological and diacritical mistakes in the Greek (now corrected in the reprints) in *Discipleship*, I was recruited to participate in the editorial board, as both translator and the lone Greek expert. I had stepped into the hermeneutical circle on the most basic level of translation and soon realized that I had entered what constitutes the initial and most basic level of translation: the translation of words.

On this basic level, translation means making intelligible the smallest units of speech – in linguistic terms, the morphemes – in a process that moves from source language to receptor language. No translator can avoid this basic task. It is the first step in the process of the transformation of meaning from one language to another one. The ideal here is synonymy in meaning, namely, that the meaning of words is synonymous in the original and receptor language. In many cases this works well: the expression *Wort*

---

[3] Cf. Martin Heidegger, *Being and Time*, translated by John Macquarrie and Edward Robinson. New York: Harper and Row Publishers 1962, 61–62, who argues that the *logos* "has the character of a *hermeneuein*, through which the authentic meaning of Being, and also those basic structures of Being which Dasein itself possess, are made known to Dasein's understanding of Being." Gerhard Ebeling, "Hermeneutik," in *Die Religion in Geschichte und Gegenwart*, Tübingen: J. C. B. Mohr, third edition 1959, 243, explicitly identifies one of the key meanings of *hermeneuein* as that of translation.

Gottes can be translated as Word of God, *Gebet* as prayer, *Kirche* as church and so on.

However, synonymy on the word level is not always successful. A good example to illustrate this point is the use of the German adjective *evangelisch*. Theological translators of German have typically translated this word as "evangelical." A prime example is Karl Barth's book, *Evangelical Theology: An Introduction*.[4] On the surface, it may seem like a proper translation, but a closer examination of this rendering reveals that it is actually problematic; this brings us to our second point.

Translation of Concepts

As the translation of the adjective *evangelisch* indicates, the meaning of words is usually embedded in the larger meaning of a phrase, expression, concept, idea and cultural milieu. In order to translate the broader meaning of a concept or expression accurately, the translator must understand the intellectual and cultural nuances of both the original and the receptor language. This is crucial for a dynamic rendering of the original language.

This point can be illustrated again with the rendering of the German adjective *evangelisch*. First, there seems to be synonymy between *evangelisch* and its translation as "evangelical." The translator of Barth's book understood the terms in this manner. This is problematic in that German *does* have another word for "evangelical" that expresses synonymy, namely, the word *evangelikal*. We can see already that a literal, synonymous translation poses a problem here. Second, the problem of synonymy was clearly perceived, and adequately dealt with, by the translators and editors of the *DBWE*. In short, given the largely American readership of *DBWE*, the adjective *evangelisch* is not identical with the American understanding of "evangelical." Evangelicalism stands for a certain theological understanding within the wide spectrum of Protestant churches and denominations in the United States and other English-speaking countries. In contrast, like Barth, Bonhoeffer employed the adjective *evangelisch* in the sense of "Protestant" as distinct from the (Roman) Catholic Church.[5] In

---

[4] Karl Barth, *Evangelical Theology: An Introduction*, translated by Grover Foley. New York: Holt, Rinehart and Winston, 1963.

[5] In *DBW* 15, 413, note 34, there is a reference to DEK, *Deutsche Evangelische Kirche*, a designation which is translated in the corresponding note 34 in *DBWE* 15, 421, as "German Evangelical Church." In this instance the translation is, in my view, mislead-

this sense, a more accurate translation of Barth's book would have been: *Protestant Theology: An Introduction.*

The broader and deeper the intellectual horizon and cultural context of the source language, the greater will be the challenge for the translator. Anyone who has attempted to read Martin Heidegger's *Being and Time* and claims to understand this philosophical opus on a first reading is hardly telling the truth. Indeed, the very concept of truth as ἀλήθεια, translated as the "unhiding" or "disclosing" of the *logos*[6] requires from the translator the mastery of German and Greek and that the reader should be steeped in the Greek philosophical traditions. As even these two examples (Barth and Heidegger) demonstrate, translation must go beyond word synonymy and consider the intellectual and cultural nuances and usages of specific words and concepts. In terms of the hermeneutical task, conceptual dynamic equivalence is arguably the most decisive criterion for a successful translation on the level of concept and discourse.

Translation of the Author

For my own hermeneutical journey, the third level is by far the most significant one. At the risk of oversimplifying, I would like to suggest that the aim of all translation must be "understanding." In other words, the ultimate hermeneutical task of translation is to bring to light the thought of an author.[7] Another possible way to express this third level of translation is to recall Anselm of Canterbury's definition of theology. We have all heard the famous words *fides quaerens intellectum,* "faith seeking understanding." For the sake of these reflections, I would like to rescript these words as *interpretatio quaerens intellectum,* "translation seeking understanding." In Anselm's view, faith is the given. Faith comes before understanding and leads to a person's deeper theological understanding of the content and coherence of that which is believed. In a similar way, I suggest, translation comes before understanding; indeed, understanding is the ultimate objective of understanding. We rely on a good translation in order to understand the thought and ideas of its author.

---

ing in that it may suggest that the struggle during the Nazification of the Church was between the German Christians and the evangelicals!

[6] Heidegger, *Being and Time*, 56–57, 270–271.

[7] Against the grain of much of contemporary hermeneutics, I do believe that an author writes with purpose and intention and communicates to make known and intelligible his or her ideas and thoughts.

At this point it is possible to interject and argue that this third level (the translation of the author) has little, perhaps nothing to do, with the task of translation proper. I admit that on the surface it may seem so, but I will argue to the contrary that this third step is not just a kind of a "bonus" of translation, but the very heart of it. Let me make my case in three steps.

1. As I worked away on my section of Bonhoeffer in *DBWE* 15, a question occurred to me repeatedly: why do we need to translate Bonhoeffer in the first place? In short, it is because we want Bonhoeffer's thought to be known and understood. Ideally this happens when we read him in German, but it also happens by translating his thought. In other words, the mastery of another language is like a window into another world. Other languages are not merely saying in other words what our own language says; rather, another language is another way of thinking, another way of perceiving the world, another vehicle of expressing a fundamental world-view. Translation of words and concepts – as accurate as it may be – is only partially able to translate the deeper structures of implicit world-views in other languages. Said negatively, translation has an implied hermeneutical boundary that cannot be overstepped. The intellectual world-view implicit in the source language can never be fully retrieved in the receptor language. This fact may be illustrated with two examples. First: as a teacher of biblical Greek I get sometimes introduced as a Greek scholar, as if Greek were my scholarly identity. This is not the case. I teach and use Greek only as the tool that makes possible a deeper reading of the biblical and philosophical texts. I understand mastery of Greek not as an end by itself but as the beginning of the path to understanding. Greek will reveal nuances in the biblical text that English translations typically fail to articulate.[8] Second: the mastery of another language in the service of translation can also be compared to scaffolding used in the construction of a building. Language is like scaffolding: it is used as the instrument to build understanding. The aim of language is understanding, in the same way that the purpose of scaffolding is to facilitate the construction of the building. Once finished, scaffolding is removed and we only see the house; analogously, once translation is completed, we treasure the understanding of the author that resulted from it.

Let me briefly return to the question that I asked earlier: why translation in the first place? We can confidently maintain that it is a good thing in-

---

[8] For example, Greek has several distinct ways of negation (indicative, non-indicative, subjunctives mood; expectation of an affirmative answer) or nuances of imperatives (present and aorist), distinct emphases in adverbial participles and subjunctive clauses etc., all of which cannot be appreciated in a translation.

deed to provide a scholarly translation of Bonhoeffer's works. This cannot mean, however, that the scholar has now a license to neglect reading Bonhoeffer in the original, in the same way that a biblical scholar cannot neglect Hebrew and Greek just because there are so many translations of the Bible available.

2. On a more important hermeneutic level, I made a rather unexpected discovery. I was assigned a section of *DBWE* 15, a rather large volume that contains Bonhoeffer's writings from the Finkenwalde years 1937–1940. Since apart from a few exceptions these writings have not been previously translated into English, I realized very soon that Bonhoeffer scholars have largely neglected the "Finkenwalde Bonhoeffer." What do I mean? It is a rather curious fact that four of the sixteen volumes in *DBWE* (vols. 4, 5, 14 and 15) originate in the period of theological education during the Finkenwalde years and shortly thereafter (more or less the years 1935–1939). While volume 4 (*Discipleship*) and volume 5 (*Life Together*) became almost instant Bonhoeffer classics, the extensive materials in volumes 14 and 15 have at the time of this writing not been translated into English.[9]

The neglect of volumes 14 and 15 in Bonhoeffer scholarship is colossal. As an even cursory glance at recent (English-speaking) scholarship indicates, these volumes hardly figure when compared to the heavyweights, such as volumes 1–8. To be fair, we may grant that the reason for this neglect lies in the very fact that these two volumes have not been translated up until now. But the problem goes deeper. On the one hand, it points to what I suggested above about the need to read Bonhoeffer in the original German; though not a requirement for lay readers, it is a basic requirement for scholars. On the other hand, is it perhaps symptomatic of Bonhoeffer scholarship that the fact of the date of publication of these two volumes – last on the list of sixteen – is an indication of the lack of importance ascribed to these volumes when compared with other volumes? But are we as scholars entitled to prefer the popular writings over those which are less popular or are as yet unknown because they are not translated?

The magnitude of the issue becomes more apparent when we consider the extent of the neglect in terms of numbers. *DBW* 14 has 1252 pages and *DBW* 15 has 762 pages (*DBWE* 14 has 1230 pages and *DBWE* 15 has 726 pages). In other words, these two volumes together contain about 2000 pages or approximately 22 per cent of all the materials in the entire *DBWE*

---

[9] Volume 15 (*Theological Education Underground 1937–1940*) has been published in 2012 and volume 14 (*Theological Education Underground 1935–1937*) as the last volume in the sixteen-volume *DBWE* in 2013. The index (volume 17) has been published in 2014.

series![10] The dilemma of the matter is that we do not yet fully understand the extent of which our neglect has presented a distorted image of Bonhoeffer and his theology. In other words, do these pages contain a wealth of materials that will shed further light on Bonhoeffer's theology to such a degree that Bonhoeffer scholarship may have to attune or even revise some of the now standard positions attributed to him?

3. In relation to the above, I often ask myself whether the time to re-examine our overall picture of Bonhoeffer's theology has arrived. As I just pointed out, there are the hundreds of yet insuffciently examined pages from the Finkenwalde period. But there is even more at stake. It is the understandable yet curious phenomenon that Bonhoeffer scholarship has been utterly intrigued with Bonhoeffer's (speculative) prison theology. When one looks at the indices of the *International Bonhoeffer Bibliography* it is immediately apparent that expressions like "religionless Christianity," "world come of age" and "non-religious interpretation" – in short, what we refer to as prison theology – are the centre and focus for much of Bonhoeffer scholarship.[11] The same is true for monographs and essays. In other words, Bonhoeffer research has up until now favoured the academic works *Sanctorum Communio* and *Act and Being*, as well as *Ethics*, and to a lesser degree the Finkenwalde classics *Discipleship* and *Life Together*. But often the most intriguing work for scholars is *Letters and Papers from Prison*.[12]

The reason why scholars and lay persons alike have been fascinated with *Letters and Papers from Prison* is self-evident, or so it seems: in prison, Bonhoeffer's life and theology came together as a unique witness to Jesus Christ. Bonhoeffer lived out in person to the very end what he himself had taught and preached. And, indeed, his life stands as a remarkable penultimate inspiration for a genuine witness to the gospel of the resurrected Christ. His example is one of the most extraordinary ones for me personally and I do not wish to distract from its power in any way.

---

[10] The 16 volumes of the *DBWE* series contain a total of 9144 pages.

[11] Cf. Ernst Feil and Barbara E. Fink (eds), *International Bibliography on Dietrich Bonhoeffer/Internationale Bibliographie zu Dietrich Bonhoeffer*. Gütersloh: Chr. Kaiser/Gütersloher Verlagshaus 1998.

[12] Jürgen Moltmann says explicitly that when he first encountered *Letters and Papers from Prison* as a student in 1949, he was captivated by the "unfinished thoughts" that stimulated his thinking. Unlike Karl Barth's polished dogmatics, Bonhoeffer drew him into the "open theological thought process;" cf. Moltmann, "Dietrich Bonhoeffer und die Theologie. Eine persönliche Würdigung," in Clifford Green and Thomas Tseng (eds), *Dietrich Bonhoeffer and Sino-Theology*, Sino-Christian Studies Supplement Series. Taipei: Chung Yuan Christian University 2008, 15–33, here 21.

However, for the sake of our discussion, let us make a distinction between his life and his theology. His life came to a momentous conclusion in prison and ultimately at the gallows in Flossenbürg. But did his theology equally come to a momentous conclusion in prison? Is his prison theology indeed the grand finale of his intellectual achievement and his theological *magnum opus*? My intention is *to raise this question* rather than attempt an answer. In 2010, Martin Marty wrote an intriguing book, *Dietrich Bonhoeffer's Letters and Papers from Prison: A Biography*.[13] If we would know next to nothing of Bonhoeffer's life – in other words, if we would be ignorant of the *Sitz im Leben* that makes his life and his theology so attractive to many Christians – then, I think, Marty is quite correct in his assessment of *Letters and Papers from Prison*: "No publisher would have seen a potentially attractive book in the letters or his other various jottings, musings, and poems written in prison."[14] The point is (almost) beyond argument: we ascribe significance to Bonhoeffer's prison theology because we associate it with his person, but not because we encounter a grand theological synthesis of his earlier theological thinking.

But Marty also points to another rather bewildering phenomenon of *Letters and Papers from Prison*. In short, it is the bizarre history of interpretation. Perhaps no other work of Bonhoeffer has been claimed in such contradictory terms. How could it be that East German communists, Evangelicals, mainline liberal Protestants, God-is-dead theologians and Catholics all alike stake out claims that make Bonhoeffer one of them? That they cannot all be right in their ideological interpretations stands to basic hermeneutical reason. Again, my intention is to raise this dilemma rather than to answer it.

Then there is Karl Barth. Arguably for Bonhoeffer there was no other contemporary theologian as important a theological *Gesprächspartner* as Barth. The two of them exchanged numerous letters and had at least six face-to-face encounters. After Bonhoeffer's death and shortly after the publication of the first edition of *Letters and Papers from Prison*, there was an exchange of letters between Barth and a pastor, Walter Herrenbrück. The latter explicitly asked Barth to respond to the ideas expressed in *Letters and Papers from Prison*; Barth did so in great detail in a letter in 1952. Barth remarks that Bonhoeffer's letters are "one deep sting" and one cannot read them without getting the impression that "there is something" in

---

[13] Martin E. Marty, *Dietrich Bonhoeffer's Letters and Papers from Prison: A Biography*. Princeton: Princeton University Press 2010.

[14] Marty, *Dietrich Bonhoeffer's Letters and Papers from Prison*, 3.

them. Nonetheless, Barth characterizes Bonhoeffer as an "impulsive, visionary thinker" who proposed ideas (in *Discipleship*, in his teaching on the mandates) and then pulled back and would probably have said things differently in a later context. "Now he has left us alone with his enigmatic statements in his letters. In many ways he indicated that he had a hunch, but he did not know how the story would be completed." In more than one way Barth continues, Bonhoeffer did not leave us anything that "was concrete in his own eyes." There may be no deeper meaning (*Tiefsinn*) to the enigmatic statements because he himself did not yet find such a deeper theological coherence. "Ohne ihn selbst fragen zu können, werden wir uns damit abfinden müssen, etwas verwirrt zurückzubleiben."[15] A few years later, in 1963, Barth once again cautioned that he did not simply want to do what is done so often: to systematize the ideas of the late Bonhoeffer.[16]

Finally, let us hear Bonhoeffer himself. On four occasions he comments in his prison letters on his theological ideas. "What might surprise or perhaps even worry you," he writes to his friend Bethge, "would be my theological thoughts and where they are leading, and here is where I miss you really very much. I don't know anyone else with whom I can talk about them and arrive at some clarity."[17] The day before the failed attempt on Hitler's life, Bonhoeffer appeals to Bethge again. In relation to the world-come-of age ideas, he says: "forgive me, this is all still put terribly clumsily and badly; I am very aware of this. But perhaps you are just the one to help me again to clarify and simplify it."[18] Finally, after the conspiracy, at the end of the outline for a planned book, he summarizes: "All this is put very roughly and only outlined. But I am eager to attempt for once to express certain things simply and clearly ... I hope in doing so I can be of some service for the future of the church."[19] Given Bonhoeffer's comments to Bethge, it seems to me that we cannot ignore his own repeated caution that he has not yet achieved clarity on these theological matters. For the moment, my own reading of *Letters and Papers from Prison* is to take these theological ideas as signposts on Bonhoeffer's much longer theological journey. I do not think that we are yet – perhaps never – in a position to take the prison letters as the pinnacle of Bonhoeffer's theology or as the starting point from which we assess retrospectively his earlier theology.

---

[15] Karl Barth, *Offene Briefe 1945–1968*. Gesamtausgabe V, 15. Zurich: TVZ 1984, 324–327.

[16] Cf. Karl Barth, *Gespräche 1963*. Gesamtausgabe IV, 41. Zurich: TVZ 2005, 281.

[17] *DBWE* 8, 362; cf. also 374.

[18] *DBWE* 8, 482.

[19] *DBWE* 8, 504.

More research needs to be done, especially in the extensive corpus of lectures in the Finkenwalde period and the relation between this period and to the ideas of the prison theology.

Conclusion

These remarks are mere personal reflections on how my engagement in translating Bonhoeffer has deepened my interest and perspective on his theology and life. Participating in the work of *DBWE* has been an unusually rewarding experience. On the one hand, I count it a privilege to bring Bonhoeffer to a wider English readership. On the other hand, my work on *DBWE* 15 has opened up a new vista of interest in his theology – namely, the hundreds of pages in volumes 14 and 15 – that, in my view, still need to be examined, first, on their own terms, and, second, in relation to the early and later Bonhoeffer. This work will be for me another station on the journey of hermeneutics, the attempt to *understand* Bonhoeffer more deeply and faithfully.

Backgrounding Bonhoeffer

4. The *Imitatio Christi* of Thomas à Kempis and Dietrich Bonhoeffer[*]

Introduction

No other spiritual classic shaped Bonhoeffer's theology of spiritual formation as much as Kempis's *Imitatio Christi*.[1] It is, therefore, a curious fact that in Bonhoeffer research there is no study that examines the influence of the medieval Augustinian monk Thomas à Kempis (1380–1471)[2] on the life and thought of Dietrich Bonhoeffer (1906–1945).[3] In view of this lacuna, the objective of this present study is to examine the thought of Kempis on the basis of his spiritual classic, the *Imitatio Christi*, a work he finished around the year 1427. Our main question is how this work shapes and influences Bonhoeffer's theological development and lifelong convictions on the spiritual life.

As a careful reading of Bonhoeffer's writings will show, the theological and spiritual insights of Kempis became critical for his theological forma-

---

[*] With gratitude I acknowledge the financial support for this research from the Social Sciences and Humanities Research Council of Canada.

[1] Not even the Spiritual Exercises of Saint Ignatius of Loyola, of which he owed a copy (cf. *DBWE* 6, 407, note 63) had such an impact on Bonhoeffer. It is noteworthy to point out that St. Ignatius treasured the *Imitatio Christi* himself very much and used it for his own spiritual exercises. Indeed, "so devoted was Ignatius to this spiritual classic that he read a chapter a day for the rest of his life and had it on a table at his bedside when he died;" cf. *The Spiritual Exercises of St. Ignatius*, translated by Louis J. Puhl, Vintage Spiritual Classic. New York: Vintage 2000, xv.

[2] For a succinct introduction on the life and thought of Kempis see Ulrich Köpf, "Thomas von Kempen," in *TRE* 33, 480–483, Nikolaus Staubach, "Thomas von Kempen," *RGG4* 8, 377 (fourth edition specified in the Abbreviations) and the older but still excellent article by Vincent Scully, "Thomas à Kempis," in *Catholic Encyclopedia*. New York: Robert Appleton Company 1912, volume 15.

[3] I was not able to access the contribution by Zen-emon Morino, "Zur Logik und Ethik der Nachfolge [Thomas a Kempis und Luther, Kierkegaard und Bonhoeffer]," in *Fukujû no Roni to Roni* (*Evangelium und Welt*) 3 (1965), 26–31. This is the only entry (#605) that specifically names à Kempis in Ernst Feil and Barbara E. Fink (eds), *International Bibliography on Dietrich Bonhoeffer/Internationale Bibliographie zu Dietrich Bonhoeffer*. Gütersloh: Chr. Kaiser/Gütersloher Verlagshaus 1998.

tion as early as his teaching career at the University of Berlin and as late as his imprisonment in Tegel. The first chronological reference to Kempis in Bonhoeffer's written oeuvre can be traced to 1932. Bonhoeffer's grandmother, Julie Bonhoeffer, expresses appreciation for her grandson's gift, apparently a copy of the *Imitatio Christi*, on the occasion of her 90th birthday. In a letter she thanks Bonhoeffer and mentions that she was already familiar with this book. Nonetheless, she says, "You gave me great pleasure with the Thomas à Kempis. I like very much to read a few sections in the mornings … Of course, I knew the little book from earlier days."[4] At the time of his grandmother's birthday in January 1932, Bonhoeffer was not yet 26 years old. Possibly he had read Kempis even during his teen years, but our sources do not allow us to draw such a conclusion.

The latest chronological datum in Bonhoeffer's life regarding Kempis can be traced to the end of 1943. According to Eberhard Bethge's masterful biography, Bonhoeffer read Kempis – in a Latin edition[5] – in his cell in Tegel prison during November and December of that year.[6] Between these two chronological markers lies the period of the Berlin, London and Finkenwalde years, namely 1932–1938 – the period that stands out as the one in which Bonhoeffer was most deeply influenced by Kempis's classic work. That influence becomes conspicuously transparent in his own spiritual classics, *Discipleship* and *Life Together*.

---

[4] *DBWE* 11, 142.

[5] Bonhoeffer's Latin edition was that of M.J. Pohl (ed), *Thomas à Kempis. Werke*, vol. 2, *Imitatio Christi*. Freiburg: Herder 1904. This Latin copy was given by Bonhoeffer's parents to Bishop George Bell on the occasion of his visit to Berlin in October 1945. It contains the following hand-written dedication: "In seinem Testament bittet unser Sohn Dietrich Ihnen, Herr Lordbischof, ein Buch aus seiner Bibliothek zur Erinnerung an ihn zu übersenden. Er hat diesen Thomas a Kempis noch im Gefängnis in Tegel bei sich gehabt. Eltern Bonhoeffer. Oktober 45." Right below these lines there is the following typed remark: "This book was sent from prison by Dietrich Bonhoeffer to be given to his friend George Bell, Bishop of Chichester, and was handed to him by his parents on October 29 1945. It was given to the Deutsche Evangelische Kirche, in memory of them both, by his wife Henrietta Bell. Saturday November 28 1959." The signature of Henrietta Bell follows. The copy is now located at the Bonhoeffer Church in Forest Hill, London. Cf. *DBWE* 8, 230–231, note 21. I was able to visit the church and examine this book in April 2005.

[6] Eberhard Bethge, *Dietrich Bonhoeffer. Theologian, Christian, Man of his Time. A Biography*, translated and revised by Victoria Barnett. Minnesota: Fortress Press 2000, 943, provides a detailed list of all the books Bonhoeffer read during his imprisonment from April 1943 until April 1945; among the 85 works listed is *The Imitation of Christ* by Thomas à Kempis.

Discipleship

Bonhoeffer lectured on the various theological aspects pertaining to discipleship when he was director of the underground seminary of the Confessing Church in Finkenwalde from 1935 to 1937.[7] Shortly after the closing of the seminary in October 1937, his book *Discipleship* [*Nachfolge*] was published in November. However, as Bethge asserts, "both the theme and the underlying thesis of *Discipleship* were already fully evolved before 1933, but the book owes its single-minded, exclusive claims to that year."[8] With Hitler's rise to power, the year 1933 foreshadowed what was to happen in Germany politically. Theologically, Bonhoeffer attempted to work out an understanding of the Christian faith that could take account of the changing ecclesiological reality. In this regard, the decade of the 1930s was decisive for shaping his overall theology. We know from the lecture notes of former students that Bonhoeffer was increasingly attentive to Kempis's *Imitatio Christi* during the winter semester 1932–1933 at the University of Berlin. According to the notes of Erich Klapproth, a student who had attended Bonhoeffer's lectures on "Schöpfung und Sünde" (Creation and Sin),[9] Bonhoeffer commented in his introduction on the importance of hearing God's word in the context of doing a spiritual exercise (*exercitium*). The significance of *exercitium* arose again during the final session of the seminar on "Theological Psychology," according to Hilde Pfeiffer's notes.[10] Another participant in the seminar and later a seminarian in the fourth course at Finkenwalde, Gerhard Krause, explicitly asserts that Bonhoeffer's exercises in that seminar "reproduced Thomas à Kempis's *Imitation of Christ*."[11] Krause thus establishes the connection between Bonhoeffer's emphasis on spiritual exercises and Kempis's *Imitatio*. Similarly, we are told by Herbert Jehle, a friend of Bonhoeffer's who studied physics at Cambridge when Bonhoeffer was in London, that during their frequent visits in London they discussed the subject of Christian community and

---

[7] For a listing of the lectures and seminars during the five courses at Finkenwalde, cf. *DBWE* 14, 1027–1036. For the seminarians' eager anticipation of the publication of *Discipleship*, cf. *DBWE* 4, 28.

[8] Bethge, *Dietrich Bonhoeffer*, 457.

[9] Published in 1933 as *Schöpfung und Fall* (*DBW* 3) and in English as *Creation and Fall* (*DBWE* 3).

[10] *DBWE* 3, 155.

[11] Cf. *DBWE* 4, 312 and Gerhard Krause's article, "Dietrich Bonhoeffer (1906–1945)," in *TRE* 7, 55–66. The friendship between Bonhoeffer and Krause eventually ended, mainly for reasons of divergent theological positions regarding the church struggle. See, for example, Krause's letter to Bonhoeffer in *DBWE* 15, 148–151.

agreed that the reading of St. Francis and Thomas à Kempis's *Imitation of Christ* would be important in that regard.[12]

A second major theological theme linking Kempis's *Imitatio Christi* and Bonhoeffer's *Discipleship* is that of *Nachfolge*, "imitation" or "following after" Christ. Chronologically, the first reference to Bonhoeffer's work on what would later become the book *Nachfolge* is found in a letter Bonhoeffer wrote at the end of April 1934 from his London pastorate to his Swiss friend Erwin Sutz, a fellow student whom he met at Union Theological Seminary. In this letter he comments on the significance of the Sermon on the Mount for the German church struggle and then, towards the end, returns to the same theme in more detail. He says: "Please write and tell me sometime how you preach about the Sermon on the Mount. I'm currently trying to do so, to keep it infinitely plain and simple, but it always comes back to *keeping* the commandments and not trying to evade them. *Following* Christi – what that really is, I'd like to know – it is not exhausted by our concept of faith. I am doing some writing that I think of as a 'spiritual exercise' – only as a first step."[13]

Here Bonhoeffer makes the connection between *Nachfolge*, the Sermon on the Mount, and *exercitium* – all subjects that figure prominently in *Discipleship*. His statement "*Nachfolge* Christi – was das ist, möchte ich wissen" sounds like an explicit allusion to Kempis's *Imitatio*. The very fact that he decided to entitle his book *Discipleship* may also point to the influence of Kempis. The editors of *Discipleship* quite correctly point out the analogy in the book titles between "*Discipleship*" and "*Imitatio Christi*."[14] It is noteworthy here that the opening of the *Imitatio* encapsulates the spirit of *Discipleship* in a most succinct manner. The first chapter has the heading "The Imitation of Christ and Contempt for the Vanities of the World." Its initial lines read as follows: "*'Whoever follows Me will not walk in darkness*,' says the Lord. These are Christ's own words by which He exhorts us to imitate His life and His ways."[15]

In the preface to *Discipleship*, the theme of the book is expressed in three crucial questions: "What did Jesus want to say to us? What does he want

---

[12] Cf. Larry Rasmussen, "Interview mit Herbert Jehle (1.3.1968)," in *Bonhoeffer Jahrbuch/Yearbook* 2 (2005–2006), 110–121, here 116.

[13] *DBWE* 13, 136. In a letter to Reinhold Niebuhr, dated 13 July 1934 (cf. *DBWE* 13, 182–184, Bonhoeffer once again remarks that he is writing on a work that addresses the questions raised in the Sermon on the Mount.

[14] See *DBWE* 4, 288 and 303.

[15] *Imitatio Christi* I 1. The English edition used in this study is that of Joseph N. Tylenda, *The Imitation of Christ*. New York: Vintage, revised edition 1998.

from us today? How does he help us to be faithful Christians today?"[16] Although Bonhoeffer does not employ the terms "to follow" or "to imitate" Christ in the preface, the substance of the whole work leaves no doubt that what it means to follow Christ is the key point on almost every page. This theme rises to a powerful crescendo on the very last page of the book: "The followers look only to the one whom they follow. But now the final word about those who as disciples bear the image of the incarnate, crucified, and risen Jesus Christ, and who have been transformed into the image of God, is that they are called to be 'imitators of God.' The follower [*Nachfolger*] of Jesus is the imitator [*Nachahmer*] of God. 'Therefore, be imitators of God, as beloved children' (Ephesians 5:1)." In a skilful play on words, Bonhoeffer marries "following Jesus" and "imitating God" by weaving together the words *Nachfolger* and *Nachahmer* into the one notion of discipleship.

It is likewise significant that while Bonhoeffer was the director of the seminary in Finkenwalde he also taught a weekly seminar on the theme of *Nachfolge* at the University of Berlin during the winter semester of 1935–1936.[17] At first glance this seems curious. Why did he dare to present a seminar on a topic that most of his colleagues would not accept as even belonging to the discipline of theology? Bonhoeffer's teacher Adolf von Harnack had so shaped the theological faculty at Berlin in the spirit of Protestant liberalism and culture that a seminar on *Nachfolge* would surely seem misplaced, to say the least, in such an academic environment. An easy answer is difficult to come by, but as we shall see below, in a very considerable sense Bonhoeffer saw the question of following Christ to be an essential theological question.[18] Yet, as his letter to Erwin Sutz indicates,[19] he himself characterizes his work on the Sermon on the Mount neither as theological interpretation – as he did with his lecture on creation and sin

---

[16] *DBWE* 4, 37.

[17] Cf. *DBWE* 14, 1017. Bonhoeffer started this seminar on 12 November 1935 (to my knowledge, there are no written records of this seminar) and possibly finished 14 February 1936, the last day of his teaching career at the University of Berlin. On 5 August 1936 Bonhoeffer's license to teach theology at the University was officially rescinded; cf. *DBWE* 14, 231.

[18] It is also evident that Bonhoeffer did not think that theological faculties were well equipped to prepare theology students for pastoral ministry. Cf. his letter to Erwin Sutz, 11 September 1934 (cf. *DBWE* 13, 217), where he declares that he never really believed in the university; instead, new theological schools are needed to teach theology students within Christian community.

[19] Cf. *DBWE* 13, 136).

during the semester at the University of Berlin[20] – nor as exegesis. Oddly, he calls it *exercitium*. Where does this designation come from?

The most plausible source is Kempis's *Imitatio Christi*, where numerous sections specifically correlate the Christian life with spiritual exercises. The heading of I 19 in the *Imitatio* reads, in the Latin, *De exercitiis boni Religiosi* [the exercises of a good religious]. Kempis speaks of the significance of exercises twice more in the same section. "If a prescribed exercise is omitted because of a brother in need," remarks the Augustinian monk, "or because we must perform some other charitable deed, the exercise may be fulfilled at a later time" (I 19, 3). Further on he exhorts, "See to it that you are not negligent in performing community exercises" (I 19, 5). Elsewhere in the *Imitatio* he remarks that the person who walks in the interior light "needs no special place nor definitive time to perform his religious exercises" (II 1, 7). At the beginning of book III Kempis asserts that "by daily prayerful exercises" the blessed understand the secrets of heaven better (III 1, 1). Finally, the heading of section IV 6 reads *Interrogatio de exercitio ante communionem* [exercises of examination before communion], and is further explained in IV 2: "Teach me the right way and give me some short exercises suitable for receiving Holy Communion."

How should we evaluate these affinities between Kempis's *Imitatio Christi* and Bonhoeffer? Given the following facts – that Bonhoeffer presented his grandmother with a copy of the *Imitatio Christi*, that he referred to *exercitium* in his teaching at Berlin, that these references can be clearly identified in Kempis, and that one student made the specific connection between these exercises and Kempis – we can sufficiently establish Kempis's influence on him. Moreover, even though Bonhoeffer does not provide any direct quotation from the *Imitatio* in the text of his *Discipleship*, the overlapping foci of both works are unmistakable. In part IV below, we will draw out the significance of these affinities in terms of Bonhoeffer's theological legacy.

Life Together

After the closing of Finkenwalde Seminary by the Gestapo in September 1937, Bonhoeffer crafted *Life Together* a year later "in a single stretch of four weeks" while he and Eberhard Bethge lived in Göttingen at the house

---

[20] The subtitle of *Creation and Fall* (*DBWE* 3) is *A Theological Exposition of Genesis 1–3*.

of the Leibholz family, who had to emigrate to England.[21] Bonhoeffer is thus looking back at his experience of living in a Christian community among young theologians who aspired to become pastors. As director of the underground seminary for two and a half years he was both the key designer of the theological curriculum and the primary professor. However, we should realize that Bonhoeffer attached as much importance to the spiritual formation of the candidates as to their theological training. *Life Together* must be read as representing some of the core aspects that for Bonhoeffer constitute a genuine Christian community. It is instructive that in this regard he refers to and cites the thought of Kempis three times in the body of the main text.

The first explicit naming of Kempis and a reference to the *Imitatio Christi* is found in the third chapter, "The Day Alone," of *Life Together*. Bonhoeffer writes: "The silence of the Christian is listening silence, humble stillness that may be broken at any time for the sake of humility. It is silence in conjunction with the Word. This is what Thomas à Kempis meant when he said: 'No one speaks more confidently than the one who gladly remains silent'."[22]

The second reference to Kempis is in the chapter entitled "Service." Bonhoeffer asserts that those wishing to serve others "must first learn to think little of themselves" and then cites Kempis's words to underscore his point: "The highest and most useful lesson is to truly know yourself and to think humbly of yourself. Making nothing of yourself and always having a good opinion of others is great wisdom and perfection (Thomas à Kempis)."[23] A few paragraphs further on in the same chapter he again insists that service for others entails recognizing that one's own sins are worse than those of others. "How could I possibly serve other persons in unfeigned humility," he asks, "if their sins appear to me to be seriously worse than my own?" To support his view, he enlists Kempis a third time as his spiritual advisor: "Do not believe that you have made any progress in the work of sanctification, if you do not feel deeply that you are less than all others (Thomas à Kempis)."[24]

Besides these three explicit references to Kempis in the main text of *Life Together*, there is at least one more direct citation from the *Imitatio Christi* that Bonhoeffer does not acknowledge. In between the second and third citations of Kempis's book, he says this: "Not considering oneself wise, but

---

[21] For details, see the introduction to *DBWE* 5, 3–4.
[22] *DBWE* 5, 85.
[23] *DBWE* 5, 96 quoting *Imitatio Christi* I 2, 5.
[24] *DBWE* 5, 98 and *Imitatio Christi* II 2, 2.

associating with the lowly, means considering oneself the worst of sinners."[25] The last phrase, "the worst of sinners," is taken straight from Kempis. In book IV of the *Imitatio*, the disciple makes the confession: "I am the worst of sinners."[26]

In addition to Bonhoeffer's acknowledged citations of the *Imitatio Christi* at several places in *Life Together*, we can discern further affinities between the two works. Even a cursory reading of both works reveals the parallel concerns of the two authors: the emphasis on silence, the Word of God, meditation, service, agapeic love and the need for confession; these topics we will further discuss in part V below. The spirit and substance of Kempis's *Imitatio Christi* is perhaps also visible in Bonhoeffer's structuring of *Life Together*, whose last chapter has as its subject the importance of "Confession and the Lord's Supper." At first glance this seems totally parallel with the *Imitatio*, at least for modern readers of that work. The reason is that most editions of it published since the 1950s place book IV, "On the Blessed Sacrament [of the Lord's Supper]," at the end. However, Bonhoeffer's Latin version reversed the order of books III and IV; that is, the topic of the Lord's Supper was not the last section of the *Imitatio*. Conceivably, Bonhoeffer also knew of a different order of the books in the *Imitatio*, perhaps from the (German?) copy he gave his grandmother as a birthday gift. Whatever the case, most relevant for our purposes is the fact that both the *Imitatio Christi* and *Life Together* discuss the significance of the Lord's Supper towards the end of their respective discourses. Given what Bonhoeffer says about the transforming power of confession and partaking in the Lord's Supper, he evidently places this chapter at the end of his work for theological reasons. What this theological significance is, we will shortly examine.

Following the closing of the Finkenwalde Seminary, Bonhoeffer continued the theological education of the pastoral candidates in the form of collective pastorates in Pomerania. One of his lectures was entitled "Thankfulness." The manuscript begins with a citation from Kempis and reads, in Bonhoeffer's German text, as follows: "Sei also dankbar für das Geringste, so wirst du würdig sein, Größeres zu empfangen." While Bonhoeffer indicates that this text is found on page 159 in his edition of the *Imitatio Christi*, the editors of the German edition identified the citation as section III 22, namely the one entitled "Remembering God's Many Benefits to Us."[27]

---

25 *DBWE* 5, 97.
26 *Imitatio Christi* IV 2, 3.
27 Cf. *DBWE* 15, 380, note 274.

However, after examining this text, it is clear that Bonhoeffer's citation is not from III 22, but from II 10, 5. Here Kempis remarks, "Be grateful, then, for even the least gift and you will be worthy of receiving greater ones."

Following the Finkenwalde years, a period for which we have ample evidence that Bonhoeffer was influenced by Kempis's *Imitatio Christi*, is followed by a second period in which Kempis seems once more a companion and theological encouragement. That period was during Bonhoeffer's imprisonment in the years 1943–1945.

Letters and Papers from Prison

We have already seen that Bonhoeffer read Kempis's *Imitatio Christi* in his Tegel prison cell in November and December 1943. In two letters from that period, he refers to it. On the fourth Sunday of advent, 19 December 1943, he finished a letter to Eberhard Bethge that he had begun the day before. There he shares with his friend that he has discovered for himself, and to his surprise, the hymn "Ich steh an deiner Krippe hier [Beside Thy Cradle Here I Stand]" composed by Paul Gerhardt.[28] Then he says this about it: "Probably one has to be alone for a long time and read it meditatively in order to be able to take it in. Every word is extraordinarily replete and radiant. It's just a little monastic-mystical, yet only as much as is warranted, for alongside the 'we' there is indeed also an 'I' and 'Christ,' and what that means can scarcely be said better than in this hymn. Only a few passages of the *Imitatio Christi*, which I am now reading occasionally in the Latin edition (which, by the way, is infinitely more beautiful in Latin than in German), also belong here."[29]

Given that Bonhoeffer composed this letter just before Christmas and that the Gerhard hymn is a traditional German Christmas piece, his dis-co-very was most likely about how it depicts the life of Jesus. For, as he says, every word is "extraordinarily rich and beautiful." Concretely, he asserts, only a few other places in Kempis's *Imitation Christi* can rival the

---

[28] This Christmas hymn, put to music by J. S. Bach in 1736, consists of ten stanzas; however, it is rather speculative to determine whether certain stanzas were more important to Bonhoeffer than others (although he cites the second part of the fifth stanza in a letter to Eberhard Bethge from Tegel prison in 1943; cf. *DBWE* 8, 230). The first stanza reads: "Ich steh and deiner Krippe hier, o Jesu, du mein Leben / ich komme, bring und schenke dir, was du mir hast gegeben / Nimm hin, es ist mein Geist und Sinn, Herz, Seel und Mut / nimm alles hin und laß dir's wohl gefallen."

[29] *DBWE* 8, 230.

hymn's depth of expressing the relation between the I, we, and Christ. What this may mean for Bonhoeffer we will examine below.

The second – and chronologically last – reference to Kempis in Bonhoeffer's oeuvre occurs in another letter, written just three days after the one mentioned above. On 22 December 1943 Bonhoeffer again wrote to Bethge. He once more refers to the *Imitatio Christi*. At the very end of the letter he notes that "In the *Imitatio Christi* I just read, Custodi diligenter cellam tuam, et custodiet te! ('Take good care of your cell and it will take care of you')."[30]

Kempis's Influence on Bonhoeffer's Theology

We have traced the influence of Kempis's *Imitatio Christi* on Bonhoeffer's writings. Now our task is to examine how and why specific theological emphases in Kempis's work found their way into Bonhoeffer's own theology. We will focus on the themes of following Christ, suffering for Christ, negation of the self, spiritual love, spiritual exercises and meditation, and the Lord's Supper.

Following Christ

Eberhard Bethge boldly asserts that the most profound idea ever expressed by Bonhoeffer is that of "discipleship as participation in Christ's suffering for others, as communion with the Crucified One."[31] Indeed, in Bonhoeffer's theology it is absolutely inconceivable that faith could exist in any form apart from following Jesus Christ and the cost of suffering that such following may entail. Against the backdrop of the contemporary Lutheran view that following the commandments of Jesus is meant more metaphorically than literally,[32] Bonhoeffer argues otherwise in *Discipleship*. In a most uncomplicated way he insists that discipleship is "commitment to Christ. Because Christ exists, he must be followed. An idea about Christ, a doctrinal system, a general religious recognition of grace or forgiveness of sins does not require discipleship."[33] His words are directed against those who reduced Jesus' commands to an "inner willingness to invest

---

[30] *DBWE* 8, 237.
[31] Bethge, *Dietrich Bonhoeffer*, 456.
[32] Cf. *DBWE* 4, 79.
[33] *DBWE* 4, 59.

everything for the kingdom of God" and thus fall prey to "the deliberate avoidance of simple, literal obedience."[34]

Why is Bonhoeffer so insistent that following Christ is the authentic hallmark of genuine faith? Why does he declare so unflinchingly that *"only the believers obey,* and *only the obedient believe."*[35] The answer, in brief, is that his conception of the significance of discipleship stems directly from his theological understanding of grace. During the second course in Finkenwalde in 1935–1936, he offered a lecture on "The Visible Church in the New Testament,"[36] in which he makes a crucial distinction between *hearing* the word of grace and *obeying* the word of grace. Those who hear God's word of grace encounter something entirely new in all their existence.[37] The word of grace demands a concrete, obedient response; otherwise it will be one's word of judgement rather than grace. The hearer of the word of grace cannot simply say that everything is fine with grace and life can go on as before. Discipleship is precisely the movement away from the word of salvific grace to obedience. In Bonhoeffer's words: "They know that wherever grace is proclaimed, people are summoned to question what they should do."[38] The emphasis on "the doing of grace" is also made explicitly in the *Imitatio Christi.* In one instance, Kempis puts these words in Jesus' mouth: "Whoever tries to withdraw himself from obedience at the same time withdraws himself from grace."[39]

For both Kempis and Bonhoeffer it seems to go against the very core of being a Christian that one could lay hold of God's grace but fail to follow Jesus' commandments in obedience. Bonhoeffer works this out more fully in the third course at Finkenwalde, in a lecture on the new life of the Christian and discipleship. There he says that the new life in Christ is not merely a new state of being [*Zustand*] but an action [*Wandeln*], taking concrete and responsible steps.[40] In the next section of the lecture he asserts that "living and walking forward within this space [in Christ] = *discipleship* among the *Synoptics.* Christian life is not a lifestyle but rather means abid-

---

[34] *DBWE* 4, 79.
[35] *DBWE* 4, 63; emphasis in original.
[36] Cf. *DBWE* 14, 434–476.
[37] Bonhoeffer says (*DBWE* 14, 440) that "something entirely new is confronting his [Peter's] existence."
[38] *DBWE* 14, 440. In his reflections on the "New Life in Paul," Bonhoeffer summarizes his understanding that grace is discipleship in the poignant expression "grace *in* discipleship;" cf. *DBWE* 14, 624.
[39] *Imitatio Christi* III 2, 1.
[40] *DBW* 14, 616.

ing completely in Christ, who has called us."[41] Clearly, in all his remarks during the Finkenwalde years Jesus' call to follow required literal obedience. "Faith is only faith in deeds of obedience," Bonhoeffer admonishes, because "faith is possible only in this new state of existence created by obedience."[42] In this respect an earlier reference in one of his letters to Erwin Sutz is crucial: *"Following* Christi – what that really is, I'd like to know – it is not exhausted by our concept of faith."[43]

Bonhoeffer's sees a necessary connection between faith, grace, obedience, and discipleship. This raises the question of why this correlation is so crucial in his theology. Why, concretely, is discipleship [*Nachfolge*] not exhausted in the concept of faith? In *Discipleship* Bonhoeffer provides a succinct answer: it is "obedience within which discipleship can become real;"[44] hence, only faith that is obedient to the call of Christ *can* become real and genuine. Because "Jesus is the Christ, it has to be made clear from the beginning that his word is not a doctrine. Instead, it creates existence anew."[45] But this new existence is not automatic. For a person who has faith in Christ, obedience "puts [that person] into the situation of being able to believe."[46] Elsewhere Bonhoeffer explains that "the external works have to take place; *we have to get into the situation of being able to believe.*"[47] Hence, what is absolutely indispensable is "a situation in which faith can begin."[48] This is the crux of every person's Christian life. Apart from a *situation* in which faith can begin, grow and mature – in other words, apart from obedience in a situation that requires obedience – faith and discipleship are mere doctrines and hence dead. Discipleship is thus "the road to faith [that] passes through obedience to Christ's call."[49]

It is difficult to decide exactly which chapters in Kempis's *Imitatio Christi* may have provided the impetus for Bonhoeffer to articulate his own theological view of discipleship in a Christian's life. But we may say with certainty that it was Kempis's work – conceivably more than anyone else's – that helped him formulate his own theology of obedient *Nachfolge* and carrying the cross of Christ.

---

[41] *DBWE* 14, 621; original emphasis.
[42] *DBWE* 4, 64.
[43] *DBWE* 13, 136.
[44] *DBWE* 4, 73.
[45] *DBWE* 4, 62.
[46] *DBWE* 4, 62.
[47] *DBWE* 4, 66; emphasis added.
[48] *DBWE* 4, 62.
[49] *DBWE* 4, 63.

Suffering for Christ

Even though Bonhoeffer says that Jesus' call to discipleship is essentially without content,[50] he nonetheless determines the focus of that call to be the cross of Christ. The correlation of the theme of discipleship – in its specific content of suffering and carrying one's cross – in both Kempis and Bonhoeffer can be further established on the basis of another text. As we mentioned above, Bonhoeffer read the section II 10, 5 in the *Imitatio Christi*[51] and cites it in the context of a discussion of the theme of thankfulness in the New Testament. Just a few lines below this very text, Kempis says this: "Jesus today has many lovers of His heavenly kingdom, but few of them carry his cross ... We all want to rejoice with Him, but few of us are willing to suffer anything for His sake ... Many admire His miracles, but few follow in the ignominy of His cross."[52]

Given the proximity of these statements to the text that Bonhoeffer cited, it seems very unlikely that he would not have known and identified with the sentiment expressed in the words just quoted. For here we have evidence that Kempis sees a correlation between following Jesus and carrying one's cross. In his own words, Bonhoeffer provides a clear echo: "Just as Christ is only Christ as one who suffers and is rejected, so a disciple is a disciple only in suffering and being rejected, thereby participating in crucifixion."[53] Moreover, just as Bonhoeffer maintains that faith is only faith in obedience, he similarly holds that "suffering becomes the identifying mark of a follower of Christ."[54] Indeed, the Christian's following of the call of Jesus culminates in a readiness to give even one's life. In Bonhoeffer's own famous and often-cited words, "Whenever Christ calls us, his call leads us to death."[55] Perhaps no passage is as profound in all of Bonhoeffer's work in expressing the interrelation between Christ, cross, suffering, grace and discipleship. In his reflections on the cross, Bonhoeffer writes: "The cross is neither misfortune nor harsh fate. Instead, it is suffering which comes from our allegiance to Jesus Christ alone. The cross is not random suffering, but necessary suffering. The cross is not suffering that stems from natural existence; it is suffering that comes from being Christian. The essence of the cross is not suffering alone; it is suffering and being

---

[50] Cf. *DBWE* 4, 58–59 and *DBWE* 14, 622.
[51] Cited in *DBWE* 15, 380.
[52] *Imitatio Christi* II 11, 1.
[53] *DBWE* 4, 85.
[54] *DBWE* 4, 89.
[55] *DBWE* 4, 87.

rejected. Strictly speaking, it is being rejected for the sake of Jesus Christ, not for the sake of any other attitude or confession. A Christianity that no longer took discipleship seriously remade the gospel into a solace of cheap grace."[56]

In light of Bonhoeffer's uncompromising view of the cross and suffering, it comes as no surprise to read that "bearing [suffering] constitutes *being* a Christian [*Im Tragen besteht das Christsein*]."[57] Here again we have another crux of the Christian life. According to Bonhoeffer, bearing – that is, suffering – *constitutes* being a Christian. Indeed, suffering is the normal characteristic of every Christian. It is not merely a temporary addition in tough circumstances or a test for the more spiritual ones among us. It is rather a defining and ontological element of being a human being – as a Christian. Hence, to venture a comment in our post-modern context, suffering is not the fate of "those less fortunate" Christians in general or of those Christians who once were forced to live under Communist rule and now perhaps live under governments that despise democracy and freedom. Bonhoeffer's implied assertion that a Christian is *essentially a suffering disciple* squarely challenges those who never associate, let alone experience, suffering as Christians. Nonetheless, because "Christ suffers as vicarious representative for the world," his cross is "the triumph over suffering."[58] That is, in Christ's resurrection the ultimate suffering – death itself – died and hence came to an end for every believer.

Like Bonhoeffer but long before him, Kempis had grasped the centrality of suffering in the life of the Christian. In a section in the *Imitatio Christi* entitled "The Royal Road to the Holy Cross,"[59] Kempis repeatedly speaks of the nexus of the cross and suffering. "Why do you then fear to carry the cross?" he asks, but then immediately affirms that "This is the way that leads to the kingdom... In the cross alone do we find the soul's eternal salvation and hope of everlasting life. *Carrying His own cross Jesus* preceded you, and on the cross He died for you ... if you are His companion in suffering you shall likewise be His companion in glory."[60] Since the theme of suffering is so prevalent throughout the *Imitatio*, there can be little doubt it influenced Bonhoeffer's theology. It is telling, for example, that Kempis ended the section with a quotation of Mark 8:34 and thus pointed to another element in the disciple's faithful obedience: the negation of the self.

---

[56] *DBWE* 4, 86.
[57] *DBWE* 4, 91; emphasis added.
[58] *DBWE* 4, 90.
[59] *Imitatio Christi* II 12.
[60] *Imitatio Christi* II 12, 2.

Negation of the Self

The disciple who follows Christ and carries his or her cross necessarily must have a certain self-understanding, namely the willingness to negate the self. Taking Jesus' words "If any want to become my followers, let them deny themselves and take up their cross and follow me"[61] literally, both Kempis and Bonhoeffer stress the act of self-negation. Kempis's *Imitatio Christi* is indeed saturated with remarks on self-negation. Throughout the text we find statements like this: "If I belittle myself, think of myself as nothing, throw off all self-regard and account myself to be dust, as I truly am, then Your grace will come upon me."[62] Elsewhere he commands the reader: "Stop loving yourself,"[63] "acquire genuine self-contempt,"[64] "realize that there is nothing more harmful to you in this world than self-love."[65] However, he also knew that no person naturally seeks to deny the self. "It is not according to man's nature to bear the cross and love it, to chastise the body and bring it into subjection, to avoid honors and be willing to suffer insults. It is not man's nature to despise one's self and to wish to be despised."[66]

We have already referred to several instances where Bonhoeffer cites from Kempis in *Life Together*. In this present context, it suffices to recall two of these. Bonhoeffer agrees with his forebear that "the highest and most useful lesson is to truly know yourself and to think humbly of yourself. Making nothing of yourself and always having a good opinion of others is great wisdom and perfection (Thomas à Kempis)."[67] Similarly, "Do not believe that you have made any progress in the work of sanctification, if you do not feel deeply that you are less than all others (Thomas à Kempis)."[68] Certainly Kempis's characteristic stress on the Christian's denial of self greatly influenced Bonhoeffer's theology. But there seems to be a decisive difference in the two theologians' interpretation of what self-denial means. Kempis's many references to the denial, abnegation and even con-

---

[61] Mark 8:34, cited in the *Imitatio Christi* in II 12, 15 and by Bonhoeffer in *DBWE* 4, 84.

[62] *Imitatio Christi* III 8, 1. Similarly IV 15, 3: "The more perfectly a man renounces the things of earth and the more quickly he dies to himself by practicing self-contempt, the more quickly does grace come to him."

[63] *Imitatio Christi* III 11, 1.

[64] *Imitatio Christi* III 13, 1.

[65] *Imitatio Christi* III 27, 1.

[66] *Imitatio Christi* II 12, 9.

[67] *DBWE* 5, 96 quoting *Imitatio Christi* I 2, 5.

[68] *DBWE* 5, 98 and *Imitatio Christi* II 2, 2.

tempt for one's self are not taken over by Bonhoeffer. For the latter, the denial of self was not primarily a psychological but a theological issue.

For Bonhoeffer, the denial of self[69] must be seen against the backdrop of sin. As he acknowledged, it is an "extreme statement" to "consider oneself the worst of sinners."[70] To recognize oneself a sinner is not a psychological but a theological insight;[71] more precisely, it is most of all a matter of revelation.[72] Hence, recognition of being the worst sinner leads into the depth of humility. For how is it possible to serve "other persons in unfeigned humility if their sins appear to me to be seriously worse than my own?"[73] In other words, a *proper* self-understanding as a sinner – and not the denial of self – are significant in Bonhoeffer's theology. Two comments are in order here.

First, while markings are rarely seen anywhere in Bonhoeffer's copy of the *Imitatio Christi*,[74] one clear pencil marking does appear in the margin of a section entitled "The Need to Look at One's Self." The two lines Bonhoeffer marked read: "If you have scurried about meddling in all sorts of things, *what good has all this done you if you have neglected your soul's welfare*? If you wish to enjoy true peace and perfect union with God you must set all things aside and keep your eyes only upon yourself."[75] The context speaks of not placing "too much trust in ourselves," nor reproaching "others for their petty faults" or making "harsh judgement against another man." It is apparent from the context and Bonhoeffer's marking that the focus is not so much on the denial of self but on the *need* to have a

---

[69] Bonhoeffer unambiguously states in *DBWE* 4, 86: "Self-denial can never result in ever so many single acts of self-mortification or ascetic exercises. It does not mean suicide, because even suicide could be an expression of the human person's own will." See now also the monograph by Lisa E. Dahill, *Reading from the Underside of Selfhood. Bonhoeffer and Spiritual Formation*. PTMS. Eugene: Pickwick Publications 2009.

[70] *DBWE* 5, 97.

[71] Cf. Bonhoeffer's affirmation of Luther's remark in the latter's *Lecture on the Letter to the Romans*: "*Sola fide credendum est nos esse peccatores* [by faith alone we know that we are sinners]" in *DBWE* 2, 136.

[72] Cf. *DBWE* 9, 300. From Bonhoeffer's student days in Berlin we have a short note on Luther's *Lectures on the Letter to the Romans* that clarifies his view of these matters: "Theological logic intends to set itself free from psychologism. It does not speak of sin and revelation as contents of consciousness. Instead, it speaks of them as realities of revelation."

[73] *DBWE* 5, 98.

[74] The author was able to examine the copy that Bonhoeffer read while in Tegel prison (for details see note 5 above).

[75] *Imitatio Christi* II 5, 2. In his copy, Bonhoeffer made a pencil mark at II 5, line 20–22 (p. 67). Cf. Bethge, *Dietrich Bonhoeffer*, 430, on Bonhoeffer's habit of not marking the books he read.

proper self. And that proper self comes into being by not neglecting the soul's welfare and by freeing oneself "from all temporal cares."[76]

Second, we have mentioned Bonhoeffer's affirmation in a letter that "alongside the 'we' there is indeed also an 'I' [*es gibt ein ich*] and 'Christ'."[77] Toward the end of his time in prison, he reflects on the 'I', 'we' and 'Christ' relation. However, he does not give us an interpretation of that relation other than to say that Gerhardt's hymn and "a few passages of the *Imitatio Christi*, which I am now reading occasionally in the Latin edition"[78] best express its meaning. We are left to speculate as to what Bonhoeffer meant, but we may venture at least a comment. In Gerhardt's hymn, in the first stanza, the Christian's relationship to Jesus is characterized as "you are my life." While a terse expression, it is conceivable that in Bonhoeffer's context of incarceration it meant what the hymn proclaims: the 'I' comes to Jesus and returns the gifts of life (spirit, purpose, heart, soul and courage). All of life is given by Jesus and all things are returned to him. In the exchange of giving, life becomes possible. Just as Jesus gave his life and thus made life possible for others, so analogously Bonhoeffer affirms the sentiment of the hymn in giving his life back to Jesus – and, a few months later, to Hitler's hangmen. The significance in all this is the paradox of receiving life by denying (but not obliterating) one's self. Christian faith that is not denying its own self cannot issue in fruitful discipleship.

Spiritual Love

In *Life Together* Bonhoeffer makes the radical differentiation between spiritual and psychological love. In his own words: "It is essential for Christian community that two things become clear right from the beginning. *First, Christian community is not an ideal, but a divine reality; second, Christian community is a spiritual [pneumatische] and not a psychic [psychische] reality.*"[79] Similarly, Bonhoeffer maintains that "because Christian community is founded solely on Jesus Christ, it is a spiritual [*pneumatische*] and not a psychic [*psychische*] reality."[80] For Bonhoeffer, this distinction is of such pertinence that without it a proper understanding and practice of Christian community becomes impossible. Underlying

---

[76] *Imitatio Christi* II 5, 3.

[77] *DBWE* 8, 230.

[78] *DBWE* 8, 230.

[79] *DBWE* 5, 35; original emphasis.

[80] *DBWE* 5, 38.

this distinction is Bonhoeffer's observation that it is quite possible to mistake a merely human community for a Christian one and for people to be drawn together on the basis of some natural affinities rather than the unconditional love of Christ.

Kempis has similar though less developed views in the *Imitatio Christi*. There he declares, in the voice of Jesus, that "some individuals, in accord with their personal piety, are drawn to one or another of the saints, but this is a human affection or preference on their part and does not come from Me."[81] A few paragraphs further in the same section Kempis criticizes those who are drawn to the saints for the wrong reasons. These people, he says, "are insufficiently enlightened from above, rarely know how to love anyone with a perfect spiritual love. Such individuals are drawn to one or another person by natural affection or human friendship."[82]

Admittedly, we have no conclusive evidence that Bonhoeffer's critical distinction between spiritual and emotional love comes from his reading of Kempis's *Imitatio Christi*. It may be the case that Bonhoeffer was shaped in this regard by both Kempis and Kierkegaard.[83] At any rate, the decisive aspect for us is that Bonhoeffer's understanding of Christian community is fundamentally indebted to the fact that only Christ's unconditional agapeic love can be the foundation of Christian community.

Spiritual Exercises: Silence and Meditation

As we saw earlier, Gerhard Krause suggests that Bonhoeffer deliberately modeled his seminar at the University of Berlin in the winter of 1932–1933, entitled "Theological Psychology," on Kempis's *Imitatio Christi*. In the course of that seminar, Bonhoeffer made these remarks on Christian character formation: "The *habitus* of a Christian character distinguishes itself from that of individuality in that it is gained through practice. ... It is a practice of formed humans to look beyond themselves. Christian character therefore carries within it a basic element of neglecting itself. The knowledge of myself as sinner, this knowledge of my justification makes charac-

---

[81] *Imitatio Christi* III 58, 3.
[82] *Imitatio Christi* III 58, 6.
[83] On Kierkegaard, see Geffrey B. Kelly, "Kierkegaard as 'Antidote' and as Impact on Dietrich Bonhoeffer's Concept of Christian Discipleship," in Peter Frick (ed), *Bonhoeffer's Intellectual Formation. Theology and Philosophy in his Thought*. Religion in Philosophy and Theology 29. Tübingen: Mohr Siebeck 2008, 145–165.

ter formation into something secondary, penultimate, yet significant as *practice.*"[84]

On the one hand, these words once more illuminate Bonhoeffer's view that a Christian's knowledge of sin leads to a neglecting of oneself and relativizes the significance of one's formation as a person. On the other hand, Bonhoeffer encourages personal formation as *spiritual* formation in two distinct but interrelated exercises.

First, he demanded the practice of silence.[85] According to Bethge, during the seminary days in Zingst and Finkenwalde, Bonhoeffer established one basic but strict rule: "never to speak about another ordinand in that person's absence or to tell that person about it afterward when such a thing did happen."[86] Bonhoeffer likely drew on Kempis's admonition (he marked the immediately following sentences of this section in his Tegel copy of the *Imitatio Christi*[87]): "The interior man places his spiritual welfare before everything else, and because he diligently attends to himself he does not gossip about the action of others. You will only arrive at a devout inner life by watching over yourself and by being silent with regard to others."[88] We have now additional evidence, however, that Bonhoeffer's introduction of the rule not to speak of an ordinand in his absence stems also from his encounter with the Bruderhof communities in Germany, where the rule was practiced.[89]

---

[84] *DBWE* 12, 231–232. Cf. *DBW* 12, 198: "Der Habitus des christlichen Charakters unterscheidet sich von dem der Individualität dadurch, daß er durch Übung erworben ist … Es ist eine Übung des über sich Hinaussehens des habituellen Menschen. Christlicher Charakter trägt also als ein Grundelement die Vernachlässigung seiner selbst in sich. Die Erkenntnis meiner selbst als Sünder, diese Erkenntnis meiner Rechtfertigung macht die Chrarakterbildung zu etwas Sekundärem, Vorletztem, doch als *Übung* bedeutsam."

[85] Cf. *DBWE* 5, 83–86.

[86] Bethge, *Dietrich Bonhoeffer*, 428. In a Finkenwalde outline for a meditation on Proverbs 3:27ff Bonhoeffer says: "*Do not talk about your brothers*! Then you can no longer speak *with* them!" (*DBWE* 14, 862; original emphasis).

[87] See note 75 above.

[88] *Imitatio Christi* II 5, 2. Elsewhere Kempis gives straightforward advice "against slanderous tongues:" "It requires much prudence on your part to keep silent when evil is being heaped upon you; turn inwardly to Me and do not be affected by human judgement. Do not have your peace depend on what other men might say about you" (III 28, 1–2). Kempis also notes: "There are many who talk overmuch, and as a result only a few men pay them much attention" (III 36, 1).

[89] Cf. the letters of Hardy Arnold, "Bruderhof-Korrespondenz," in which he describes his meetings with Bonhoeffer in London and the latter's interest in community in *Bonhoeffer Jahrbuch/Yearbook* 2 (2005–2006), 75–109, on the rule of silence, 86, note 38.

What, then, is the theological significance of silence for Bonhoeffer? On a practical level, "there is a wonderful power in being silent – the power of clarification, purification, and focus on what is essential." Hence, in silence "much that is unnecessary remains unsaid."[90] On a spiritual level, that which is essential is brought about in the practice of silence: "In the end, silence means nothing other than waiting for God's Word and coming from God's Word with a blessing."[91] In that sense, silence must be seen "in its essential relationship to the Word, as the simple act of the individual who falls silent under the Word of God."[92] Silence as such is not a spiritual exercise; it becomes one only by virtue of its focus on the Word of God. This is precisely Bonhoeffer's intent in teaching his seminarians, namely to help them understand that the practice of silence enables genuine speech which, in turn, comes from the hearing of God's word in meditation.

Second, the spiritual exercise of silence bears fruit in meditation on a text of Scripture. The practice of meditation was so important to Bonhoeffer that he drafted an "Introduction to Scriptural Meditation [*Anleitung zur Schriftmeditation*]" in May 1936 as part of the circular letter that he and Bethge regularly sent to the Finkenwalde brothers who were then working in various pastorates.[93] Later these instructions – in an abbreviated form – became part of Bonhoeffer's reflection on Christian community in *Life Together*. Bonhoeffer identifies "three things for which the Christian needs a regular time during the day: *meditation on the Scripture, prayer* and *intercession*. All three should find a place in the *daily period of meditation*."[94] In order to preclude any misunderstanding, he makes it abundantly clear not to "expect from silence anything but a simple encounter with the Word of God … It [meditation] serves no other purpose. Spiritual experiments have no place here."[95] Elsewhere he repeats: "It is not necessary for us to find new ideas in our meditation [and] above all, it is not necessary for us

---

[90] *DBWE* 5, 85.
[91] *DBWE* 5, 85.
[92] *DBWE* 5, 84.
[93] Cf. *DBWE* 14, 931–936.
[94] *DBWE* 5, 86; original emphasis. Cf. Kempis: "Set aside an opportune time for deep personal reflection and think often about God's many benefits to you. Give up all light and frivolous matters, and read what inspires you to repentance of soul and not what just entertains the mind. If you abstain from unnecessary conversation and useless visiting, as well as from listening to idle news and gossip, you will find sufficient and suitable times for your meditation" (I 20, 1. This section in the *Imitatio Christi* is called "The Love of Silence and Solitude." Bonhoeffer cites a later sentence from this section in *DBWE* 5, 85).
[95] *DBWE* 5, 86.

to have any unexpected, extraordinary experiences while meditating."[96] In his "Guide to Scriptural Meditation," Bonhoeffer offers four reasons why one should meditate: (1) For a Christian, every day without a deeper knowledge of God is a lost day; (2) A preacher of the Word cannot preach that Word unless it speaks to the preacher him/herself; (3) We need a well-established discipline of prayer; and (4) Preachers need help against the impious haste and unrest of daily life.[97]

In practical terms, "in our personal meditation on Scripture we stick to a brief selected text that will possibly remain unchanged for an entire week … here we are guided into the unfathomable depths of a particular sentence and word."[98] The whole point of the spiritual exercise of scriptural meditation is thus crystal clear: "We are reading the Word of God as God's Word for us. Therefore, we do not ask what this text has to say to other people. For those of us who are preachers that means we will not ask how we should preach or teach on this text, but what it has to say to us personally … we are rather waiting for God's Word to us."[99] Meditation on Scripture has nothing to do with exegesis, theology or any other academic reflection. It focuses neither on the practice of silence as such nor on reading a biblical passage in a most concentrated manner, but exclusively on the encounter with God.[100]

The Lord's Supper

Bonhoeffer's presentation of the nature of Christian community in *Life Together* reaches an unequivocal crescendo in the last chapter, entitled "Confession and the Lord's Supper." As we mentioned above, unlike his version of the *Imitatio Christi* – which discusses "The Blessed Sacrament" in the penultimate chapter – in *Life Together* Bonhoeffer deliberately placed the discussion of the Lord's Supper at the end of the book. The rea-

---

[96] *DBWE* 5, 88. Bonhoeffer then continues: "We must not get stuck in such experiences. Above all, we must not allow them to dissuade us from observing our period of meditation with great patience and fidelity."

[97] Cf. *DBWE* 14, 931–932.

[98] *DBWE* 5, 87.

[99] *DBWE* 5, 87.

[100] For a possible dependence on Kempis, cf. *DBWE* 5, 89, note 14. At the very beginning of the *Imitatio Christi*, after mentioning the following after and imitating of Jesus, Kempis concludes the first paragraph with these words: "Let it then be our main concern to meditate on the life of Jesus (*Summum igitur studium nostrum, sit in vita Jesu meditari*)" (*Imitatio Christi* I 1). For Kempis, the content of one's meditation is thus clearly staked out: it is the life and teaching of Jesus (cf. *Imitatio Christi* I 25, 6).

son is an obvious theological one: only in the confession of one's sins and the forgiveness of those sins in the celebration of the Lord's Supper lies the unshakable foundation for the continuity of Christian community.

Kempis believed that preparation for the Lord's Supper needed to include "some short exercise."[101] For him, this meant to "meditate on your transgressions."[102] "In general," he says, "be sorry for all your sins, but in particular, you must grieve and bewail those offenses you commit every day."[103] Bonhoeffer likewise places great emphasis on the confession of sins. Indeed, the act of confession is so vital and crucial that without it "the final breakthrough to community"[104] remains illusory. The real test for Christian community lies in accepting one another not as fellow believers but as sinners. Only when "another Christian hears our confession of sin in Christ's place, forgives our sins in Christ's name" can genuine Christian community begin to take shape. The formation of that kind of genuine community is characterized by Bonhoeffer's word "breakthrough" [*Durchbruch*]. In practicing the confession of sins and the celebration of the Lord's Supper there is a fourfold breakthrough – to community, to the cross, to new life, and to assurance.[105]

Underlying Bonhoeffer's insistence on confessing concrete sins and receiving forgiveness in the celebration of the Lord's Supper is the conviction, that within Christian communities, confession of sins often amounts to nothing more than a superficial self-forgiveness rather than a contrite confession before God and humanity. Here Bonhoeffer asks the pointed question: "Is not the reason for our innumerable relapses and for the feebleness of our Christian obedience to be found precisely in the fact that we are living from self-forgiveness and not from real forgiveness of our sins? Self-forgiveness can never lead to the break with sin."[106] Since it is the nature of sin "to remain unknown" and shun the light, "sin must be brought into the light."[107] Unless sin is confessed, its power is not broken. For Bonhoeffer, "Sin that has been spoken and confessed has lost all of its power. It has been revealed and judged as sin. It can no longer tear apart the community."[108] That is, since even in the *sanctorum communio* the committing of

---

[101] *Imitatio Christi* IV 6, 2.

[102] *Imitatio Christi* IV 12, 1.

[103] *Imitatio Christi* IV 7, 1. Cf. I 1, 3: "It is better to experience remorse than to know its definition," a saying Bonhoeffer marked in his edition of the *Imitatio Christi*.

[104] *DBWE* 5, 108.

[105] Cf. *DBWE* 5, 110–113.

[106] *DBWE* 5, 113.

[107] *DBWE* 4, 110.

[108] *DBWE* 4, 110.

sins still occurs, it is precisely here where the power of sin must be brought to light and thus be broken. Unconfessed sins in the Christian community eventually tear it apart or else reduce it to a mere superficial gathering of well-meaning people who are bound together not so much by Christ himself as by some other social purpose.

Conclusion

Although we can find only about a dozen direct citations from Thomas à Kempis's *Imitatio Christi* in Bonhoeffer's writings, the influence of Kempis on Bonhoeffer far exceeds that number. The weight of this influence must be measured not so much in terms of the number of citations but of conceptual affinities. Unquestionably, in this respect the *Imitatio Christi* had virtually a lifelong impact on Bonhoeffer's view of the theology and practice of Christian community. This is most evident in the Finkenwalde and imprisonment periods.

The convergence of the main ideas in the *Imitatio Christi* and Bonhoeffer's writings, most notably *Discipleship* and *Life Together*, is so substantial and obvious as to leave no doubt of Bonhoeffer's deep theological appreciation for Kempis's work. The themes of divine and human suffering, following the call and imitating the life of Christ, carrying one's cross, and practicing spiritual exercises such as silence and meditation are fundamental to both. For Bonhoeffer, the paradoxical and kenotic circle of following Christ, self-denial and carrying one's cross leads to the exclamation that "discipleship is joy."[109] Ultimately Bonhoeffer's *theologia crucis* that was so decisively shaped by Kempis may even today inspire the church to become a joyous *ecclesia crucis*.[110]

---

[109] *DBWE* 4, 40.

[110] Cf. Douglas John Hall, "Ecclesia Crucis: The Disciple Community and the Future of the Church in North America," in Wayne Whitson Floyd, Jr. and Charles Marsh (eds), *Theology and Practice of Responsibility. Essays on Dietrich Bonhoeffer.* Valley Forge: Trinity Press International 1994, 70–73.

5. Friedrich Nietzsche's Aphorisms and Dietrich Bonhoeffer's Theology

Introduction

Dietrich Bonhoeffer's first encounter with both the philosophy of Ludwig Feuerbach and Friedrich Nietzsche was during his early teen years. According to Eberhard Bethge, when Karl-Friedrich, Bonhoeffer's oldest brother, returned from World War I at the age of nineteen he read Feuerbach and discussed his writings with the family.[1] At the end of the First World War in 1918, Dietrich Bonhoeffer was no more than twelve years old. During that age, Bonhoeffer also had his first encounter with the thought of Friedrich Nietzsche. This first encounter came by way of a teacher, Martin Havenstein, during the time when Dietrich Bonhoeffer attended Grunewald *Gymnasium*. Havenstein was a Nietzsche expert and wrote the work *Nietzsche als Erzieher*.[2] Whether the high school student Bonhoeffer read this work cannot be known for certain. It seems conceivable, however, to surmise that a teacher who is absorbed in the thought of Nietzsche to the extent that he wrote a work on the philosopher would share some of his insights with his students.[3] From Bonhoeffer's biographer, Eberhard Bethge, we know that in preparation for writing his book *Ethics*, Bonhoeffer's reading included Karl Jaspers' introduction on Nietzsche, a work entitled *Nietzsche*.[4] According to Bethge, Bonhoeffer owned eight of the sixteen volumes of the Nietzsche works edited by

---

[1] Cf. *DBWE* 7, 7.

[2] Cf. *DBWE* 9, 569, note 49 and Martin Havenstein, *Nietzsche als Erzieher*. Berlin: E. S. Mittler 1922.

[3] The editors of *DBWE* 9, 569, note 49 speak of the young Bonhoeffer as writing under "the influence of his philosophy professor," namely Havenstein, when he worked on his *Abitur* essay on the philosophy of Euripides.

[4] Cf. Eberhard Bethge, *Dietrich Bonhoeffer. Theologian, Christian, Man of his Time. A Biography*. Translated and revised by Victoria Barnett. Minnesota: Fortress Press, 2000, 715 and *DBWE* 6, 222, note 19. Cf. also Karl Jaspers. *Nietzsche: Eine Einführung in das Verständnis seines Philosophierens*. Berlin: Walter de Gruyter 1936.

Nietzsche's sister.[5] We also know from a remark of Bethge's that the young Bonhoeffer "read all of Nietzsche very carefully."[6]

Friedrich Nietzsche (1844–1900)

A study of Nietzsche[7] and Bonhoeffer is telling in that the first came from the church and ended up entirely as the prodigal son who never returned from the world while the latter came from the world and discovered the church. As each of them began his intellectual quest at the opposite end from the other, somewhere along the trajectories of those two journeys, Bonhoeffer encountered Nietzsche long enough, as it were, to breath in the philosophical air of the wayward son of a Lutheran pastor. In several volumes of the *Dietrich Bonhoeffer Werke/Works*, we have explicit references to the philosophy of Nietzsche. In a first step, we will survey Bonhoeffer's engagement with the philosophy of Nietzsche in a chronological order; in other words, we will focus on specific passages or allusions to Nietzsche's aphorisms as they appear in Bonhoeffer's work and do so, deliberately, with a minimum of interpretive comments in order to let Bonhoeffer's use of Nietzsche emerge as objectively as possible. In a second step, we will then examine how Nietzsche's philosophy shaped Bonhoeffer's own theological formation.

Nietzsche's Aphorisms in Bonhoeffer's Works until 1939

In Berlin in 1926, the student Bonhoeffer presented a meditation for children entitled "Address on the Decalogue." He asks the children the rhetori-

---

[5] Nietzsche scholars are suspicious of this edition; cf. *DBWE* 6, 222, note 19.

[6] Eberhard Bethge, "The Challenge of Dietrich Bonhoeffer's Life and Theology," in *WCA*, 22–88, here 27. Later in the same essay Bethge repeats: "Bonhoeffer had been an ardent reader of Nietzsche in his youth" (76).

[7] For this essay I have used the collected works published by Giorgio Colli and Mazzino Montinari, *Kritische Studienausgabe* (*KSA*). Munich: dtv, 1980, in 15 volumes. The first six volumes are Nietzsche's writings, usually understood as aphorisms rather than philosophical discourses. Volumes 7–13 are a collection of his fragments and letters and volumes 14 and 15 consist of introduction, commentary, index etc. Reference to English translations of Nietzsche's work is provided in the footnotes. Good recent studies of Nietzsche as a philosopher are Eugen Fink, *Nietzsche's Philosophy*. New York: Continuum 2003, Lawrence J. Hatab, *Nietzsche's Life Sentence. Coming to Terms with Eternal Recurrence*. New York/London: Routledge 2005 and Stephen Williams, *The Shadow of the Antichrist. Nietzsche's Critique of Christianity*. Grand Rapids: Baker Academic 2006.

cal question whether "freedom or force" is better. If someone prefers force over freedom, Bonhoeffer answers himself, "that kind of person has the soul of a slave."[8] About a year later, the student Bonhoeffer writes for a seminar a meditation on "Honour." He opens his meditation by questioning how "honor, Christianity, young people ... can be brought together?" Then he adds: "The Nietzsche complex about the slave morality of Christianity comes into play here."[9] In both instances Bonhoeffer sees the dangers of young people having the misconception that Christianity may be reduced to a restrictive morality, in Nietzsche's term, a slave morality. In a third instance of that same period, in one of Bonhoeffer's sermons (on James 1:21–25) prepared in the summer of 1926, Nietzsche is cited twice by name and referred to several times in allusions. Bonhoeffer proclaims the transformative power of God's word and then says: "We have arrogantly and conceitedly driven it [God's word] from us. We have uttered impressive words, mumbled something about philosophy and Nietzsche and about being bigger than our sins,[10] and have carried our wise heads exceedingly high."[11] A few paragraphs further into the sermon, Bonhoeffer comes to speak of obedience. "Obedience," he laments, "is a word that we don't like to hear very much today and whose meaning we don't want to understand. It is a word that, since the time of Nietzsche, we have contemptuously driven out from ethics and especially from religion."[12] Finally, Bonhoeffer proclaims: "Jesus Christ is the path from God to humanity," and hence all other paths are false, no matter where they may lead, including to the *Übermensch*.[13]

Nietzsche's thought plays only a minor role in Bonhoeffer's two academic dissertations. In the doctoral dissertation *Sanctorum Communio* there is only one brief citation of Nietzsche. In the context of arguing for the validity of prayer and intercession, Bonhoeffer cites the philosopher's statement "'waiting for God to draw near' (Nietzsche),"[14] but *de facto* reverses the statement's original meaning rather than taking it as the criticism of prayer that Nietzsche intended it to be.[15]

---

[8] *DBWE* 9, 456. Cf. Nietzsche, *Genealogy* I, 10.

[9] *DBWE* 9, 529.

[10] *Genealogy* 3, 20.

[11] *DBWE* 9, 494–495.

[12] *DBWE* 9, 495.

[13] *DBWE* 9, 496.

[14] *Beyond Good and Evil*, 58. Nietzsche says (*KSA* 5, 75) that "Gebet [ist] eine beständige Bereitschaft für das 'Kommen Gottes'."

[15] In *Act and Being* there is no citation of Nietzsche's works, only the vague possibility that Bonhoeffer's critique of philosophical systems may have been inspired to a cer-

Bonhoeffer's year (1928–1929) as a vicar in Barcelona was the first substantiated period in which he seems to have read and reflected on Nietzsche's philosophy. In his congregational lecture on "Jesus Christ" Bonhoeffer makes the first explicit references to Nietzsche. There he notes that "everywhere there is a terrible refusal to obey the harsh demands of Jesus words. These are for heroes and those on the way to the overman [*Übermensch*]."[16] Further into the same lecture Bonhoeffer notes that being a Christian is essentially not something religious since religion remains "menschlich-allzumenschlich."[17] Finally, he also speaks of Jesus' life as one that revaluates all traditional values.[18] The theme of revaluation of traditional, Christian values is a major theme in Nietzsche and thus becomes, as we shall see, also crucial to Bonhoeffer, especially in his articulation of ethics. This is already evident in Bonhoeffer's second congregational lecture in Barcelona on the topic "What is a Christian Ethic?" There he says plainly: "Hence the discovery of the world beyond good and evil is by no means to be attributed to the enemy of Christianity Friedrich Nietzsche, whose polemic against the self-righteousness of Christianity derived from this perspective. It belongs rather to the original, albeit concealed material of the Christian message."[19] A few pages further on Bonhoeffer returns to the same theme. "Christians create their own standards for good and evil; only Christians themselves provide the justification for their acts, just as they alone bear responsibility for them. Christians create new tables, new decalogues, as Nietzsche said of the Overman. Indeed, Nietzsche's Overman is not, as he imagined, the opposite of the Christian; without realizing it, Nietzsche imbued the Overman with many features of the free Christian as described and conceived by both Paul and Luther."[20] At the end of his

---

tain degree by Nietzsche's critique; cf. editor's reference to Kierkegaard and Nietzsche in *DBWE* 2, 67, note, 69.

[16] *DBWE* 10, 350, note 22.

[17] *DBWE* 10, 358. The reference to "menschlich-allzumenschlich" is of course an allusion to Nietzsche's work of the same title.

[18] Cf. *DBWE* 10, 352, note 32. Bonhoeffer says (*DBW* 10, 314): "Alle überkommenen Werte scheinen zu stürzen, umgewertet zu werden." Nietzsche spoke of the "Umwertung aller Werte" (*Ecce Homo, KSK* 6, 365). In the prologue (9) to *Zarathustra*, Nietzsche speaks of "the one who breaks the tablets of values [der, der zerbricht ihre Tafeln der Werthe]" and the one "who will write new values on new tablets [die, welche neue Werthe auf neue Tafeln schreiben]."

[19] *DBWE* 10, 363. Cf. *DBW* 10, 327: "Die Entdeckung des Jenseits von Gut und Böse gehört also durchaus nicht dem Christentumsfeind Fr. Nietzsche, der von hier aus gegen das Moralin des Christentums polemisiert, sondern sie gehört zum freilich verschütteten Urgut der christlichen Botschaft."

[20] *DBWE* 10, 366–367; cf. note 21.

lecture, Bonhoeffer refers to the saga of the giant Antaeus who could not be defeated "until during one battle his adversary lifted him up off the ground, whereupon the giant lost the power that had flowed into him only from his contact with the earth."[21] Bonhoeffer uses this saga in analogy to human life. "Those who would abandon the earth, who would flee the crisis of the present, will lose all the power still sustaining them by means of eternal, mysterious power."[22] In August 1928 Bonhoeffer preached in Barcelona on 1 John 2:17: "And the world and its desire are passing away, but those who do the will of God live forever." In the context of speaking of eternity Bonhoeffer cites Nietzsche: "Yet all joy wants eternity – wants deep, wants deep eternity."[23]

After his return to Berlin from Barcelona, Bonhoeffer entered the academy once more in order to write his *Habilitation* and then as a lecturer in theology. In July 1930 Bonhoeffer submitted an essay on the topic of how to selection and determine the significance of a biblical text for a sermon. In passing he observed that some preachers use extra-biblical texts, such as Goethe or Nietzsche texts, to appeal to a more educated audience. For Bonhoeffer, however, this is a severe mistake [*Irrweg*]. "That precisely the Bible is God's word, however, and a religious poem by Nietzsche is not, is the irresolvable mystery of God's revelation in hiddenness."[24]

During the winter semester of 1931–1932 Bonhoeffer presented a lecture at the University of Berlin on the "The History of Systematic Theology in the Twentieth-Century." Nietzsche is mentioned six times in the course of those lectures. In his social analysis of German society at the turn of the century, Bonhoeffer refers, among many others, also to Nietzsche, whom he understands to attack the spirit of scepticism with his "eschatological anticipation of an Overman [*Übermensch*]."[25] In a discussion of religion, Bonhoeffer refers to Nietzsche a second time. "Friedrich Nietzsche," explains Bonhoeffer, "took up Feuerbach's doctrine of the whole human being [*Lehre vom ganzen Menschen*]. [A human being is] not a transcendent being that only appears to exist [*Scheinwesen*] but is *ens realissimum* [the most real being]."[26] After several more sections Bonhoeffer treats the issue of culture and ethics. "Nietzsche," he declares, "rejected Christianity entirely, as the most disastrous inhibition of autonomous culture. For him,

---

[21] *DBWE* 10, 377.
[22] *DBWE* 10, 377–378.
[23] *DBWE* 10, 517 citing *Zarathustra*, "The Sleepwalker Song," 12.
[24] *DBWE* 10, 382–383.
[25] *DBWE* 11, 180.
[26] *DBWE* 11, 186.

compassion is basically and principally unnatural in human beings, and he considered it the principle of Christian ethic."[27] A little further in the same lecture Nietzsche is mentioned as one who supported a "culture of personality" [*Persönlichkeitskultur*].[28] In the section on "Preaching," Nietzsche is mentioned once more. Bonhoeffer postulates that there is no such thing as a Christian way to God and not even faith is a religious path. That Christians have, nonetheless, lived as if faith is a religious possibility and thus become boastful has been clearly perceived by Nietzsche in "his critique of glorifying in one's servitude" [*Knechtsseligkeit*].[29]

On the day of his birthday in 1932, the young Bonhoeffer gave a public lecture at the Technical University in Berlin on the topic of self-determination. In passing he mentions Nietzsche's Zarathustra who, similar to the prophet Jeremiah, curses the day of his birth.[30] There are also two[31] sermons of the year 1932 in which Bonhoeffer draws on Nietzsche without mentioning his name. In a sermon on Colossians 3:1–4, Bonhoeffer opens his deliberations by questioning whether those who "set their minds on things that are above, not on things that are on earth" (verse 2) would not do better by destroying old tablets and making new ones. "Because of sentences like this, 'Set your mind on things that are above and not on things that are on earth,' ... Christianity is accused of betraying the earth."[32] As before in the lecture in Barcelona, here too, Bonhoeffer appeals to Nietzsche's dictum to be faithful to the earth.[33] In another sermon, Bonhoeffer preached on John 8:32: "The truth will make you free." "The human being who loves," he proclaims boldly, "because [he] has been made free by God's truth is the most revolutionary human being on earth. He is the overturning of all values; he is the explosive material in human society;

---

[27] *DBWE* 11, 219. The editors (cf. note 223) refer to Nietzsche's work *The Anti-Christ*, 7, as a possible parallel to Bonhoeffer's discussion. There Nietzsche says: "Christianity is called the religion of *pity*. – Pity is the opposite of the tonic affects that heighten our vital feelings: pity has a depressive effect. And pity further intensifies and multiplies the loss of strength."

[28] Cf. *DBWE* 11, 224.

[29] Cf. *DBWE* 11, 236. The editors point out (in note 305) that the term "Knechtsseligkeit" is not extant in Nietzsche's writings. The suggestion that Bonhoeffer may have been thinking of *The Anti-Christ* 24, does not seem compelling.

[30] Cf. *DBWE* 11, 253.

[31] The editors of *DBWE* 11 point to two other sermons that may go back to Nietzsche's thought. The evidence is not, however, strong enough to establish Bonhoeffer's dependence on Nietzsche; cf. *DBWE* 11, 410, note 10 and 446, note 17.

[32] Cf. *DBWE* 11, 458.

[33] *Zarathustra*, "Prologue," 3.

he is the most dangerous human being."[34] Here we have an allusion to Nietzsche in the words "the overturning of all values" even though Bonhoeffer employs the word *Umsturz* rather than the usual *Umwertung*.

In his lecture at the University of Berlin on "Creation and Sin" in 1932–1933, Nietzsche was an important – although incognito – partner in theological dialogue. There are several unambiguous allusions to Nietzsche's thought even though his name was never mentioned. The most unmistakable allusion is found in the context of Bonhoeffer's discussion of Genesis 2:8–17. Bonhoeffer interprets these verses to mean that "Adam knows neither what good nor what evil is and lives in the strictest sense *beyond good and evil*; that is, Adam lives out of the life that comes from God, before whom a life lived in good, just like a life lived in evil, would mean an unthinkable falling away."[35] The reference to "beyond good and evil" is, of course, the exact title of one of Nietzsche's works, *Beyond Good and Evil*, and was hinted at in the earlier work *Thus Spoke Zarathustra*.[36]

In his interpretation of the fall of humanity in Genesis 3:6, Bonhoeffer remarks that "the extent of the fall is such that it affects the whole of the created world. From now on that world has been robbed of its creatureliness and drops blindly into infinite space, like a meteor that has torn itself away from the core to which it once belonged. It is of this fallen-falling world that we must now speak."[37] Many scholars find it quite likely that Bonhoeffer was drawing on a parallel idea in Nietzsche's *The Gay Science*, where the latter asks: "are we not continually plunging downward? And backward, sideways, forward, in all directions? Is there still any up or down? Do we not wander as though through and endless nothing? Do we not feel empty space breathing upon us?"[38] Apparently, in Bonhoeffer's copy, this passage was marked.[39]

Other allusions to Nietzsche are less obvious. On his reflections on Genesis 1:1–2, Bonhoeffer says: "the thinking of fallen humankind, lacks a beginning because it is a circle. We think in a circle. But we also feel and will in a circle. We exist in a circle."[40] Commentators have seen a parallel with Nietzsche's aphorism in *Thus Spoke Zarathustra*. In "Concerning the

---

[34] *DBWE* 11, 471.

[35] *DBWE* 3, 87–88; original italics.

[36] *KSA* 4, 208 ("Vor Sonnen-Aufgang"): "Denn alle Dinge sind getauft am Borne der Ewigkeit und jenseits von Gut und Böse; Gut und Böse selber aber sind nur Zwischenschatten und feuchte Trübsale und Zieh-Wolken."

[37] *DBWE* 3, 120.

[38] *DBWE* 3, 120, note 11; citation from *The Portable Nietzsche*, 95.

[39] *DBWE* 3, 120, note 11.

[40] *DBWE* 3, 26.

Virtuous," he says: "The circle's thirst is within you; every circle curves and turns in order to catch itself up again."[41]

In his interpretation of Genesis 2:7 Bonhoeffer observes that "the human being whom God has created in God's image – that is, in freedom – is the human being who is taken from earth. Even Darwin and Feuerbach could not use stronger language than is used here."[42] As the editors of this volume rightly point out, Nietzsche, and in turn Bonhoeffer, employ Feuerbach's characterization of the human being as *ens realissimum* [the most real being] in their own philosophical reflections.[43]

In his discussion of good and evil Bonhoeffer explains that "the words tob and ra speak of an ultimate split [*Zwiespalt*] in the world of humankind in general that goes back behind even the moral split, so that tob means also something like 'pleasureable' [*lustvoll*] and ra 'painful' [*leidvoll*]."[44] The editors refer to Nietzsche who also combines the pairs good and evil and pleasure and pain in his *Thus Spoke Zarathustra*.[45]

In his interpretation of Genesis 3:7 Bonhoeffer once more may have drawn on Nietzsche. He suggests that sexuality is a "passionate hatred of any limit" since sexuality seeks to possess the other person and thereby "destroy[s] the other person as a creature, robs the other person of his or her creatureliness, lays violent hand on the other person's limit, and hates grace."[46] Nietzsche's definition of love in *Ecce Homo* similarly portrays love as war and ultimately as "the deadly hatred of the sexes."[47]

Also during the winter semester 1932–1933 Bonhoeffer delivered a public lecture on the kingdom of God. He begins the very first sentence with these words: "We are otherworldly [*Wir sind Hinterweltler*] or we are secularists; but in either case this means that we no longer believe in God's kingdom."[48] It may be the case that Bonhoeffer employed the term *Hinterweltler* in analogy to Nietzsche. In *Thus Spoke Zarathustra*, Nietzsche entitled one of the sections "On the Hinterlanders [*Von den Hinterweltlern*]."[49] The following two sentences refer several times to the earth, our

---

[41] *DBWE* 3, 26, note 7; cf. *KSA* 4, 121 ("Von den Tugendhaften"): Des Ringes Durst ist in euch: sich selber wieder zu erreichen, dazu ringt und dreht sich jeder Ring."

[42] *DBWE* 3, 76.

[43] *DBWE* 3, 76, note 7. Cf. above *DBWE* 11, 186.

[44] *DBWE* 3, 88.

[45] *DBWE* 3, 88, note 25. Cf. *Zarathustra*, "On the Afterworldly." Cf. also *DBWE* 3, 90, note 32.

[46] *DBWE* 3, 123.

[47] Cf. *DBWE* 3, 123, note 10.

[48] *DBWE* 12, 285.

[49] Walter Kaufmann translates this section "On the Afterwordly" (*The Portable*

mother, a motive that Bonhoeffer used before in one of his Barcelona lectures.[50] The topic of the earth plays also an important part in the section "On the Hinterlanders" in *Thus Spoke Zarathustra*.

In one of his London sermons, delivered in English, Bonhoeffer preached on 2 Corinthians 12:9: "my strength is made perfect in weakness." In exposition of this text he notes: "What is the meaning of weakness in this world? We know that Christianity has been blamed ever since its early days for its message to the weak. Christianity is a religion of slaves, of people with inferiority complexes; it owes its success only to the masses of miserable people."[51] Toward the end of the same sermon, Bonhoeffer uses a Nietzschean concept once more, but reverses it completely: "Not the powerful is right, but ultimately the weak is always right. So Christianity means a devaluation of all human values and the establishment of a new order of values in the sight of Christ."[52] Here Bonhoeffer turns Nietzsche upside-down. Whereas Nietzsche proclaimed the revaluation of all values as a feat of the overman,[53] Bonhoeffer assigns the creation of values exclusively to Christ. In another sermon, on the occasion of the wedding of Albrecht and Hilde Schönherr in April 1936, Bonhoeffer addresses the groom directly with these words: "Albrecht, become a joyful pastor! Whoever knows himself to be one with Jesus Christ also knows that he is redeemed, and hence the one who also looks redeemed will be an enormous help to his congregation."[54] Possibly Bonhoeffer was thinking of Nietzsche's reproach of priests: "Better songs they will have to sing for me before I learn to believe in their redeemer; more redeemed his disciples would have to look."[55]

It is telling that Bonhoeffer's two spiritual classics, *Discipleship* and *Life Together*, make no reference to Nietzsche. How can we explain this lacuna? The answer, it seems, is straightforward. As a philosopher, Nietzsche raised and debated philosophical issues which, to be sure, do impinge on the crucial issues of the Christian faith to some extent. But his intention as such was not to discuss matters of spiritual direction. Nietzsche's aphorisms were far from Bonhoeffer's interest in the spiritual life, discipleship

---

Nietzsche, 142) and Del Caro and Pippin (*Zarathustra*, 20), as "On the Hinterworldy." Both translations do not make it very clear that Nietzsche is speaking of people and not merely of an idea, although the idea of a *Hinterwelt* is implicated.

50 Cf. *DBWE* 10, 377.
51 *DBWE* 13, 402.
52 *DBWE* 13, 403.
53 Cf. *Zarathustra*, "Prologue," 9.
54 *DBWE* 14, 915.
55 *Zarathustra*, "On Priests."

and costly grace and thus had no value for Bonhoeffer with regard to the Christian life discussed in these two books.

Nietzsche's Aphorisms in Bonhoeffer's Writings after 1940

After the closing of the underground seminary in Finkenwalde, Bonhoeffer continued to teach the seminarians of the Confessing Church in the collective vicariates in Pomerania. In the winter of 1939–1940 Bonhoeffer presented his meditation on Psalm 119. In contrast to genuine thankfulness, "the thanksgiving of the world always refers ultimately to itself; through gratitude one seeks merely their higher confirmation and consecration of one's own happiness."[56] In a similar vein, in another session in July 1940 the topic was also that of thankfulness. After looking at the biblical evidence, he cites the views of a few select thinkers: Thomas à Kempis, Larochefoucauld, Rousseau and then Nietzsche. He quotes two sentences, but in reversed order from Nietzsche, from an aphorism in *Human, All too Human*. Bonhoeffer begins with the statement: "Gratitude... is a milder form of revenge," and then proceeds to cite the answer to the question which Nietzsche actually posed, namely: "what is the reason for the thankfulness of the powerful?" The answer is this: "through his good deed, his benefactor has, as it were, violated the powerful man's sphere and penetrated it."[57]

In *Ethics* the philosophy of Nietzsche figures more prominently and deliberately than in his other writings. Most notable are Bonhoeffer's allusions to *Thus Spoke Zarathustra* and, to a lesser extent, allusions to *Ecce Homo* and *Beyond Good and Evil*. In the section "Christ, Reality and Good," Bonhoeffer speaks of ultimate reality: "That God alone is the ultimate reality," he proposes is "not an idea meant to sublimate the actual world, nor is it the religious perfecting of a profane worldview. It is rather a faithful Yes to God's self-witness, God's revelation. If God is merely a religious concept, there is no reason why there should not be, behind this apparent 'ultimate' reality, a still more ultimate reality: the twilight or the death of the gods."[58] The reference to "the twilight or the death of the

---

[56] *DBWE* 15, 508–509. Note 47 points to the fact that Bonhoeffer wrote the word "Nietzsche" in the margin of the manuscript and refers as a possible parallel to *Zarathurstra*, the section on "Old and New Tablets." However, it is more likely that Bonhoeffer was thinking of another context; cf. the following note below.

[57] *DBWE* 15, 380 and *Human, All too Human, KSK* 2, 66.

[58] *DBWE* 6, 48, note 10.

gods" is, of course, unmistakably Nietzschean, except that Nietzsche combines the death of the gods and the coming of the overman [*Übermensch*].[59]

Pilate's acclamation – "look, what a person!" – when Jesus appeared before him during his trial (cf. John 19:5) has been used by Bonhoeffer – in the rendering of the Vulgate: *ecce homo* – on several contexts in the section "Ethics as Formation."[60] Since Nietzsche has entitled one of his works *Ecce Homo*, interpreters are quick to point out that Bonhoeffer may have deliberately used Nietzsche's title to set it in stark relief to his portrayal of Jesus Christ.[61] It is impossible to make a judgement with certainty and the question needs to remain open.[62] There is, however, solid evidence that a few pages further into his discussion in the same section, Bonhoeffer does deliberately invoke a concept of Nietzsche, only to rebut it "The human being should and may be human," Bonhoeffer affirms, but then continues: "All super-humanity [*Übermenschentum*], all efforts to outgrow one's nature as human, all struggle to be heroic or a demigod, all fall away from a person here, because they are untrue."[63]

In Bonhoeffer's first draft of "History and Good [1]" Nietzsche is cited once by name. After he rejects the view that ethics can be reduced to a categorical knowledge of good and evil,[64] Bonhoeffer argues that freedom underlies all concrete ethical behaviour and hence "the action of the responsible person is most profoundly in accord with reality."[65] He continues to say that "this concept of 'accordance with reality' [*das Wirklichkeitsgemäße*] requires further clarification. A misunderstanding would lead to that 'servile attitude toward the facts' (Nietzsche) that always retreats wherever pressure is greater, that justifies success on principle, and that in any given situation chooses the expedient as being in accord with reality.

---

[59] Cf. *Zarathustra*, "On the Bestowing Virtue." Zarathustra says: "Dead are all gods; now we want the overman to live."

[60] *DBWE* 6, 82, 83, 84, 88, 91.

[61] Cf. *DBWE* 6, 82, note 22.

[62] Likewise, I am also rather skeptical as to Bonhoeffer's reference to people as "failures [*gescheiterte Existenzen*]" and a possible parallel in Nietzsche's lament that "with the Jews the slave revolt in morality begins;" cf. *DBWE* 6, 90, note 58.

[63] *DBWE* 6, 94.

[64] Bonhoeffer also wrote "A Theological Position Paper on State and Church," a piece that was originally published in the various editions of *Ethics*, but now appears in *DBWE* 16, 502–528. In the course of his discourse Bonhoeffer says: "Like everything that exists, government is also in a certain sense beyond good and evil" (*DBWE* 16, 513). The phrase "beyond good and evil" is of course Nietzschean, but Bonhoeffer's exposition does not contribute to a greater understanding how he employed Nietzsche in this context.

[65] *DBWE* 6, 222.

Misunderstanding accordance with reality in this sense amounts to irresponsibility."[66] For Bonhoeffer, however, "the most fundamental reality is the reality of the God who became human."[67] Below we will return to a discussion of what these reflections on reality mean for Bonhoeffer vis-à-vis Nietzsche.[68]

In the section "History and Good [2]," Bonhoeffer refers to Nietzsche by name and then quotes a passage from *Thus Spoke Zarathustra*. "Unknowingly," Bonhoeffer comments, "Nietzsche speaks in the spirit of the New Testament when he chides the legalistic and narrow-minded misunderstanding of the commandment to love your neighbor with the following words: 'You crowd around your neighbor and have fine words for it. But I say unto you: your love of the neighbor is your bad love of yourselves. You flee to your neighbor from yourselves and would like to make a virtue out of that: but I see through your "selflessness." … Do I advise love of those nearest to you [*Nächstenliebe*]? Sooner I should even advise you to flee from those nearest you and to love those farthest away [*Fernstenliebe*]."[69] To illustrate the concreteness of a person's love for the neighbour far away, Bonhoeffer recalls the following incident. "In a terrible miscarriage of justice in the United States in 1931, nine young black men accused of raping a white girl of dubious reputation were sentenced to death even though their guilt could not be proven. This triggered a storm of outrage that found expression in open letters from the most respected European public figures" except from Germans who hid behind their "'Lutheran' understanding of vocation."[70] Regarding this incident Bonhoeffer wonders whether Jesus' call to love the neighbour who is far away "lead[s] us here to understand Nietzsche's statement: 'My brothers, love of the neighbor I do not recommend to you: I recommend to you love of the farthest'?"[71]

---

[66] *DBWE* 6, 222–223. On Bonhoeffer's appropriation of this Nietzschean aphorism, see *DBWE* 6, 222, note 19.

[67] *DBWE* 6, 223.

[68] In the second draft of the section "History and Good [2]" Bonhoeffer repeats, almost verbatim, what he has said about Nietzsche in the first draft of "History and Good [1]"; cf. *DBWE* 6, 261. The Editors of *DBW/E* 6 suggest in this section Bonhoeffer may also be drawing on Nietzsche when he notes that "love for human beings leads into the solidarity of human guilt." Though possible, it seems to me that the allusion to Nietzsche's notion of guilt is not strong enough to substantiate such a claim; cf. *DBWE* 6, 233, note 59.

[69] *DBWE* 6, 294. Bonhoeffer cites from (and slightly alters) the section "On Love of the Neighbour." Cf. *DBWE* 10, 630.

[70] *DBWE* 6, 295.

[71] *DBWE* 6, 295 and *Zarathustra*, "On Love of the Neighbour."

In the section "Heritage and Decay," Bonhoeffer refers to Nietzsche three times by name. "From Win[c]kelmann to Nietzsche," Bonhoeffer elucidates, "in Germany there is a deliberately anti-Christian appropriation of the Greek heritage. The reason for this particular relation to the heritage of antiquity, so different from that of the more western European peoples, lies doubtless in the form that the gospel assumed through the Reformation in Germany. Nietzsche could have arisen only from the soil of the German Reformation. Here, the contradiction between the natural and grace is starkly opposed to the reconciliation of nature with grace in the Roman heritage. From a Greek point of view, Nietzsche could receive a positive assessment from German Reformation theology – something incomprehensible for Western peoples."[72] Further on in the same section, Bonhoeffer discusses western godlessness as the result of the French Revolution. The tragedy, Bonhoeffer laments, is that "this godlessness is emphatically Christian. In every possible Christianity – nationalist, socialist, rationalist, or mystical – it turns against the living God of the Bible, against Christ. Its God is the new human being, whether the 'factory of new humanity' is Bolshevist or Christian."[73] According to the editors notes of *Ethics*, Bonhoeffer wrote the word "Nietzsche" in the margin of his manuscript besides these lines.[74] The association with Nietzsche in this context suggests that Bonhoeffer may have been thinking of Nietzsche's *Übermensch* or *Übermenschentum*; as we saw already, the latter term he employed earlier in *Ethics*.[75]

Bonhoeffer cites Nietzsche twice in the section "God's Love and the Disintegration of the World." In the first instance, Bonhoeffer discusses the meaning of shame following the fall. "Covering is necessary," notes Bonhoeffer, "because it keeps shame alive, reminding them [Adam and Eve, humanity] of their estrangement from the origin; it is also necessary because human beings must now just endure themselves and live a hidden life as the estranged and divided beings they are. Otherwise they would betray themselves. 'Every deep spirit needs a mask' (Nietzsche)."[76] In the second instance, Bonhoeffer is exegeting Jesus' saying in the Sermon on the Mount: "Do not judge, so that you may not be judged" (Matthew 7:1). Bonhoeffer rejects judging as reprehensible "not because it springs from

---

[72] *DBWE* 6, 106–107.
[73] *DBWE* 6, 122–123. The reference to the "factory of new humanity" is the title of a book, published in 1935, by the Russian Alexandra Rachmanova.
[74] Cf. *DBWE* 6, 123, note 93.
[75] *DBWE* 6, 94.
[76] *DBWE* 6, 304.

dark motives, as Nietzsche thought, but because judging is itself the apostasy from God."[77]

Bonhoeffer opens the section entitled "Church and World [1]" with these words: "We begin this section by calling attention to one of the most astounding experiences we have had during the years of trial for all that was Christian. Whenever, in the face of deification of the irrational powers of blood, of instinct, of the predator within human beings, there was an appeal to human reason."[78] Köster correctly identified that Bonhoeffer's words "the predator within human beings [*das Raubtier im Menschen*]" is an allusion to Nietzsche's expression that the human being is the best of predators.[79]

Bonhoeffer's *Fiction from Tegel Prison* has no mentioning of Nietzsche and, following the editors of this volume, conceivably only a handful of allusions. These are as follows: In the Drama, scene 1, Grandmother reads to little brother, a ten year old boy. The story is that of a hunter who shoots a "wondrous beast."[80] The editors suggest that Bonhoeffer may have thought of Nietzsche's image of the hunter,[81] an image Bonhoeffer had incorporated into a sermon in London to describe the calling of the prophet Jeremiah.[82] In scene 2 of the Drama Bonhoeffer puts these words in the mouth of Ulrich: "Suddenly, there in the middle of hell, I met – God." The editors refer to Nietzsche's *Thus Spoke Zarathustra* as a possible source for this saying.[83] In scene 3 of the Drama, the Stranger says that "dying is interesting, not being dead. Dying takes a long time and is just as varied as life."[84] Here again the editors point to Nietzsche as a possible source, conceivably the section "On Free Death" in *Thus Spoke Zarathustra* where Nietzsche contrasts death and dying. In the section entitled "The Major's Story" in Bonoeffer's prison novel, Hans speaks of "all kinds of flying vermin [*Ungeziefer*] – bumblebees, mosquitoes, horseflies – stinging, biting, and tormenting me horribly."[85] Again, it is conceivable that Nietzsche's

---

[77] *DBWE* 6, 315.

[78] *DBWE* 6, 339–340.

[79] Cf. Peter Köster, "Nietzsche als verborgener Antipode in Bonhoeffers 'Ethik'," in *Nietzsche Studien* 19 (1990), 397, note 140. Cf. *Zarathustra*, "On Old and New Tablets." Del Caro and Pippin (*Zarathustra*, 169) translate the expression as "the human being is, after all, the best beast of prey."

[80] *DBWE* 7, 26–27.

[81] Cf. *Zarathustra*, "The Magician."

[82] Cf. *DBWE* 13, 349–350.

[83] *DBWE* 7, 41. Cf. *Zarathustra*, "On the Pitying," where Nietzsche says: "Thus the devil once spoke to me: 'Even God has his hell: it is his love for mankind'."

[84] *DBWE* 7, 57.

[85] *DBWE* 7, 150.

Thus Spoke Zarathustra may have been Bonhoeffer's inspiration behind these lines; for Nietzsche does, indeed, speak of vermin, although mostly of poisonous flies.[86] Further on in the same section, Franz reminisces about an old teacher who himself reflects on the theme of "historiography" and the fact that history reveals the viewpoint of those who succeeded. That, however, "is barbarism over and over again, because it systematically makes people savage and base."[87] Once more, the editors refer to Nietzsche who may have guided Bonhoeffer in his musings. It seems to me that all these possible allusions to Nietzsche cannot be established with any degree of certainty. To be sure, there are conceptual parallels between Bonhoeffer and Nietzsche on the points mentioned. However, the evidence is not conclusive to determine the degree of Bonhoeffer's dependence on Nietzsche as his source.[88]

It is a bewildering and curious fact that in *Letters and Papers from Prison* the thought of Nietzsche plays a very inconsequential, if any, role. Given Bonhoeffer's repeated attempts to conceptualize a "religionless Christianity" within the context of a "world come of age," one would think that Nietzsche's critique of the traditional forms of Christianity may have animated Bonhoeffer's thinking to a certain degree. Surprisingly, however, Bonhoeffer does not even hint at such Nietzschean ideas as the coming of the *Übermensch*, the revaluation of old values, faithfulness to the earth or a new ethical framework beyond good and evil. There are three allusions to Nietzsche in *Letters and Papers from Prison* that strike the reader to be more cursory than substantial. The first one in a letter to Eberhard Bethge, dated 12 February 1944. Bonhoeffer notes that he reminisces about his childhood and thinks of the many impressions of nature. Beside "the Harz Mountains, the Thuringian Forest, or the Weser Mountains" there is also "a fashionable and a Nietzschean Engadin."[89] In a letter to Eberhard Bethge of 9 March 1944 Nietzsche – together with Kierkegaard – is briefly mentioned, among many others, as having a different kind of *hilaritas* (*Heiterkeit*; serenity) than Michelangelo, Burckhardt, Mozart, Luther, Barth and others.[90] In a third instance, again in a letter to Eberhard Bethge, dated 25 March 1944, Nietzsche is mentioned in the context of Bonhoeffer and Bethge's discussion of landscape painting. "We go along all too easily with

---

[86] Cf. *Zarathustra*, "On the Flies of the Market Place."

[87] *DBWE* 7, 164.

[88] This caution also applies to another place in the novel; cf. *DBWE* 7, 172 where Bonhoeffer refers to "salves" and the editors suggest parallels with Nietzsche.

[89] *DBWE* 8, 294.

[90] *DBWE* 8, 319.

Nietzsche's primitive alternatives, as if the 'Apollonian' concept of beauty, and the 'Dionysian,' the one we call demonic nowadays, are the only ones."[91]

There are, however, two instances in which Bonhoeffer employs an expression that, to my knowledge, have never been traced back to Nietzsche. In a letter to Eberhard Bethge of 29 May 1944, Bonhoeffer relates that he was in the process of reading Weizsäcker's book *The World-View of Physics*. This book, he says, "has again brought home to me quite clearly that we shouldn't think of God as a stopgap [*Gott als Lückenbüßer*] for the incompleteness of our knowledge ... God is not a stopgap. We must recognize God not only where we reach the limits of our possibilities. God wants to be recognized in the midst of our lives."[92] The editors of *DBW* 8 quite correctly point out that the phrase "God as a stopgap [*Gott als Lückenbüßer*]" was used by Paul Tillich in his book *Die religiöse Lage der Gegenwart*, a work Bonhoeffer consulted for his lecture on the "History of Theology in the Twentieth Century" in the winter semester of 1931–1932.[93] The fact that Tillich used the expression should not detract from the more important fact that he did not coin it. Its author is actually Nietzsche. In *Thus Spoke Zarathustra*, Nietzsche says "Aus Lücken bestand der Geist dieser Erlöser; aber in jede Lücke hatten sie ihren Wahn gestellt, ihren Lückenbüßer, den sie Gott nannten (The spirit of these redeemers consisted of gaps; but into every gap they had plugged a delusion, their stopgap, whom they named God)."[94] The same allusion to God as stopgap is repeated once more. In his "Outline for a Book" of August 1944, Bonhoeffer wants to include the following in the first chapter: "The religionlessness of the human being come of age. 'God' as a working hypothesis, as stopgap for our embarrassments, has become superfluous (as indicated previously)."[95]

Nietzsche's Influence on Bonhoeffer's Theology

Above we saw that Bonhoeffer draws on Nietzsche in many different ways. Our task now is to discuss those salient features in Nietzsche that shaped Bonhoeffer's own theology in response to the challenges posed by the philosopher. Being mindful not to systematize unduly – either Nietzsche

---

[91] *DBWE* 8, 331.
[92] *DBWE* 8, 405–406.
[93] Cf. *DBWE* 8, 405, note 5.
[94] *Zarathustra*, "On Priests."
[95] *DBWE* 8, 500.

or Bonhoeffer – there are several interrelated themes that are decisive for both of them, albeit in their idiosyncratic contexts. We will briefly discuss each of them.

Critique of Christendom

If a person has any knowledge of the philosophy of Friedrich Nietzsche it is typically the impression that it is blatantly anti-Christian. This impression is of course the intentional creation of Nietzsche himself. He not only entitled one of his writings *The Antichrist*, but the numerable aphorisms throughout his oeuvre leave no doubt as to his unconcealed view, bitter critique and at times sacrilegious and grotesque attack on Christianity and on Jesus Christ.[96] Much could be speculated about Nietzsche's (mis)interpretation and (mis)understanding of Christianity, but for our purposes it suffices to articulate the *cantus firmus* of Nietzsche's disparaging of Christianity.

In Nietzsche's estimate "Christianity has sided with all that is weak and base, with all failures; it has made an ideal of whatever *contradicts* the instinct of the strong life to preserve itself; it has corrupted the reason even of those strongest in spirit by teaching men to consider the supreme values of the spirit as something sinful, as something that leads into error – as temptations."[97] The cynic Nietzsche continues: "Christianity is called the religion of *pity* [*Religion des Mitleidens*]. Pity stands opposed to the tonic emotions which heighten our vitality: it has a depressing effect. We are deprived of strength when we feel pity ... Under certain circumstances, it [pity] may engender a total loss of life and vitality out of all proportions to the magnitude of the cause (as in the case of the death of the Nazarene) ... Pity negates life and renders it *more deserving of negation*. Pity is the *practice* of nihilism."[98]

---

[96] For a recent study on Nietzsche and his relation to Christianity, see Williams, *The Shadow of the Antichrist. Nietzsche's Critique of Christianity*. For an assessment of Nietzsche and the biblical tradition, see Hans Hübner, *Nietzsche und das Neue Testament*. Tübingen: Mohr Siebeck 2000.

[97] *The Anti-Christ*, 5.

[98] *The Anti-Christ*, 7. Bonhoeffer also interprets Feuerbach in this vein: "The primal drive of the ego is the drive to live, [the] primal inhibition is death; all religion [originates] from the experience of death as inhibition, from the fear of death. In praying to God, the human being prays to the idealized form of his drive toward life. That is why there has always been only anthropology in Christianity. Feuerbach thinks highly of humankind because of this elevated capacity that human beings have... Feuerbach was

These words leave no doubt as to Nietzsche's repugnance with Christianity: *it denies life*! The state of the Christian is the worst in the hierarchy of sentient beings. Out of fear, Nietzsche claims, humanity unfolded in this downward spiral: "the domestic animal, the herd animal, the sick human animal – the Christian."[99] Ultimately, the reason for such a low view of life has its momentum in the Christian conception of God. In Christianity, "God degenerated into the *contradiction* of life, instead of being its transfiguration and eternal Yes! God as the declaration of war against life, against nature, against the will to live! God – the formula for every slander against 'this world,' for every lie about the 'beyond'! – God the deification of nothingness, the will to nothingness pronounced holy!"[100] The great tragedy for Nietzsche is that "in Christianity neither morality nor religion has even a single point of contact with reality. Nothing but imaginary *causes* ('God,' 'soul,' 'ego,' 'spirit,' 'free will' – for that matter, 'unfree will'), nothing but imaginary *effects* ('sin,' 'redemption,' 'grace,' 'punishment,' 'forgiveness of sins")."[101] In sum, for Nietzsche, the religion that is based on the εὐαγγέλιον, the *good* news for humanity, has become the very epitome of the devaluation of life in general and the human being in particular. To repeat a citation from above, Bonhoeffer clearly perceives that Nietzsche "rejected Christianity entirely, as the most disastrous inhibition of autonomous culture. For him, compassion is basically and principally unnatural in human beings, and he considered it the principle of Christian ethic."[102] In other words, the correlation between Christianity and "human anti-nature" is so deeply entrenched in Nietzsche's thinking that the second cannot be rehabilitated apart from the first. And this is precisely the issue at which Bonhoeffer and Nietzsche part their ways. Whereas for Nietzsche the sequence is logically from the life-denial forces of Christianity to human anti-nature for Bonhoeffer the power of the resurrected Christ leads to the fullness of human life. These two worlds are so far apart that they cannot be reconciled.

And yet, Bonhoeffer accepts to a certain degree Nietzsche's stinging criticism that Christians all too often forfeit their most basic humanity.

Schleiermacher's most consistent pupil, but he regarded as an illusion what for Schleiermacher was an unproved assumption" (*DBWE* 11, 185).

[99] *The Anti-Christ*, 3.

[100] *The Anti-Christ*, 18. Nietzsche has a particularly difficult time with the concept of sin. For him, sin "ist bisher das grösste Ereignis in der Geschichte der kranken Seele gewesen; in ihr haben wir das gefährlichste und verhängnisvollste Kunststück der religiösen Interpretation" (*Genealogy*, KSA 5, 389).

[101] *The Anti-Christ*, 15.

[102] *DBWE* 11, 219.

This is most evident in his later writings, especially in *Letters and Papers from Prison*. On 18 July 1944, two days before the failed conspiracy on Hitler, Bonhoeffer writes in a letter to his friend Eberhard Bethge: "'Could you not stay awake with me one hour?' Jesus asks in Gethsemane. That is the opposite of everything a religious person [*der religiöse Mensch*] expects from God. The human being [*der Mensch*] is called upon to share in God's sufferings at the hands of a godless world. Thus we must really live in a godless world and not ty to cover up or transfigure its ungodliness some-how with religion. Our lives must be 'worldly,' so that we can share pre-cisely so in God's suffering; our lives are allowed to be 'worldly,' that is, we are delivered from false religious obligations and inhibitions."[103] Here Bonhoeffer insists that a Christian person must and *may* live in a secular, godless world without diminishing either the world's godliness or the per-son's humanity. The day after the failed conspiracy, on 21 July 1944, Bon-hoeffer writes another letter to Bethge and comes back to the theme of how one should live. "Later on I discovered, and am still discovering to this day, that one only learns to have faith by living in the full this-worldliness of life... one throws oneself completely into the arms of God, and this is what I call this-worldliness [*Diesseitigkeit*]: living fully in the midst of life's tasks, questions, successes and failures, experiences and perplexities – then one takes seriously no longer one's own sufferings but rather the sufferings of God in the world. Then one stays awake with Christ in Gethsemane. And I think this is faith; this is μετάνοια [repentance]. And this is how one becomes a human being, a Christian."[104]

Precisely at this point it becomes clear that Bonhoeffer overcomes Nietzsche's charge that in "Christianity neither morality nor religion has even a single point of contact with reality." There is perhaps no theologian of the twentieth century who emphasized "this-worldly" living as much as did Bonhoeffer. Just as Nietzsche was ready to affirm all of life uncondi-tionally without recourse to an "other-worldly" reality,[105] Bonhoeffer likewise calls the Christian to a life that is unconditionally rooted in all of this world's reality. Only then "one becomes a human being [*ein Mensch*], a Christian." In other words, Bonhoeffer stresses the symbiotic relation between becoming a human being and living fully entrenched in this world's reality and – at the same time and without contradiction – being a Christian. A passage from *Ethics* says it most eloquently: "As reality is *one*

---

103 *DBWE* 8, 480.
104 *DBWE* 8, 486.
105 Cf. Hatab, *Nietzsche's Life Sentence. Coming to Terms with Eternal Recurrence*, 20, 148–151.

in Christ, so the person who belongs to this Christ-reality is also a whole. Worldliness does not separate on from Christ, and being Christian does not separate one from the world. Belonging completely to Christ, one stands at the same time completely in the world."[106]

What living unreservedly in the world means for Bonhoeffer is nicely expressed in his essays "After Ten Years." In the section on optimism he writes: "in its essence optimism is not a way of looking at the present situation but a power of life, a power of hope [*eine Lebenskraft, eine Kraft der Hoffnung*] when others resign, a power to hold our heads high when all seems to be have come naught, a power to tolerate setbacks, a power that never abandons the future to the opponent ... no one ought to despise optimism as the will for the future ... it is the health of life."[107] In terminology reminiscent of Nietzsche himself Bonhoeffer points to the Christian's expression of life in strength, fullness and vitality. For him, being Christian and being fully human are not mutually exclusive,[108] as for Nietzsche, but indissolubly joint together in the reality of Christ.

Beyond Good and Evil; Revaluation of all Values

Nietzsche seems to have shaped Bonhoeffer's theology in an interesting way with respect to the notion of good and evil. As we noted above, Bonhoeffer addressed this question in a lecture in Barcelona on the topic "What is a Christian Ethic?" followed by his interpretation in *Creation and Fall*. To repeat, for Bonhoeffer, "the discovery of the world beyond good and evil is by no means to be attributed to the enemy of Christianity Friedrich Nietzsche, whose polemic against the self-righteousness of Christianity derived from this perspective. It belongs rather to the original, albeit concealed material of the Christian message."[109] Bonhoeffer agrees with Nietzsche – but for different reasons – that the distinction between good and evil is a fragile conception. Whereas Nietzsche's anthropology simply disregarded such a distinction as the invention of human feebleness, Bon-

---

[106] *DBWE* 6, 62.

[107] *DBWE* 8, 50–51.

[108] Cf. Bonhoeffer's letter of 8 July 1944, in which he argues that from a biblical perspective, the human being is always understood as the "whole human being" (*DBWE* 8, 456) and not separated into an "inner" and "outer" person. Bonhoeffer further says that "one must simply recognize that the world and humankind [*Menschen*] have come of age. One must not find fault with people in their worldliness but rather confront them with God where they are strongest" *DBWE* 8, 457.

[109] *DBWE* 10, 363.

hoeffer employs it in the course of coming to terms with ethics. Audaciously he declares: "The knowledge of good and evil appears to be the goal of all ethical reflection. The first task of Christian ethics is to supersede that knowledge."[110] Why is Bonhoeffer so adamant about deconstructing traditional Christian approaches to ethics? His answer is lucid: "In knowing about good and evil, human beings understand themselves not within the reality of being defined by the origin, but from their own possibilities, namely, to be either good or evil. They now *know themselves beside and outside God*, which means they know nothing but themselves, and God not at all. For they can only know God by knowing God alone. The knowledge of good and evil is thus disunion with God. Human beings can know about good and evil only in opposition to God."[111] Elsewhere in *Ethics* Bonhoeffer asks the rhetorical question: "Does this mean negating the distinction between good and evil? No, but it means that human beings cannot justify themselves by doing good."[112]

It is crucial to understand that Bonhoeffer is not arguing that there is no reality or distinction between good and evil; given the historical context within which he wrote the *Ethics* manuscript, it would be absurd to think that he has given up the belief that good and evil are tangible realties. Here he is merely contending that the distinction between good and evil cannot be the foundation upon which a Christian ethic should be constructed. Christian ethics is beyond the distinction of good and evil. Everything hinges on the little word *beyond*. Christian ethics is beyond good and evil for two chief reasons.

First, the knowledge of good and evil is the result of the fall of humanity; only as a sinner is the human being preoccupied with this distinction. As Williams puts it: "The knowledge of good and evil, as the biblical narrative of the fall tells us, is a sign of disunity and not a knowledge on which humanity is originally perched in authentic creatureliness."[113] Hence, any human attempt to catalogue deeds into good and evil is thus the attempt to retract to a state before the fall or, as Bonhoeffer puts it, a refusal "of being defined by the origin." Accordingly, because of the fall into sin, there exists no possibility[114] of a person to know the difference between good and evil. The sinner, even the redeemed sinner, cannot place her/himself into the

---

[110] *DBWE* 6, 299.

[111] *DBWE* 6, 300; emphasis added.

[112] *DBWE* 6, 227. Cf. also Williams, *The Shadow of the Antichrist*, 243.

[113] Williams, *The Shadow of the Antichrist*, 242.

[114] See our discussion below on Bultmann and Tillich and the reasons why Bonhoeffer rejected that there is such a thing as "possibility" or "potentiality" in theology.

truth of knowing the difference between good and evil. Second, and very briefly, the reality of the redemptive act of God in Jesus Christ becomes tangible in the world not by recourse to deeds catalogued as either good or evil, but only in the obedient pursuit to do the will of God in responsible action – a point we will return to below.

Given Nietzsche's ultra-pessimistic analysis of Christianity as a whole and of its life-sapping morality in particular it comes of no surprize that Nietzsche calls for a radical revaluation [*Umwertung*] of all ethical values. Since his culture and personal milieu were overwhelmingly Christian, Nietzsche is essentially calling for a revaluation of all *Christian* values. Moreover, since he fundamentally rejects a morality that is predicated on the basic categories of good and evil, it follows as a logical consequence that he postulates values that are beyond good and evil. Curiously employing biblical terminology, Zarathustra shouts: "Break, break me these old tablets of the pious, my brothers! Gainsay me the sayings of the world slanderers!"[115] And again he announces: "Look at the faithful of all faiths! Whom do they hate the most? The one who breaks their tablets of values, the breaker, the lawbreaker – but he is the creative one. Companions the creative one seeks and not corpses, nor herds and believers. Fellow creators the creative one seeks, who will write new values on new tablets."[116] But for the moment Zarathustra has to comfort himself: "Here I sit and wait, old broken tablets around me and also new tablets only partially written upon. When will my hour come?"[117]

At first glance it seems that Bonhoeffer largely agrees with Nietzsche's deconstruction of laws and values. In his lecture "Basic Questions of a Christian Ethic?" delivered during the year in Barcelona, Bonhoeffer daringly declares: "There are no acts that are bad in and of themselves; even murder can be sanctified. There is only faithfulness to or deviation from God's will. There is no law with a specific content, but only the law of freedom, that is, bearing responsibility alone before God and oneself. The law has been overcome once and for all. It follows from the Christian idea of God that there can be no more law. It is from this same perspective that we must thus understand the ethical commandments and apparent laws we find in the New Testament itself."[118] It is decisive at this point to understand that Nietzsche's revaluation of all values is tied to the coming of the

---

[115] *Zarathustra*, "On Old and New Tablets," 15.
[116] *Zarathustra*, "Zarathustra's Prologue," 9.
[117] *Zarathustra*, "On Old and New Tablets," 1.
[118] *DBWE* 10, 367.

overman and hence, as Bonhoeffer clearly recognizes,[119] is a futuristic, eschatological event. But for Bonhoeffer, a Christian's new humanity, though in its full realization also an eschatological event, is already reality in this fallen and broken world.[120] This new humanity begs the question of how one should live and what the criteria are for one's ethical framework and moral actions? And here Bonhoeffer parts ways with Nietzsche once again. For in Bonhoeffer's view, it is Jesus Christ himself who is the source and power for the revaluation of all traditional values.[121] In a sermon given in London, Bonhoeffer unequivocally affirmed that "Christianity means a devaluation of all human values and the establishment of a new order of values in the sight of Christ."[122] Moreover, in the Barcelona lecture Bonhoeffer elucidates:

"Christians create their own standards for good and evil; only Christians themselves provide the justification for their acts, just as they alone bear responsibility for them. Christians create new tables, new decalogues, as Nietzsche said of the Overman. Indeed, Nietzsche's Overman is not, as he imagined, the opposite of the Christian; without realizing it, Nietzsche imbued the Overman with many features of the free Christian as described and conceived by both Paul and Luther."[123]

What Bonhoeffer assumes here is the underlying principle of freedom which finds it tangible manifestation in the acts of love. As Bonhoeffer confidently remarked in a sermon on John 8:32 ("The truth shall make you free"): "the human being who loves because [he] has been made free by God's truth is the most revolutionary human being on earth. He is the overturning of all values; he is the explosive material in human society; he is the most dangerous human being."[124] Paradoxically, Christian freedom is always bound to the will of God. Put otherwise, Christian values are free in the sense that they are always a response to the search for the will of God. Bonhoeffer puts it this way: "Traditional morals – even if propagated

---

[119] Cf. *DBWE* 11, 180.

[120] Cf. Clifford Green, *Bonhoeffer. A Theology of Sociality.* Grand Rapids: Eerdmans, revised edition 1999, 52–65.

[121] Cf. *DBWE* 10, 352, note 32.

[122] *DBWE* 13, 403. Bonhoeffer's notion of freedom may well go back to Nietzsche. In *Creation and Fall*, Bonhoeffer says emphatically that "there is no 'being-free-from' without a 'being-free-for'" (*DBWE* 3, 67). Nietzsche expresses very similar sentiments: "You call yourself free? Your dominant thought I want to hear, and not that you have escaped from a yoke ... Free *from* what? As if that mattered to Zarathustra! But your eyes should tell me brightly: free *for* what" (*Zarathustra*, in *The Portable Nietzsche*, 175).

[123] *DBWE* 10, 366–367.

[124] *DBWE* 11, 471.

for Christians – or public opinion can never provide the standards for the actions of Christians. Christians act according to how God's will seems to direct them, without looking sideways at others, that is, without considering what is usually called morals. No one but Christians and God, however, can know whether they are indeed acting rightly or wrongly. Ethical decisions lead us into the most profound solitude, the solitude in which a person stands before the living God. Here no one can help us, no one can bear part of the responsibility; here God imposes a burden on us that we must bear alone."[125]

New Humanity and Faithfulness to the Earth

Given Nietzsche's unrelenting critique of Christianity and his desire for a revaluation of all values, it follows for him that *human beings as such* are inextricably intertwined in these two predicaments and hence constitute much of the cause of the problem. Since human beings alone are the bearers of both Christianity and all moral values, for Nietzsche it is in one way or another inexorable that current humanity is largely superfluous.[126] The answer Nietzsche proposes to overcome the life-sapping reality of Christianity and the dysfunction of moral values vis-à-vis the human being lies in the coming of a new human being. The "human being is something that must be overcome," he proclaims loudly, "overcome yourself even in your neighbour; and you should not let anyone give you a right that you can rob for yourself!"[127]

Superfluous humanity is the cosmos's predicament that must be overcome. Nietzsche announces the new being, most extensively in *Thus Spoke Zarathustra*, as the coming of the overman. In the *Prologue* Nietzsche sets out his ideas: "*I teach you the overman (Übermensch)*. Human being is something That Must be overcome. What have you done to overcome him? ... Behold, I teach the overman! The overman is the meaning of the earth.

---

125 *DBWE* 10, 367.
126 Cf. *Zarathustra*, "On the New Idol:" "Far too many are born; the state was invented for the superfluous! ... Just look at these superfluous! They steal for themselves the works of the inventors and the treasures of the wise: education they call their thievery – and everything turns to sickness and hardship for them! Just look at these superfluous! They are always sick, they vomit their gall and call it the newspaper. They devour one another and are not even able to digest themselves. Just look at these superfluous! They acquire riches and yet they become poorer. They want power and first of all the crowbar of power, much money – these impotent, impoverished ones!."
127 *Zarathustra*, "On Old and New Tablets," 4.

Let your will say: the overman *shall be* the meaning of the earth!"[128] And elsewhere Zarathustra says: "Uncanny is human existence and still without meaning: a jester can spell its doom. I want to teach humans the meaning of their being, which is the overman, the lightning from the dark cloud 'human being'."[129] "It was there too that I picked up the word 'overman' (*Übermensch*) along the way, and that the human is something that must be overcome, – that human being is a bridge and not an end; counting itself blessed for its noon and evening as the way to new dawns ... I taught them all *my* creating and striving: to carry together into one what is fragment in mankind and riddle and horrid accident – as poet, riddle guesser and redeemer of chance I taught them to work on the future, and to creatively redeem everything that *was*. To redeem what is past in mankind and to recreate all 'It was' until the will speaks: 'But I wanted it so! I shall want it so.' This I told them was redemption, this alone I taught them to call redemption. – Now I wait for *my* redemption – so that I can go to them for the last time."[130]

In the face of Nietzsche's violent claim to dispense with superfluous humanity in favour of the coming *Übermensch* Bonhoeffer proclaims: "Jesus Christ is the path from God to humanity," and hence all other paths are false, no matter where they may lead, including the path that leads to the *Übermensch*.[131] It is decisive here to recognize, as Hatab argues, that Nietzsche's notion of the *Übermensch* is to be understood as "a structural model for a new way of *experiencing* the world, rather than a new type of person," namely a "structural concept that prepares the possibility of life-affirmation."[132] As a "structural model," "the overman is the meaning of the earth" and calls humanity "to remain faithful to the earth."[133] Nietzsche's passionate plea to affirm (by means of *überwinden*) unconditionally the purely immanent life of physical existence on this earth as the *meaning* of life comes in a sense close to Bonhoeffer's own affirmation that Nietzsche "took up Feuerbach's[134] doctrine of the whole human being

---

128 *Zarathustra*, "Zarathustra's Prologue," 3.
129 *Zarathustra*, " Zarathustra's Prologue," 7.
130 *Zarathustra*, "On Old and New Tablets," 3.
131 *DBWE* 9, 496.
132 Hatab, *Nietzsche's Life Sentence. Coming to Terms with Eternal Recurrence*, 55.
133 *Zarathustra*, "Prologue," 3.
134 Elsewhere Bonhoeffer credits Feuerbach for his insight that humanity and earth are inseparable entities. The chief significance of Genesis 2:7, says Bonhoeffer, is that "the human being whom God has created in God's image – that is, in freedom – is the human being who is taken from earth. Even Darwin and Feuerbach could not have used stronger language than is used here. Humankind is derived from a piece of earth. Its

[*Lehre vom ganzen Menschen*]. [A human being is] not a transcendent being that only appears to exist [*Scheinwesen*] but is *ens realissimum* [the
most real being]."[135] Both agree that the essence of humanity lies not in its
transcendent horizon, but in its immanent, earthly affirmation of life in all
its manifestations. Only in the total affirmation of all of life is the affirmation of all of humanity, and vice-versa. For Nietzsche, this affirmation is
the end in itself, the meaning of both the overman and earth; for Bonhoeffer, it is the hallmark of following Christ, whose reality brings about on
this earth the very groundedness and life-affirmation that Zarathustra announces. As Green suggests, Nietzsche's critique of religion as dehumanizing "people by robbing them of their strength and creativity" finds its
ally in Bonhoeffer in that "the constructive significance of Bonhoeffer's
non-religious *theologia crucis* may be appreciated for its originality and its
historical contribution."[136] For just like Nietzsche, Bonhoeffer craved so
deeply for a life unflinchingly rooted in the reality of this earth. For Bonhoeffer, however, that life was possible in Christ's reality and power. And
precisely at this point Bonhoeffer's *amor mundi* comes as close to the centre of his theology and life as that is possible. But this love for the world is
not merely a component of or an addition to his faith or an anticipatory
foreshadowing of what we call now a "theology of the earth." Quite to the
contrary, as Sabine Dramm says so concisely: "love for the world springs
from the midst of this faith. It is the basis for Christian existence in the here
and now of the world. It embraces the person as a whole. From it come the
understanding and practice of a worldly Christian existence, one that is
fully in accordance with Bonhoeffer's own way. It is precisely the very core
of his thought that love for the world is grounded in the Christ event – and
even more – it only comes into being in Him. In Christ, assent to the
worldliness of the world becomes definitive."[137] Because Bonhoeffer conceived of the love for the world in such a radical but christocentric manner
was he able to stand so firmly rooted in his own life and take Nietzsche
seriously.[138] For him the power of the reality of Christ is such that it can
transform all worldly and human reality in precisely the terms that

---

bond with the earth belongs to its essential being" (*DBWE* 3, 76). On Nietzsche's adaptation of Feuerbach, cf. Williams, *The Shadow of the Antichrist*, 26–27.

[135] *DBWE* 11, 186.

[136] Green, *Bonhoeffer. A Theology of Sociality*, 272.

[137] Sabine Dramm, *Dietrich Bonhoeffer. An Introduction to His Thought.* Peabody:
Hendrickson 2007, 106.

[138] Bethge, "The Challenge of Dietrich Bonhoeffer's Life and Theology," 78, suggests that "Bonhoeffer liberates the Christians so that they can listen to Feuerbach and
Nietzsche and give them their honest share for their contribution. These people now

Nietzsche envisioned. In the words of Green, "the weak and suffering Christ, then, is the ultimate critic of religion. The transformation of human life brings people from the periphery of life to its center, from a fragmented existence to an integrated life, from otherworldliness to a historical life in the world, from episodic regression to a faith which informs their whole life, from subjective inwardness to responsibility in public life, from dishonest and humiliating apologetics to meaningful acceptance or reality, from individualistic self-preoccupation to 'existing for others'."[139] In Bonhoeffer's own words: "As reality is *one* in Christ, so the person who belongs to the Christ-reality is also a whole. Worldliness does not separate one from Christ, and being Christian does not separate one from the world. Belonging completely to Christ, one stands at the same time completely in the world."[140]

---

give us a bad conscience when we make the Christian faith a shop for religious needs or a skilful technique for avoiding this world."

[139] Green, *Bonhoeffer. A Theology of Sociality*, 271.

[140] *DBWE* 6, 62.

6. Nietzsche's *Übermensch* and Bonhoeffer's *mündiger Mensch*: Are They of Any Use for a Contemporary Christian Anthropology?*

Introduction

In order to frame our topic, let me begin with a citation from the young Bonhoeffer. The twenty year old student of theology was preparing an exegesis and sermon for a homiletics seminar on the text of James 1:21–25. The sermon was aimed at "young people 16–20 years old."[1] In the course of that sermon Bonhoeffer proclaims: "God is revealed in God's holy word. Jesus Christ is the path from God to humanity. All human road signs [*Wegtafeln*] are subject to rigorous questioning when seen in the light of this path, regardless of the words they carry; to God, to the mysteries, to the world of the spirits, to the soul, or to a super-human race [*Übermensch*]."[2]

Bonhoeffer's words in this sermon stake out in a nutshell the theme that is central to this essay. I would like to examine and correlate how Bonhoeffer's fundamental conviction that "Jesus Christ is the path from God to humanity" squares with his critique of Nietzsche's *Übermensch* and his own idea, formulated in a prison cell at Tegel, of the *mündige Mensch*. The characterizations of the *Übermensch* and the *mündige Mensch* are both anthropological designations, each embedded in the unique intellectual milieu of its author. The objective of this essay is thus an examination of how Nietzsche's unrelenting call to overcome humanity in the form of the *Übermensch* and Bonhoeffer's notion of *mündiger Mensch* may be interpreted in the context of a contemporary Christian anthropology. Both thinkers agree that religion as such and Christianity in particular have left the human being, and especially Christians, with a crippling inability to embrace life in its fullness. Nietzsche, being the more radical of the two,

---

* This essay was first presented at the International Bonhoeffer Congress, Prague, Czech Republic, in June 2008.
[1] *DBWE* 9, 493.
[2] *DBWE* 9, 496.

rejects Christianity wholesale since it engenders only the weakest and most loathsome of human beings. Bonhoeffer, however, while he agrees with Nietzsche's critique to a certain degree, seeks to articulate theological and ethical avenues by which the *mündige Mensch* may actually overcome the life-denying forms of Christianity that Nietzsche so devastatingly attacks. How do these separate visions of humanity address the real issues of the contemporary person – both as a human being and as a Christian? What aspects of Nietzsche and Bonhoeffer's anthropology can Christians still appropriate today in order to embrace life in its fullness?

I will proceed in a first section to give an explication of Nietzsche's view of humanity and the *Übermensch*, followed by a second section on Bonhoeffer's basic anthropological assumptions vis-à-vis Nietzsche. The focus will be on the third part of the essay in which I will explore how both Nietzsche's and Bonhoeffer's anthropological assumptions may be interpreted in the context of our contemporary world. The question I will pursue regards the extent to which Bonhoeffer's anthropology allows a Christian to have the kind of fulfilling life Nietzsche was demanding so adamantly.

Nietzsche on Humanity

Since all philosophy and all theology are necessarily contextual to a person's idiosyncratic *Sitz im Leben*, it follows that we cannot understand Nietzsche's view of the human being apart from his own social and intellectual milieu. There can be no doubt that Nietzsche's peculiar upbringing with his mother and two aunts coupled with his adult life-experiences in the second half of the nineteenth century are the main reasons why he developed such an eccentric hatred of Christianity.[3] Nonetheless, in spite of the violent attacks on Christianity and Christians alike, there is a theme in Nietzsche that is likewise of great importance to Bonhoeffer. It is the question of what constitutes the human being; what does it mean to be fully human. Nietzsche's relentless axe-grinding against Christianity was ultimately directed at Christian anthropology, since for him the substructure of the Christian tradition lay in the question of humanity. If that substructure could only produce a certain kind of human being, Nietzsche argued, then that structure must itself be the problem. In a nutshell, his argument

---

[3] Cf. Hans Hübner, *Nietzsche und das Neue Testament*. Tübingen: Mohr Siebeck 2000, 71. See also Stephen N. Williams, *The Shadow of the Antichrist. Nietzsche's Critique of Christianity*. Grand Rapids: Baker Academic 2006.

was that Christianity utterly destroys the basic humanity of the Christian person and, as an inescapable consequence, destroys life itself by its failure to affirm it. Let us now briefly sketch out his position and arguments.

Jesus and Paul

Nietzsche's tirades against Christianity[4] follow the interpretive trajectory from Jesus to Paul to theology to the concreteness of the Christian life. Although academic assessments of how Nietzsche viewed Jesus vary considerably, he "placed Jesus in a certain antithesis to Christianity" without feeling "the hostility provoked by the religion that bears his name."[5] The Nietzschean oeuvre makes it clear that as a rule Jesus' simple gospel had a clear edge compared to the devastating theology of the Apostle Paul. And yet, the fact that Nietzsche speaks of Jesus as "the noblest human being"[6] and "the only Christian"[7] should not blind us to the fact that what he says of Jesus is primarily negative. Nietzsche's bone of contention with Paul is that he is the inventor of all that could have possibly gone wrong with the message of Jesus. How did this happen?

The Bible, Nietzsche mocks, "contains the history of one of the most ambitious and importunate souls, of a mind as superstitious as it was cunning, the history of the apostle Paul... But without this remarkable history, without the storms and confusions of such a mind, of such a soul, there would be no Christianity; we would hardly have heard of a little Jewish sect whose master died on the cross."[8] Thus, for Nietzsche, the origin of Christianity amounts to the vision of a tormented man who had an epileptic seizure! "With that the intoxication of Paul is at its height... This is the first Christian, the inventor of Christianness [*Christlichkeit*]!"[9] The good news about the master who was crucified was followed up with the vilest news of all: namely by Paul, the "dysangelist."[10]

---

[4] In what follows I am drawing on my study, "Friedrich Nietzsche's Aphorisms and Dietrich Bonhoeffer's Theology."

[5] Williams, *The Shadow of the Antichrist*, 187.

[6] *Human, All too Human*, 475.

[7] *The Anti-Christ*, 39.

[8] *Daybreak*, 68.

[9] *Daybreak*, 68.

[10] Cf. *The Anti-Christ*, 42. See also Jörg Salaquarda, "Dionysus versus the Crucified One: Nietzsche's Understanding of the Apostle Paul," in James C. O'Flaherty, Timothy F. Sellner and Robert M. Helm (eds), *Studies in Nietzsche and the Judeo-Christian Tradition*. Chapel Hill/London: The University of North Carolina Press 1985, 100–29, who argues that "it is not until *The Antichrist* that Nietzsche achieves an unequivocal

God, Transcendence and Sin

Concretely, Nietzsche faults Paul for the inventions of God, sin and immortality. Regarding the concept of God, Nietzsche reduces Paul's view of God to the formula: *deus, qualem Paulus creavit, dei negatio* ("the God, whom Paul invented, is the negation of God").[11] Nietzsche debunks Paul's invented God "as miserable, as absurd, as harmful, not merely an error but a crime against life. We deny God as God."[12] For how can one speak of "a God of goodness"[13] or of a God of love and holiness and sinlessness when "he creates sin and sinners and eternal damnation and a vast abode of eternal affliction and eternal groaning and sighing!"[14] Nietzsche's atheism is thus not a mere intellectual rejection of a metaphysical idea, but a deeply felt inner struggle questioning why a supposedly loving and caring God has demands that seem to squarely negate life.

In accordance with his atheism is Nietzsche's disdain for a belief in immortality that has its locus in the future. For Nietzsche, such transcendental speculation is tantamount to the inadmissible devaluation of earthly life. It is the Apostle "Paul's invention" and his "method of priestly tyranny," namely "the belief in immortality [*Unsterblichtkeit*] – which is to say the doctrine of the 'judgment'."[15] Indeed, "Paul himself" taught this "outrageous doctrine of personal immortality"[16] and thus planted in Christianity the emphasis on the "state after death."[17] The problem, as Nietzsche sees it, is as follows: "When the emphasis of life is put on the 'beyond' rather than on life itself – when it is put on nothingness –, then the emphasis has been completely removed from life."[18] The very idea of nothingness stems from Christianity itself. Nietzsche maintains that "Christianity is called the religion of pity [*Religion des Mitleidens*]. –Pity is the opposite of the tonic affects that heighten the energy of vital feelings; pity has a de-

---

differentiation of the roles of Jesus and Paul in the origin of Christianity, and at the same time arrives at an unrestrained opposition to the Apostle" (104).

[11] *The Anti-Christ*, 47.
[12] *The Anti-Christ*, 47.
[13] *The Anti-Christ*, 91.
[14] *The Anti-Christ*, 113.
[15] *The Anti-Christ*, 42. In *Daybreak*, 72, Nietzsche claims: "Paul knew of nothing better he could say of his Redeemer than that he had *opened* the gates of immortality to everyone ... it was only now that immortality had *begun* to open its doors – and in the end only a very few would be selected: as the arrogance of the elect cannot refrain from adding."
[16] *The Anti-Christ*, 41.
[17] *The Anti-Christ*, 41.
[18] *The Anti-Christ*, 43.

pressing effect. You lose strength when you pity ... Schopenhauer was right here: pity negates life, it makes life worthy of negation, –pity is the practice of nihilism ... pity wins people over to nothingness! ... You do not say 'nothingness': instead you say 'the beyond'; or 'God'; or 'the true life'."[19] Nietzsche's verdict is thus clear: at the core of Christianity lies the practice of pity and love of neighbour, a practice which at once denies the vitality of life and thereby postpones "the true life" to the realm beyond. In a nutshell, earthly life is devalued and forfeited for life in the future.

The Denial of Life

For Nietzsche, the devaluation of earthly life is also brought about by another Pauline teaching. Just as Paul is the inventor of Christianity and the inventor of the idea of immortality, so likewise he is the inventor of the concept of sin. In an aphorism entitled "Belief in the Sickness as Sickness," Nietzsche comes straight to his point: "It was Christianity which first painted the Devil on the world's wall; it was Christianity which first brought sin into the world."[20] Paul, Nietzsche sneers, "invented the repellent flaunting of sin, it introduced into the world sinfulness one has lyingly made up."[21] Elsewhere he declares that "sin, this supreme form of human self-desecration, was invented to block science, to block culture, to block every elevation and ennoblement of humanity; the priests rule through the invention of sin."[22] All of this "imaginary sinfulness"[23] weakens and destroys life rather than celebrates it. At times, Nietzsche's rage is so unrestrained that he thinks the only "presupposition of Christianity [is] that all men are great sinners and do nothing but sin."[24] Elsewhere he provides a summary description of what he thinks is the problem with Christianity: the great tragedy is that "in Christianity neither morality nor religion has even a single point of contact with reality. Nothing but imaginary causes ('God,' 'soul,' 'ego,' 'spirit,' 'free will'—for that matter, 'unfree will'), nothing but imaginary effects ('sin,' 'redemption,'[25] 'grace,' 'punishment,' 'for-

---

[19] *The Anti-Christ*, 7.
[20] *Human, All too Human*, "The Wanderer and his Shadow," 78.
[21] *Daybreak*, 29.
[22] *The Anti-Christ*, 49. Elsewhere, *Genealogy* 3, 20, Nietzsche maintains that sin "has been the greatest event in history of the sick soul up till now: with sin we have the most dangerous and disastrous trick of religious interpretation."
[23] *Human, All too Human*, "The Religious Life," 141.
[24] *Human, All too Human*, "The Wanderer and his Shadow," 156.
[25] Cf. *Human, All too Human*, "A Glance at the State," 476.

giveness of sins').”[26] In short, Nietzsche believes that all of these staples of Christian doctrine are essentially destructive of all positive, vital, cultural and human manifestations of life and what it means to become human.

For Nietzsche, the problem with Christianity's "imaginary causes" and "imaginary effects" is that "Christianity has sided with all that is weak and base, with all failures; it has made an ideal of whatever contradicts the instinct of the strong life to preserve itself; it has corrupted the reason even of those strongest in spirit by teaching men to consider the supreme values of the spirit as something sinful, as something that leads into error – as temptations.”[27] All the constituents necessary for the unqualified affirmation of life, as Nietzsche desires it, are short-circuited and actually contradict and destroy life itself at the root. In the life of Christians, Nietzsche concludes, "God degenerated into the contradiction of life, instead of being its transfiguration and eternal Yes! God as the declaration of war against life, against nature, against the will to live! God – the formula for every slander against 'this world,' for every lie about the 'beyond'! – God the deification of nothingness, the will to nothingness pronounced holy!”[28] In other words, the irredeemable drama of the Christian life is that transcendence has wholly swallowed up immanence; earthly life is forfeited for a life in the beyond – and that for Nietzsche is the epitome of nihilism.

Moreover, congruent with Nietzsche's non-metaphysical and non-transcendent conception of life is the claim that human life is limited to the sphere of immanence, concretely to ethics and morality. Indeed, "the question of the origin of moral values," declares Nietzsche, "is a question of the first rank for me because it determines the future of humanity.”[29] As is well known, Nietzsche characterizes Christian ethics as a "slave morality,”[30] namely a morality that enslaves the human being by virtue of its transcendent horizon. This is exactly the dilemma that Nietzsche wants to overcome. "I am negating a type of morality that has attained dominance and validity in the form of morality as such, – decadence morality or, to put it plainly, Christian morality.”[31] Hence, "the uncovering of Christian morality is an event without equal, a real catastrophe. Anyone who knows about this is a force majeure, a destiny.”[32] This is the task of Zarathustra.

---

26 *The Anti-Christ*, 15.
27 *The Anti-Christ*, 5.
28 *The Anti-Christ*, 18.
29 *Ecce Homo*, "Daybreak," 2.
30 Cf. *Genealogy*, 1, 10.
31 *Ecce Homo*, "Why I am a Destiny," 4.
32 *Ecce Homo*, "Why I am a Destiny," 8.

The Übermensch

Given the irredeemable "human anti-nature" [*Unnatur*][33] of the Christian, the Nietzschean solution is to overcome humanity in a new human being which he calls the *Übermensch*. The "human being is something that must be overcome," he decrees loudly, "overcome yourself even in your neighbour; and you should not let anyone give you a right that you can rob for yourself!"[34]

In the Prologue Nietzsche sets out his ideas: "I teach you the overman (*Übermensch*). Human being is something That Must be overcome. What have you done to overcome him? ... Behold, I teach the overman! The overman is the meaning of the earth. Let your will say: the overman shall be the meaning of the earth!"[35] And elsewhere Zarathustra says: "Uncanny is human existence and still without meaning: a jester can spell its doom. I want to teach humans the meaning of their being, which is the overman, the lightning from the dark cloud 'human being'."[36] "It was there too that I picked up the word 'overman' (*Übermensch*) along the way, and that the human is something that must be overcome, – that human being is a bridge and not an end; counting itself blessed for its noon and evening as the way to new dawns ... I taught them all my creating and striving: to carry together into one what is fragment in mankind and riddle and horrid accident – as poet, riddle guesser and redeemer of chance I taught them to work on the future, and to creatively redeem everything that was. To redeem what is past in mankind and to recreate all 'It was' until the will speaks: 'But I wanted it so! I shall want it so.' This I told them was redemption, this alone I taught them to call redemption. – Now I wait for my redemption – so that I can go to them for the last time."[37]

In subliminal messianic terminology Nietzsche speaks of the final redemption of humanity by the hand of the *Übermensch*, a humanity that is fully tied to the earth. In a nutshell, for Nietzsche the human being is essentially non-transcendent and immanent. "The overman is the meaning of the earth," Nietzsche announces and then demands further: "Let your will say: the overman shall be the meaning of the earth!"[38] But, Nietzsche laments, at the moment it is precisely because human beings let themselves

---

[33] This is Bonhoeffer's expression in *DBW* 11, 186.
[34] *Zarathustra*, "Prologue," 4 and *The Anti-Christ*, 3.
[35] *Zarathustra*, "Prologue," 3.
[36] *Zarathustra*, "Prologue," 7.
[37] *Zarathustra*, "On Old and New Tablets," 3.
[38] *Zarathustra*, "Prologue," 3.

be tied to transcendent reality that they fail to shape their own meaning apart from God. How Nietzsche conceives of such humanity free of transcendent shackles will be discussed further below.

Bonhoeffer's Theological Anthropology

It is perplexing and curious that in *Letters and Papers from Prison* Nietzsche's thought plays no obvious role for Bonhoeffer. Somewhat astoundingly, Bonhoeffer neither mentions nor hints at such Nietzschean ideas as the *Übermensch*, the revaluation of values beyond good and evil, or faithfulness to the earth.[39] And yet, as the letters from prison make abundantly clear, Bonhoeffer was increasingly thinking of an anthropological conception that both built on the presuppositions worked out in his early academic works and did justice to a secular humanity increasingly estranged from the church. *Mündigkeit*, as Bonhoeffer understood it, was a form of human self-understanding that took full account of a "world come of age" and an increasingly "religionless Christianity" that took seriously Nietzsche's critique of traditional forms of Christianity. In working out Bonhoeffer's anthropology of human *Mündigkeit*, we will concentrate on three basic presuppositions underlying his notion of humanity. The first is ontological, the second epistemological and the third ethical.

Basic Ontological Presupposition: Christuswirklichkeit

Arguably the most fundamental category underlying all of Bonhoeffer's thought – his philosophy, theology and ethics – is that of reality or, in his own term, *Wirklichkeit*. Already in *Sanctorum Communio* he proposes that "one can never arrive at the reality of the other by means of epistemology and metaphysics. Reality is simply not deducible, but given – to be acknowledged or rejected. It can never be explained theoretically; likewise it is only given for the whole person as an ethical being."[40] In other words, Bonhoeffer's conception of reality as "given" implies that reality has a basic

---

[39] Bonhoeffer mentions Nietzsche three times in *Letters and Papers from Prison*. The most important one is a passing remark on the Nietzschean distinction between the Dionysian and Apollonian; cf. the letter dated 25 March, 1944 (*DBWE* 8, 331). On the question of faithfulness to the earth, cf. Nicoletta Capozza, *Im Namen der Treue zur Erde: Versuch eines Vergleichs zwischen Bonhoeffers und Nietzsches Denken*. Münster: LIT Verlag 2003.

[40] *DBWE* 1, 53 note 68. See also *DBWE* 2, 66.

ontological structure.[41] For him, the "given" of reality also means that it is independent of and outside of either construction or deconstruction. Moreover, Bonhoeffer characterizes reality as "ultimate reality" and even more precisely notes that "God alone is the ultimate reality."[42] "That God alone is ultimate reality, is, however, not an idea meant to sublimate the actual world, nor is it the religious perfection of a profane worldview. It is rather a faithful Yes to God's self-witness, God's revelation."[43] For Bonhoeffer this means that God's revelation is inextricably linked to the incarnation of Jesus. In his own words, "for a disciple of Jesus, 'God-given realities' exist only through Jesus Christ."[44] Moreover, "only insofar as the ultimate reality is revelation, that is, the self-witness of the living God, is its claim to ultimacy fulfilled. But then the decision about the whole of life depends on our relation to God's revelation."[45] We will return to the question of why Bonhoeffer's understanding of ultimate divine reality revealed in Christ is crucial for engaging Nietzsche and post-modern humanity.

Since for Bonhoeffer reality in its totality is constituted, centered and fulfilled in Jesus Christ, it follows that there is no reality that is not part of the one divine reality revealed in Christ.[46] Our contemporary reality – whether we explicate it as postmodern, secular or godless – is part of the one Christ reality. As such, contemporary reality is neither more nor less real than any other reality. In Bonhoeffer's scheme of ultimate reality, the question is not how Christ or Christianity fit into our contemporary reality but how the contemporary world understands itself vis-à-vis the ultimate reality of God in Christ. Or, in view of a contemporary Christian anthropology, the question is not how the Christian faith should be made attractive to a postmodern person, but rather how the postmodern subject may be able to embrace the actuality of *Christuswirklichkeit*. To put the issue in the most lucid terms: it is the contemporary, postmodern person who must justify him/herself vis-à-vis *Christuswirklichkeit* and not the

---

[41] Peter Dabrock, "Responding to 'Wirklichkeit.' Reclaiming Bonhoeffer's Approach to Theological Ethics between Mystery and the Formation of the World," in Kirsten Busch Nielsen, Ulrik Nissen and Christiane Tietz (eds), *Mysteries in the Theology of Dietrich Bonhoeffer: A Copenhagen Bonhoeffer Symposium*, Forschungen zur systematischen und ökumenischen Theologie 119. Göttingen: Vandenhoeck & Ruprecht 2007, 55, notes perceptively that "it is by no means a given to concede a central place in moral discourse to a term [*Wirklichkeit*] with ontological connotations."

[42] *DBWE* 6, 48.

[43] *DBWE* 6, 48.

[44] *DBWE* 4, 95.

[45] *DBWE* 6, 48–49.

[46] Cf. *DBWE* 6, 58: "The world has no reality of its own independent of God's revelation in Christ."

other way round. Expressed differently, the path of the *humanum* must always lead to *Christuswirklichkeit*.

Basic Epistemological Presupposition: The Limited Self

Corresponding to Bonhoeffer's basic ontological category – that all reality is constituted and "given" by God in Jesus Christ – is a second basic ontological distinction. In *Act and Being*, Bonhoeffer maintains that part of the one given reality is that no human being is "untouched by sin."[47] "Being in Adam" is an ontological designation for being a sinner. But being a sinner entails not only *cor curvum in se* (a heart turned in upon itself) but even more so excludes the epistemological possibility "that human beings could place themselves into the truth."[48] In other words, the given reality of human life as a life disfigured by sinfulness precludes a person's ability to analyze, comprehend and rectify the dilemma of life itself.[49] Why this epistemological impasse?

For Bonhoeffer all thinking is self-limiting and self-enclosed. Since every self is distorted by sin, its very own efforts of thinking will never be able to attain a self-knowledge that could break and overcome the limits set by sin. If thinking undistorted by sin were a possibility, then sin would not really be a power that enslaves and, as a consequence, the salvific and redemptive work of Jesus Christ would be rendered meaningless. In other words, the I, the self, cannot come to itself because its ontological reality is distorted by sin; the very essence of sin is such that it cannot be known by a self that is itself corrupted by sin. In philosophical discourse, Bonhoeffer observes, "the I, now thinking itself, simply becomes the point of departure instead of the limit-point of philosophy. But thinking cannot do this without losing two very different things, reality and transcendence, that is, the one through the other. Philosophy, thinking, the I, all come under the power of themselves, rather than transcendence ... Thinking languishes in

---

[47] *DBWE* 2, 136.
[48] *DBWE* 2, 136.
[49] Bonhoeffer also rejects Schleiermacher's *a priori* religiosity: "A person is born with the religious capacity as with every other, and if only his sense is not forcibly suppressed, if only that communion between a person and the universe ... is not blocked and barricaded, then religion would have to develop unerringly in each person according to his own individual manner" (*On Religion,* 146). Cf. Christiane Tietz, "Friedrich Schleiermacher and Dietrich Bonhoeffer," in Peter Frick (ed), *Bonhoeffer's Intellectual Formation. Theology and Philosophy in his Thought.* Religion in Philosophy and Theology 29. Tübingen: Mohr Siebeck 2008, 121–143, here 140.

itself; precisely where it is free from the transcendent, from reality, there it is imprisoned in itself."[50]

These words point to a fundamental difference between Nietzsche and Bonhoeffer. While the latter argues that any form of thinking that seeks to free itself from the fetters of a transcendent reality will inevitably imprison itself and be unable to come to itself, the former wants absolutely nothing of a thinking that orients itself toward a transcendent reality. Indeed, Nietzsche's position is nothing but a paradigm for how humanity should get away from life-denying thinking that predicates itself on a transcendent reality. Nietzsche's *Übermensch* must live for himself apart from a transcendent reality. Bonhoeffer roots the *humanum* in the reality of Christ, being at once fully immanent within a transcendent horizon.

Basic Ethical Presupposition: Creation of Values

Already during his year in Barcelona the young Bonhoeffer elucidates: "Christians create their own standards for good and evil; only Christians themselves provide the justification for their acts, just as they alone bear responsibility for them. Christians create new tables, new decalogues, as Nietzsche said of the Overman [*Übermensch*]. Nietzsche's Overman is not, as he imagined, the opposite of the Christian; without realizing it, Nietzsche imbued the Overman with many of the features of the free Christian as described and conceived by both Paul and Luther."[51] Perhaps surprisingly, Nietzsche finds here a strong supporter in Bonhoeffer. Like Nietzsche, Bonhoeffer thinks that the task of ethics is the creation – or in Nietzschean terms, the revaluation – of (new) values, but he does so for reasons that are quite different from the philosopher. With an almost Nietzschean pathos Bonhoeffer declares: "The knowledge of good and evil seems to be the goal of all ethical reflection. The first task of Christian ethics is to supersede that knowledge." Bonhoeffer wants to go beyond good and evil because "the mere possibility of knowing about good and evil is already a falling away from the origin [*Ursprung*],"[52] that is to say, a being hopelessly tied to sin or the reality of one's own imprisoned self. "The knowledge of good and evil is thus disunion with God."[53]

---

50 *DBWE* 2, 39.
51 *DBWE* 10, 366–367.
52 *DBWE* 6, 300.
53 *DBWE* 6, 300.

Bonhoeffer's starting point for constructing an ethic lies entirely elsewhere: "The source of a Christian ethic is not the reality of one's own self, not the reality of the world, nor is it the reality of norms and values. It is the reality of God that is revealed in Jesus Christ." Even more to the point, he says: "The subject matter of a Christian ethic is God's reality revealed in Christ becoming real [*wirklichwerden*] among God's creatures."[54] When the focus is shifted away from the self as the criterion for ethics to the reality of God, "the question of the good becomes the question of participating in God's reality revealed in Christ. Good is no longer an evaluation of what exists, for instance my essence, my moral orientation [*Gesinnung*], my actions, or of a state of affairs in the world. It is no longer a predicate that one can apply to something that exists of itself. Good is the real itself [*das Wirkliche*], that is, not the abstractly real that is separated from the reality of God, but the real that has its reality only in God. Good is never without this reality. It is no general formula."[55]

The Humanum in Nietzsche and Bonhoeffer

Following the above clarification of the presuppositions undergirding both Nietzsche and Bonhoeffer's anthropological framework, we will now examine in greater detail how each of them conceptualizes the *humanum* in concrete terms. We will first articulate Nietzsche's project of the human being, then look at the common ground and finally the differences between Nietzsche and Bonhoeffer.

Nietzsche's Vision of a New Humanity

(1) Nietzsche explains: "The problem I am posing is not what should replace humanity in the order of being (– the human being is an endpoint –): but instead what type of human should be bred, should be willed as having greater value, as being more deserving of life, as being more certain of a future."[56] Here we have a very clear indication of how Nietzsche thinks of the human being. The reference to the human being as "an endpoint" is his attempt to free the human being once more from the impediment of transcendence. For Nietzsche, "endpoint" always means that the human being

---

[54] *DBWE* 6, 49.
[55] *DBWE* 6, 50.
[56] *The Anti-Christ*, 3.

as such, all by itself, is sufficient simply as a self-referential being. As recent interpreters put it: "In Nietzsche's nontranscendent worldview the *humanum* is fulfilled without reference to transcendence: in the Overman [*Übermensch*]. For the Christian definition of man, the *humanum* is fulfilled in the ecclesia, which is open toward transcendence."[57] The main point here is that the human being does not need any reality – that is principally a transcendent reality – beyond itself in order to have a sufficient ground on which to affirm life. In other words, there is no need for God and no place for any of the ideas that the apostle Paul invented such as sin, salvation and redemption.

Moreover, Nietzsche's claim that humanity can be bred and willed indicates a further dimension of his purely immanent conception of humanity, namely the human potential for personal growth and development. The creation of humanity is then not so much an act of God as it is the motivation that is immanent in the human being as such. Hatab speaks therefore quite correctly of Nietzsche's "self-creating individual."[58] What is the significance of this for Nietzsche?

In order to answer this question, let us return to a comment we made earlier in relation to Nietzsche's *Übermensch*. We pointed out that Nietzsche sees the idea of the *Übermensch* as the meaning of the earth. I agree with Hatab that the notion of the *Übermensch* "should not be taken as a hyperextension of the master type or as the promise of a higher, progressive type of human being."[59] Expressed differently, Nietzsche's term *Übermensch* precisely does not point to something new beyond the human being, some sort of super-humanity yet to be created. On the contrary, the mysterious word *Übermensch* functions primarily as "a structural model for a new way of experiencing the world, rather than a new type of person."[60] Nietzsche's proposal that the *Übermensch* is a model for "experiencing the world" once again underlines the absolute immanence of his anthropological conception. It is to experience the world as it exists and not merely to believe in a world beyond. As a "structural model," "the overman is the meaning of the earth" and calls humanity "to remain faith-

---

[57] Wolf-Daniel Hartwich, Aleida Assman and Jan Assman, afterword to Jacob Taubes, *The Political Theology of Paul*, Stanford: Stanford University Press 2004, 135.

[58] Lawrence J. Hatab, *Nietzsche's Life Sentence. Coming to Terms with Eternal Recurrence*. New York: Routledge 2005, 54. Nietzsche also often speaks of the human being he envisions as a "free spirit;" cf. Williams, *The Shadow of the Antichrist,* 101–105, 218–219.

[59] Hatab, *Nietzsche's Life Sentence*, 55.

[60] Hatab, *Nietzsche's Life Sentence*, 55.

ful to the earth."[61] The earth alone is the place where human beings must live!

(2) Above, we clarified that Nietzsche sees the great failure of Christianity in its denial of life. The counterpoint that Nietzsche thus proposes in the *Übermensch* is an immanent type of human being that makes life-affirmation possible. Indeed, crucial to Nietzsche's immanent understanding of the *Übermensch* is that as a "structural concept" it "prepares the possibility of life-affirmation."[62] In this regard, Nietzsche makes the distinction between life-enhancement [*Erhöhung*] and life-affirmation [*Bejahung*], "where the former is Nietzsche's ideal and the latter can be attributed even to ideals that are life-denying in Nietzsche's sense."[63] Life denial, for example, is detected by Nietzsche in aristocratic societies, in that it creates a certain type of person tied to morality and ultimately humanity's self-overcoming.[64] Christianity falls within this category; it is life-enhancing[65] and yet still life-denying. Hatab suggests that even though life-enhancement is an instance of the "creative will to power" and does bring about high forms of culture, in the end it is not identical with what Nietzsche calls life-affirmation. Christianity, its slave morality notwithstanding, has no doubt made immense contributions to culture, but in its essence it is not, for Nietzsche, fully life-affirming. Life-affirmation requires two basic predispositions. First, life-affirmation requires affirming oneself in the affirmation of conflict, and second, it requires the affirmation of otherness.[66]

(3) The affirmation of oneself in the midst of conflict and the affirmation of the other are embedded in Nietzsche's distinction between "being" and "becoming." Nietzsche wants to prevail over the Western theological and philosophical tradition with its penchant of dividing reality into the binary opposites of "being" and "becoming." Opposites such as good and evil, time and eternity, spirit and nature, reason and passion, truth and appearance etc. are not mutually exclusive and cannot, therefore, be set against each other.[67] The fundamental error of the metaphysicians is precisely that at the expense of "becoming" they focus on "being" as the unchangeable, as grounded in God, as the thing-as-such. Quite to the contrary, Nietzsche asserts, "what constitutes the value of the good and revered

---

61 *Zarathustra*, "Prologue," 3.
62 Hatab, *Nietzsche's Life Sentence*, 55.
63 Hatab, *Nietzsche's Life Sentence*, 44.
64 Cf. *Beyond Good and Evil*, 257.
65 Cf. *The Anti-Christ*, 39.
66 Cf. Hatab, *Nietzsche's Life Sentence*, 47.
67 Hatab, *Nietzsche's Life Sentence*, 13.

things is precisely that they are insidiously related, tied to, and involved with these wicked, seemingly opposite things."[68] Only in "becoming" can the conflicting forces of opposites be harnessed for the affirmation of life. Put differently, the Christian denial of life, which has its roots in the static realm of being, must overcome "being" and embrace "becoming" in the midst of the fluid, dynamic, unstable, and changeable conditions of life. As Hatab puts it, "The innocence of becoming is Nietzsche's alternative to all Western moralistic scripts that portray the life-world as a fallen or flawed condition, which would require reparation according to transcendent or historical forms of transformation."[69] For Nietzsche, it is therefore nearly impossible to create a "becoming" person unless the Western intellectual tradition forfeits its view of the world as "being" in sin, guilt, and full of a bad conscience. Applied to the anthropological question, it is evident that life-affirmation is ensconced in the flux of becoming. It is precisely in this ebb and flow and the cycles of becoming that the affirmation of oneself amounts to an agonistic conflict. The very nature of changing conditions, circumstances and challenges implies that self-affirmation cannot escape conflict. Human becoming is dynamic, it is not a static being. The affirmation of life as a self in the agonistic struggle of becoming necessarily includes the affirmation of the other. Hatab puts it well: "the self is formed in and through agonistic relations. So in a way, openness toward one's Other is openness toward oneself."[70]

(4) The sphere of life that is for Nietzsche in need of a most radical transformation is probably that of morality. Given Nietzsche's view that Christians are entrapped in a slave-morality it comes as no surprise that he hardly misses an occasion to call for a re-valuation [*Umwertung*] of all values. It is now decisive to understand just how radical Nietzsche's demands are: He is not asking his readers to be just a little more open-minded or to embrace the spirit of enlightenment rationalism more whole-heartedly, nor is he suggesting that new governments or societies should re-write the moral books of nations. On the contrary, Nietzsche is placing full responsibility on the emerging[71] human being as he envisions that being in *Thus Spoke Zarathurstra*. The task of the coming *Übermensch* as announced by Zarathustra is clearly anticipated in the Prologue: "Break, break me these old tablets of the pious, my brothers! Gainsay me the say-

---

[68] *Beyond Good and Evil*, 2.
[69] Hatab, *Nietzsche's Life Sentence*, 62.
[70] Hatab, *Nietzsche's Life Sentence*, 47.
[71] *Zarathustra*, "On Old and New Tablets," 1: "Here I sit and wait, old broken tablets around me and also new tablets only partially written upon. When will my hour come?"

ings of the world slanderers!"[72] And again he announces: "Look at the faithful of all faiths! Whom do they hate the most? The one who breaks their tablets of values, the breaker, the lawbreaker – but he is the creative one. Companions the creative one seeks and not corpses, nor herds and believers. Fellow creators the creative one seeks, who will write new values on new tablets."[73] In a later section, in "On the Way of the Creator," Zarathustra utters one of his most demanding claims: "Can you give yourself your own evil and good and hang your will above yourself like a law?"[74] Here we have in one sentence Nietzsche's programmatic agenda for the *Übermensch*. "Can you," that is to say the new *humanum*, the new subject, create "your own evil and good." In other words, Nietzsche demands that the person as such become the criterion over good and evil. As a consequence, the new *humanum* "hangs" the decision over good and evil "like a law" above her/himself. In this very process, the new *humanum* has de-valued the old Christian values, taken the authority of judging over good and evil, created new and re-valued tablets – and all of this on a purely immanent, non-transcendent basis.

In sum, it is evident that Nietzsche's conception of humanity is always involved in the dynamic process of becoming, tied to the agonistic struggles of this world alone without recourse to any transcendent reality. The *humanum* does not simply have being, but is always in the open-ended processes of becoming; humanity is always a work in progress.

Common Ground between Nietzsche and Bonhoeffer

(1) Conceivably the most significant agreement between Nietzsche and Bonhoeffer is their unreserved affirmation of all of life, including not only those things and events that are good and enjoyable, but also those that create struggle, challenge, defeat and agony. At the very end of his treatise, On the Genealogy of Morality, Nietzsche provides a succinct and provoking summary of what is wrong with the Christian view of morality. He argues that the ideal of suffering and asceticism – both deeply entrenched in the Christian tradition – have serious consequences for a proper view of humanity. They lead, he says, to "hatred of the human, and even more of the animalistic, even more of the material, this horror of the senses, of the reason itself, this fear of happiness and beauty, this longing to get away

---

[72] *Zarathustra,* "On Old and New Tablets," 15.
[73] *Zarathustra,* "Prologue," 9.
[74] *Zarathustra,* "On the Way of the Creator."

from appearance, transience, growth, death, wishing, longing itself – all that means, let us dare to grasp it, a will to nothingness, an aversion to life, a rebellion against the most fundamental prerequisites of life."[75] If we now take these denunciations and restate them positively, it follows that Nietzsche is advocating a life that affirms life in the broad spectrum from the basic human elements such as the senses, happiness and beauty to desire, change and death. In other words, Nietzsche's plea is for the unconditional and unabbreviated affirmation of all spheres of life.

Bonhoeffer presents a striking parallel to Nietzsche's sentiments in one of the letters he wrote from prison. The day after the failed conspiracy, on 21 July 1944, Bonhoeffer writes a letter to Bethge in which he ponders: "Later on I discovered, and am still discovering to this day, that one only learns to have faith by living in the full this-worldliness of life. If one has completely renounced making something of oneself – whether it be a saint or a converted sinner or a church leader (a so-called priestly figure!), a just or an unjust person, a sick or a healthy person – then one throws oneself completely into the arms of God, and this is what I call this-worldliness [*Diesseitigkeit*]: living fully in the midst of life's tasks, questions, successes and failures, experiences and perplexities – then one takes seriously no longer one's own sufferings but rather the sufferings of God in the world. Then one stays awake with Christ in Gethsemane. And I think this is faith; this is μετάνοια [repentance]. And this is how one becomes a human being, a Christian."[76]

Bonhoeffer's remarks that one should live "unreservedly in life's duties, problems, successes and failures, experiences and perplexities" not only deeply echo Nietzsche's ideas but come to a decisive finale: the acceptance of these things will help one to "become a human and a Christian." Like Nietzsche, Bonhoeffer ties the unconditional affirmation of life to the fuller and deeper "becoming" of what it means to be human.

(2) The unconditional affirmation of life includes, first, the affirmation of the other. Nietzsche's agonistic struggle with the other is part of the formation of the self and the acceptance of the self. In a manner reminiscent of Nietzsche, Bonhoeffer too understands personhood as being shaped and defined by the other. He reminds his readers that "the individual exists only in relation to an 'other'; individual does not mean solitary. On the contrary, for the individual to exist, 'others' must necessarily be

---

[75] *Genealogy* 3, 28.
[76] *DBWE* 8, 486.

there."[77] Concretely, this implies that a person's existence is always one in community with another person. A key purpose of that other person, the You, is that it "sets the limit for the subject." In other words, because the other You becomes the subject's "reality-form [*Wirklichkeitsform*]" it follows that "the other can be experienced by the I only as You, but never directly."[78] Bonhoeffer thus maintains, like Nietzsche, that there is no such thing as an isolated, non-communicative self. Personhood necessarily involves the other and the limit or agony the other constitutes for the self.

Second, and related to the affirmation of the other, is a specific conception of freedom that has amazing parallels in Nietzsche and Bonhoeffer. In one passage from *Thus Spoke Zarathustra*, we read: "You call yourself free? Your dominating thought I want to hear, and not that you escaped from a yoke. Are you the kind of person who had the right to escape from a yoke? There are some who threw away their last value when they threw away their servitude. Free from what? What does Zarathustra care! But brightly your eyes should signal to me: free *for what?*"[79]

The distinction between "free from what" and "free for what" is so close to Bonhoeffer – conceptionally and terminologically – that one wonders whether Bonhoeffer is indebted to Nietzsche without giving him due credit. At any rate, in *Creation and Fall*, Bonhoeffer contends that "freedom is not a quality that can be uncovered; it is not a possession, something to hand; instead it is a relation and nothing else." To be more precise, "there is no 'being-free-from' without a 'being-free-for' ... Without God, without their brothers and sisters, human beings lose the earth."[80] The parallels between Nietzsche and Bonhoeffer are indeed striking as neither of them has a merely abstract – let alone post-modern – understanding of the concept of freedom. Freedom necessarily includes the other and is directed toward him/her. For both thinkers, the "other" is not merely a post-modern or politically correct element of a philosophical system but rather the "other" constitutes the very core in the dynamic process of self-becoming. Apart from the other, my own becoming will remain incomplete.

(3) A third common ground between Nietzsche and Bonhoeffer is their understanding of ethics. Both speak of the creation of new values and Bonhoeffer does so explicitly by following Nietzsche: "Christians create their own standards for good and evil; only Christians themselves provide the

---

[77] *DBWE* 1, 51.

[78] *DBWE* 1, 51.

[79] *Zarathustra,* "On the Way of the Creator." For a brief discussion of the notion of freedom in Nietzsche, cf. Hatab, *Nietzsche's Life Sentence,* 53–54.

[80] *DBWE* 3, 67.

justification for their acts, just as they alone bear responsibility for them. Christians create new tables, new decalogues, as Nietzsche said of the Overman [*Übermensch*]. Nietzsche's Overman is not, as he imagined, the opposite of the Christian; without realizing it, Nietzsche imbued the Overman with many of the features of the free Christian as described and conceived by both Paul and Luther."[81]

In order to do justice to both Nietzsche and Bonhoeffer, it is crucial to understand that their common ground lies in the creation of new values, but not in their respective grounding of their suggested revaluation. Nietzsche, in short, grounds his revaluation of morality upon his conviction that conventional Christian morality leads to anthropological impoverishment and thus proposes that the new human being, the coming *Übermensch*, be grounded solely on the earth for his/her moral values. The love of earthly life becomes the criterion of what is good and evil. The new human being, and not God, religion or any other metaphysical speculation, becomes the judge over good and evil. Bonhoeffer, however, grounds his notion of ethics precisely in a transcendent reality. But the reality of God revealed in Jesus Christ is not the kind of abstract and life-denying reality that Nietzsche so vehemently critiqued. As we noted above, for Bonhoeffer, the Christian attempt to catalogue good and evil is futile because such an endeavour is the desire to relativize the fall of humanity and to deny the new powerful reality of God in Jesus Christ. The biblical narrative, he notes, "is concerned only with the realization [*Wirklichwerden*] of the Christ-reality in the contemporary world that it already embraces, owns, and inhabits."[82] The task of the Christian is thus to embrace, love and live in the world, to have the courage to create new values as the Spirit of God interprets the will of God in concreteness.

Nietzsche and Bonhoeffer: Parting Visions of Humanity

(1) The most divergent elements in Nietzsche's and Bonhoeffer's anthropologies are the immanent vis-à-vis transcendent spheres. I have repeatedly pointed out Nietzsche's purely immanent and thus one-dimensional horizon within which a person must find being and becoming. For Nietzsche, heaven is kept away from earth so as not to interfere with the dynamics of becoming. Bonhoeffer, in contrast, while also fully emphasizing the immanent realm of humanity, nonetheless grounds it in transcendence. For

---

[81] *DBWE* 10, 366–367.
[82] *DBWE* 6, 58; emphasis added.

him, the *humanum* is a transcendent self which is transfigured immanently. In this sense, his anthropology has a two-dimensional horizon. Earth is always in view of heaven and heaven never forgets the earth.

(2) Given the divergent positions on immanence versus transcendence it is congruent that Nietzsche and Bonhoeffer also differ significantly in their understanding of the ability of the self to come to itself. In Nietzsche's immanent universe, the self becomes the main persona in the drama of becoming human. Nietzsche assumes that the self is not limited to become itself or that the self has enough a priori potential "to become itself in its becoming." All of this is different in Bonhoeffer. In his two-dimensional understanding of humanity, the fact of the fall places irreversible ontological and epistemological limits upon the self. In short, as we said above, the self cannot come to itself. Human self-understanding comes only from the outside, from above, from revelation. For Bonhoeffer, a person cannot find adequate self-understanding apart from the revelatory power of Christ. But even then, it remains always fragmentary; indeed, given its limits, on earth the self can never come to know itself fully.

(3) Nietzsche's emphasis on "becoming" human over "being" human undoubtedly stems, as we saw, from a deep reflection of human nature. While it is true that in the Christian tradition, as Bonhoeffer understands it, there is also ample room for a person's "becoming," there is however a decisive element of "being." The apostle Paul long ago spoke of those who live in the new reality of Christ as "being a new creation" (2 Corinthians 5). For Paul, and subsequent Christian theology, being a new creation means being in the reality and power of Christ – a fact that Bonhoeffer calls an "ontological designation."[83] On this point, Nietzsche is worlds apart from Bonhoeffer and the Christian tradition. Nonetheless, even though being in Christ and being a new creation focuses on a person's new state of being, it does not – indeed it cannot – mean that "becoming" in the Nietzschean sense has come to an end for the person who is such a "new creation." Again in a Pauline context, there are many instances in which the apostle points to elements that are matters of human becoming, most notably his teaching on the fruits of the Spirit in Galatian 5.

(4) Nietzsche's immanent, non-transcendent conception of humanity must reject any form of holy, revealed scriptures. For him, the only "scriptures" are the new values created in the process of the coming and becoming of the *Übermensch*. Bonhoeffer, however, reckons fundamentally with the power of God's word. For him, God's word is *selbstwirksam*, that is to

---

[83] Cf. *DBWE* 2, 136.

say, God's word is the power of God himself to effect real transformation in a person's being and becoming. Since God's word is the revealed and recorded will of God about humanity – from sin and alienation to salvation and redemption – a person's full humanity must be shaped in relation to the power of that divine claim and presence. The affirmation of life cannot happen apart from the power of God's word.

(5) Ultimately, Bonhoeffer's anthropology envisions the "becoming" of the Christian *humanum* in the secular world. Even the church is not excluded from the secular sphere, as Bonhoeffer once noted: "There is no form of the church as such that preserves it fundamentally from secularization."[84] That even the church is part of the secular sphere lies in Bonhoeffer's understanding of the unity of all reality. "There are not two realities, but only one reality, and that is God's reality revealed in Christ in the reality of the world. Partaking in Christ, we stand at the same time in the reality of God and in the reality of the world. The reality of Christ embraces the reality of the world in itself. The world has no reality of its own independent of God's revelation in Christ. It is a denial of God's revelation in Jesus Christ to wish to be 'Christian' without being 'worldly,' or [to] wish to be worldly without seeing and recognizing the world in Christ. Hence there are not two realms, but only the one realm of the Christ-reality [*Christuswirklichkeit*], in which the reality of God and the reality of the world are united."[85]

Conclusion

Wayne Floyd once remarked that "for the proto-deconstructionist Bonhoeffer, an irony lies at the heart of all late-modern and postmodern attempts to free the subject from any encumbrances of transcendence; for in attempting to free the subject from heteronomy, they actually leave the subject imprisoned with only itself, unable to allow the approach of that which is genuinely other."[86] Floyd's assessment of Bonhoeffer vis-à-vis postmodernism fits squarely with our attempt to examine how Bon-

---

[84] *DBWE* 15, 453. Cf. *DBW* 15, 449: "Es gibt keine Gestalt der Kirche, die als solche grundsätzlich vor der Säkularisierung bewahrt."

[85] *DBWE* 6, 58. On the postmodern condition and the unifying reality of Jesus Christ, cf. Michael Trowitzsch, "Jesus Christus: Wahrheit der Kirche, Einheit der Wirklichkeit – oder: Bonhoeffer und die Postmoderne," in Michael Trowitzsch (ed), *Über die Moderne hinaus: Theologie im Übergang*. Tübingen: Mohr Siebeck 1999, 159–173.

[86] *DBWE* 2, 39 note 14.

hoeffer's and Nietzsche's idiosyncratic visions of humanity address the issues of the contemporary person. Both want an unqualified affirmation of life in which the *humanum* does not disappear but comes to itself in the midst of all challenges, struggles and joys. The path to that type of *humanum*, as we saw, is both similar and dissimilar for the two thinkers. Nietzsche wants it all apart from religion, faith and a transcendent hope. For Bonhoeffer, the affirmation of life entails that every *humanum* is deeply and immanently grounded with both feet in the *mündige Welt* while stretching out one's arms to the transcendent reality mediated in Jesus the Christ. On 18 July 1944, two days before the failed conspiracy on Hitler's life, Bonhoeffer writes to Bethge: "The human being [*der Mensch*] is called upon to share in God's sufferings at the hands of a godless world. Thus we must really live in that godless world and not try to cover up or transfigure its godlessness somehow with religion. Our lives must be 'worldly,' so that we can share precisely so in God's suffering; our lives are *allowed* to be 'worldly,' that is, we are delivered from false religious obligations and inhibitions."[87] Echoes of these words could already be found in a sermon from Barcelona: "Christians are neither modern nor unmodern," and, we may add, postmodern. "Rather, they serve their own time, that is they worry not about human beings but about God. And yet – they serve their own time, and that means they step into the midst of it with all its problems and difficulties, with its seriousness and its distress, and there they serve. Christians are people of the present in the most profound sense."[88]

---

[87] *DBWE* 8, 480.
[88] *DBWE* 10, 529.

7. Rudolf Bultmann, Paul Tillich and Dietrich Bonhoeffer[*]

Introduction

The year 1924 at the University of Marburg was historically unique in that three thinkers who shaped Bonhoeffer's theology in substantial ways all taught in the same university for that short period: Rudolf Bultmann (1884–1976) came to Marburg to the faculty of theology in 1921 and stayed there for the rest of his life, Paul Tillich (1886–1965) was appointed to teach systematic theology and philosophy in 1924 and Martin Heidegger (1889–1976) was appointed to the faculty of philosophy between 1923 and 1928. In this study we will focus on the first two thinkers.[1] The main questions we will examine are the extent to which Bonhoeffer's thought betrays the theological contours of Bultmann and Tillich as found in his written legacy and why Bonhoeffer engaged these two theologians in his own theological construction. In other words, our objective is to ascertain the theological significance of Bultmann and Tillich in Bonhoeffer's theology.

[*] I wish to acknowledge the financial support for this research from the Social Sciences and Humanities Research Council of Canada.

[1] For Heidegger's influence on Bonhoeffer's thought, see Stephen Plant, "'In the Sphere of the Familiar.' Heidegger and Bonhoeffer," in Peter Frick (ed), *Bonhoeffer's Intellectual Formation. Theology and Philosophy in his Thought*. Religion in Philosophy and Theology 29. Tübingen: Mohr Siebeck 2008, 301–327. On Heidegger's influence on Bultmann, see the study by Hans-Georg Gadamer, "Martin Heidegger und die Marburger Theologie" in Erich Dinkler (ed), *Zeit und Geschichte*. Dankesgabe an Rudolf Bultmann zum 80. Geburtstag. Tübingen: J.C.B. Mohr (Paul Siebeck) 1964, 479–490 and Hans Hübner, "'Existentiale' Interpretation bei Rudolf Bultmann und Martin Heidegger," in *ZThK* 103 (2006), 533–567. On Heidegger's relation to theology, see John Caputo, "Heidegger and Theology," in *CCH*, 326–344.

Rudolf Bultmann

Bultmann's Thought in Bonhoeffer's Writings

In order to be in a position to assess Bultmann's influence on Bonhoeffer we will present a succinct review of how the latter incorporates and interprets the work of the former in his writings. In his doctoral dissertation, *Sanctorum Communio*, the young Bonhoeffer argued that Christian love "loves the real neighbor."[2] In a discussion that was later deleted from the published version of the dissertation but included as a footnote in the recent volume of the *Dietrich Bonhoeffer Works*, Bonhoeffer argues against Karl Barth's interpretation of the love commandment. He protests: "Who gives Barth the right to say that the other is 'as such infinitely unimportant' when God command us to love precisely that person? God has made the 'neighbor as such' infinitely important, and there isn't any other 'neighbor as such' for us."[3] Then Bonhoeffer draws on Bultmann's recent book, simply entitled *Jesus* (published in 1926).[4] Bonhoeffer cites Bultmann to refute Barth and to strengthen his own understanding of Jesus' commandment to love one's neighbour. To this end, he approvingly cites Bultmann: "Whatever of kindness, pity, mercy I show my neighbor is not something that I do for God ...; the neighbor is not a sort of tool, by means of which I practice the love of God ... As I can love my neighbor only when I surrender my will completely to God's will, so I can love God only while I will what [God] wills, while I really love my neighbor."[5]

In his *Habilitation*, entitled *Act and Being*, completed in 1930 and published in 1931, Bonhoeffer refers among many others to Bultmann[6] as one

---

[2] *DBWE* 1, 169.

[3] *DBWE* 1, 170 note 28.

[4] For a concise introduction to the life and work of Bultmann see Walter Schmithals, "Rudolf Bultmann," in *TRE* 7, 387–396.

[5] *DBWE* 1, 170, note 28. The young Bonhoeffer also lists Bultmann's *Jesus* in the list of works he consulted in preparation for the sermon he submitted as part of his first theological examination in 1927; cf. *DBWE* 9, 180. During the same period, Bonhoeffer also refers to Bultmann's essay "Die Bedeutung der neuerschlossenen mandäischen und manichäischen Quellen für das Verständnis des Johannesevangeliums," in *ZNW* 24 (1925), 100–146. In a study of John and Paul, Bonhoeffer rejects the Mandean parallel (regarding the question of the meaning of the vine in John 15) Bultmann had suggested in his exegesis of that passage (cf. *DBWE* 9, 395).

[6] Bonhoeffer employed the following studies of Bultmann in his *Act and Being*: "What does it Mean to Speak of God" (1925), in Rudolf Bultmann, *Faith and Understanding*, volume 1, edited by Robert W. Funk. London: Harper & Row 1969, 53–65; "The Question of Dialectic Theology: A Discussion with Peterson" (1926), in James M. Robinson (ed), *The Beginnings of Dialectic Theology*. Richmond: John Know Press

of those thinkers who in "the most recent developments in theology ... attempt to come to an agreement about the problem of act and being,"[7] the very problem Bonhoeffer himself made the focus of his study. It is therefore not surprising that Bultmann's writings become a critical point of reference for the development of Bonhoeffer's own positions in *Act and Being*.

Bonhoeffer's first major debate with Bultmann's theology centers on the question of the relation, on the one hand, between philosophy and theology, and on the other hand, between philosophy/theology and revelation. In a long note,[8] Bonhoeffer briefly describes Bultmanns's understanding of that relation in these terms: According to Bultmann "the task of philosophy [is] to examine phenomenologically those structures of Dasein which represent the existential-ontological possibilities (as distinct from ontic ones, of course) for believing and unbelieving Dasein ... The theme of philosophy is existentiality [*Existenzialität*], whereas the theme of theology is concrete (believing) existence [*Existenz*]."[9] Bonhoeffer continues by saying that Bultmann's line of thinking is also evident in his understanding of revelation when he asserts that "believers can state no more accurately or completely than unbelievers what revelation is."[10] Believers only know that revelation touched them, that they found grace and that they are forgiven. Hence, for Bultmann, notes Bonhoeffer, "the event-character [*Ereignis-charakter*] of revelation and the event-character of faith can be thought of within the existential-ontological possibilities of Dasein."[11] Bonhoeffer sees the assumptions for Bultmann's thought rooted in the latter's unexplained assertion that "believing Dasein is still Dasein, in every instance."[12]

Precisely here, however, Bonhoeffer detects "the roots of the unbounded claim of philosophy ... [for] it must be asked whether one can assert this

---

1968, 257–274; "On the Question of Christology" (1927), in *Faith and Understanding*, 116–144; "The Significance of 'Dialectical Theology' for the Scientific Study of the New Testament" (1928), in *Faith and Understanding*, 145–164 and "The Historicity of Man and Faith" (1930), in Rudolf Bultmann, *Existence and Faith*, edited by Schubert M. Odgen. Cleveland/New York: World Publishing Co. 1960, 92–110.

[7] *DBWE* 2, 25.

[8] The editor of *DBW* 2 correctly surmises that Bonhoeffer may have added the note after he had the manuscript of *Act and Being* already finished. On the one hand, the note is excessively long and of such an importance that it belongs in the main body of the text, and on the other hand, some of the literature Bonhoeffer refers to appeared most likely after he had completed the manuscript.

[9] *DBWE* 2, 77, note 89. Bonhoeffer refers to Bultmann's "The Historicity of Man and Faith."

[10] *DBWE* 2, 77, note 89.

[11] *DBWE* 2, 77, note 89.

[12] *DBWE* 2, 78, note 89. Cf. Bultmann, "The Historicity of Man and Faith," 94.

[unity of Dasein], even only of its existential-ontological possibilities, apart from revelation without making revelation impossible. If the answer is 'yes,' then believers do in fact know nothing 'more' about revelation than unbelievers."[13] Not surprisingly, Bonhoeffer rejects this position. For him, "the letting go of the ontic by retreat into the ontological [unity of Dasein] is considered futile by revelation. In the *existentiell* event of revelation, the *existential* structure of Dasein is touched and changed. There is no second mediator, not even the existential structure of Dasein. For revelation, the ontic-existentiell and ontological-existential structures coincide."[14]

In the following chapter in *Act and Being*, in the section entitled *Knowledge of Revelation*, Bonhoeffer refers to Bultmann's view that "talk of God is possible 'only as talk of ourselves,' since 'to apprehend our existence' would mean 'to apprehend God'."[15] This view sits uneasy with Bonhoeffer for whom talking of God enables a person to talk of oneself. Put otherwise, Bultmann's statement seems to ignore "the fact that faith can be directed solely and exclusively to God."[16] A few pages further in Bonhoeffer's study, we find what may well be one of the most important theological engagements between Bonhoeffer and Bultmann. About half through his work, Bonhoeffer draws a grand conclusion: He explains: "For human beings, to exist means to stand, act, and decide under God's claim. Existence is in pure actuality. Consequently, self-understanding is given only in the act itself. There are no concepts of existence prior to existence. The existence of human beings is either in sin or in grace. Through revelation there is only sinful or pardoned existence, without potentiality."[17] The crux of Bonhoeffer's argument is that he wants to safeguard any attempt – theological or philosophical – to arrive at an understanding of human existence apart from revelation. In this regard, he sees Bultmann's attempt to explain human existence along Heideggerian lines leaning in just that false direction. In Bonhoeffer's own words, "the danger of a concept of exist-

---

13 *DBWE* 2, 78, note 89.

14 *DBWE* 2, 78, note 89; emphasis added. A little further into his study, Bonhoeffer refers once more to Bultmann. In a note he compares the understanding of Barth and Bultmann respectively and seems to agree with the latter, which he defines in these terms: "'Dialectical' does not mean so much 'determined by the opposite' as determined by historical reality, by the concrete question of the context and by God's answer;" cf. *DBWE* 2, 85, note 9 and Bonhoeffer's reference to Bultmann's study "The Significance of 'Dialectical Theology' for the Scientific Study of the New Testament," 163–164. See also Christiane Tietz-Steiding, *Bonhoeffers Kritik der verkrümmten Vernunft*, Beiträge zur historischen Theologie 112. Tübingen: Mohr Siebeck 1999, 181–183.

15 *DBWE* 2, 95.

16 *DBWE* 2, 95.

17 *DBWE* 2, 97.

ence derived apart from revelation lurks in Bultmann's attempt to inter-pret the insecurities of Dasein in the sense of 'always-being-already-guilty', on the basis of its historicity."[18] Why Bonhoeffer is so insistent in linking revelation and human existence, we will discuss below.

While Bonhoeffer worked on *Act and Being*, he also produced several other studies. In his essay, "Die Frage nach dem Menschen," Bonhoeffer remarks that a person's self-understanding is always dependent on the Word of God that comes from the outside – namely by revelation – and constitutes an absolute limit. Bultmann, Bonhoeffer claims, uses Heidegger's philosophy to show that a person has "the possibility of being" [*sein Sein ist Sein-können*], either in sin or in God. But since for Bonhoeffer revelation is the limit of human self-knowledge it is only a logical consequence for him to ban the concept of possibility from theology. In his own words: "The concept of potentiality has no right in theology and hence in theological anthropology."[19] In a seminar on theological psychology that Bonhoeffer held during the winter semester 1931–1933 at the University of Berlin, he makes a brief mention of Bultmann. He explains that in Barth's theology the I breaks apart into an old and a new I at the expense of a unified I [*Gesamt-Ich*]. The same split is the case in Bultmann's thought, but the continuity of the new I comes at the expense of the new I even though Bultmann is concerned with the *Gesamt-Ich*.[20]

Bultmann's theology has no discernible influence in Bonhoeffer's classic works *Discipleship* and *Life Together*, except that he apparently consulted Bultmann's study "Das christliche Gebot der Nächstenliebe" while he was preparing the manuscript for *Life Together*.[21]

In his *Ethics*, Bonhoeffer refers to Bultmann on several occasions. In Bonhoeffer's second version of the section entitled "History and the Good," he discusses what it means to say that Christ is life and cites Bultmann's commentary on John. Bonhoeffer quotes Bultmann's translation of John 1:4a "What has come into being – in it he was life."[22] In the next paragraph,

---

[18] *DBWE* 2, 97.

[19] *DBWE* 10, 403. In Bonhoeffer's words: "*the concept of possibility has no place in theology and thus no place in theological anthropology*" (original emphasis).

[20] *DBWE* 12, 221. Also in the early 1930s Bonhoeffer encouraged his American friend Paul Lehman, who planned a study tour to Europe, to study either with Barth or Bultmann; cf. *DBW* 17, 107, 112 and 136.

[21] Cf. *DBWE* 5, 186.

[22] *DBWE* 6, 250, note 13; cf. Rudolf Bultmann, *The Gospel of John. A Commentary*. Philadelphia: Westminster Press 1971, 39. Bonhoeffer's citation is not entirely accurate as Bultmann's original translation ("Was da geworden ist, – in dem war er (der Logos) das Leben") is more precise in specifying the role of the Logos.

Bonhoffer says in typical fashion that "Christ is the life that we cannot give ourselves, but which comes to us completely from the outside, completely from beyond ourselves ... This new life is not present other than hidden under the mark of death." The expression that life is under "the mark of death" is taken straight from Bultmann's commentary on John 11:26[23] which, in turn, is probably an allusion to Heidegger's philosophy.

During the years of Bonhoeffer's involvement in the conspiracy, there are several important letters in which Bonhoeffer defends Bultmann. In a letter of March 1942 to Ernst Wolf, the editor of the journals *Evangelische Theologie* and *Verkündigung und Forschung*, Bonhoeffer relates the following: "I take great pleasure in the new Bultmann volume.[24] The intellectual honesty of his work never ceases to impress me. Apparently Dilschneider recently disparaged you and Bultmann quite stupidly here at a Berlin pastors' meeting; and, as I was told, the meeting came within a hair's breadth of sending you a protest against Bultmann's theology! And from Berliners, of all people! I would like to know if any of them has actually worked through the commentary on John. This arrogance, which flourishes here – under the influence of several blowhards, I think – is a real scandal for the Confessing Church."[25] What impressed Bonhoeffer so much about Bultmann's work is made explicit in a letter he wrote in July 1942 to his Marburg friend Winfried Krause (who died in Marburg in 1943). "Now as to Bultmann," explains Bonhoeffer, "I belong to those who welcomed his writing – not because I agree with it. I regret the twofold approach it takes (the argument deriving from John 1:14 and from the radio should not be mixed together; I do consider even the latter to be a valid argument, but the distinction should be clearer) – in this regard perhaps I have remained Harnack's student to this day. To put it bluntly: Bultmann has let the cat out of

---

[23] Cf. *DBWE* 6, 25 and Bultmann, *The Gospel of John*, 404.

[24] Bonhoeffer refers to Bultmann's monograph *New Testament and Mythology*. Philadelphia: Fortress Press, 1984. In a letter to Karl Barth of May 1942, Bonhoeffer notes: "The most recent theological happening for us was the Bultmann volume, which gave rise to a fiery dispute between Asmussen and Wolf and beyond. Despite it all, I took great joy in the essays" (*DBWE* 16, 277).

[25] *DBWE* 16, 260–261. Karl Barth, in a letter to Otto Solomon of May 1942, remarks that he has heard "of the repercussions of the most recent Bultmann furor." Then he laments: "Oh, if only our dear friends in the Confessing Church would leave all that and would finally begin to rack their brains, five minutes before midnight, whether there is anything, anything, they could do to deal with the inexorable coming disaster! The demythologized New Testament is truly only the dotting of an I, that is, in comparison with all that the Germans have done and daily continue to do in the occupied regions, stirring up a cloud of wrath. But I am afraid that all their eyes are still closed and behind them they are only dreaming, dreaming" (*DBWE* 16, 275).

the bag, not only for himself but for a great many people (the liberal cat out of the confessional bag), and in this I rejoice. He has dared to say what many repress in themselves (here I include myself) without having overcome it. He thereby has rendered a service to intellectual integrity and honesty. Many brothers oppose him with a hypocritical faith and that I find deadly.[26] Now an account must be given. I would like to speak with Bultmann about this and open myself to the fresh air that comes from him. But then the window has to be shut again. Otherwise the susceptible will too easily catch a cold. If you see Bultmann, please give him my greetings ... Tell him that I would like to see him, and how I see these things."[27]

As is well-known, during his imprisonment in Berlin, Bonhoffer wrote several letters to his friend and biographer Eberhard Bethge in which he dared to share some of the fresh thoughts he had gained in his theological reflections. In a letter dated 5 May 1944, Bonhoeffer returns to a topic he had written about in earlier letters: "A few more words about 'religionlessness.' You probably remember Bultmann's essay on 'demythologizing the New Testament.' My opinion of it today would be that he went not 'too far,' as most people thought, but rather not far enough. It's not only 'mythological' concepts like miracles, ascension, and so on (which in principle can't be separated from concepts of God, faith, etc.!), that are problematic, but 'religious' concepts as such. You can't separate God from the miracles (as Bultmann thinks); instead, you must be able to interpret and proclaim them *both* 'nonreligiously.' Bultmann's approach is still basically liberal (that is, it cuts the gospel short), whereas I'm trying to think theologically ."[28] Bonhoeffer was exceedingly anxious to hear Bethge's reaction to his thoughts expressed on Bultmann. In a subsequent letter he wonders whether Bethge did indeed receive, as he himself called it, his "Bultmann letter" of 5 May. But Bethge did not, not even a month later; he eventually received it on 26 June 1944.[29] In the meantime, however, on 8 June 1944, Bonhoeffer

---

[26] In another letter to Ernst Wolf in September 1942 Bonhoeffer protests: "As I hear from Marburg, the Council of Brethren there is presently in the midst of deciding about the expulsion of Bultmann from the Confessing Church! These theological hypocrites, so works-righteous! Were it actually to come to expulsion ... I think I would have to have myself expelled as well, not because I agree with Bultmann, but because I consider the others' attitude by far more dangerous than Bultmann's" (*DBWE* 16, 359).

[27] *DBWE* 16, 347.

[28] *DBWE* 8, 372. The reference is to Rudolf Bultmann, "Neues Testament und Mythologie. Das Problem der Entmythologisierung der neutestamentlichen Verkündigung," in idem, *Offenbarung und Heilsgeschehen*. Munich: Lempp 1941, 27–69.

[29] On Bonhoeffer's eagerness to know about the fate of the letter, cf. *DBWE* 8, 410, 412, 423, 432, 445.

wrote another long letter in the course of which he discusses Barth, Tillich and Bultmann at some length. About Bultmann he says this: "As for Bultmann, he seems to have sensed Barth's limitation somehow, but misunderstands it in the sense of liberal theology, and thus falls into typical liberal reductionism (the 'mythological' elements of Christianity are taken out thus reducing Christianity to its 'essence'). My view, however, is that full content, including the 'mythological' concepts, must remain – the New Testament is not a mythological dressing up of a universal truth, but this mythology (resurrection and so forth) is the thing itself! – but that these concepts must now be interpreted in a way that does not make religion the condition for faith ... Only then, in my opinion, is liberal theology overcome ... but at the same time the question it asks is really taken up and answered ... The fact that the world has come of age is no longer an occasion for polemics and apologetics, but is now actually better understood than it understands itself, namely from the gospel and from Christ." [30]

Bultmann's Influence on Bonhoeffer's Theology

As we noted above, Bonhoeffer was extremely impressed with Bultmann's courage and intellectual honesty in articulating crucial issues for contemporary German theology. Indeed, Bonhoeffer saw a good deal of intellectual sincerity and personal integrity in Bultmann's attempt to work out a theology that attempted to do full justice to both human existence and the divine answer to the dilemmas of that existence. At the risk of oversimplifying a complex matter, I propose that Bonhoeffer's dialogue with Bultmann's theology focussed on primarily two broad issues. On the one hand, it is the question to what extent Bultmann's program of demythologizing the Bible may have shaped Bonhoeffer's own theses regarding "religionless Christianity," and on the other hand, it is the issue of how a person may attain a theologically adequate and proper self-understanding.[31] We shall briefly sketch out both of these complex issues.

Clifford Green notes quite correctly that "in some quarters Bonhoeffer's project [of a religionless Christianity in a world come of age as articulated in the letters from prison] was seen as parallel to Rudolf Bultmann's demy-

---

[30] *DBWE* 8, 430–431.

[31] Cf. Tietz-Steiding, *Bonhoeffers Kritik der verkrümmten Vernunft*, 191: "Was Bonhoeffer mit seiner Kritik an Bultmann abwehren will, dürfte klar sein. Philosophie ist nicht in der Lage, dem Menschen ein theologisch angemessenes Selbstverständnis zu ermöglichen."

thologizing proposal"[32] while Hans-Richard Reuter, the editor of *DBW* 2, maintains that "the systematic affinity of Bonhoeffer to Rudolf Bultmann's theological thought – which in *Act and Being* is hard to deny – has not as a rule had much exposure."[33] In other words, the question before us is whether Bultmann's notion of demythologizing the biblical narratives is the backbone for Bonhoeffer's conceptualization of a "religionless Christianity?" This question, to be sure, defies an easy answer. No doubt, there are "parallels" and "affinities" between Bultmann and Bonhoeffer; nonetheless, I am inclined to think that the differences between their theological conceptions warrant the conclusion that their proposals are sufficiently nuanced, unique and independent.[34]

Bonhoeffer agreed with Bultmann that the unscientific worldview of the Bible presents a problem for a modern, enlightened, technologically oriented person. In short, the biblical worldview is a problem in that it requires of the modern person a *sacrificius intellectus*. Bonhoeffer similarly understood that the *mündige* person can no longer simply believe as if science and biblical scholarship did not exist. For example, in his interpretation of creation in Genesis 1:6–10, Bonhoeffer boldly asserts: "Here the ancient image of the world confronts us in all its scientific naïvité. To us today its ideas appear altogether absurd."[35] Both Bonhoeffer and Bultmann agree that to a person who is wholly and completely entrenched in all of life, with body and mind, the current scientific worldview has made religion problematic.

In spite of this agreement in terms of the unscientific, mythological worldview of the biblical texts, their respective proposals are distinct, at least methodologically and in terms of their ultimate objectives. Bult-

---

[32] *DBWE* 6, 2; cf. also *DBWE* 6, 435. One of the first scholars to articulate the parallel between Bultmann and Bonhoeffer was Gerhard Ebeling, "Die 'nicht-religiöse Interpretation biblischer Begriffe'," in idem, *Wort und Glaube.* Tübingen: J. C. B. Mohr (Paul Siebeck), third edition, 1967, 90–160. It is, moreover, interesting to note that Bonhoeffer's cousin, Hans-Christoph von Hase, in a letter addressed to Bonhoeffer when he was at Union Theological Seminary, says that he himself was thinking of "questions in contemporary theology" and was tempting to place you [Bonhoeffer] together with Bultmann behind Ritschl" (*DBWE* 10, 253). At any rate, his cousin clearly understood the affinities between Bonhoeffer and Bultmann. For a discussion of Bonhoeffer's notion of "religionless Christianity," see Clifford J. Green, *Bonhoeffer. A Theology of Sociality.* Grand Rapids/Cambridge: Eerdmans, second edition, 1999, 269–282.

[33] *DBWE* 2, 170.

[34] Contra Gerhard Krause, "Dietrich Bonhoeffer und Rudolf Bultmann," in Erich Dinkler (ed), *Zeit und Geschichte*, 439–460, who seems to press the evidence of the sources too much in terms of possible affinities and agreements between Bultmann and Bonhoeffer.

[35] *DBWE* 3, 50.

mann's program of demythologizing is essentially a hermeneutical and existential attempt to remove the unscientific stumbling block of the kerygma so that the modern person can hear it anew and accept it by means of a clear decision and with faith. For Bonhoeffer, however, Bultmann's proposal remained essentially a liberal one.[36] Bonhoeffer's musings on "religionless Christianity," while not entirely void of hermeneutical elements, have as the main objective precisely the overcoming of the kind of liberal "reductionism"[37] espoused by Bultmann. There is really no term that fittingly expresses the type of theology Bonhoeffer was envisioning; the kind of theology he began to construct, at least in its fragmentary conception in his letters from prison,[38] had not yet been articulated, not even by himself. To some extent Bonhoeffer's theological vision was liberal, existential, ontological, biblical, systematic etc. and yet, paradoxically, it was neither eclectic nor uncritical.[39] Only one thing was sure: it was a theology that had a Christocentric focus and aimed at nothing less than life in its fullness. Bonhoeffer's construction of theology – in distinction to Bultmann, Tillich and Barth – was fundamentally rooted in the desire to articulate a theology of life that was unshakably anchored in the perennial question "Who is Christ for us today?" In that sense, as Bethge comments, "Bonhoeffer's Christological 'reality' stands against Bultmann's anthropological 'potentiality'."[40] Bonhoeffer's was a theology that took seriously human exist-

---

[36] Cf. *DBWE* 8, 372.

[37] Cf. Gerhard Ebeling, "Die 'nicht-religiöse Interpretation biblischer Begriffe'," 135, who argues that Bonhoeffer is mistaken in characterizing Bultmann's program of demythologizing as a liberal reductionism. Bultmann himself was interested, as Bonhoeffer, in *interpreting* mythological concepts in the biblical narratives rather than merely eliminating them.

[38] I agree with the critique of Karl Barth when he cautions against taking the isolated sayings on "religionless Christianity" in the prison correspondence as the cornerstone for much of Bonhoeffer's theology. Cf. Karl Barth, *Offene Briefe 1945–1968.* Gesamtausgabe V, 15. Zurich: TVZ 1984, 324–327 and idem, *Gespräche 1963.* Gesamtausgabe IV, 41. Zurich: TVZ 2005, 281. For the details of the discussion, cf. Gerhard Krause, "Dietrich Bonhoeffer und Rudolf Bultmann," 447.

[39] Cf. Götz Harbsmeier, "Die 'nicht-religiöse Interpretation biblischer Begriffe' bei Bonhoeffer und die Entmythologisierung," in Ernst Wolf, Charlotte von Kirschbaum and Rudolf Frey (eds), *Antwort.* Karl Barth zum Siebzigsten Geburtstag am 10. Mai 1956. Zurich 1956, 544–561. Harbsmeier notes that "weder im positiven noch im negativen Sinne darf der Bonhoeffersche Gedankengang als Beitrag zu einer existentialentheologischen Hermeneutik genommen werden ... Bonhoeffer steht ganz außerhalb einer derartigen Grundkonzeption der Hermeneutik. Er macht jedenfalls die für Bultmann so grundlegende Unterscheidung von existential und existentiell, ontologisch und ontisch nicht zum Fundament aller weiteren Erwägungen" (546).

[40] Eberhard Bethge, "The Challenge of Dietrich Bonhoeffer's Life and Theology," in *WCA*, 22–88, here 84.

ence and literally the "mythological" account of Christ's resurrection. Bonhoeffer is clear on that point. To repeat his view once more: "My view, however, is that full content, including the 'mythological' concepts, must remain – the New Testament is not a mythological dressing up of a universal truth, but this mythology (resurrection and so forth) is the thing itself! – but that these concepts must now be interpreted in a way that does not make religion the condition for faith."[41]

The issue at stake between a religionless interpretation of Christianity and the program of demythologizing the biblical world view is still most aptly illuminated by Bethge. His comments are worth to be cited it at length. Bethge assumes that Bonhoeffer's "non-religious interpretation speaks of a dimension different from Bultmann's existential interpretation" and then explains: "Bultmann, the professor in the lecture-room, gives an account of the process of interpretation ... and builds up a systematic epistemology of it. Bonhoeffer thinks about the God-forsaken world. Bultmann's problem is that of faith and understanding. This problem is not to be found in Bonhoeffer's letters ... The hindrance with Bonhoeffer is not just misunderstanding, but God's absence and hiddenness."[42]

Put differently, Bonhoeffer's religionless interpretation aims at a theological reconception that claims a person's entire life[43] in the very encounter with Jesus Christ. "Religionless Christianity," then, seems to suggest that there is no religious, cultural, intellectual or any other precondition that makes a person *a priori* open to matters of the Christian faith in a modern context. The transforming and life-changing encounter with Christ himself is the "thing as such," but its character is not religious, experiential but personal-Christological.[44] But how is such an encounter possible, how can it be explicated in theological stringent terms? For an answer, let us turn to our second question, namely how a person can attain a theologically proper self-understanding.

As we saw, Bonhoeffer discusses Bultmann very substantially in *Act and Being*. One of the most pressing questions for Bonhoeffer was the issue of how a person can come to have proper self-knowledge and knowledge of God. In a nutshell, Bonhoeffer rejects what he understands to be Bult-

---

[41] *DBWE* 8, 430.

[42] Eberhard Bethge, "The Challenge of Dietrich Bonhoeffer's Life and Theology," 84.

[43] Cf. Green, *Bonhoeffer. A Theology of Sociality*, who notes that in his interpretation of biblical concepts Bonhoeffer "is clearly after something more than conceptual alteration; he is, as stated before, trying to describe a new *psychic posture* which affects a person's whole life" (269).

[44] Cf. the comments of the editors of *DBWE* 8, 588–589.

mann's position, namely, that a person has the ontological-existential possibility to arrive at a proper understanding of self based on a (Heideggerian) analysis of self and (almost) apart from revelation.[45] Decisive for this complex discourse are the concepts of "possibility"[46] or "potentiality" and "revelation." In Bonhoeffer's own words: "The concept of possibility ... is clearly suggested to Bultmann by Heidegger's existential-ontological analysis of Dasein as the possibility of ontic existence.[47] Consequently, it includes the possibility of an ontological[48] understanding of Dasein unaffected by revelation. But, seen from the position of revelation, 'to be possible' in relation to sin or grace (whether *existential* or *existentiell*) always means to be already really in one or the other."[49]

Why Bonhoeffer rejects the notion of "possibility" so radically is most evident in his view of the ontological status of a person's being either in Adam or in Christ. "Were it really a human possibility for persons themselves to know that they are sinners apart from revelation, neither 'being in Adam' nor 'being in Christ' would be existential designations of their being. For it would mean that human beings could place themselves into the truth, that they could somehow withdraw to a deeper being of their won, apart from their being sinners, to be regarded as a potentiality of a more profound 'possibility of being in the truth'. It would rest on being untouched by sin."[50] In other words, for Bonhoeffer there is no such thing as

---

[45] Cf. *DBWE* 2, 97: "the danger of a concept of existence derived apart from revelation lurks in Bultmann's attempt to interpret the insecurities of Dasein."

[46] For a detailed discussion of Bultmann's concept of possibility, see Tietz-Steiding, *Bonhoeffers Kritik der verkrümmten Vernunft*, 184–193.

[47] *DBWE* 2, 96, note 24. See also Martin Heidegger, *Being and Time*, translated by John Macquarrie and Edward Robinson. New York: Harper and Row Publishers 1962, 183: "The kind of Being which Dasein has, as potentiality-for-Being, lies existentially in understanding. Dasein is not something present-at-hand which possesses its competence for something by way of an extra; it is primarily Being-possible. Dasein is in every case what it can be, and in the way in which it is its possibility." For a discussion of potentiality in Heidegger and Bonhoeffer, cf. Charles Marsh, *Reclaiming Dietrich Bonhoeffer. The Promise of his Theology*. New York: Oxford University Press 1994, 120–125.

[48] On Bonhoeffer's attempt to construct a "theological ontology" in *Act and Being*, see the study by Robert P. Scharlemann, "Authenticity and Encounter: Bonhoeffer's Appropriation of Ontology," in *Theology and the Practice of Responsibility. Essays on Dietrich Bonhoeffer*, edited by Wayne W. Floyd and Charles Marsh. Valley Forge: Trinity Press International 1994, 253–265.

[49] *DBWE* 2, 96, note 24.

[50] *DBWE* 2, 136. Already in *Sanctorum Communio*, Bonhoeffer had rejected the Heideggerian category of "possibility" as belonging to theological discourse. Cf. *DBWE* 1, 143: If "one regarded revelation only as beginning (potentiality), and not at the same time also as completion (reality), this would take away what is decisive about

an ontological-existential possibility of a person's coming to understand her/himself as a sinner by means of Dasein's structural analysis. Knowledge of sin can only come by means of revelation. Here Bonhoeffer flatly rejects what he thinks Bultmann has taken from Heidegger's dictum that "Dasein is not something present-at-hand which possesses its competence for something by way of an extra; it is primarily Being-possible."[51] Heidegger's expression "the way of an extra" Bonhoeffer conceptualizes concretely as revelation. Bonhoeffer repeatedly stressed that "it is the genuine 'from outside' that gives us an understanding of Dasein, that makes it intelligible that this 'from outside' is what places us into truth."[52] Concretely – since "revelation is essentially an event of God's free activity [and] supersedes and challenges also the existential-ontological possibilities of Dasein"[53] – knowledge of sin, and consequently the forgiveness of sins and faith, is not a mere matter of philosophy but becomes a moment in the transformation of one's life. "In the existentiell event of revelation," says Bonhoeffer, "the existential structure of Dasein is *touched* and *changed*."[54]

In all fairness to Bultmann, it may have been the case that Bonhoeffer saw the gap between them as too wide. Bultmann himself seems to suggest this much in an essay written in 1963, entitled "The Idea of God and Modern Man."[55] In this study Bultmann affirms that "Christian faith speaks of a *revelation*, by which it understands God's act as an event ... which does not communicate doctrines, but concerns the existence of man and teaches him, or better, enables him to understand himself as sustained by the transcendent power of God."[56] Bultmann goes on to say that theologians like Tillich, Ebeling and others agree that the transcendent must be sought not beyond but in the midst of the world. Then he cites a letter from Bonhoeffer *expressis verbis*: "God's 'beyond' is not what is beyond our cognition! Epistemological transcendence has nothing to do with God's transcendence. God is the beyond in the midst of our lives."[57] Bonhoeffer him-

---

the revelation of God, namely that God's word became history;" cf. also note 40, where Bultmann is mentioned. See further Ernst Feil, *The Theology of Dietrich Bonhoeffer*, translated by Martin Rumscheidt. Philadelphia: Fortress Press 1985, 29–32, 37–39.

[51] Martin Heidegger, *Being and Time*, 183.

[52] *DBWE* 2, 110. In the next sentence Bonhoeffer remarks that a philosophy of the possibility of Dasein has no room for "the occurrence of revelation in the cross and resurrection in the Christian church."

[53] *DBWE* 2, 78, note 89.

[54] *DBWE* 2, 78, note 89.

[55] First published in *ZThK* 60 (1963); English translation in *WCA*, 256–273.

[56] *WCA*, 265.

[57] *WCA*, 265–266 citing *DBWE* 8, 367. In the next paragraph, Bultmann cites Bonhoeffer once more approvingly, once again an excerpt from a letter he wrote from Tegel

self wanted to pursue these ideas further in the book he planned in prison. Chapter Two was to examine how "the transcendent is not the infinite, unattainable tasks, but the neighbor within reach in any given situation."[58]

Paul Tillich

Tillich's Early Theology in Bonhoeffer's Writings

Compared to Bultmann, there are not as many references to Tillich in Bonhoeffer's writngs.[59] One of the first substantive discussions of Tillich is in *Sanctorum Communio*, where Bonhoeffer discusses Tillich's work *Masse und Geist*.[60] Bonhoeffer asks himself whether there is "such a thing as a Protestant community constituted as a mass [*Massengemeinde*]"[61] similar to the Roman Catholic understanding of Christian community or church. His answer includes a reference to Tillich. "Prompted by the well-founded sense that the 'spirit' withdraws from the masses," he comments, "Tillich has attempted to uncover a direct relation between the two; he sees the holiness of the formless mass in the fact that it can be given form by the revelation of the forming absolute. But this no longer has anything to do with Christian theology. We know only that holiness of God's church-community that is bound to and formed by the word in Christ. The word is received only by personal appropriation, which is why God's church-community is impelled away from the mass. But Tillich has nevertheless pointed out something important. The church-community must be engaged with the mass; it must hear when the masses are calling for community, such as in the Youth Movement or in sports, and must not fail to proclaim its word about the *sanctorum communio* within their very midst. The basic rule, however, remains unchanged: the Christian concept of the church-community is the criterion for evaluating the notion of the mass, and not the other way around."[62]

---

prison: "And we cannot be honest unless we recognize that we have to live in the world 'etsi deus non daretur.' And this is precisely what we do recognize – before God! God himself compels us to recognize it" *DBWE* 8, 478.

[58] *DBWE* 8, 501.

[59] On the relation between Tillich and Bonhoeffer, cf. the remarks by Bethge, "The Challenge of Dietrich Bonhoeffer's Life and Theology," 83.

[60] *Masse und Geist. Studien zur Philosophie der Masse.* Berlin: Verlag der Arbeitsgemeinschaft 1922.

[61] *DBWE* 1, 239.

[62] *DBWE* 1, 239–240.

In *Act and Being*, Bonhoeffer discusses Tillich in the following manner: "If Paul Tillich believes that there is no possibility of distinguishing between philosophical and theological anthropology (*Religiöse Verwirklichung*, Berlin 1930, 300), one need only refer to the concept of revelation. If, from the viewpoint of revelation, theological anthropology sees human existence as essentially determined by guilt or by grace – and not merely as 'under threat in an unconditional sense' – then philosophical anthropology is able to adopt such concepts from theology only at the expense of bursting its own framework. For in doing so, philosophical anthropology turns its analysis of human existence, too, into an analysis of humanity's attempt to lay hold of itself; that is to say, it can do so only at the expense of becoming theological anthropology. This leaves the question of truth untouched. It is to be tested only in conjunction with the concept of contingency inherent in revelation."[63]

Moreover, during his inaugural lecture at the University of Berlin in July 1930, on the topic "The Anthropological Question in Contemporary Philosophy and Theology," Bonhoeffer comments again on Tillich's anthropology. The human being, Bonhoeffer asserts, is a self-questioning being by virtue of his or her essence, but in such a way that a person cannot simply discover answers to these questions in the deeper strata of the soul. A person is bound to the questionability of his or her existence. The answers to human existence, according to Bonhoeffer's review of Tillich may be conceptualized in this manner: "Paul Tillich, whose thought begins at this point, views the human being as a finite being [Wesen] characterized by not coming to his own essence through himself, since there is absolutely no secure, unified point from which self-understanding might be possible. The human being is not is not able to elevate himself to lord over the world because all that is human is basically called into question [by the ground of all being,] [all that is finite by the infinite]. Hence the person comes to his essence only where, standing at his boundary [Grenze], he experiences the inbreaking of the infinite ... The absolute *boundary* is the inbreaking of the absolute itself; the absolute 'No' *is* the absolute 'Yes'. The human being understands himself on the basis of this boundary."[64] Similar ideas are also discussed in Bonhoeffer's lecture on the "The History of Twentieth-Century Systematic Theology."[65] Once again he mentions

---

[63] *DBWE* 2, 77.

[64] *DBWE* 10, 397–398.

[65] Bonhoeffer presented this lecture during the winter semester 1931–1932 at the University of Berlin. Cf. *DBWE* 11, 177–244. In addition to the instance discussed above, Tillich is mentioned several times more in the same lecture within contexts that

Tillich. "This is the essential difference from Tillich. It is at the boundaries of our existence that [according to Tillich], we experience the radical No; if we accept this boundary situation [*Grenzsituation*] we find ourselves affirmed. In recognizing that we are sinners, in essence we already have the recognition of mercy.[66] This identification (Holl) must be broken; it means preemption, by our own power, of God's act of grace. [God] is completely free, even above and beyond the recognition of sin."[67] Further in the same lecture Bonhoeffer remarks that it is possible to speak differently than Tillich of the "humankind" [*Mensch*] and "transcendence."[68] Regarding the human being, Bonhoeffer characterizes Tillich's view briefly as including the newness of created life, community and a new discovery of transcendence. Transcendence, says Bonhoeffer, means for Tillich a widening of perspectives.

Other, more sporadic references in Bonhoeffer's writings to Tillich's theology occur in the following contexts. In his lecture on "The Nature of the Church" during the summer semester 1932 Bonhoeffer approvingly refers to Tillich's critique of the civilizing process [*Verbürgerlichung*] of the German church.[69] Elsewhere, in one of the letters written during his imprisonment, Bonhoeffer makes reference to the expression "Gott als Lückenbüßer." Tillich employed this essentially Nietzschean[70] expression in his work *Die religiöse Lage der Gegenwart*, a book Bonhoeffer had probably read as early as 1928 during his year in Barcelona.[71] If so, the citation of the expression gives testimony both to Bonhoeffer's good memory and the significance he attached to the phrase.

More substantial is Bonhoeffer's discussion of Tillich in a long letter written from Tegel prison on 8 June 1944 and addressed to his friend Eber-

---

are not crucial for the development of Bonhoeffer's arguments; cf. 178, 179, 181, 220, 226, 234.

[66] According to the editors of *DBWE* 11, 237, note 308, this sentence ("in recognizing that we are sinners, in essence we already have the recognition of mercy [*Gnadenerkenntnis*]") cannot be located in Tillich's works.

[67] *DBWE* 11, 237.

[68] Cf. *DBWE* 11, 228.

[69] *DBWE* 11, 277.

[70] On Nietzsche and Bonhoeffer see my studies in this volume.

[71] Cf. *DBWE* 8, 405, note 5. Fuller (Eberhard Bethge [ed], *Letters and Papers from Prison*, translated by Reginald Fuller. New York: Macmillan Publishing 1971, 311) translates the words "Gott als Lückenbüßer" as "God as stop-gap." Bonhoeffer knew Tillich's work *Die religiöse Lage der Gegenwart* (Berlin 1926), reprinted in Paul Tillich, *Main Works/Hauptwerke*, vol. 5, edited by Robert P. Scharlemann. Berlin/New York: Walter de Gruyter 1988, 91. In preparation for a lecture he planned to give for his congregation in Barcelona in 1928, Bonhoeffer had requested a copy of this book from Walter Dress; cf. *DBW* 17, 88.

hard Bethge. In the course of his theological reflections, he also mentions Tillich. In Bonhoeffer's view, "Tillich undertook the religious interpretation of the development of the world itself – against its will – giving it its form through religion. That was very brave, but the world threw him out of the saddle and galloped on by itself. He too thought he understood the world better than it understood itself, but the world felt totally misunderstood and rejected such an insinuation. (The world *does* need to be understood in a better way than it does itself! but not 'religiously,' the way the religious socialists want to)."[72]

Tillich's Influence on Bonhoeffer's Theology

It is noteworthy that in retrospect Tillich remarks of Bonhoeffer's *Letters and Papers from Prison*: "In these letters Bonhoeffer dealt with the same problem that I have dealt with in all my books, namely, the problem of seeking a solution to the conflicts between the religious tradition and the modern mind."[73] Even though, any attempt to determine Paul Tillich's theological influence in Bonhoeffer's thought must reckon with the crucial datum, as Bethge reminds us, that "all Bonhoeffer knew of Tillich was what had been published before the Nazi period. It was this he had in mind when he argued for or against Tillich."[74] In other words, modern interpreters must be mindful to resist the temptation to judge that influence in terms of Tillich's post-war works, such as his *Systematic Theology*[75] and other writings.

Tillich's theology prompted for Bonhoeffer questions that were similar to those raised by Bultmann's work. In a broad sense, these were the two issues of the meaning of religion in the world and a precise conception of theological anthropology.

---

[72] *DBWE* 8, 428.

[73] *A History of Christian Thought*. New York: Harper & Row 1968, 359.

[74] Eberhard Bethge, *Dietrich Bonhoeffer*, 857–858. One of the puzzling questions for Bonhoeffer scholars is whether the two men ever met face to face either in Germany or at Union Theological Seminary in New York. There is evidence for a face to face meeting between the two men. In a letter (dated 5 December 1938) Bonhoeffer replies to Gerhard Leibholz's question, whether he knew Tillich, in these words: "You asked about Tillich. I know him, that is, I got to know him during his work for two days here … tell him that I recall the conference with his friends in Wannsee with pleasure" (*DBWE* 15, 86). Regarding Tillich's view of Bonhoeffer, we know that he thought very highly of him and wished to bring him to the United States in 1939; cf. *DBWE* 15, 173–174.

[75] *Systematic Theology*, 3 volumes. Chicago: Chicago University Press 1951, 1957, 1963.

In one sense, Bonhoeffer applauds Tillich's objective to work out a proper relation between the Christian world as a mass [*Massengemeinde*] and the role and need of religion; but in another – and more decisive – sense, he critiques Tillich for precisely his theological attempt to do so. For in Bonhoeffer's theological reasoning, the significance of the masses of people gains its shape not by "the revelation of the forming absolute" but only in the encounter of "the word of Christ."[76] Tillich's reference to "revelation" and the "forming absolute" are far too vague for Bonhoeffer and are a far cry from Christian theology. For him, the masses of people are not so much formed or shaped by a "forming absolute" but only as a church–community that is in turn constituted by the word of Christ. Here Bonhoeffer's christocentric focus to sociality is abundantly evident. It is not the case that the masses need more religion. In a strict sense, the masses do not need Christianity or even a "non-religious" form of Christianity. It is not the mass that determines what it needs vis-à-vis religion. Quite to the contrary, "the Christian concept of the church-community is the criterion for evaluating the notion of the mass, and not the other way around."[77] By criticizing Tillich on this point he is in a sense foreshadowing what he later penned in *Ethics* under the rubric of "Ethics as Formation." There he says plainly: "The church's concern in not religion, but the form of Christ and its taking form among a band of people."[78] In the next sentence, Bonhoeffer makes a pronouncement that seems to be tailor-made as a critique for the kind of program Tillich had in mind. "If we let ourselves stray even the least bit from this perspective," warns Bonhoeffer, "we fall unavoidably into those programs of ethical or religious world-formation from which we departed above."[79] In one of the letters from prison he says of Tillich, to repeat: "The world *does* need to be understood in a better way than it does itself! but not 'religiously,' the way the religious socialists want to."[80] Hence, for Bonhoeffer, it is not a religious or socialist form that the world needs, but exclusively the form of Christ.

When Bonhoeffer claims that the world needs the form of Christ there seems to be some affinity with Tillich's idea that for modern humanity God

---

[76] *DBWE* 1, 239–240.

[77] *DBWE* 1, 240.

[78] *DBWE* 6, 97. In the same context Bonhoeffer remarks: "The church is nothing but that piece of humanity where Christ really has taken form. It is solely the form of Christ that matters, not any form besides Christ's own... Therefore [the church's] first concern is not with the so-called religious function of human beings, but with the existence in the world of whole human beings in all their relationships."

[79] *DBWE* 6, 97.

[80] *DBWE* 8, 428.

is often merely a "gap stop" or "gap-filler." In one of his early works, *Die Religiöse Lage der Gegenwart* (1926) [*The Religious Situation*], Tillich broadly analyzes the contemporary German context of science, art, politics and religion. He asserts that the church lost the battle between the claims of faith and knowledge and that science is now autonomous. On the one hand, the triumph of science brings "an end to all attempts to deduce proofs of the eternal from the finite and its forms. It made impossible the use of gaps in scientific knowledge for the sake of introducing God as gap-filler in the scientific description of the world. It forced the recognition that the eternal appears at a deeper level than the level of rational thought."[81] But on the other hand, the understanding of the non-scientific realm as "feeling … led to the separation of the whole sphere of truth from religion. Religion left it alone to work out its finite realization. And religion itself was dealt with as a matter of subjective moods which could make no claims to understand or reform the world."[82] According to Tillich's theological analysis, German Protestantism thus failed in articulating a proper relation between science and faith. God was consequently reduced to a mere "gap-filler," a second rate recourse to cheap explanations of scientific phenomena. God was thus pushed to the periphery. Although Bonhoeffer does not disagree with Tillich's view of God as a "gap-filler," precisely at this point he goes beyond Tillich. If Tillich pointed to the question, Bonhoeffer attempts to give an answer. In Bonhoeffer's conception of reality there is an unshakable *cantus firmus*: "Christ is the center and power of the Bible, of the church, of theology, but also of humanity, reason, justice and culture."[83] Elsewhere he avows: "The whole reality of the world has already been drawn into and is held together in Christ. History moves only from this center and toward this center."[84] In other words, a "gap-filler" God cannot give any form to the world, neither can religion. The form of the world is Christ alone; he is the center of all reality, including science, culture and faith. The separation of science and faith surely produced a second rate concept of God and yet "the reality of Christ embraces the reality of the world in itself. The world has no reality of its own independent of God's revelation in Christ."[85] Expressed differently, a proper conception of the one reality of the world places God, in Christ, at the centre and not at the periphery of all of life.

---

[81] Paul Tillich, *Main Works/Hauptwerke*, vol. 5, 91. Translation is from *The Religious Situation,* translated by H. Richard Niebuhr. New York 1956, 204.
[82] *The Religious Situation*, 204–205.
[83] *DBWE* 6, 341.
[84] *DBWE* 6, 58.
[85] *DBWE* 6, 58.

Regarding Bonhoeffer's critique of Tillich's anthropology, he treated it in a manner that was not unlike his criticism of Bultmann's theological anthropology. The main issue is once more the question of revelation. Bonhoeffer agrees with Tillich's basic analysis of human existence in that a finite person cannot come to one's own self-understanding "since there is absolutely no secure, unified point from which self-understanding might be possible."[86] But Bonhoeffer rejects Tillich's view that human self-understanding might somehow come into sharper relief when a person stands at one's limit and "experiences the inbreaking of the infinite … The absolute *boundary* is the inbreaking of the absolute itself; the absolute 'No' *is* the absolute 'Yes'. The human being understands himself on the basis of this boundary."[87] Although Bonhoeffer may grant what Tillich views as the incursion of the absolute into human finiteness, he himself expressed these matters in a non-abstract manner. For Bonhoeffer, arguably, Tillich's language is too ambiguous in saying exactly what is meant by the incursion of the absolute. Bonhoeffer perceives Tillich's notion of "inbreaking" as the event of revelation and "the absolute" as God. In other words, Tillich's "inbreaking of the infinite" is expressed more sharply – and traditionally – by Bonhoeffer as "the revelation of God." Moreover, what Tillich terms "the absolute boundary" corresponds to Bonhoeffer's notion of sin and the claim that "being in Adam" is an ontological category. Here, too, Bonhoeffer holds against Tillich what he already critiqued in Bultmann: "Were it really a human possibility for persons themselves to know that they are sinners apart from revelation, neither 'being in Adam' nor 'being in Christ' would be existential designations of their being. For it would mean that human beings could place themselves into the truth, that they could somehow withdraw to a deeper being of their own, apart from their being sinners, to be regarded as a potentiality of a more profound 'possibility of being in the truth'. It would rest on being untouched by sin."[88] Whereas in Bultmann the notion of "possibility" was the issue for Bonhoeffer, in view of Tillich's concept of the inbreaking of the infinite into a person's limit, Bonhoeffer sees the danger of somehow leaving a small window open that would make knowledge of one's own sinfulness possible, no matter how deficient that knowledge may be. Against these notions Bonhoeffer never wavers in postulating that human self-knowledge cannot in any way mean that a person could come to have an autonomous understanding as a sin-

---

[86] *DBWE* 10, 397.
[87] *DBWE* 10, 397–398.
[88] *DBWE* 2, 136.

ner.[89] No existential analysis of *Dasein* and no inbreaking of the infinite into a person's limits can accomplish this. Only God himself in the revelation[90] of Jesus as the Christ can break into that reality and bring about self-knowledge that is adequate.

Conclusion

The lives of Bultmann, Tillich and Bonhoeffer were characterized by two essential common denominators. One was the historical context of a native country that was overrun – ideologically, politically, culturally, socially and religiously – by Nazi propaganda and the ensuing destruction of human lives; the other was the fact that all three were theologians deeply concerned with the contemporary situation vis-à-vis the question of how the biblical kerygma can become a transforming reality in lives of godless and religionless people who are either explicitly or implicitly participating in one of the twentieth century's most atrocious tyrannies. The theological and personal answers these three thinkers provided in that context took on different form, radicality and cost.

To recall Tillich's words once more, both he and Bonhoeffer were dealing with "the problem of seeking a solution to the conflicts between the religious tradition and the modern mind."[91] Even though Bonhoeffer took both Bultmann and Tillich very seriously as theological and philosophical thinkers, in the end he judged their theological programs as not entirely convincing, or at least as not going far enough. As we saw, the crux of the difference between himself and their theologies lies in the estimation of the role of revelation in a person's self-understanding. Bonhoeffer believed that his own theological attempt to work out a *"genuine ontology"*[92] went

---

[89] Regarding a person's knowledge of sin, Bonhoeffer invoked Luther's dictum: *sola fide credendum est nos esse peccatores* [we know by faith alone that we are sinners]; cf. *DBWE* 2, 135. Hence, even the knowledge that we are sinners cannot come to us apart from revelation.

[90] Bonhoeffer's understanding of Tillich's view of revelation begs the question of whether he understood Tillich correctly. For by 1930 Tillich had written two articles on the subject of revelation, namely "Die Idee der Offenbarung" (1927) in Paul Tillich, *Main Works/Hauptwerke*, volume 6, edited by Gert Hummel. Berlin/NewYork: Walter de Gruyter 1992, 99–106 and "Offenbarung: Religionsphilosopisch" (1930) in Paul Tillich, *Main Works/Hauptwerke*, volume 4, edited by John Clayton. Berlin/NewYork: Walter de Gruyter 1987, 237–242. It cannot be discerned from Bonhoeffer's writings whether he knew of these essays.

[91] Tillich, *A History of Christian Thought*, 359.

[92] Cf. *DBWE* 2, 109.

beyond both Bultmann and Tillich. A true ontology, Bonhoeffer argued extensively in *Act and Being*, cannot be conceived of apart from revelation. For revelation alone is the guarantor of the continuity between the old and new "I," the old "I" trapped in the ontological category of "being in Adam" and the new "I" transformed into the new ontological category of "being in Christ."

8. Dietrich Bonhoeffer and Gerhard Ebeling: An Encounter of Theological Minds

> Die tiefsten und verborgensten
> Verständnisschwierigkeiten, die uns als
> Theologen selbst erwachsen, haben darin
> ihren Grund, dass wir mit unserer
> Theologie am falschen Ort sind.[1]

Bonhoeffer on Ebeling

Dietrich Bonhoeffer met Gerhard Ebeling, a fellow Berliner, for the first time at the underground Finkenwalde Seminary of the Confessing Church during the fourth theological course in the winter of 1936–1937. It took Bonhoeffer very little time to realize that Ebeling was an exceptionally gifted theological thinker; it is fair to say that Bonhoeffer discovered the theological genius in Ebeling. On his own initiative, Bonhoeffer wrote to Martin Albertz, superintendent of the Confessing Church responsible for theological education, to recommend Ebeling for further theological education, stating: "I consider him to be an extraordinarily gifted and capable scholar and theologian... capable of exceptional scholarly work."[2] As Bonhoeffer continued, because of a "dangerous decline of theological expertise recently and presumably also in the near future, it is becoming ever more urgent that we [the Confessing Church] have at least a few genuinely solid theologians."[3] Moreover, since an "unusually propitious opportunity has

---

[1] Gerhard Ebeling, "Hauptprobleme der protestantischen Theologie in der Gegenwart. Anfragen an die Theologie," in idem, *Wort und Glaube,* vol. 2. Tübingen: J. C. B. Mohr [Paul Siebeck] 1969, 69: "The deepest and most concealed issues of understanding that we theologians face have their reason in that we show up in the wrong places with our theology."

[2] *DBWE* 14, 290.

[3] *DBWE* 14, 290. Ebeling affirms this point later in the interview "Gespräch über Dietrich Bonhoeffer," in idem, *Wort und Glaube,* vol. 4. Tübingen: J. C. B. Mohr [Paul Siebeck] 1995, 650.

recently emerged for Ebeling to go to Zürich for a year,"[4] namely to do doctoral work under Emil Brunner, Bonhoeffer urged Albertz to release Ebeling from pastoral and congregational work for the time of his academic work.[5] Albertz granted Bonhoeffer's request and, in the spring of 1937, Ebeling began his doctoral studies at the University of Zurich – albeit under the supervision of Fritz Blanke and not Emil Brunner, with a dissertation on Luther's exegesis of the Gospels,[6] a work that he finished in the summer of 1938. In May of 1939 Ebeling got married to his Swiss bride, Kometa Richner. They returned to Germany and Ebeling became the illegal pastor of a Confessing Church congregation in Berlin.[7]

Bonhoeffer continued to stay in contact with Ebeling after he had returned to Germany.[8] That he thought of Ebeling not only as a gifted theologian but also as a man with pastoral gifts is evident in the fact that Bonhoeffer entrusted Ebeling with various official ecclesial practices, even in his own extended family. To this effect there is the interesting letter that Bonheoffer's mother wrote to him when he was already incarcerated in Tegel prison. In May 1943, just shortly after his arrest, Eberhard Bethge and Renate Schleicher, Bonhoeffer's niece, got married. Gerhard Ebeling was the minister who officiated at that wedding. Since Bonhoeffer had to miss the wedding, his mother filled him in on some of the details: "The minister [Ebeling] spoke very well and very seriously, perhaps a little too seriously for such a young woman. He emphasized the responsibility of a marriage perhaps more than happiness. However, I told myself that it is perhaps not really his task to talk about that aspect; each person bears that within himself."[9]

A few weeks later, when Bonhoeffer was not released from prison as he had hoped, he drafted a last will and testament. In addition to bequeathing Ebeling one of his books,[10] Bonhoeffer added an addendum stating that he

---

[4] *DBWE* 14, 291.

[5] In retrospect Ebeling says that he went to Zurich on Bonhoeffer's "urging" ("auf Drängen Bonhoeffers"); cf. Gerhard Ebeling, *Umgang mit Luther*. Tübingen: J.C.B. Mohr [Paul Siebeck] 1983, 205.

[6] Cf. Gerhard Ebeling, *Evangelische Evangelienauslegung: eine Untersuchung zu Luthers Hermeneutik*. Darmstadt: Wissenschaftliche Buchgesellschaft 1962 [orig. 1942]. On the work on the dissertation, cf. Albrecht Beutel, *Gerhard Ebeling. Eine Biographie*. Tübingen: Mohr Siebeck 2012, 54–62.

[7] Cf. Beutel, *Gerhard Ebeling*, 66–86.

[8] Ebeling confirms this point in the interview "Gespräch über Dietrich Bonhoeffer," 650–651.

[9] *DBWE* 8, 90.

[10] *DBWE* 8, 159, 194.

would be happy if Ebeling, amongst a handful of other possible candidates, could preside over his funeral.[11]

Ebeling on Bonhoeffer

There is clearly enough evidence that Bonhoeffer thought of Ebeling as an exceptionally gifted theologian and pastor. But what does Ebeling reveal of Bonhoeffer's influence on him? How explicit is Ebeling on the significance that Bonhoeffer may have had in shaping his own theological development and life? The answer, in short, is that both Ebeling and his interpreters leave no doubt that Bonhoeffer had indeed a significant influence on Ebeling's theological development. In his masterful recent biography of Ebeling, Beutel dedicates several pages exclusively to Bonhoeffer's influence on Ebeling. Beutel suggests that Bonhoeffer left a deep impression [*Prägung*] on the young Ebeling who was theologically still coming into his own. Ebeling was aware of this decisive shaping of his theology and expressed deep thankfulness for his encounter with Bonhoeffer throughout his life.[12] Let us examine some of his own affirmations.

It is curious that Ebeling did not contribute to *I Knew Dietrich Bonhoeffer*, as it includes the reflections of a number of other Finkenwalde students.[13] Nonetheless, from the many scattered references to Bonhoeffer throughout his prolific career, Ebeling does provide a very clear and decisive assessment of Bonhoeffer's influence on him. In a lecture delivered in Basel in 1960 on the theme "Hauptprobleme der protestantischen Theologie in der Gegenwart,"[14] Ebeling concludes by saying, "I mentioned at the beginning that I am grateful to a number of theological contemporaries. At the end I would at least like to mention by name two theologians who were our contemporaries. Both have understood with exceptional clarity what I am trying to say somehow more tentatively. I am thinking, as you can probably guess, but I will not go into any explanation, of Dietrich Bonhoeffer.[15]

---

[11] *DBWE* 8, 160.

[12] Beutel, *Gerhard Ebeling*, 196.

[13] Wolf-Dieter Zimmermann and Ronald Gregor Smith (eds), *I Knew Dietrich Bonhoeffer: Reminiscences by his Friends*. New York: Harper and Row Publishers, 1966.

[14] "Main Problems in Contemporary Protestant Theology."

[15] Gerhard Ebeling, *Wort und Glaube*, vol. 2, 70, my translation. The second theologian Ebeling mentions in the context of his lecture is the French priest Henri Perrin.

That missing explanation was provided in much more detail in a 1978 interview, published as "Gespräch über Dietrich Bonhoeffer."[16] The interviewer opened the conversation by reminding Ebeling that in 1951 he had self-identified as *Bonhoeffer-Schüler*[17] and asked whether he would still stand by that statement. Ebeling's answer was equally to the point. He noted that he was a Bonhoeffer-student in only a limited sense since he had other theological teachers such as Bultmann and above all Luther. If there is any person, Ebeling admits, then it was Luther who provided the theological impulses for his thinking, especially the systematic-theological and hermeneutical ones. But these remarks are not to be taken, Ebeling concludes, to infer that he would not be tremendously grateful to Bonhoeffer – humanly speaking and theologically.[18] For Ebeling, Bonhoeffer represented "an unusually ingenious combination of theology and church." Even though, as a "personality, he was not a pure academic, but an inimitable blend of academic and church person – in the best and widest sense – and a person of the world. He was extraordinarily worldly (*weltmännisch*), an accomplished piano and ping-pong player."[19]

Let us now examine in greater detail the specific theological topoi that Ebeling inherited from Bonhoeffer. In Beutel's view, there are six key areas: the genuine interconnectedness of the spiritual and the human in the documents from prison with a focus on Christology, the question of law and gospel, the correlation between gospel and religion, theological thinking in the mold of the development of the Western intellectual tradition, the Christian understanding of reality and, finally, the pinnacle of all theological work in the act of preaching.[20] Let us now turn to some of these and other theological topoi and examine how Ebeling formulated and reformulated the topoi as central building blocks in his own emerging theological work.

Hermeneutics

As we noted above, when Bonhoeffer "discovered Ebeling" he convinced the Confessing Church leadership to grant Ebeling a leave of absence from pastoral work in order to write a dissertation. The firstfruits of Ebeling's

---

16   "Conversation About Dietrich Bonhoeffer." See note 3.
17   Eberhard Bethge, *Theologian, Christian, Man of his Time. A Biography*, translated and revised by Victoria Barnett. Minnesota: Fortress Press 2000, 889.
18   Cf. Ebeling, *Wort und Glaube*, vol. 4, 647.
19   Ebeling, *Wort und Glaube*, vol. 4, 653.
20   Ebeling, *Wort und Glaube*, vol. 4, 198–201.

theological output was published as *Evangelische Evangelienauslegung: Eine Untersuchung zu Luthers Hermeneutik.*[21] As the subtitle indicates, Ebeling thought of his dissertation as a contribution to hermeneutics, a topic Bonhoeffer was keenly interested in during the Finkenwalde years. In a letter to Erwin Sutz, in October 1936, he says that he was in the process of finishing "his book," a veiled reference to *Discipleship*. Then he continues to remark, "I would really like to try my hand at a book on hermeneutics. There seems to me to be a very great gap here."[22]

What do we know of Bonhoeffer's position on hermeneutics? Wilhelm Rott, one of students who belonged to the inner circle of Finkenwaldian brothers, notes: "Like Karl Barth whose "every word" he had read, Bonhoeffer approached the texts as a dogmatist and a preacher; the question of method hardly arose at that time. All the same, he was acquainted with the idea and matter of hermeneutics – not every theologian of those times knew the word – he was reading Hofmann's *Hermeneutics*. Bonhoeffer was determined to make the texts speak to our time."[23]

The key to Bonhoeffer's understanding of hermeneutics lies in the phrase "to make the texts speak to our time." Like Barth, Bonhoeffer went consciously beyond the confines of the historic-critical method and as early as 1925 called for a *philosophical-methodological* interpretation of the biblical texts.[24] In his 1932–1933 lecture on creation and sin,[25] Bonhoeffer understood his task as providing a *theological* explication of Genesis 1–3. In other words, for Bonhoeffer the task of hermeneutics is to demonstrate how, by means of theological-philosophical interpretation, the words of Scripture speak to our time as he makes clear in *Discipleship*. For a christologically shaped hermeneutic, he argues, "the problem of following Christ shows itself here to be a hermeneutical problem"[26] in that the interpreter must avoid an anachronistic comparison between Jesus and our own time and context. "Simple obedience would be misunderstood hermeneutically," Bonhoeffer cautions, "if we were to act and follow as if we were con-

---

[21] "Protestant Interpretation of the Gospels: An Examination of Luther's Hermeneutics."

[22] Cf. *DBWE* 14, 273.

[23] Zimmerman and Smith (eds), *I Knew Dietrich Bonhoeffer*, 133.

[24] See for example his essay "Paper on the Historical and Pneumatological Interpretation of Scripture," *DBWE* 9, 285–300, prepared for a seminar offered by Reinhold Seeberg in the summer semester 1925. Bonhoeffer does not employ the term "hermeneutics" but the substance of the paper examines essentially the hermeneutic question.

[25] Published as *Creation and Fall*, cf. *DBWE* 3.

[26] *DBWE* 4, 82.

temporaries of the biblical disciples."[27] The upshot of these remarks is that Bonhoeffer had a very keen perception of the need to reflect systematically on how Scripture is to be interpreted. Even though he hardly employed the term "hermeneutics," it is nonetheless the case that his attempts to correlate concepts such as epistemology, method, revelation, Holy Spirit, human word, divine utterance, etc. is at core the attempt that later became known, as Ebeling's work demonstrates, under the rubric of the hermeneutic question.

Bethge recalls explicitly that Bonhoeffer influenced Ebeling's "choice of the theme of hermeneutics."[28] Nonetheless, it is nearly impossible to decide the precise role and influence that Bonhoeffer actually had on Ebeling's lifelong interest in the subject of hermeneutics. Bethge's claim stands in tension with Ebeling's later recollection. In fact Ebeling claims that the "theme [*Thematik*] of his dissertation"[29] arose already during his first semester at the University of Marburg in 1930–1931; during four semesters at Marburg he attended the enormous number of forty-two academic offerings.[30] In the first semester, he attended a seminar that dealt with the topic of Luther's interpretation of the first commandment. Ebeling became so fascinated that he was hooked forever. In the same semester he attended Rudolf Bultmann's lecture on "Theological Encyclopaedia" with the result that the "hermeneutical question" strongly influenced him.[31] It seems fair to say that Bultmann left such a great impression on the young student, so much so that Ebeling never really lost his interest in the questions of theological method and hermeneutics. Beutel brings it to the point when he says that Ebeling's thinking was from the beginning of his theological formation characterized by the question of hermeneutics, an interest that arose during his student days with Bultmann and found further interest in the circle around Bonhoeffer.[32]

Whatever the precise impetus for Ebeling's interest in hermeneutics, the more important matter is that in all of his theological work the question of hermeneutics played a consistently significant role. Evan a cursory review of his authorship reveals the continued presence of hermeneutics at the heart of Ebeling's thought, and led him to found the "Institut für Hermeneutik" in Zurich and the monograph series "Hermeneutische Untersuch-

---

[27] *DBWE* 4, 82.
[28] Bethge, *Dietrich Bonhoeffer*, 568.
[29] Ebeling, *Wort und Glaube*, vol. 4, 651.
[30] Beutel, *Gerhard Ebeling*, 11.
[31] Cf. Ebeling, *Wort und Glaube*, vol. 4, 651.
[32] Beutel, *Gerhard Ebeling*, 258.

en zur Theologie," published to this day by Mohr Siebeck in Tübingen. For Ebeling the question of hermeneutics is the fundamental challenge to understand (existentially) the ever-changing conditions that illuminate life's meaning in the horizon of history, language, biblical text, Word of God, theology, and reality in order to remove the hindrances for faith.[33]

Law and Gospel

When Bonhoeffer and Ebeling met during the fourth course at Finkenwalde – a course, according to Bethge, "distinguished by an insatiable theological hunger"[34] – Ebeling's theological promise was duly noted by Bonhoeffer. In the context of Bonhoeffer's lecture "Concrete Ethics in Paul,"[35] and perhaps prompted by Karl Barth's reversal of the traditional Lutheran understanding of "law and gospel" into "gospel and law," the seminarians were charged to organize and present a seminar on the question of the relation between law and gospel, in particular the question of how the church should preach the law. As one of the key organizers, Ebeling's presentation was entitled "Theses on the Question: How Does the Church Preach the Law?"

The context of his theses must be placed in the larger context of the Lutheran doctrine of the *triplex uses legis*, the three-fold use of the law.[36] In order to understand Ebeling's theses, let us examine two theses in particular. The first one is III.6: "Because Christ redeemed not only the Jews but also the entire world from the power of sin and the curse of the law, the church preaches the law of Christ equally to both Jews and gentiles as those who were separated according to the plan of salvation history by the

---

[33] A still excellent introduction to Ebeling's understanding of hermeneutics is his article, "Hermeneutik," in *Die Religion in Geschichte und Gegenwart*, Tübingen: J.C.B. Mohr [Paul Siebeck], third edition 1962, vol. 3, 242–262. See also Ebeling, "Word of God and Hermeneutics," in *Word and Faith*. Philadelphia: Fortress Press 1963, 305–332.

[34] Bethge, *Dietrich Bonhoeffer*, 565.

[35] Cf. *DBWE* 14, 718–729.

[36] See Robert Kolb and Timothy J. Wengert (eds), *Book of Concord: Confessions of the Evangelical Lutheran Church*, Minneapolis: Fortress Press 2000: "The law of God is used (1) to maintain external discipline and respectability against dissolute, disobedient people and (2) to bring such people to a recognition of their sins. (3) It is also used when those who have be born again through God's Spirit, converted to the Lord, and had the veil of Moses removed for them live and walk in the law" (587.1). Ebeling sees a qualitative difference between the first use and the second/third uses of the law (see thesis IV.5). Bonhoeffer similarly separates them, cf. "The Doctrine of the Primus Usus Legis according to the Confessional Writings and their Critique," in *DBWE* 16, 584–612.

revelatory sphere of the law, but who now are equally revealed as sinners within the one effective sphere of the law and who through Christ's fulfillment of the law have become members of the same body of Christ."[37] The second thesis is IV.8: "Hence the *usus* doctrine is merely a systematic auxiliary construction."[38]

Theses III.6 articulates one of the key terms for Ebeling: that salvation must be understood in a historical-theological dynamic as "the plan of salvation history" (*Plan der Heilsgeschichte*). For Ebeling this means that law and its functions are not independent entities, but are always in relation to the other entities of that plan, namely first and foremost the gospel of the revealed Christ. In short, the coordinates of the plan of salvation are Jew, law, gentile, gospel, and all are related to Christ.

In order to understand the full impact of the use of the law within the plan of salvation, we must place it into the context of the Lutheran distinction between law and gospel. Ebeling not only follows this distinction in virtually all of his theological thinking from beginning to end, but does so more stringently than many Lutheran theologians, including Bonhoeffer. Suffice it here to note that in the concluding work of his theological oeuvre, his three-volume *Dogmatik des christlichen Glaubens*, the distinction between law and gospel receives once more a lengthy and competently argued discussion in § 35.[39] This distinction entails "the very logic of the matter of theology"[40] and is for this reason absolutely indispensable. What is at stake?

Ebeling understands law as something which is always present in the reality of life. He contends that in order to understand what law is, one "must look at the totality and reality of all life [*gesamte Lebenswirklichkeit*]."[41] What he means by the totality of all life experience is, more precisely, that law is the measure of a certain aspect of reality or the means by which a specific aspect of life can be assessed in terms of a standard. The total life-reality Ebeling has in mind is nothing but that aspect of life which he characterizes as the destruction of life; as a theological category, it is the life that is destroyed by sin. In his own words, law has the function "to preserve life under the conditions of sin which bring about the destruction of life, but also to recognize life in its state of destruction and thereby be-

---

[37] *DBWE* 14, 778.
[38] *DBWE* 14, 785.
[39] Gerhard Ebeling, "Die Unterscheidung von Gesetz und Evangelium," in *Dogmatik des christlichen Glaubens*, vol. 3, Tübingen: Mohr Siebeck, fourth edition 2012, 288–295.
[40] Ebeling, "Die Unterscheidung von Gesetz und Evangelium," 289.
[41] Ebeling, "Die Unterscheidung von Gesetz und Evangelium," 290.

come prepared for a genuine life which is being opened up by the gospel as the word of life."[42] Ultimately, Ebeling asserts, the fundamental distinction [*Fundamentalunterscheidung*] between law and gospel has its origin in the antagonism between sinner and creator and thereby in the sinner's own rejection of his creatureliness.

Law and gospel thus serve, respectively, as ciphers for finiteness/destruction/death and infinity/redemption/life. To be clear, this is not to say that law *is* in fact destruction or death and that gospel *is* the same as life. What the distinction implies rather is that law is the means by which the reality of destruction and death can be measured, can be articulated and thereby people can understand that they are inescapably part of this destructive reality. Likewise, gospel is in itself not identical with life but its words, its content points to the person Jesus of Nazareth who as the resurrected Messiah is the power that constitutes life. In other words, Ebeling follows the Lutheran theological tradition that employed the distinction between law and gospel in the conviction that it was dogmatically the most appropriate expression to address the poles of all life experiences within the matrix of the plan of salvation.

To what extent does Ebeling's position reflect that of Bonhoeffer? Although there are about two dozen references to the theme "law and gospel" in Bonhoeffer's writings, they are mostly secondary in relation to his main points. Hence, it is impossible to construct a complete systematic outline of his position and to compare it with Ebeling's view. Nonetheless, for our purposes we may draw on the essay "A Theological Position Paper on the *Primus Usus Legis*,"[43] Bonhoeffer's only substantiated discussion of the theme. While the focus of Bonhoeffer's review is on the first use of the law, he does conclude the essay with a section on "Some conclusions and questions" and a final section as an overarching "*Critique of the usus doctrine.*" This structure indicates sufficiently that Bonhoeffer judged the teaching on law and gospel at least as problematic as it was helpful for theological discourse. While he criticizes a lack of clarity, the danger of forcing a "method" on Christian proclamation, Bonhoeffer's main critique is that this traditional Lutheran teaching needs renewal [*Erneuerung*]. The lack of clarity whether there is a duplex, triplex, or quadruplex *usus legis* merely points to the confusion of key dogmatic questions. Moreover, Bonhoeffer's hesitation to adopt the distinction of law and gospel with the same enthusiasm as Ebeling is also evident in an earlier reference in the essay where he

---

[42] Ebeling, "Die Unterscheidung von Gesetz und Evangelium," 289.
[43] Cf. *DBWE* 16, 584–601.

explicitly affirms that the (Barthian) sequence of "'gospel and law' has its own validity."[44]

In that light it is certainly problematic that Ebeling imposed on Bonhoeffer the category "law and gospel" to interpret some of his writings, most notably in his essay "The 'Non-Religious Interpretation of Biblical Concepts.'" As the editors of *DBW/E* 6 discerned correctly, this category was not central to Bonhoeffer himself.[45] Although it remains a speculation, I am sceptical that Bonhoeffer would have made this category central to his thought should he have had a possibility to provide us with a full-scale outline of his theology.

The Concept of *Wirklichkeit*

What we have said so far on the themes of hermeneutics, law, and religion has in a sense a common denominator in Ebeling's concept of reality. Here we stand on surer ground than elsewhere in that we can identify Bonhoeffer's influence on Ebeling. As is well known, Bonhoeffer placed decisive significance on the notion of reality (*Wirklichkeit*); arguably, it may be the most fundamental category underlying all of his philosophy, theology, and ethics. Since for Bonhoeffer reality in its totality is constituted, centered, and fulfilled in Jesus Christ, it follows that there is no reality that is not part of the one divine reality revealed in Christ.[46] "There are not two realities, but *only one reality*, and that is God's reality revealed in Christ in the reality of the world. Partaking in Christ, we stand at the same time in the reality of God and in the reality of the world. The reality of Christ embraces the reality of the world in itself. The world has no reality of its own independent of God's revelation in Christ. It is a denial of God's revelation in Jesus Christ to wish to be "Christian" without being "worldly," or [to] wish to be worldly without seeing and recognizing the world in Christ. Hence there are not two realms, but only *the one realm of the Christ-reality* [*Christuswirklichkeit*], in which the reality of God and the reality of the world are united."[47]

---

[44] *DBWE* 16, 596.

[45] Cf. *DBWE* 6, 435.

[46] Cf. "The world has no reality of its own independent of God's revelation in Christ" (*DBWE* 6, 58).

[47] *DBWE* 6, 58. On the postmodern condition and the unifying reality of Jesus Christ, cf. Michael Trowitzsch, "Jesus Christus: Wahrheit der Kirche, Einheit der Wirklichkeit – oder: Bonhoeffer und die Postmoderne," in Michael Trowitzsch (ed),

Bonhoeffer's concept of the unity of reality is also a cornerstone for Ebeling's theology. This is made clear in a short biographical essay Ebeling wrote in 1958, simply called "Dietrich Bonhoeffer."[48] Ebeling correctly points out that Bonhoeffer's theology can only be understood as being intertwined with his life as a servant of the church to which he sacrificed his academic career. The one overarching conclusion that Ebeling draws in his reflections is that Bonhoeffer's theology was guided by the basic impulse (*Grundimpuls*) that faith has to do with reality.[49] In Ebeling's words: "faith has to do with reality. The concept of reality runs through the whole of Bonhoeffer's theological work alongside the concept of the church. It is the very fact of being engaged with the question of reality that raises... the question of the concrete reality of the church... [and] also criteria by reference to which theological thinking has to be tested in intellectual history."[50]

Ebeling examines these ideas on reality further in his essay "Theology and Reality," the published version of his inaugural lecture at the University of Zurich in 1956.[51] Although Bonhoeffer is not mentioned by name, the theological tone of the essays shows echoes of Bonhoeffer's own ideas. Ebeling affirms that theology does not only speak of "a special reality of divine revelation, a history of salvation with its saving acts. Theology surely speaks, to say the least, *also* of the world, of history, of man, and thus of all things which everyone encounters as reality... not in unrelated juxtaposition, but in such a way that speaking of God and of his revelation it has no other aim whatsoever than to speak correctly of the world, of history, of man." Like Bonhoeffer, Ebeling expends much energy in making his case that God's reality is not a mere abstract notion, but a relation that can be verified in the world, in history among human beings. It is therefore hardly surprising that Ebeling included a section in his *Dogmatik* entitled "The Reality of Redemption."[52] And, again like Bonhoeffer, Ebeling also places a significant weight on the power of the revealed and proclaimed Word of God. Against the charge that the Christian message speaks all too often past the realities of the world, Ebeling argues that "proclamation does not seek to be realized by man, but man is to be realized by the mes-

---

Über die Moderne hinaus. Theologie im Übergang. Tübingen: Mohr Siebeck 1999, 159–173.

[48] Gerhard Ebeling, *Word and Faith*, 282–287.

[49] Ebeling, *Word and Faith*, 284.

[50] Ebeling, *Word and Faith*, 284–285.

[51] Gerhard Ebeling, "Theology and Reality," in *Word and Faith*, 191–200. See also "Faith and Unbelief in Conflict about Reality," in *Word and Faith*, 374–406.

[52] Gerhard Ebeling, "Die Wirklichkeit der Versöhnung," in *Dogmatik des christlichen Glaubens*, vol. 2, Tübingen: Mohr Siebeck, fourth edition 2012, 225–228.

sage – i.e. exposed to the whole truth of reality... the message has no wish to be illuminated by our reality, but our reality is to be illuminated by the message."[53]

The Reality of Religion

To his credit, Ebeling was the first post-war theologian who took Bonhoeffer's theological statements made in his prison correspondence seriously and devoted a long essay to their interpretation. In 1955 he wrote "The Non-Religious Interpretation of Biblical Concepts"[54] and thus started a long chain of (sometimes rather curious) interpretive attempts of these – in Karl Barth's words[55] – enigmatic statements from prison.[56] Ebeling acknowledges that Bonhoeffer's initial remarks reached near "canonic status" but also warns of the danger not merely to repeat but to advance Bonhoeffer's "exciting impulse (*erregender Anstoss*)."[57] As expected, the notion of religion plays a prominent role in such a discussion; but startlingly, perhaps, Ebeling does so also by recourse to the notion of law. He asks quite insightfully whether there is a "theological category" that is "suited to define the place of religion and non-religiousness in theology?"[58] He takes the clue to understanding from Bonhoeffer's own musing: "The Pauline question of whether περιτομή is a condition for justification is today, in my opinion, the question of whether religion is a condition for salvation. Freedom from περιτομή is also freedom from religion."[59]

Ebeling grants that "Bonhoeffer sensed with a sure instinct the [theological] category" that was necessary to unravel the question of why religion cannot be a condition for salvation in view of the nature of the gospel; un-

---

[53] Ebeling, *Word and Faith*, 198.

[54] Ebeling, *Word and Faith*, 98–161.

[55] Karl Barth, *Offene Briefe 1945–1968*, Gesamtausgabe V 15. Zurich: TVZ 1984, 325. Elsewhere Ebeling remarks: "Die bekannten Stichworte Dietrich Bonhoeffers wie 'Ende der Religion,' 'mündige Welt' und 'religionsloses Christentum' waren bei ihm selbst das gärende Produkt einer Mischung der Barthschen Antithetik von Glaube und Religion mit einer geistesgeschichtlichen Analyse im Hinblick auf das bereits säkularisierte neuzeitliche Religionsverständnis;" see Ebeling, *Wort und Glaube*, vol. 3. Tübingen: J. C. B. Mohr [Paul Siebeck] 1975, 420–421; see also 546–547.

[56] See for a discussion see Ralf Wüstenberg, *A Theology of Life: Dietrich Bonhoeffer's Religionless Christianity*. Grand Rapids: Eerdmans 1998.

[57] Cf. "Profanität und Geheimnis," in *Wort und Glaube*, vol. 2, 184.

[58] Ebeling, *Word and Faith*, 141.

[59] *DBWE* 8, 365–366.

fortunately, "he did not make thoroughgoing use of it after all."[60] Just as religion cannot be a condition for salvation, Bonhoeffer says elsewhere, so likewise biblical concepts "must now be interpreted in a way that does not make religion the condition for faith (cf. the περιτομή in Paul)."[61] All of this amounts for Ebeling to the "decisive starting-point from which to reach a comprehensive theological solution of the problem of non-religious interpretation. The analogy with circumcision points to the law."[62]

At first glance, the suggestion to make sense of biblical concepts with non-religious language in a world come of age with the category of a concept that had its origin nearly five hundred years ago in Reformation theology seems striking, to say the least. And today in our postmodern context, where the axis of being and action seems to be autonomy, will the category of law not be merely a reinstatement of heteronomy? The answer depends crucially on Ebeling's understanding of law, or as noted above, more precisely, on his distinction between law and gospel. Ebeling himself offers us several points of clarification. First, he says that "religious interpretation is interpretation based on law. Non-religious interpretation means interpretation that distinguishes law and Gospel."[63] In other words, neither religion nor the law are categories that are able to yield a christological, concrete interpretation of the faith, however much they try. Second, Ebeling warns his readers that "introduction of the concept of law naturally does not imply the identification of religion and law."[64] To prove his point, Ebeling asserts conversely that religionlessness is not the same as lawlessness, a position he attributes to Bonhoeffer. Third, "the introduction of the concept of law implies rather that the phenomenon of religion... has its place in theology within the problem of the law."[65] But since law and gospel are essentially a unity and since the law is only understood in the light of the gospel, it follows that religion can likewise only be understood in the light of the gospel.

In what sense does Ebeling interpret the dynamic of law/gospel as the appropriate category to make sense of Bonhoeffer's ideas on religion/religionlessness? Ebeling argues that the preaching of the gospel necessarily includes the proclamation of the law. Without the proclamation of the law, the gospel is no longer gospel; otherwise the gospel itself becomes a *lex*

---

[60] Ebeling, *Word and Faith*, 141.
[61] *DBWE* 8, 430.
[62] Ebeling, *Word and Faith*, 141.
[63] Ebeling, *Word and Faith*, 142; translation slightly altered.
[64] Ebeling, *Word and Faith*, 142.
[65] Ebeling, *Word and Faith*, 142.

nova. As we saw above, the proclamation of the law and gospel is always a matter of addressing the reality of our world and thus Ebeling asks: "What do Bonhoeffer's observations on religion and non-religiousness contribute towards the problem of the preaching of the law, or as we can now also say, of the coming to expression of the *reality that concerns us*?"[66] Ebeling proposes two ways in which Bonhoeffer does this:

1. "The basic structure of 'religion' is the supplanting of reality by God."[67] For Ebeling this is the common denominator for everything Bonhoeffer postulates about religion. Concrete examples are: the two spheres of religion, making room for God, God the stop-gap, exploiting human weakness to create room for God, understanding God epistemologically and metaphysically, individual salvation, inwardness, and many others.[68] The problem is at hand: religious efforts try to add an element to faith and the practice of faith that is otherwise seen as incomplete. Because God's mysterious being is not enough, the believer tries to add another dimension of reality to his/her faith or experience of God. But any endeavour that supplants reality through adding God ultimately "misses both the right understanding of the law and also the right understanding of the Gospel."[69]

2. "The basic structure of 'non-religiousness'... is coping with reality without God."[70] The reverse of supplanting reality through God is simply to subtract God from reality. A nonreligious person "does not have God as compensation for his weakness, as the Beyond over his boundaries, as prolongation of the world, as extension of reality. He is wholly dependent on this world, utterly exposed to the pressure of reality and therewith to its claims."[71] This nonreligious person is the one come of age and has no recourse to God as the stop-gap, but is ultimately – if intellectually honest – all alone in his/her reality.

Even such an abbreviated sketch of Ebeling's unravelling of Bonhoeffer's statements on religion and nonreligiousness indicate that the nonreligious person can ultimately also not escape the law. As Ebeling admits, such an assertion is of course only possible as a theological assertion.[72] Nonetheless, every nonreligious person's experience of reality is such that it contains experiences of the destruction of life. As we said above, the law is

---

[66] Ebeling, *Word and Faith*, 148; italics added.
[67] Ebeling, *Word and Faith*, 148.
[68] Cf. Ebeling, *Word and Faith*, 148–150.
[69] Ebeling, *Word and Faith*, 150.
[70] Ebeling, *Word and Faith*, 150.
[71] Ebeling, *Word and Faith*, 154.
[72] Cf. Ebeling, *Word and Faith*, 155.

exactly the benchmark of the reality that uncovers the destructive side of life, the side marred by the reality of sin.[73] Moreover, since law and gospel are a dialectical unity, it follows in Ebeling's theological discourse that law and gospel must equally be proclaimed and addressed to both the religious and nonreligious person.

Ebeling's lens – some may call it imposition – of law and gospel through which he examined Bonhoeffer's statements from prison may seem at times questionable, perhaps even forceful. Nonetheless, the appreciation that Ebeling has for his former teacher are beyond doubt. In almost poetic language he addresses all theologians interested in the subject. "It is necessary to emphasize that the expression non-religious interpretation was not coined in order to loosen the reins of theological study but to tighten them, not in order that the traditional biblical and theological concepts could be cheerfully thrown overboard but in order to regain them, not in order to succumb to a snobbish freebooter jargon but to strive for new expression of the Word of God, not in order to play off life against doctrine, action against thought, but to incorporate life really in doctrine and action really in thought, not purely and simply in order to enable the non-believer to understand but in order that we ourselves, we theologians, should come to the right understanding, not in order that we should now proclaim non-religious interpretation as Gospel but in order that, if we should prove appropriate, we should really proclaim the Gospel in non-religious interpretation?"[74]

Theological Language

Very briefly, one final point. In his essay "The 'Non-Religious Interpretation of Biblical Concepts,'" Ebeling notes in passing that the entire dialectic of law and gospel raises other theological and ontological questions, such as "the connexion between being, word and language."[75] Given that, in good Lutheran fashion, Ebeling assigns the Word of God a central place in his theological conception, coupled with his interest in hermeneutical theology, it is almost predictable that the subject of theological language also figures in his discourse. Already in the early stages of his career, Ebeling wrote essays such as "Word of God and Hermeneutics," "Rudimentary Reflexions on Speaking Responsibly of God," and "Worldly Talk of

---

[73] Ebeling, *Wort und Glaube*, vol. 2, 67.
[74] Ebeling, *Word and Faith*, 128.
[75] Ebeling, *Word and Faith*, 143.

God."[76] As these titles indicate, from the beginning Ebeling saw it as a key theological task to reflect on how theology employs language, even "worldly talk" (Bonhoeffer is not mentioned in that essay), to speak responsibly of God in the world.

What precisely he has in mind, may best be seen in one of the many section on *Sprache* in his *Dogmatik des christlichen Glaubens*. In a section with the telling heading "The basic human constitution as language-constitution" (*Die Grundsituation des Menschen als Sprachsituation*), Ebeling (perhaps following Karl Jaspers) defines the basic human situation as one in which the ability to speak is constitutive; speaking is our distinct basic human quality. In his own words: "the basic human situation is a language-situation… because in it occur various language-events [*Sprachgeschehen*]."[77] Concretely, this means for Ebeling that we find in the sphere of language our "ultimate being-encountered [*letztinstanzliches Angegangensein*],"[78] and this in three distinct ways. In our being-encountered by language-events, we are called to respond to the encounter and can do so by negating, corresponding, or making a promise.

Theological language, as the language of the Word of God, is always embedded and directly related to the basic human constitution as language-constitution. Hearing and speaking about God is the ultimate human encounter of a person vis-à-vis his or her total reality (*Wirklichkeit im ganzen*) and challenges the entirety of one's life. In a language-event the listener is called to respond, to say yes or no. The criterion is always how the theological language-event is able to address the basic human situation and makes room for faith, hope, and love.[79]

Conclusion

Both Dietrich Bonhoeffer and Gerhard Ebeling were Lutheran theologians. Bonhoeffer ends his lecture on "The History of Twentieth-Century Systematic Theology" with the question "*Who will show us Luther?*"[80] and Ebeling became a life-long admirer of Luther since his first semester at the University of Marburg. It seems to me that Ebeling was the more traditional Lutheran thinker. While he held to the theological staples of Lutheran

---

[76] See *Word and Faith*, respectively 305–332, 333–353, 354–362.
[77] Ebeling, *Dogmatik des christlichen Glaubens*, vol. 2, 189.
[78] Ebeling, *Dogmatik des christlichen Glaubens*, vol. 2, 189.
[79] Ebeling, *Dogmatik des christlichen Glaubens*, vol. 2, 191.
[80] *DBWE* 11, 244.

theology, such as the distinction of law and gospel, the four *solas*, and the two-kingdom doctrine, Bonhoeffer seemed to have been more willing to charter new paths on the old, proven Lutheran doctrines. Perhaps one case in point that illustrates the difference between Bonheoffer and Ebeling is their conception of reality. Both agree on the absolute centrality of the concept in terms of theological discourse, but Bonhoeffer was rejecting the traditional Lutheran understanding of the two-kingdom doctrine, mainly on theological grounds but conceivably also because of the political misuse of the doctrine by Nazi ideologues.

More important, however, is the fact that both Bonhoeffer and Ebeling were gifted and keen theological thinkers. What unites them is the attempt to locate their theological conceptions in the real world, in the midst of real people with real needs. To both thinkers it was absolutely crucial *that their theology was at the right place at the right time* – whether it be in prison, in the clutches of a dictatorship, on the pulpit, or in the halls of the academy. Ebeling especially laments the fact that all too often theologians are in the wrong place with their theology. In short, Ebeling pleads that contemporary theology be in that place where Jesus was, namely with human beings to whom the gospel belongs.[81] Bonhoeffer, I think, would wholeheartedly agree.

Finally, and most significant, both Bonhoeffer and Ebeling were independent theological thinkers. Even though both admit that Luther played a decisive influence on their theological development, as did Barth for Bonhoeffer and Bultmann for Ebeling, and still others for both of them, the hallmark of a good theologian is not merely the acknowledgement of significant forebears in the guild, but the freshness of independent thinking in (necessarily) a context that differs from that of the forebears. No theologian wants to be a mere parrot announcing what others have already announced loud and clear. The genius of both Bonhoeffer and Ebeling was precisely that: They gratefully acknowledged their theological forefathers, build on the best of their ideas, but were fiercely independent when they were convinced the context required that they do theology precisely in the place where Jesus was, with real human beings with real needs and hopes.

---

[81] Cf. Ebeling, *Wort und Glaube*, vol. 2, 69.

9. Bonhoeffer and Philosophy

Bonhoeffer – A Philosopher?

Most scholars consider Dietrich Bonhoeffer to be among the foremost theological thinkers of the twentieth century, but few would count him among philosophical thinkers. Even after six decades of Bonhoeffer research, scholars have paid relatively little attention to the philosophical influences that shaped Bonhoeffer's intellectual formation. In this regard, the state of research resembles an unplowed field. To be sure, there are exceptions. Nonetheless, Wayne Floyd's characterization of the state of philosophical research on Bonhoeffer is fitting. When it comes to understanding "Bonhoeffer's unique contributions" to questions of philosophical theology, notes Floyd, "it is not so much that the philosophical influences on Bonhoeffer's early work have been misrepresented as that they have not yet been reconstructed in anything approaching a comprehensive manner."[1] The issue as such is that without a proper reconstruction of the philosophical influences on Bonhoeffer's thought his theology is in danger to be disfigured and misrepresented. The issue, therefore, is not primarily that there is a dearth of scholarly work examining these questions, but that the lack of such works portrays Bonhoeffer's person and his theology in a one-sided manner.[2]

There is evidence that Bonhoeffer's philosophical interests emerged already in his youth, but especially during his studies at the universities of Tübingen and Berlin and his relatively short academic career at the latter institution. His deeper interests in philosophy can be traced to the first semesters in Tübingen. According to Eberhard Bethge, Bonhoeffer attended lectures and seminars on philosophy.[3] During his years in Berlin, his

---

[1] *DBWE* 2, 8.

[2] Cf. Charles Marsh, *Reclaiming Dietrich Bonhoeffer. The Promise of His Theology.* Oxford: Oxford University Press, x.

[3] Eberhard Bethge, *Dietrich Bonhoeffer. Theologian, Christian, Man of his Time. A Biography*, translated and revised by Victoria Barnett. Minnesota: Fortress Press 2000, 53–56.

interests in philosophy did not subside, as can be reconstructed from his letters. Alongside a number of theologians, Bonhoeffer studied independently Kant, Husserl and "Hegel's Bestimmung des objectives Geistes."[4] In addition Bonhoeffer attended a lecture on epistemology and seminar on the topic of freedom and necessity in the philosopher Heinrich Maier, a lecture on the "History of Logic" with Rieffert and a seminar with Eduard Spranger on the theme of "Philosophy of Culture."[5]

Bonhoeffer's enduring interest in philosophy manifests itself in his *Habilitationsschrift*, *Act and Being*, especially in the subtitle *Transcendental Philosophy and Ontology in Systematic Theology*. The entire work is the attempt of the young theologian to demonstrate the relevance of philosophical questions for systematic theology. Following his *Habilitation*, there are two more indicators of Bonhoeffer's philosophic interest. The first is his inaugural lecture at the end of July 1930 and the second a seminar he offered on Hegel's philosophy of religion during the summer semester 1933. Unfortunately, the only record of the seminar is a reconstructed text based on student notes.[6]

The specific philosophical questions that interested Bonhoeffer vis-à-vis systematic theology we will now examine more closely in the following sections, in such a way that we will focus on the particular philosophers who shaped his theological thinking the most.

Classical Philosophers

Like all thinkers before him fascinated with the intellectual history of the west, Bonhoeffer too was drawn to Greek philosophy, principally its two chief representatives, Plato and Aristotle, and by extension to the Christian thinkers shaped by them, namely Augustine and Thomas of Aquinas.

Aristotle. Bonhoeffer discussed Aristotle already in his first academic work, *Sanctorum Communio*. The first question of the dissertation, "the question of the philosophical foundation for a Christian doctrine of person and community"[7] leads Bonhoeffer to an examination of Aristotle's concept of person. Drawing on Windelband's *A History of Philosophy*, Bonhoeffer notes the following: for Aristotle human beings are "persons" by

---

[4] Bethge, *Dietrich Bonhoeffer*, 73.
[5] Bethge, *Dietrich Bonhoeffer*, 72.
[6] Cf. Ilse Tödt, *Dietrich Bonhoeffers Hegel-Seminar 1933. Nach Aufzeichnungen von Ferenc Lehel*. Munich: Chr. Kaiser 1988.
[7] *DBWE* 1, 41, note 20.

virtue of their essential belonging to the universal reason of the species. Just like the divinity participates in *nous* (mind) so likewise the human species and the individual human person participate in nous. Accordingly, for Aristotle, the essential human being is "a ζῷον πολιτικόν [political animal]."[8] This means that human beings can exercise their minds only within the state; "thus by definition the state is to be regarded as prior to all individual existence."[9]

For Bonhoeffer, related is Aristotle's concept of God. God's essential being (*Sein*) is his thinking, but not in the sense of a personal being or a personal concept of God. Rather, God's thinking "is the nature of the universal, highest form of thinking" void of "any fundamental voluntarism." Hence, Aristotle has an "intellectualist-monotheistic concept of God."[10] Both Aristotelian concepts – those of person and divinity – are too limited for Bonhoeffer in order to be fruitful for his theology of sociality.

In *Creation and Fall* Bonhoeffer employs another fundamental Aristotelian concept. In his interpretation of Gen. 3:1, regarding the question of the serpent ("Did God say..."), Bonhoeffer comments: "in this question what is possible [Möglichkeit] is played off against reality [Wirklichkeit], and what is possible undermines reality. In relation of human beings to God, however, there are no possibilities: there is only reality."[11] Here Bonhoeffer introduces the Aristotelian distinction of potentiality/actuality (δύναμις/ἐνέργεια) into theological discourse. The importance of this distinction was already hinted at by Bonhoeffer in *Sanctorum Communio* but its full significance came to the fore only in his dialogue with Heidegger (see below) in *Act and Being*.

Plato. Bonhoeffer's engagement with Platonic philosophy is not substantial. We find neither in *Sanctorum Communio* nor in *Act and Being* an independent assessment of the great Greek philosopher. For the most part Bonhoeffer repeats the positions that he gleaned from the secondary literature he had surveyed. Plato is referenced only occasionally in footnotes and seems to have no significant impact on Bonhoeffer's theology as a whole.

An important aspect of the Platonic tradition, more precisely Middle Platonism, is the distinction between the existence and being of God. This distinction was taken over by Thomas Aquinas and briefly discussed by Bonhoeffer. The Greek terms ὕπαρξις (existence) and οὐσία (being) are in-

---

8 *DBWE* 1, 35, note 2. Cf. Aristotle, *Pol.* 1253a 3.
9 *DBWE* 1, 35, note 2.
10 *DBWE* 1, 35, note 2.
11 *DBWE* 3, 108–109.

troduced by Aquinas into his theological discussions, but he does so in terms of their Latin equivalents *essentia* (essence) and *esse* (being). As we noted, Bonhoeffer attempts to construct an ontological foundation for a theology of being that does justice to both his concepts of person and God. In this regard, he mentions "the Thomist principle of the *analogia entis.*"[12] While *essentia* and *esse* coincide in God, because "God essentially is always what God should be,"[13] they are separate in human beings. But it would be wrong to understand that separation as if "the *esse* of human beings is divine and the *essentia* nondivine, or the reverse." Rather, "the ontological relationship of human beings to God lies in the entirety of the *essentia-esse* difference of human beings and not the *essentia-esse* identity of God." [14] The analogical relationship is precisely in that human beings are in "becoming" while God is in "being." God "is the eternal 'is' that abides in all 'was' and 'will be'."[15] Even though, God is not exhausted in his being and neither is being in God. God is always his own "absolute originality" (*absolute Eigenständigkeit*) just as human beings have their "relative but authentic reality" (*relative Eigenwirklichkeit*) vis-à-vis God.[16]

Bonhoeffer's understanding of the divine-human relation confronts him with the question of possibility in theology. On the one hand, the Thomist doctrine of being opens up space for the full creatureliness of human beings, that is to say that there is a genuine continuity between human beings in *status corruptionis* and in *status gratiae*. On the other hand, there is the difficulty to arrive at a genuine concept of sin and grace. Why is this so? The issue is that human beings who live in the tension of the *essentia-esse* dynamic still have some innate possibility to resolve this tension in favour of the *essentia-esse* identity.[17] The ensuing theological predicament is that "human existence is, once again, comprehensible through itself and also has access to God."[18] To what extent the young Bonhoeffer interpreted Aquinas correctly and was able to integrate these matters properly into his own philosophical theology remains a question that has not yet been satisfactorily answered in Bonhoeffer scholarship.[19]

---

[12] *DBWE* 2, 73.
[13] *DBWE* 2, 73.
[14] *DBWE* 2, 73.
[15] *DBWE* 2, 73.
[16] Cf. *DBWE* 2, 74.
[17] Cf. *DBWE* 2, 75.
[18] *DBWE* 2, 75.
[19] Cf. Barry Harvey, "Augustine and Thomas Aquinas in the Theology of Dietrich Bonhoeffer," in Peter Frick (ed), *Bonhoeffer's Intellectual Formation*. Tübingen: Mohr Siebeck 2008, 11–29.

Immanuel Kant

As noted above, the young student Bonhoeffer did not only attend formal academic lectures and seminars on philosophy but also did not spare the effort to study philosophical literature on his own. An example is Bonhoeffer's study of Kant's *Critique of Pure Reason*, as can be seen from a letter of the Tübingen student.[20] It is impossible, however, to say with certainty that Bonhoeffer studied all of Kant's works. The editor of *Akt und Sein*, Hans-Richard Reuter, maintains in the Afterword of that volume that Bonhoeffer's knowledge of European philosophy was second-hand and that he gained his knowledge of Kant from the interpretation of the philosopher Hinrich Knittermeyer.[21] Nonetheless, when Bonhoeffer was working on the manuscript of *Ethics* in Ettal, he asked his friend Bethge to send him a six-volume edition of Kant's works.[22] Whether Bonhoeffer worked his way through these volumes, and if so, to what extent and depth he did we can no longer ascertain.

There are two instances in *Ethics* in which Bonhoeffer deals with Kant directly. First, Bonhoeffer rejects Kant's dictum "truthfulness as a principle"[23] as a grotesque claim. Kant's example – to speak the truth, when asked by a murderer, whether one is hiding the person the murderer pursues – destroys the legitimate claim that God and my neighbour poses for my ethical responsibility.[24] Second, Bonhoeffer wants to correct Kant's attitude toward prayer. According to Kant, his experience of shame when he prays is an argument against prayer. Bonhoeffer counters that "by its very nature, prayer belongs in a locked room."[25] There is a further reference to Kant in *Ethics*, namely Bonhoeffer's freely paraphrased citation from *Critique of Practical Reason*, to the effect that "the maxim of an action" should become "a principle of universal law."[26] Bonhoeffer rejects such a criterion because it does not help the real person before God.

Given the context of the philosophical questions discussed in *Sanctorum Communio* and *Act and Being*, it comes of no surprise that Bonhoeffer was especially attentive to Kant's epistemology. Bonhoeffer suggests that the task of theology is to engage the philosophical question of the possibility

---

[20] Cf. *DBW* 9 63.

[21] Cf. *DBW* 2, 166.

[22] Cf. *DBW* 16, 81. Bonhoeffer was asking for Wilhelm Weischedel (ed), *Immanuel Kant. Werke in sechs Bänden*. Wiesbaden/Darmstadt: Insel 1956–1964.

[23] *DBWE* 6, 279.

[24] Cf. *DBWE* 6, 279–280.

[25] *DBWE* 6, 305.

[26] *DBWE* 6, 99.

of human understanding by means of reason. This philosophical, epistemological question is largely shaped by Kant's concept of the person. For
Kant, fundamental is the knowing I as the starting point for philosophy.
The synthesis of the I-You relation and the subject-object relation are overcome in an intellectualist view of the spirit.[27] In spite of a person's participation in "universal reason" Kant's philosophy does not provide a genuine
epistemology of "concrete community, since his concept of the person ultimately remains apersonal as well."[28] The same may be said about Kant's
"obvious flaw" in understanding the church. According to Kant, Bonhoeffer argues, the empirical form of the church is merely "a manifestation
of the normal, ideal church of the future… unattainable in this world."[29]
Kant also fails to understand the Christian concept of sin and the empirical
reality of the church because he does not rigorously apply his concept of
"radical evil" also to the empirically sinful – and not just imperfect – nature of the church.[30]

In *Act and Being*, Bonhoeffer engages the philosophical master in a rather peculiar manner. Kant, claims Bonhoeffer, is the one who is responsible
for all the philosophical questions examined vis-à-vis theology in *Act and
Being*. Concretely, Bonhoeffer attempts a clarification of theological concepts that do justice to both a transcendental-philosophical and an ontological interpretation of theological concepts. That is to say, Bonhoeffer is
set on demonstrating theologically the meaning of "the being of God" in
revelation and the relation between faith as act and revelation as being, or
"how human beings stand in light of revelation."[31] In this regard, Bonhoeffer admits in a footnote, that his entire Kant interpretation is somewhat stylized. He presents Kant as the transcendental philosopher "which
he never was entirely, even though in our view he intended to be."[32]

Bonhoeffer expresses the key question for transcendental thinking
within the context of act and being in these terms: the basic epistemological position "is the attempt of the I to understand itself. I reflect on myself;
I and myself move apart and come together again."[33] Bonhoeffer – most
likely following his teacher Wilhelm Lütgert – welcomes Kant's insight "to

---

[27] Cf. *DBWE* 1, 42.
[28] *DBWE* 1, 197, note 68.
[29] *DBWE* 1, 210–211.
[30] *DBWE* 1, 212.
[31] *DBWE* 2, 27–28; emphasis original.
[32] *DBWE* 2, 33, note 1.
[33] *DBWE* 2, 33; cf. Christiane Tietz-Steiding, *Bonhoeffers Kritik der Vernunft*. Beiträge zur historischen Theologie 112. Tübingen: Mohr Siebeck 1999, 24–35.

place reason within its rights precisely by defining its limit."[34] Because reason encounters its own limits it becomes its own crisis and is placed in its "primordial legitimacy." Expressed differently, "human beings understand themselves... not from the transcendent but from themselves, from reason."[35] This "internal contradiction" cannot be overcome by any transcendental epistemology.

Georg Wilhelm Friedrich Hegel

Bonhoeffer's interest in Hegel, similar to that of Kant, was limited to his academic years, that is to say, mainly to his academic works *Sanctorum Communio*, *Act and Being* and a seminar on Hegel offered by Bonhoeffer in the summer semester 1933. One of the participants of the seminar, the Hungarian student Ferenc Lehel, remembers the following of Bonhoeffer's approach to Hegel. "Bonhoeffer las die Philosophie Hegels als Theologe, und zwar als ekklesiologisch eingestellter Theologe. Er suchte im Philosophischen das Theologische ... In einem bestimmten Sinne behandelte Bonhoeffer Hegel eklektisch, indem er die Religions-Philosophie Hegels prüfte und das hervorhob, was ihm, dem Theologen, wertvoll erschien. Das war spannend für uns Studenten."[36] Moreover, judging from Bonhoeffer's edition of the works of Hegel, it is clear that he studied Hegel in great detail.[37]

What themes in Hegel interested the theologian Bonhoeffer in *Sanctorum Communio*? For one, it was Hegel's "monumental perception" that "the principle of spirit is something objective, extending beyond everything individual – that is that there is an objective spirit, the spirit of sociality which is distinct in itself from all individual spirit."[38] According to Bonhoeffer, Hegel maintained a sense for the concrete forms of life of the individual person, but only as a form of universal spirit. But everything hinges for Bonhoeffer on the spirit of sociality. This spirit is in its essence beyond individualism and manifests itself as the Hegelian objective spirit concretely in human history and communal life. Moreover, the sociological concept of unity is anchored theologically in an "immanentist concept of God or the identification of human and divine spirit."[39] Accordingly, "once the

---

[34] *DBWE* 2, 34.
[35] *DBWE* 2, 36.
[36] Ilse Tödt (ed), *Dietrich Bonhoeffers Hegel-Seminar 1933*, 10.
[37] Cf. Tödt (ed), *Dietrich Bonhoeffers Hegel-Seminar 1933*, 22.
[38] *DBWE* 1, 74.
[39] *DBWE* 1, 197, note 68.

human spirit had become aware in Christ of its identity with the divine
Spirit, and through the death of death itself finitude had been destroyed,
what has become manifest in Christ must now be realized effective in the
church."[40] Hence, Bonhoeffer rewrites Hegel's "God existing as community"[41] as "Christ existing as church-community,"[42] most likely under the
influence of his doctoral supervisor Reinhold Seeberg.[43] In church community individuals are united in the unity of the spirit. The awareness of
both the spirit and the unity becomes effective and concrete in faith. In
other words, faith in its historical dimension is the starting point for the
spirit.[44]

But precisely at that point – at the historical concreteness of the objective
spirit in the church-community – locates Bonhoeffer the weakness of Hegel's conceptualization. Just as Kant before him, Hegel likewise overlooks
the fact that the community of saints always has been and always remains
a community of sinners.[45] In the end it is not simply the matter that human
reason is somehow able to overcome sin and that the absolute spirit enters
into the subjective spirits and thus manifests itself in an objective community of spirit. From a theological point of view the issue is that sin can only
be overcome in faith: as the church of word and faith "we can see nothing
but our sin, and accept our holiness in faith."[46]

Bonhoeffer sees a further weakness in Hegel's philosophy in his conception of God. In his "Lectures on Christology" in the summer semester of
1933 Bonhoeffer accuses Hegel of Docetism. In Hegel's penchant for the
perfected philosophical system, Bonhoeffer argues, God's appearance "is
necessarily the taking shape of the idea... God appears by necessity. That is
the nature of God. God is only God by appearing in history. It is precisely
this *necessity* of the incarnation, God's becoming human, that is dangerous. It makes a principle out of something that cannot and should not be a
necessity."[47] When Bonhoeffer discusses Hegel in *Act and Being*, initially
he affirms that "Idealism, especially Hegel, actually appear to have reached
or attained a synopsis of act and being that would be capable of satisfying

---

[40] *DBWE* 1, 198, note 68.
[41] Cf. Georg W. F. Hegel, *Lectures on the Philosophy of Religion*, volume 3. Edited by
Peter C. Hodgson. Berkeley and Los Angeles: University of California Press 1984, 331
and *DBWE* 1, 198, note 68.
[42] Cf. *DBWE* 1, 121, 141, 189, 190, 199, 207.
[43] Cf. *DBWE* 1, 198, note 218.
[44] Cf. *DBWE* 1, 198–199.
[45] Cf. *DBWE* 1, 212.
[46] *DBWE* 1, 212.
[47] *DBWE* 12, 337.

the demands of the problem," but immediately Bonhoeffer retracts his approval because idealistic philosophers falter "on the resistance of their own reality... Hegel wrote a philosophy of angels, but not of human beings as Dasein [*menschliches Dasein*]. Even the philosopher simply is not in full possession of the spirit."[48] Bonhoeffer critiques Idealism, that is to say Hegel, because "the movement of the spirit is turned in upon itself"[49] and the spirit wants to understand itself out of itself. But this is humanly impossible because sin turns the spirit upon itself (*ratio in se ipsam incurva*; Bonhoeffer alters the Lutheran dictum and replaces *cor* with *ratio*) and thus the spirit itself is unable to come to a proper self-understanding. For Bonhoeffer the outcome is clear: people who "need only come to themselves, in order to be in God, are doomed to hideous disillusion in the experience of being-, persisting-, and ending-up-turned-in-upon-themselves utterly – the experience of utmost loneliness in its tormenting desolation and sterility."[50] From an epistemological point of view human beings always remain with themselves and cannot do otherwise but attempt to understand themselves by their encapsulating reason. Bonhoeffer called this kind of self-directed thinking "religion."[51] It remains religion even if, to speak with Hegel, it seeks to open up space for revelation by means of reason.

In terms of the ontological question of the act-being problem Bonhoeffer credits Hegel to have understood its significance and enthroned ontology again after Kant had dethroned it. For in a *genuine* ontology being is prior to consciousness, that is to say that the task of ontology is to demonstrate real being [*Seiendes*] outside of human consciousness and the sphere of limited reason.[52]

Friedrich Nietzsche

It seems likely that Bonhoeffer studied Nietzsche more than any other philosopher, especially in view of Nietzsche's attempt to lead Christianity *ad absurdum*. The young Bonhoeffer had a first encounter with Nietzsche's ideas already during his years at Grunewald Gymnasium. One of his teachers, Martin Havenstein, was interested in Nietzsche and in 1922 pub-

---

[48] *DBWE* 1, 42.
[49] *DBWE* 1, 41.
[50] *DBWE* 1, 42.
[51] Cf. *DBWE* 2, 52.
[52] Cf. *DBWE* 2, 59.

lished the work *Nietzsche als Erzieher*.[53] We also know that Bonhoeffer owned eight of the 16 volumes of the edition that Nietzsche himself had published during his lifetime.[54] Bethge notes in retrospect that the young Bonhoeffer read Nietzsche with great interest.

In *The Anti-Christ*, Nietzsche attacks Christianity without restraint. Christendom, he sneers, is an expression of a life of weakness, the lowly and everything that failed. Christendom presupposes an ideal but is actually in opposition to all the primordial instincts of a life of strength.[55] For this reason Christianity has become a "religion of pity." Pity robs life of its emotional strength because it is contrary to the energy of life and the higher feelings that spring from it. Christianity leads to depression. The human being loses strength when showing pity.[56] The outcome of Christian pity is devastating. It brings about "a total ... life denying tendency."[57]

The Christian tendency to deny life corresponds further to the Christian notion of God. For Nietzsche "God is in contradiction to life,"[58] precisely because the God of Christianity is in enmity against the will to live, nature and life itself. God becomes a formula for the denial of earthly life and a cheap comfort for the life beyond. Such a negative concept of God, Nietzsche thinks, has unavoidable consequences for a distorted reality of daily life. The teachings of Christianity have little in common with the reality of the world. God, soul, spirit are imaginary causes; sin, redemption, grace, punishment, forgiveness are imaginary effects.[59]

Bonhoeffer discusses Nietzsche's ideas several times in his Berlin University lecture "The History of Twentieth-Century Systematic Theology" during the winter semester 1931–1932. "Nietzsche," ventures the young lecturer, "rejected Christianity entirely, as the most disastrous inhibition of autonomous culture. For him, compassion is basically and principally unnatural in human beings, and he considered it the principle of Christian ethics."[60] Bonhoeffer agrees with Nietzsche inasmuch as Christianity denies life and cheapens being and culture; that is to say he does not want to dismiss Nietzsche's critique of Christianity. Nietzsche is correct when he mocks that the good news, the εὐαγέλλιον, turns out among Christians to be without foundation in reality and often is mere adversity to life. But

---

[53] Martin Havenstein, *Nietzsche als Erzieher*. Berlin E. S. Mittler 1922.
[54] Cf. *DBWE* 6, 222, note 19.
[55] Cf. *The Anti-Christ*, 5.
[56] Cf. *The Anti-Christ*, 6.
[57] *The Anti-Christ*, 7.
[58] *The Anti-Christ*, 18.
[59] Cf. *The Anti-Christ*, 15.
[60] *DBWE* 11, 219.

Bonhoeffer does not agree with all of Nietzsche's critique. Nietzsche's understanding of Christianity as radically life-denying leads him to attack Christians as such he is devaluing human beings; it also leads him to undervalue the religion that brings forth human beings even though some may seem to be out of touch with reality. It may be the case that there are indeed Christians who live disconnected from reality and deny life, but the genuine following of Jesus Christ leads a person deeply into the reality of the world with all things good and evil. This incongruity in one's understanding of the essence of Christianity cannot be overcome. Still in Tegel prison, Bonhoeffer writes to Bethge: "The human being is called upon to share in God's suffering at the hands of a godless world. Thus we must really live in that godless world and not try to cover up or transfigure its godlessness somehow with religion. Our lives must be 'worldly,' so that we can share precisely so in God's suffering; our lives are *allowed* to be 'worldly,' that is, we are delivered from false religious obligations and inhibitions."[61] Bonhoeffer want to make crystal clear that as human beings we are allowed to really live and do not need to be in the world in some sort of artificial life. But unlike Nietzsche, for him this real life is bound to Christ.

In view of Nietzsche's extremely pessimistic analysis of a supposedly life-denying form of Christianity, it comes of no surprize that Nietzsche also calls for a radical revaluation of all values [*Umwertung aller Werte*]. In principle and concretely this means for Nietzsche the revaluation of all Christian values. But since Christian moral values are fundamentally predicated on the categories of good and evil, his idea of revaluation is precisely a devaluation of these categories. In a rather pious but thoroughly ironic language Nietzsche's Zarathustra demands: "Look at the faithful of all faiths! Whom do they hate the most? The one who breaks their tablets of values, the breaker, the lawbreaker – but he is the creative one... Fellow creators the creative one seeks, who will write new values on new tablets."[62] And in a similar tone: "Break, break me these old tablets of the pious, my brothers! Gainsay me the sayings of the world slanderers."[63]

The young vicar accepted Nietzsche's challenge already in Barcelona. "The discovery of the world beyond good and evil is by no means to be attributed to the enemy of Christianity Friedrich Nietzsche, whose polemic against the self-righteousness of Christianity derived from this perspective. It belongs rather to the original, albeit concealed material of the

---

61 *DBWE* 8, 480.
62 *Zarathustra*, "Prologue" 9.
63 *Zarathustra*, "On Old and New Tablets," 15.

Christian message."[64] But unlike Nietzsche, Bonhoeffer's argument is theological and not ethical. "The knowledge of good and evil is thus disunion with God. Human beings can know about good and evil only in opposition to God"[65] because they have already lost their origin, that is to say, that they are marked by the inescapable power of sin. In everyday life it is the responsibility of Christians both to create the standards for good and evil and to bear the responsibility for those standards. Bonhoeffer calls explicitly on Nietzsche in that Christians should create their own new tablets and new decalogues just as Nietzsche had asked of the overman [*Übermensch*].[66] For a merely traditional morality cannot serve Christians as the standard for ethical responsibility. But what is the ethical standard for Christian behaviour? Bonhoeffer hints at a possible answer in a sermon preached in London. Christianity devalues all human values and re-establishes new values in view of Christ.[67] Christians act ethically in their freedom in Christ, searching for the will of God without looking sideways at what is conventional morality. Whether such ethical acting is good or evil can only be known by the acting person and ultimately by God.[68]

The person acting beyond good and evil is for Nietzsche not merely a progressive Christian. For the world does not need religiously reformed people but a completely new kind of human being. In his *Zarathustra* Nietzsche speaks of the appearance of that person, the overman [*Übermensch*]. What precisely Nietzsche meant with the expression *Übermensch* is a matter of debate among scholars. It is likely the case that *Übermensch* does not designate the cipher of a new, futuristic genus of human being, but rather an anthropological concept that expresses the human possibility of full life affirmation.[69] Along those lines Nietzsche asks "what type of human being should be *bred*, should be *willed* as having greater value, as being more deserving of life, as being more certain of the future."[70]

Nietzsche himself combines the *Übermensch* with task of devaluation of all values and faithfulness to the earth. "*I teach you the overman (Übermensch)*. Human being is something That Must be overcome. What have you done to overcome him? ... Behold, I teach the overman! The overman is the meaning of the earth. Let your will say: the overman *shall be* the

---

[64] *DBWE* 10, 363.
[65] *DBWE* 6, 300.
[66] Cf. *DBWE* 10, 367.
[67] Cf. *DBWE* 13, 403.
[68] Cf. *DBWE* 10, 366–367.
[69] Cf. Lawrence Hatab, *Nietzsche's Life Sentence. Coming to Terms with Eternal Recurrence*, New York: Routledge 2005, 55.
[70] *The Anti-Christ*, 3.

meaning of the earth!"[71] In this combination Nietzsche calls human beings to the unconditional affirmation of life. Such affirmation he envisions in completely immanent terms and without any relation to the Christian faith. The purpose of being human is on earth and not in a comfort for the afterlife. In this regard Bonhoeffer agrees with Nietzsche when he says that "Nietzsche took up Feuerbach's doctrine of the whole human being. [A human being is] not a transcendent being that only appears to exist but is *ens realissimum*, with regard not only to thoughts but also to drives."[72] While for Nietzsche this kind of immanent human being is the purpose of *Dasein* as such, for Bonhoeffer the purpose of earthly *Dasein* springs from faith and leads to God in the following of Jesus Christ. In the end, for Bonhoeffer faith is foundation for our love for the world. For Christ himself spoke an unconditional yes to the world and in this yes the constituted his love for the world.[73]

Martin Heidegger

The young Bonhoeffer wrote his dissertation *Sanctorum Communio* without any reference to the philosophy of Heidegger. Heidegger's *magnum opus*, *Being and Time*, was published in February 1927 while Bonhoeffer handed in his dissertation in July of the same year. A few years later, when Bonhoeffer was working on his *Habilitation*, *Act and Being*, things had changed considerably. In this work Heidegger turned out to be a significant philosophical interlocutor. It is immediately apparent that Bonhoeffer leans closely on Heidegger's vocabulary, especially terminology such as *Dasein*, existence, ontological, ontic, existential, *existentiell*, possibility etc.

Bonhoeffer perceives a philosophically most important question for theology discussed in Heidegger's philosophical ideas, namely the question of the human possibility for self-knowledge and the knowledge of God. Is it possible for human beings to understand themselves and to know God? While in *Sanctorum Communio* Bonhoeffer examined "the category of *possibility*"[74] without recourse to either Heidegger or any other philosophical thinker, in *Act and Being* he engages Heidegger's concept of possibility explicitly. He agrees with Heidegger who "interprets being essentially in

---

[71] *Zarathustra*, "Zarathustra's Prologue," 3.

[72] *DBWE* 11, 186.

[73] Cf. Sabine Dramm, *Dietrich Bonhoeffer. Eine Einführung in sein Denken*. Gütersloh: Gütersloher Verlag 2001, 128.

[74] *DBWE* 1, 127.

terms of temporality."[75] Human existence is *Dasein*, but not merely as something present-at-hand, but, in Heidegger's own formulation, *Dasein* "is primarily Being-possible. Dasein is in every case what it can be, and in the way in which it is its possibility."[76] *Dasein* is always fallen in the world. But inasmuch as Dasein has death as its end, it is able to escape from the fallenness and head the call to come back to "itself upon its ownmost *potentiality-for-Being*."[77] "Insofar as Dasein lays hold of the possibility, the existence, most authentic to it, Dasein grasps its own wholeness."[78]

Bonhoeffer sees the problem of the category of possibility in the following: "The concept of possibility... includes the possibility of an ontological understanding of Dasein unaffected by revelation. But seen from the position of revelation, 'to be possible' in relation to sin or grace (whether existential or existentiell) always means to be already really in one or the other."[79] Bonhoeffer is convinced that human self-understanding is marked by sin and unattainable apart from revelation. Heidegger was correct in seeing that Dasein must be interpreted ontologically, but according to Bonhoeffer, he was incorrect in that he does not recognize sin as an "ontological designation"[80] and the fact that human beings cannot be understood independent of sin (and God's grace). Concretely this entails that "for human beings, to exist means to stand, act, and decide under God's claim. Existence is in pure actuality. Consequently, self-understanding is given only in the act itself. There are no concepts of existence prior to existence. The existence of human beings is either in sin or in grace. Through revelation there is only sinful or pardoned existence, without potentiality."[81] If it were otherwise, "it would mean that human beings could place themselves into the truth, that they could somehow withdraw to a deeper being of their own, apart from their being sinner, their 'not being in the truth.' Being in Adam would, consequently, have to be regarded as a potentiality of a more profound 'possibility of being in the truth.' It would rest on a being untouched by sin."[82]

Both the transcendental and the ontological attempt to arrive at human self-understanding cannot overstep the boundaries set by sin. Neither ontological analysis of Being nor understanding of act can reach God. Even

---

[75] *DBWE* 2, 68.
[76] Martin Heidegger, *Being and Time*, 182.
[77] Heidegger, *Being and Time*, 322.
[78] *DBWE* 2, 70.
[79] *DBWE* 2, 96, note 24.
[80] *DBWE* 2, 136.
[81] *DBWE* 2, 97.
[82] *DBWE* 2, 136.

for the philosophically thinking human being there is no possibility for the knowledge of God. In Bonhoeffer's words: "There is, therefore, no method for the knowledge of God; human beings cannot place themselves into the existential [existentiell] situation from which they could speak of God, for they a are not able to place themselves into the truth."[83]

In the end Bonhoeffer overcomes the inadequacy of the philosophical idea of possibility on the basis of theological thinking. Since God cannot merely be "an object of consciousness," every attempt at knowledge of God – and correspondingly any human attempt at self-understanding – must acknowledge God as the subject by means of revelation. "This cognition of revelation is called 'believing,' what is revealed is called Christ, and the subject of understanding is God as Holy Spirit. God is in revelation only in the act of understanding oneself. The reflection on this act will never meet God in my consciousness."[84]

Bonhoeffer's rejection of Heidegger's idea of possibility closes the circle that began with Aristotle. The Aristotelian differentiation between potentiality and actuality (δύναμις and ἐνέργεια) and Heidegger's philosophy of possibility Bonhoeffer rejects as unfitting concepts for theology. There simply is no human possibility to reach epistemologically beyond sin. Bonhoeffer never lets go of this conviction, not even in Tegel prison, but at that point in his life more poetically than theologically. In his poem "Stations on the Way to Freedom" he says "Hover not over the possible, but boldly reach for the real."[85]

Conclusion: Philosophy and Theology

Over two decades ago Heinz Eduard Tödt wrote for the editors of the *Dietrich Bonhoeffer Werke*: "Die Rezeption der Theologie Bonhoeffers scheint mir trotz vieler zum Teil hochqualifizierter Untersuchungen erst in den Anfängen zu stehen."[86] Morevoer, Tödt also suggested that we have "ein volleres Verständnis und ein tieferes Wirken von Bonhoeffers Theologie nicht hinter uns, sondern größtenteils noch vor uns."[87] There can be little doubt that Tödt's sentiments are largely valid today, especially in view of the research that still needs to be carried out vis-à-vis the philosophical

---

[83] *DBWE* 2, 92.
[84] *DBWE* 2, 92.
[85] *DBWE* 8, 513.
[86] *DBW* 1, XIV.
[87] *DBW* 1, XIX.

underpinnings of Bonhoeffer's theology. As noted before, such philosophical investigations are rather the exception in Bonhoeffer scholarship, even after several decades of research. There are no larger academically solid works on the philosophy of Kant and Hegel on Bonhoeffer and only a few studies that have examined thinkers such as Kierkegaard, Dilthey, Fichte, Scheler, Knittermeyer and others. Indeed, Bonhoeffer research has focussed too narrowly on theological themes such as Christology, ecclesiology, ethics and the consistently raised question of religionless Christianity. All of these themes are of course significant topics and building blocks for Bonhoeffer's theology and have their place in his oeuvre. And yet, a theologically one-sided research trend runs the risk to interpret and understand Bonhoeffer's theology out of itself. Such an endeavour is legitimate to a certain degree, to be sure, but it falls short on the appropriate recognition of the philosophical underpinnings of his theology.

In what way can we now characterize in Bonhoeffer the formal relation between philosophy and theology? Why was Bonhoeffer intensely interested in philosophy, at least during his short academic career in Berlin? The methodological question of the proper relation between philosophy and theology can best be illustrated in his academic works. In both *Sanctorum Communio* and *Act and Being* Bonhoeffer sustains a constant tension between the two disciplines. Although Bonhoeffer understood philosophy and theology as independent disciplines he acknowledged the dynamic tension between them, but in such a way that theology had the upper hand over philosophy. Metaphorically speaking, philosophy belongs to the household, but only as the handmaid to theology. Still, Bonhoeffer's subservience of philosophy to theology does not mean that he appropriated the latter in an eclectic and dilettante manner. One example must suffice to illustrate the relation between philosophy and theology.

Bonhoeffer's rejection of the philosophical premise – both in the transcendental and ontological dimensions – that the autonomous self can come to itself is based on the counter premise, namely that the autonomous self can never come to itself apart from revelation. Methodologically Bonhoeffer proceeds from the starting point of his theological thesis, namely the conviction that human beings apart from Christ are always "in Adam" and inescapably tied to the realities *cor curvum in se* and *ratio curva in se*. In summary: human beings who are enslaved by the power of sin have no innate possibility (against Aristotle and Heidegger) to understand sin and overcome it for their salvation. If there would be a possibility of understanding of sin apart from revelation, then sin's sting of death would *de facto* be relativized. This epistemological impasse cannot be overcome.

Only in the light of revelation do human beings come to themselves and know who they are, both as sinners and believers.[88] The sketch of this example shows how Bonhoeffer resolves the dynamic tension between philosophy and theology. The theological premise of revelation functions both as his foundational thesis and the main argument to render apart philosophical epistemology. In other words, for Bonhoeffer philosophy is important for his theological reflections, but always in the sense that philosophical insights must support his theological thinking and not undermine it.

---

[88] Cf. *DBWE* 2, 80.

Foregrounding Bonhoeffer

10. Notes on Bonhoeffer's Theological Anthropology: The Case of Racism

> Progressive white theologians, with few exceptions, write and teach as if they do not need to address the radical contradiction that racism creates for Christian theology. James Cone[1]

> The way the southerners talk about the Negroes is simply repugnant, and in this regard the pastors are no better than the others. Dietrich Bonhoeffer[2]

Introduction

Racism is diabolic. Racism is dehumanizing. Racism is a sin. Racism is the Berlin Wall of America. Racism is America's "national sin."[3] These statements have an absolute ring to them and precisely for this reason they demand a response from Christian theologians. James Cone has repeatedly challenged white theologians to break the silence and speak out against "white theology's amnesia about racism."[4] The purpose of this paper is to respond in a small way to Cone's rightful challenge and offer a theological critique of the multifaceted phenomenon of racism[5] on the basis of Dietrich Bonhoeffer's theological anthropology.[6]

---

[1] James Cone, *Risks of Faith: The Emergence of a Black Theology of Liberation, 1968–1998.* Boston: Beacon Press 1999, 130.

[2] *DBWE* 10, 269, in a letter to his brother, 2 January 1931.

[3] J. Deotis Roberts, *Bonhoeffer and King: Speaking Truth to Power.* Louisville: Westminster John Knox Press 2005, 43.

[4] For example, in his plenary address to the American Academy of Religion in Denver, November 2001. Cf. also James Cone, "White Theology Revisited," in his *Risks of Faith*, 130–137.

[5] Although in itself a very complex issue, in this study I will treat the relation between the concepts of racism, anti-Semitism, white racism etc. as phenomena that stem from the same root, namely the hierarchical (de)valuation of human beings based on the colour of their skin.

[6] Cone acknowledges that Bonhoeffer was one of the theologians who shaped the

Bonhoeffer's own life and theology may at least partially be understood as a remarkable attempt to overcome both a country and a church that had been utterly led astray by the fabricated lies of the ideologues of racism. Bonhoeffer was one of the few who cried out against a racism that erupted as blatant anti-Semitism; but as he tried to break the silence, the others' silence broke him.[7] In view of Bonhoeffer's personal encounter with American racism and his active resistance against the Nazi regime and a church sold out to that evil regime, it seems that of all white privileged theologians he is the one who is closest to the experiences, struggles, alienation, and theological expression of African American theologians. Indeed, Cone himself affirms that much when he acknowledges that Bonhoeffer is one of the few white theologians who have not constructed a theology apart from "any reference to the oppressed of the land."[8]

Ideological Roots of Racism

Long before the insidious propaganda and industrial gas chambers of Hitler, the arch-racist of the twentieth century, the roots of what would centuries later blossom as ideological racism had long been planted in the soil of western intellectual history. Aristotle proposed (cf. *Politics* 1254a19–1255b15), grounded as he saw it in both reason and fact, that some human beings are by nature free and others slaves; hence, the first are meant to rule while the latter are meant to serve. The slave, for Aristotle, therefore, belongs to the master as he constitutes "a living but separated part of his bodily frame" (*Politics*, 1255b11–12). Similarly, just as the Hellenes are superior to barbarians, so are men superior to women. Moving from the Aristotelian classification of the individual human being to that of peoples, the Roman Tacitus declared (*Germania* 98) that the Germanic people of antiquity were the virile and courageous children of nature; these ideas

---

development of his theology and credits Bonhoeffer as an example of one who challenged the Nazi regime. Cf. *Risks of Faith*, 10, 12, 31, 75.

[7] See, for example, Wolfgang Gerlach, *And the Witnesses Were Silent: The Confessing Church and the Persecution of the Jews*, translated and edited by Victoria J. Barnett. Lincoln: University of Nebraska Press 2000. See also Daniel Jonah Goldhagen, *Hitler's Willing Executioners: Ordinary Germans and the Holocaust.* New York: Knopf 1996 and Rudolf Kreis, *Antisemitismus und Kirche: In den Gedächtnislücken deutscher Geschichte mit Heine, Freud, Kafka und Goldhagen.* Hamburg: Rowohlt 1999.

[8] James H. Cone, *A Black Theology of Liberation.* Philadelphia: J.B. Lippincott 1970, 28, note 4; cf. also 61, 88, 131, 167–68 and his *Risks of Faith*, 10, 12, 31, 75.

were later married to the white, superior Aryan race myth and thus became the ground for ideological racism.[9]

In the western world, a radical transition from merely subscribing to a racist ideology to putting into practice scrupulous racist measures was marked by the year 1492. Columbus himself, as his diary entries and other writings make abundantly clear, held the natives of South America in low regard, brought them to Spain as slaves, and was, according to Barolomé de Las Casas, "the origin of the mistreatment that [the natives] have later had to suffer."[10] In the decades and centuries following Columbus, the history of Latin America stands as an iniquitous monument reminding us of the mind-boggling genocides of native peoples, namely sins committed because of the pursuit of gold or in the attempt to save souls in the name of Christ.[11] In a parallel development, the derogatory stigmatization of the Jewish people of the Iberian Peninsula as marranos, "pigs," was in full swing. Under Ferdinand and Isabella, about 3000 Jews were burned for the crime of being outwardly baptized Christians and inwardly practicing Jews.[12] In 1492, incidentally the same year as Columbus left Spain "to discover the new world," the Jewish people were expelled from Spain. Whatever the justifications, the assumptions that made possible unimaginable human atrocities are the same in the cases of Spain, South America, American racism and Nazi-Germany: it is the assertion of human superiority of Europeans and its corollary, namely the inferiority of non-European or native peoples.[13] Measured in terms of the colour of a person's skin: white

---

[9] Cf. Alan Davies, "The Ideology of Racism," in *Concilium* 151 (1982), 11–16, here 12. On the development of racist thinking, cf. Dwight N. Hopkins, *Being Human: Race, Culture and Religion*. Minneapolis: Fortress Press 2005, 131–143.

[10] Gustavo Gutiérrez, *Las Casas. In Search of the Poor of Jesus Christ*. Maryknoll: Orbis Books 1993, 24.

[11] For an overview of the history of Latin America during the last 500 years, see the classic work by Eduardo Goleano, *Open Veins of Latin America. Five Centuries of the Pillage of a Continent*. New York: Monthly Review Press, 1973. From a theological perspective, cf. Jon Sobrino, "Five Hundred Years. Structural Sin and Structural Grace," in idem, *The Principle of Mercy. Taking the Crucified People from the Cross*. Maryknoll: Orbis Books 1994, 69–82.

[12] Cf. Rudolf Kreis, *Antisemitismus und Kirche*, 127–128. Anti-Semitism has its roots in antiquity and was continued in Europe in the centuries that followed. The church is forever inculpably tied to that development. For example, whatever theological catharsis Martin Luther accomplished in his struggles with Rome, the reformer himself went astray in his judgement of Jews and Turks.

[13] Gutiérrez, *Las Casas*, 341. John Wesley, the founder of the Methodist Church, was appalled by the atrocities the Europeans committed. In a sermon he preached in 1774, entitled "A Caution against Bigotry," he says: "It were to be wished, that none but heathens had practised such gross, palpable works of the devil. But we dare not say so. Even

skin is superior over dark skin, to the degree that the darker the skin the more inferior the human being. This, in a nutshell, is the assumption underlying all racism, this is the great lie.[14]

In the modern age of awakening reason, the hierarchical view of the human race was expressed with little inhibitions. "I am apt to suspect," writes David Hume, that "the negroes and in general all the other species of men [are] naturally inferior to the whites."[15] Kant agreed with him and Hegel added his own caricature: "We must lay aside all thought of reverence and morality – all that we call feeling – if we would rightly comprehend him [the Negro]; there is nothing harmonious with humanity to be found in this type of character."[16] Similar sentiments were disseminated by Arthur de Gobineau, often identified as the father of racism, especially in his essay (1853–1855) "L'essai sur l'inégalité des races humaines."[17] In France, Gobineau was pessimistic about democracy and so wanted to transcend it by means of the Aryan racial genius. In England, Robert Knox[18] proclaimed the rise of the democratic genius of the Anglo-Saxon race. In both cases, the roots were the same: the conviction of white European superiority over peoples of colour. As one commentator notes, "despite their differences,

---

in cruelty and bloodshed, how little have the Christians come behind them! And not the Spaniards or Portuguese alone, butchering thousands in South America: not the Dutch only in the East Indies, or the French in North America, following the Spaniards step by step: our own countrymen, too, have wantoned in blood, and exterminated whole nations; plainly proving thereby what spirit it is that dwells and works in the children of disobedience" (http://wesley.nnu.edu/john-wesley/the-sermons-of-john-wesley-1872-edition/sermon-38-a-caution-against-bigotry). Cf. also his "Thoughts Upon Slavery," published in the same year. He not only sharply condemns the practice of American and British slavery, but goes into great detail to point out the many virtues of the peoples kidnapped and stolen as slaves from their African lands.

[14] For a recent analysis of the correlation of racism and skin colour, see Margaret L. Hunger, *Race, Gender, and the Politics of Skin Tone*. New York and London: Routledge 2005.

[15] Cited by Alan Davies, "The Ideology of Racism," 15. For an analysis of racist ideologies in Continental Philosophy, cf. Robert Bernasconi and Sybol Cook (eds), *Race and Racism in Continental Philosophy*. Bloomington: Indiana University Press 2003.

[16] Cf. Josiah U. Young, *No Difference in the Fare: Dietrich Bonhoeffer and the Problem of Racism*. Grand Rapids: Eerdmans, 1998, 76–77. This work is a thorough and detailed treatment of the topic American racism in the writings of Bonhoeffer. See now also Reggie L. Williams, *Bonhoeffer's Black Jesus. Harlem Renaissance Theology and an Ethic of Resistance*. Waco: Baylor University Press 2014.

[17] Cf. Janine Buenzod, *La formation de la pensée de Gobineau et l'essai sur l'inégalité des races humaines*. Paris: Librairie A.-G. Nizet 1967 and Michael D. Biddis, *Father of Racist Ideology: The Social and Political Thought of Count Gobineau*. London: Weidenfeld and Nicholson 1970.

[18] Robert Knox, *Races of Man: A Fragment*. Philadelphia: Lea and Blanchard 1850.

the Anglo-Saxon and Aryan race myths were the fabrications of the western psyche fixated on itself during the radical changes, impossible dreams and profound insecurities of the modern age. The proper term for such self-infatuation is narcissism."[19]

The historical explosion of this racist ideology happened in two distinct ways. In Europe, where only few people of colour lived, the form of racial superiority manifested itself as anti-Semitism and came to an irruption under Hitler's Nazi regime; in the United States, where large numbers of African Americans lived, racial ideology had incarnated itself very early into the American dream of life in the form of slavery. For this reason, in America, the history of racism is closely tied to the practice of slavery. Indeed, as Deotis Roberts has noted recently, there is a clear correlation between slavery and racism in that the "roots of racism are in the tradition of slavery."[20]

Bonhoeffer's Encounter with Racism in America

The young Bonhoeffer's insights into the social, ecclesiological, and theological issues that racism poses for a Christian bear witness to his growing sensitivity of what he later termed the following after Christ or discipleship. Very early in his pastoral life he reflected on the nexus between social issues and theology. Before he came to New York, he had encountered concrete human issues in Barcelona with his congregation and, after his return from New York, in Berlin with his confirmands and their families. In those years, Bonhoeffer himself referred to these issues as "the social question."[21] As a pastor he did not shy away from the social crises of people but showed personal interest and sometimes offered concrete help. In other words, even before he arrived in New York he was exposed to and had analyzed social issues from both the perspectives of human existence and theological reflection. It is hence of little surprise that he showed a great curiosity to penetrate the racial issue in America.[22] Indeed, on more than one occasion, he wondered whether he had spent too much time with the question of racism.[23]

When Bonhoeffer came to America in 1930 to study at Union Theological Seminary in New York, the slave trade had been abolished officially for

---

[19] Davies, "The Ideology of Racism," 12.
[20] Roberts, *Bonhoeffer and King*, 43.
[21] Cf. *DBWE* 10, 62. See also *DBWE* 11, 73–74.
[22] See the excellent study by Young, *No Difference in the Fare.*
[23] Cf. *DBWE* 10, 293.

about 65 years. The issue of racism, however, was a living reality and was palpably evident to the young German visitor. At Union, Bonhoeffer found a good friend in Franklin Fisher, an African American fellow student from Alabama. Fisher's friendship was decisive for Bonhoeffer's first-hand encounter with the lives, questions and struggles of the African American community and his subsequent ability to unmask anti-Semitism in his native Germany. Fisher introduced Bonhoeffer to the Abyssinian Baptist Church in Harlem where he became an active participant. Bonhoeffer writes home that he works regularly in a "negro boys club."[24] In a report for the church officials of the Lutheran Church upon his return to Germany, Bonhoeffer lists the following: that together with his friend Fisher and sometimes in his absence he taught Sunday school regularly for more than half a year, that he held bible studies for women, that once a week he helped out in "weekday church school," that he made many friendships with African Americans and was allowed into their homes and that his friend introduced him to the leaders of the black movement at Howard College.[25] Bonhoeffer spent Easter Morning 1931 on a trip with a group of young African Americans boys.[26]

In all these encounters, the young Bonhoeffer had ample opportunity to hear the personal stories and read the literature[27] of African Americans in a land dominated by white Christians. Bonhoeffer's impression of white racism is expressed in a letter he wrote to his older brother Karl Friedrich, dated 8 January 1931. Intriguingly, he comes to the topic of racism in America. He explains: "The separation of whites from blacks in the southern states really does make a rather shameful impression... The way the southerners talk about the Negroes is simply repugnant, and in this regard the pastors are no better than the others. I still believe that the spiritual songs of the southern Negroes represent some of the greatest artistic achievements in America.[28] It is a bit unnerving that in a country with so

---

[24] *DBWE* 10, 267.
[25] *DBWE* 10, 314.
[26] *DBWE* 10, 295.
[27] Bonhoeffer read many works by African American writers. Cf. *DBWE* 10, 421–422 and Josiah U. Young, "Dietrich Bonhoeffer and Three Black Writers: James W. Johnson, Langston Hughes and Countee Cullen," in Peter Frick (ed), *Bonhoeffer and Interpretive Theory. Essays on Methods and Understanding*. International Bonhoeffer Interpretations 6. Frankfurt: Peter Lang 2013, 85–98.
[28] Bonhoeffer took some records of African American spirituals back to Berlin and later played these for his students; see Eberhard Bethge, *Dietrich Bonhoeffer: Theologian, Christian, Man for His Times. A Biography,* translated and revised by Victoria Barnett. Minnesota: Fortress Press 2000, 150.

inordinately many slogans about brotherhood, peace, and so on, such things still continue completely uncorrected."[29]

Several comments on Bonhoeffer's remarks are in order. First, as a keen observer he harshly condemns the way southerners speak of African Americans. His point is clear: language is a vehicle for racism. Even worse, the pastors, those who have God's words on their lips and should be exemplary in witnessing the love of Jesus Christ, their speech, too, is as repugnant as that of anyone else. Second, Bonhoeffer's impression is not that there is a (merely neutral) separation of white and black persons, but that the whites separated *from* the blacks (*die Separation der Weißen von den Schwarzen*). This is important. As his choice of the preposition *von* suggests, Bonhoeffer determines that the origin of the racial separation lies with white people. They are the ones who are responsible for racist ideology and racist measures, such as the segregation in railway cars etc. Third, the young visitor clearly detected the incompatibility of a nation that employs "so inordinately many slogans about brotherhood, peace" and does so little to correct unconcealed acts of racism. Here, without saying so explicitly, we may infer that Bonhoeffer points out the mutually exclusive claims of Christian teaching and civil liberties, on the one hand, and the tolerated practices of racism within church and state, on the other hand.

Bonhoeffer's Awakening To Racial Anti-Semitism in Germany

Even before Bonhoeffer returned to Germany he became aware that a racial problem was looming in his own country. In February 1931 Bonhoeffer received a very long and informative letter from his friend Helmut Rößler. In the letter Rößler spoke quite openly about what he saw as the coming challenges for the church in Germany. Among many other things he wrote: "I think the greatest tragedy of the church and of our people . . . is that the powerful *völkisch* movement is combining a purified, red-hot national feeling with a new paganism . . . The basis of this neopagan religion is the assertion of the proven unity between *religion* and *race*, more specifically the Aryan (Nordic) race . . . *All* the basic critical notions of this religion toward Christianity have been taken from the intellectual arsenal of racial ressentiment whose scholarly integrity is in part highly questionable."[30]

---

[29] *DBWE* 10, 269.
[30] Cf. *DBWE* 10, 283–284.

It would have been uncharacteristic of Bonhoeffer to be blind to Rößler's contention that something evil was gaining shape in his home country. Notwithstanding the unique context of American racism and German Anti-Semitism, Rößler's words make a connection between race and, as he mentions earlier in the letter, the increasing public resentment against the Jews. When Bonhoeffer returned to Germany, Hitler soon came to power in January 1933 and Nazi ideology grew to dominate all aspects of the nation. The rhetoric about the superior Aryan race and the propaganda against Jews issued in the Aryan clause of April 1933.[31] It is crucial to note that Bonhoeffer's stay in America sharpened his eyes to recognize that German anti-Semitism was a radicalized form of racism. During his time in Berlin, London and Finkenwalde, Bonhoeffer was able to recognize with utmost clarity that ant-Semitic legislation by the Nazi government had grave theological consequences for the church. This is not the place to discuss the details of this phase of Bonhoeffer's life and struggles. Suffice it to say that it was during this period that the young theologian wrote the essay "The Church and the Jewish Question" in 1934.[32] Bonhoeffer was not satisfied with the Confessing Church's watering down of the Barmen confession, precisely because it did not have a clear stand in condemning the flagrant anti-Semitic attacks on Jewish people.

After the closing of the underground seminary in Finkenwalde by the Gestapo, in the fall of 1937, Bonhoeffer travelled a second time to America. Uneasy about his "escape" into security in a far-away land he returned to his own country in anticipation of a war and his own responsibility in re-building his country and church after the war. It is significant that upon his immediate return, just before the beginning of the Second World War, Bonhoeffer wrote an article entitled, "Protestantism without Reformation." In it he reflected on Church and Theology in America and included a section called "The Negro Church." He provides a brief historical introduction: "The slave masters agreed that the gospel may be preached among the slaves only after the bishop of Lo[n]don wrote a fateful letter to calm things down. In it he reassured the white masters that nothing whatsoever

---

[31] For historical details and the significance of the Aryan clause for the church, see Bethge, *Dietrich Bonhoeffer,* 304–323.

[32] Cf. *DBWE* 12, 361–373. Even though Bonhoeffer stood apart in his personal and theological views of Jewish people, it is also the case that "his arguments [are not always] convincing or compatible with contemporary, post-Holocaust political and theological perspectives;" cf. Ruth Zerner, "Church, State and the 'Jewish Question,'" in *CCDB*, 193 and Victoria J. Barnett, "Dietrich Bonhoeffer's Relevance for a Post-Holocaust Christian Theology" in Peter Frick (ed), *Bonhoeffer and Interpretive Theory. Essays on Methods and Understanding,* 213–237.

had to change in the outward conditions of the slaves who were baptized, since baptism signified the deliverance from sin and evil lust, and not so much a release from slavery or any other such external fetters."[33]

The words with which the Bishop assured the slave masters that "nothing whatsoever had to change in the outward conditions of the slaves who were baptized, since baptism signified the deliverance from sin and evil lust" must be understood against Bonhoeffer's writing *Discipleship*. Cheap grace is exactly this: an existence in the name of Christ that has no consequences in the concrete realities of daily life. An individual's following Christ is one thing for Bonhoeffer; it is quite another matter how the demands of costly grace must transform a Christian community. In this regard, Bonhoeffer seems to imply, American churches have not done well. There can be no doubt that Bonhoeffer deems the exclusion of African Americans from full participation in a church that carries the name of Christ as utterly unacceptable. He continues: "So it happened that Negroes became Christians and were allowed... to partake of communion – as the last guests. Any further participation in the life of a congregation was ruled out; all the offices of the congregation and ordination remained the privileges of the whites... Once all attempts had failed to be recognized as equal members in the church of Jesus Christ, Negroes made an effort to organize themselves in their own congregations."[34]

The reference that African Americans wish "to be recognized as equal members in the church of Jesus Christ" points to the fact that for Bonhoeffer the issue of racism within the Christian church is a very grave ecclesiological and theological problem.

Racism: A Theological and Ecclesiological Issue

Given Bonhoeffer's personal experiences in the context of racial America and anti-Semitic Germany, he did not hesitate to expose the wickedness of racism as both a theological and ecclesiological issue. Racism is a theological issue inasmuch as racism goes contrary to God's design and affirmation of every person's intrinsic human dignity; racism is an ecclesiological issue inasmuch as it surfaces as a reality within the church, often characterized by Bonhoeffer as "Christ existing as community." Expressed differently, racism is one issue for the church, but it has different, mutually implicit, dimensions. In what follows, we will examine how the issue of racism is

---

[33] *DBWE* 15, 457.
[34] *DBWE* 15, 457.

grounded in Bonhoeffer's theology and then discuss its implication for the Christian church as a whole.

Racism as Sin. The theological premise that constitutes the starting point for deconstructing racism is that racism is an act of sin. Racism is sin and therefore it must be situated in a theology of sin. It is crucial to understand that for the white Christian church, racism cannot be a theologically neutral topic. Racism cannot be neutral because it is the shameful display of a hierarchical judgement of the value of human beings as determined by one group of persons over against another. The fact that it is Christians that make such judgements over other Christians is without excuse—theologically, psychologically and ethically.

Within an ontology of sin, what is the root of racism? It is decisive to recognize the distinction between sin, in the singular, and sins, in the plural. The first points to the vertical disruption between God and all humanity, the second points to the horizontal acts of sin, the sins committed because of a person's being under the power of sin.[35] Sins follow from sin. Sin is an ontological gap that separates humanity from God, sins are the acts that disrupt human relationships and all other aspects of life. The irruption of sins may be characterized as a psychological disruption, intellectual limitation, ethical dilemma, sexual confusion, ecological irresponsibility, social disintegration, structural evil, and racial discrimination. Whereas sin must be overcome, and has been overcome in Jesus the Christ and is known theologically as salvation, racial discrimination belongs to the realm of the horizontal level of sin and must correspondingly be addressed as an aspect of a Christian's redemptive living empowered by God's Spirit.

In Bonhoeffer's view, sin is "the will that in principle affirms as valuable only itself, and not the other, and that acknowledges the other only on its own terms."[36] In relation to the racist, these words mark the racist as a person who lives by the illusion that he or she can come to a self-understanding on the basis of placing one's own self above those of other selves. Hence, the racist becomes the benchmark for measuring the value of other selves on the basis of his/her own estranged self. "The other will is not ignored and negated," Bonhoeffer notes, "rather, one seeks to force it onto one's own will and thus overcome it."[37]

---

[35] Cf. the discussion of sin and racism in J. Deotis Roberts, *Liberation and Reconciliation: A Black Theology*. Philadelphia: The Westminster Press 1971, 109. Roberts works with the distinction of vertical and horizontal aspects of sin.

[36] *DBWE* 1, 118 note 22.

[37] *DBWE* 1, 86. Whether the racist holds his/her view consciously or unconsciously matters little (cf. 1 Corinthians 4:3–4).

The deeper issue with the sin of racism, as with the sin of anti-Semitism, is the disturbing reality that such acts are hardly perceived to be sin. In this regard, Roberts has provided some sobering remarks: In matters of racism, he notes, there is "the *indifference* of the North. The racist of the North does not hate the black man; he does not know that he *exists*. Because he ignores the black man's very presence, he is not aware of any race problem or his complicity in it. There is no need for forgiveness, for he is not conscious of any sin."[38] The dilemma of the Christian racist is thus evident. On the one hand, his/her sin of not really seeing the existence and presence of the African American person is tantamount to declaring that a brother or sister, in the language of Gustavo Gutiérrez, is a non-person.[39] The mere toleration of a person is already a sin but the ignorance of a person is a very grave sin. For in merely tolerating or ignoring a person who is created in the image of God, God's good creation is rejected and thus God himself is assaulted in the sin. On the other hand, the racist is equally destroyed in his racist ideology. Paradoxically, even though racism denies the full humanity of another person, the racist is principally *self*-destructive. For racism is the symptom of the racist's own distortion, disruption, dysfunction, and lack of humanity – namely his or her sinfulness understood as the universal power unto death (*Todesverhängnis*).[40] Because, as Bonhoeffer insisted, no one can come to his or her own self apart from the self of others, the racist who is not in communion with others cannot do so either.[41] Unrepentant racists will necessarily remain estranged from life as they deny the beauty of God's image in themselves and others.

Racism as the Destruction of the Imago Dei. Between his first and second visit to America, Bonhoeffer presented a series of lectures at the University of Berlin on the topic of creation and sin, which were subsequently published as *Creation and Fall* (*DBWE* 3). In the course of that lecture, Bonhoeffer explained that in a person, "freedom is not a quality that can be uncovered; it is not a possession, something to hand, an object; nor is it a form of something to hand; instead, it is a relation and nothing else. To be more precise, freedom is a relation between two persons. Being free means 'being-free-for-the-other,' because I am bound to the other. Only by being in relation with the other am I free."[42]

---

[38] Roberts, *Liberation and Reconciliation*, 103–104.
[39] Cf. Gustavo Gutiérrez, *The Power of the Poor in History: Selected Writings.* Maryknoll: Orbis Books 1983, 92, 193.
[40] Cf. *DBWE* 1, 110 note 11.
[41] Cf. *DBWE* 2, 31.
[42] *DBWE* 3, 63.

For Bonhoeffer, the freedom inherent in a person's creation *imago dei* is not characterized, as in classical theology, as *analagia entis* but as an *analogia relationis*. That is, human likeness to the divine is not one of being but one of relation. The freedom we have as created beings is a freedom given to us by the Holy Spirit. But precisely as such, a person is free only inasmuch as "one creature exists in relation to another."[43] This is essential human creatureliness. It can only be defined "in terms of the existence of human beings over-against-one-another, with-one-another, and in-dependence-upon-one-another."[44] But, as Green has pointed out, the relationship is not just "a relationship per se... It is a *particular* relationship which constitutes the *imago*: just as the true Lordship of the Creator is God's being free for the creation, so the true humanity of God's creatures is co-humanity in being free for others on the basis of their freedom for God through Christ. Most specifically, this social freedom of the Creator and humanity is the freedom of love."[45]

The racist violates the other person by denying a physical feature, namely that of skin colour, as an essential feature of the person who was created in God's image. By denying the other's full creatureliness, the racist implicitly also rejects his own. For by not accepting the other brother or sister as the person made in God's image, the racist thereby denies being in relation or in-dependence-upon the other. As a result, one loses both the neighbour in Christ and oneself. As Bonhoeffer notes, "God does not want me to mold others into the image that seems good to me, that is, into my own image. Instead, in their freedom from me God made other people in God's own image."[46] The fact that God himself deem it right and good to create persons with utter uniqueness, with their own specific imprint of God's image entails that "the complete diversity of individuals in the community is no longer a reason to talk and judge and condemn, and therefore no longer a pretext for self-justification. Rather, this diversity is a reason for rejoicing in one another and serving one another."[47] Hence, the attempt to rise above racism requires from the Christian community to celebrate the visible image of God in every *person* of colour. As Josiah Young has convincingly shown, everything depends on encountering the *person* as such and not merely "the Negro." It is not simply enough to embrace the

---

[43] *DBWE* 3, 64.

[44] *DBWE* 3, 64.

[45] Clifford J. Green, *Bonhoeffer: A Theology of Sociality*. Grand Rapids: Eerdmans, revised edition 1999, 192.

[46] *DBWE* 5, 95.

[47] *DBWE* 5, 95.

"Negro" but the fact that the "Negro" is a *person* with a unique and important *African* history.[48]

Racism as the Betrayal of the Church. When individual Christians hold
racist opinions they are guilty of individual sins. When the church community holds racist opinions and silently permits racist measures, then it is
guilty of collective sin. Above we cited Bonhoeffer's remarks on how African Americans were deliberately segregated in the churches by not being
allowed to participate in the service and by receiving communion last.
Since "all attempts had failed to be recognized as equal members in the
church of Jesus Christ" the African American church began to organize
itself out of necessity. "For American Christendom *the racial issue* has
been a real problem from the beginning... This is one of the dangerous
sings of the church's guilt [*ein bedrohliches Zeichen einer Schuld der
Kirche*] in past centuries and a grave problem for the future. The fact that
today the 'black Christ' of a young Negro poet is pitted against the 'white
Christ' reveals a deep destructive rift [*eine tiefe Zerstörung*] within the
church of Jesus Christ."[49]

Bonhoeffer's sentiments express two key issues for the white church,
namely the "guilt of the church" and the "deep destructive rift within the
church." These two issues are correlated in that the rift caused by white
church is its guilt. The rift in the church, namely the separation brought
about by the white church on the African American members of the
church, is *destructive*. In *Life Together*, Bonhoeffer leaves no doubt that a
church that is divided in the one body of Christ destroys Christian community. Because all Christians *are* part of the one body of Christ, every
member of that body is necessary for the health of the body.[50] Since Christians can encounter each other only through the mediation of Christ, a
body that is divided along the lines of colour does not allow Christ to be
the only mediator between Christians. Apart from Christ, Bonhoeffer explains further, we cannot know God, neither the brother nor ourselves.[51]
Racists who force members of colour out of the church thus sin against the
body of Christ, the fellow brother and sister and against themselves. The
destruction of the one body of Christ works on all of these levels.

The guilt of the white church in causing segregation in the body of
Christ is obvious. The admission of guilt is Bonhoeffer's pronouncement
rather than the admission of the white church. However, the significance of

---

[48] Young, *No Difference in the Fare*, 87–89.
[49] *DBWE* 15, 456.
[50] Cf. *DBWE* 5, 92.
[51] Cf. *DBWE* 5, 33.

guilt lies precisely in owning up to the sin that underlies the guilt. In regards to racism, the guilt of the church is the denial of its own racism. Without a genuine admission of the church's guilt in standing silently by or even condoning racism, it is extremely difficult if not impossible to overcome racism in a substantial manner. Unless deep-seated held racist convictions are utterly abandoned, the body of Christ will continue to be divided.

If racism stands uncorrected in the church community it is sin. But if racism is admitted, confessed and forgiven, then genuine Christian community can be restored. Bonhoeffer's words on the nature of true Christian community are among his most prophetic ones. In the first chapter in *Life Together*, he provides the blueprint for how authentic Christian relationships are possible. For him, it is crucial recognize that relationships between Christians are not possible in a direct manner, in a direct relation from person to person, from soul to soul. Such an attempt at unmediated human relationship is the attempt of the self enslaved in sin, an attempt that is rooted in what he calls psychological or emotional love [*seelische Liebe*]. In contrast, genuine human relationships are only possible with Jesus Christ being the mediator. In other words, all relationships among Christians are mediated by Christ; there are no unmediated, direct relationships between Christians. Those relationships mediated by Christ are rooted in spiritual love [*geistliche Liebe*].[52] For Bonhoeffer, the difference between emotional and spiritual love is as follows: emotional love is akin to eros in that it is rooted in the soul and urges of a person and seeks its own advantage. Eros, though not evil in itself, nonetheless seeks to control and bind the other person to itself.[53] Spiritual love, on the contrary, is rooted in the love of God and displays itself as the humble service of agape-love directed toward one another; in Bonhoeffer's words, this kind of love is "unsophisticated, nonpsychological, unmethodical, helping love."[54]

It is evident that for Bonhoeffer the mere toleration of, or exclusion of, a person of colour from a Christian community would make that community inauthentic and thereby cease to be a Christian community. A church community that is not characterized by unconditional agapeic acceptance of every person, or expressed differently, one that has certain criteria by which to exclude certain persons, violates the fundamental faith that Christ alone is the mediator and peace between human beings.

---

52 Cf. *DBWE* 5, 40–42.
53 Cf. *DBWE* 5, 40.
54 *DBWE* 5, 40.

Conclusion

In this study I have attempted to examine the sin of racism by looking at Bonhoeffer's struggle against specific forms of racism in Germany and, to a lesser extent, in America. In conclusion, and in view of the needed discussion of racism within Christian churches, I would like to underscore the following five points:

1. Although we have examined the issue of racism as a theological and ecclesiological issue for the church, these categories serve only the function of analysis. The real issue of racism is not of a theological nature; rather, the problem is that racism degrades real *persons*. As such, racism is not a theoretical, but a concretely human predicament. Correspondingly, the solution to racism lies not in understanding the complexities of an issue, but in changing one's behaviour in concrete acts of unconditional love so that the lives of *persons* are changed.

2. Since racism is predicated on the assumption of white persons' superiority over persons of colour, every attempt to unmask racism must squarely deal with that assumption as a fabricated lie. It is not enough for a white Christian to become merely nicer, more accepting, more inclusive or more open toward the sister or brother of colour. Nor is it good enough to change one's attitude because of an academic insight, a church program, political or denominational correctness. Since the root cause of racism is at the very core of how one person judges the value of another fellow human being, the change must be effected on that root level. In other words, racism must be overcome, individually and collectively, by an act of genuine repentance, absolution for that sin and unconditional agapeic acceptance of every person of colour. The moment God's Spirit brings a white Christian to the unadulterated conviction that before God and within the human family every person is equal, irrespective of colour, racism can be overcome. [55]

3. As Bonhoeffer insisted in *Life Together*, unconditional agapeic acceptance is decisive for genuine Christian community; indeed, apart from it, Christian community remains a wishful thinking. Only when the other person is encountered as the person made in God's image is there *Christian* community, because Christ stands between the persons. Only in spiritual community is the other person welcomed as made in God's image. Only agapeic acceptance welcomes the other person unconditionally without

---

[55] See, for example, the concluding chapter in Dwight N. Hopkins, *Introducing Black Theology of Liberation*. Maryknoll: Orbis Books 1999.

any attempt to re-create the other or to think less of a sister or brother of colour than of oneself.

4. When Christians of various colours encounter each other in unconditional agapeic community they are united in true faith. But they are also empowered to stand together in the solidarity of concrete actions and deeds. Hence, active solidarity of a black-and-white congregated church community is the starting point for genuine spiritual community.

5. Christians must own without flinching the conviction that racism and the Christian faith are mutually exclusive. Racism is simply incompatible with the life and teaching of Jesus himself.

11. Bonhoeffer's Theology and Economic Humanism: An Exploration in Interdisciplinary Sociality

> Tatenloses Abwarten und stumpfes Zuschauen
> sind keine christlichen Haltungen. Den Christen
> rufen nicht erst die Erfahrungen am eigenen
> Leibe, sondern die Erfahrungen am Leibe der
> Brüder, um derentwillen Christus gelitten hat, zur
> Tat und zum Mitleiden.[1]

Introduction: The Economic Downward Spiral

The aim of this essay is an examination of Bonhoeffer's theology vis-à-vis economics. Admittedly, at first glance, this may appear as a rather far-fetched idea since Bonhoeffer was neither trained nor known as an economist and has left us no systematic treatment of his thought on that subject. Yet, there is the curious fact that Bonhoeffer's entire adult life unfolded within an inexorable economic downward spiral. The height of that spiral was for Bonhoeffer in all probability the granting of his doctoral degree in theology in 1927. The bourgeois élan of the Bonhoeffer family, embedded as it was in intellectual elitism and relative economic wealth, had borne another fruit with the legendary academic achievement of the youngest son, at a mere 21 years of age. There is little doubt that the prism through which the newly minted Dr. Dietrich Bonhoeffer looked at the world in 1927 was "from above." Yet from now on, slowly but surely, his vantage point of the world was about to change and Bonhoeffer was drawn into these changes, not as a spectator, but increasingly more as one of the protagonists. The year in Barcelona (1928–1929) opened his eyes for the social issues of both the business class and those on the margins of society. Then, in 1929, the Wall Street Crash happened and shortly thereafter Bonhoeffer visited New York City as a post-doctoral student at Union Theological Seminary. During that year, his eyes were opened for the social issues in

---

[1] *DBW* 8, 34.

the United States, most of all the ill of racism and its economic impact on the lives of African-Americans. When he returned to Berlin, the economic constraints of the Weimar Republic made themselves felt with his students and society. Germany was plagued with extremely high unemployment, nearly 30 % by 1932. Even though the rise of Nazism in 1933 temporarily improved economic conditions, as the economy now geared up for the industrial output of war machinery, within the next decade all of Germany was faced with the impending total collapse of its economy. Bonhoeffer himself walked to the gallows with literally no possessions. He, too, had lost everything. His life journey "from above" now ended in the deepest "here below."

Against the foil of Bonhoeffer's own experience of an economic downward spiral, the objective of this essay lies in the exploration of what he had to say of the complex interdisciplinary matrix between theology and economy. What is the relation between these two disciplines? How are the brute realities of economic suffering for the masses to be correlated with the gospel of Jesus Christ? In what manner should theology address economic issues? What is the role of the church between theology and economics? I will examine these questions in several steps. I will first p resent B on-hoeffer's own pronouncement of the emergence of the humanistic side of his theology, followed by an analysis of his basic theological assumptions in relation to his statements on the questions of economics. I will finally, and more tentatively, sketch a brief outline for the development of a critical theology that provokes the emergence of authentic humanistic economies.

The Humanizing of Bonhoeffer's Theology

Since Bonhoeffer was foremost a theologian, I will correspondingly address our key question of the relation between theology and economics from Bonhoeffer's theological perspectives, a path that he himself would have followed. The discipline of theology was the lens through which he analyzed almost all of the spheres around him. That is to say, a theological analysis of the questions of economics would at least have been his starting point in coming to terms with the complex relation between theology and economies.

To repeat what I indicated above, Bonhoeffer's own experience of the downward economic spiral, the descent from a life "above" to the suffering world "below" happened in various stages. Two such crucial stages in this journey were the experiences in Barcelona and New York City. In 1928,

Bonhoeffer went a year to Barcelona in order to be an assistant pastor to a German Lutheran congregation. On his way there, he visited a high mass in Paris that was attended by many prostitutes. The emotional reaction of the young pastor was profound: "It was an enormously impressive picture, and once again one could see quite clearly how close, precisely through their fate and guilt, these most heavily burdened people are to the heart of the gospel."[2] Here we have one of the earliest utterances of Bonhoeffer's emerging social conscience. He speaks of the "most heavily burdened people," burdens often brought about by "fate and guilt." The number of burdened people in his life was to grow steadily, as during the year in Barcelona. There his eyes and heart were opened to a reality of what he termed the "social question."[3]

Interestingly, Bonhoeffer's biographical encounter with the underside of social realities during the Barcelona year had as its correlative a re-conception of his theology. In an entry in his diary, he notes: "My theology is beginning to become humanistic; what does that mean? I wonder whether Barth ever lived abroad?"[4] Here Bonhoeffer gives us a glance into his theological formation. Prompted by his personal experiences of the "social question" he is thinking about theology in a new key. It is taking shape in a more "humanistic" fashion, even though he does himself not quite know what "humanistic" means. Given his reference to living "abroad" we may surmise that perhaps a "humanistic" kind of theology is one that emerges both in the academy and in the encounters with other human beings and their cultures. Or more precisely, academic theology is fine-tuned in the academy of life, namely in the social, political and economic structures in which people live. Something to this effect Bonhoeffer alludes to in a sermon. Although he does not address the question of theology as such, he ventures a few comments on what we can argue to be one of the goals of theology, namely the empowering of Christians to live a fully human life. "Christians," he proclaims, "serve *their own time*, and that means they step into the midst of it with all its problems and difficulties, with it seriousness and distress, and there they serve. Christians are people of the present in the most profound sense. Be it *political* and *economic* problems, *moral* and

---

[2] *DBWE* 10, 59.

[3] *DBWE* 10, 62, 69. The social question emerged as Bonhoeffer witnessed both the extravagance of the German business community (cf. *DBWE* 10, 69, 78), human hardship (cf. *DBWE* 10, 78: financial difficulties) and social marginality (cf. *DBWE* 10, 110). According to his own description, he encountered globetrotters, vagrants, escaped criminals, hired killers, legionnaires, circus people, dancers.

[4] *DBWE* 10, 64.

religious decline, concern for the present generation of young people – everywhere the point is to enter into the problems of the present."[5]

Although Bonhoeffer does not use the word "*humanisitic*" in this sermon, his reflection leaves no doubt: theology is not a mere abstract academic undertaking but must relate in a most concrete manner to the social realities of *human* beings, including the realm of economics.

In New York, we observe a subtle yet important terminological change in Bonhoeffer's characterization of social realities. Whereas in Barcelona he spoke in general terms of the "social question," now in New York, he speaks of the "social problem."[6] Why this adaptation in expression? Without overstating the case, could it be that Bonhoeffer's exposure to the social realities in Barcelona were still more coloured by his life "from above." While not denying that social issues did exist, the young Bonhoeffer still judged those somewhat disinterestedly, hence the expression "social question." A question does not per se imply an issue. In New York, however, Bonhoeffer took his own sermon from Barcelona to heart, especially in his confrontation with racism[7] in Harlem and the full-fledged economic crisis following the Wall Street collapse a year earlier. Racism and economics were not mere academic issues or neutral social realities. They were concrete social evils and problems. Now Bonhoeffer understood unmistakably: social realities imply tremendous issues, suffering, imbalances, dysfunction and destruction. What was at stake was not theology, but human lives uprooted because of economic collapse; hence, theology must address these social issues in a manner that human life is transformed into new ways of humane and equitable existence.

In the middle of his journey "from above to below," Bonhoeffer penned down the now famous recollection for his fellow-conspirators at New Year's Eve 1943, entitled "After Ten Years." Even though he had still not arrived at the bottom himself, he ponders: "It remains an experience of incomparable value that we have for once learnt to see the great events of world history from below, from the perspective of the outcast, the suspects, the maltreated, the powerless, the oppressed and the reviled, in short from the perspective of the suffering."[8]

---

[5] *DBWE* 10, 529.

[6] *DBWE* 10, 307.

[7] Cf. my essay, "Dietrich Bonhoeffer's Theological Anthropology: The Case of Racism," in this volume.

[8] *DBWE* 8, 52.

Economics and Theology: Basic Assumptions

On a global scale, "those who suffer" includes vast numbers of people who suffer because of the negative effects brought about by the economic structures that govern their everyday lives. This is no different in Bonhoeffer's time from our own at the beginning of the twenty-first century. Yet – as we noted already – because Bonhoeffer was primarily a theologian and a preacher and not an economist or a social worker, he was interested in articulating theology and not advance economic theories. Moreover, given his own experiences of the economic spiral, it should not come as a surprise that Bonhoeffer did on occasion discuss the questions of economics. Our task is now to articulate the three basic theological and "humanistic" assumptions he brings to bear on his understanding of economics.

Economics as a Reality Dependent on the Reality of Christ

Likely, late in the summer of 1942, Bonhoeffer wrote a lengthy review of a monograph by Otto Dilschneider, entitled *Die evangelische Tat: Grundlagen und Grundzüge der evangelischen Ethik* (Gütersloh: Bertelsmann 1940). According to Bonhoeffer, the thesis of the book was vintage Lutheran: Protestant ethics addresses exclusively the question of the personhood of the human being and that all other spheres in the world remain untouched by this key question. Bonhoeffer remarks that "these assertions are intended to prove that Christian ethics does indeed have to do with the Christian businessman, Christian statesman, etc., but not with economics, politics, etc."[9] Dilschneider proposes – by employing the notions of *Personalethos* and *Realethos* – the separation of the person (Christian man or woman) and the realm in which one's personhood (businessperson) becomes actualized (realm of economics). For Bonhoeffer the overarching question thus becomes whether "*in the realm of Christian ethics it is possible to make statements about worldly orders and conditions, thus, e.g., about state, economy, science ... or whether these things of the world are in fact 'ethically neutral'.*"[10]

Bonhoeffer places his critique of Dilschneider's basic thesis in the context of liberal theology and religious socialism. The former misread the gospel as a merely religious message mostly irrelevant to social, worldly realities and orders, while the latter emphasised the "social-revolutionary

---

[9] *DBWE* 16, 540–541.
[10] *DBWE* 16, 541; original emphasis.

character of Jesus' words about the poor and the rich, about justice and peace." In effect, Bonhoeffer argues, "both have read past the center of the New Testament, namely, the *person of Jesus Christ as the salvation of the world*. The ethical question is resolved in the question of Christ, and the question of the gospel's relation to the worldly orders can be answered only from the New Testament answer to the question of Christ." [11] Furthermore, Bonhoeffer contends, "all created things are through and for Christ and exist only in Christ (Colossians 1:16), i.e., there is nothing that would stand outside the relation to Christ, neither persons nor things; indeed, in relation to Christ do created things have their being, not only human beings but also state, economy, science nature, etc." [12]

Bonhoeffer's sentiment expressed in these words takes on an even more crystallized form when placed into the context of his conception of reality (*Wirklichkeit*). One of the most basic presuppositions of all of Bonhoeffer's thought is his critique of what he calls the "pseudo-Lutheranism" of the post-Reformation period, in particular the emphasis on Luther's doctrine of the two kingdoms. [13] In the section "Christ, Reality and the Good" in his *Ethics*, Bonhoeffer boldly declares: "There are not two realities, but *only one reality*, and that is God's reality revealed in Christ in the reality of the world... The world has no reality of its own independent of God's revelation in Christ. It is a denial of God's revelation in Jesus Christ to wish to be 'Christian' without being 'worldly,' or to wish to be worldly without seeing and recognizing the world in Christ. Hence there are not two realms, but only *the one realm of the Christ-reality* [*Christuswirklichkeit*], in which the reality of God and the reality of the world are united." [14]

Bonhoeffer's view of the unity of reality because of Jesus Christ thus precludes the autonomy of economics. Even though de facto much of our contemporary world functions as if economics is an independent reality, Bonhoeffer's theological premise of the one reality in Christ calls the Christian to be an economic agent within the one structure of reality created and sustained by God.

---

[11] *DBWE* 16, 542–543.
[12] *DBWE* 16, 543.
[13] In *DBWE* 6, 114, Bonhoeffer asserts that Luther's doctrine of the two kingdoms had since the Reformation been misunderstood in that "government, reason, economy, and culture each claimed the right to autonomy."
[14] *DBWE* 6, 58.

The Bourgeois Church and the Proletariat

Already in his dissertation *Sanctorum Communio*, the young Bonhoeffer had included a discussion of capitalism, the proletariat and the church. Reinhold Seeberg, his doctoral supervisor, was rather critical of those pages and wondered if they belonged to the dissertation at all. Not surprising, then, those pages had suffered the fate of obscurity in the first published editions until the new critical edition in the *Dietrich Bonhoeffer Werke* restored them to their proper place, albeit tucked away in elongated and tedious footnote.

Bonhoeffer's discussion is framed by Troeltsch's question to what extent the church offers a solution to contemporary social issues. The latter asserts that "the social problem is vast and complicated. It includes the problem of the capitalistic economic period and of the industrial proletariat created by it" but also matters such as the growth of military, super states, colonialism, trade and the treatment of "people and labor like machines."[15]

As Seeberg correctly detected, Bonhoeffer's discussion of the questions raised by Troeltsch is indecisive as he struggles to do justice to a theology of the church, contemporary social issues and his own privileged upbringing. Notwithstanding Seeberg's reluctant criticism, it is crucial to keep in mind that here we have one of the earliest indications in Bonhoeffer's work that he clearly perceived the correlation between theology and practice, between the church and society, between the privileged and the unprivileged. How these correlations are articulated theologically and how they actually shape the church or contemporary society is another question. For now, the young doctor of theology wrestles with these issues, and this is to his credit more than it is a criticism. As he matures in age, gains broader theological insights and experiences the world more and more "from below," the answers to these early questions come increasingly into sharper focus.

The young Bonhoeffer acknowledges that "Christian social work has accomplished admirable things," but the key question for him lies elsewhere. He wonders: "where is the real discussion among gospel, church-community, and proletariat?"[16] The framing of the question with these three nouns is significant. Concisely, they represent for Bonhoeffer the pillars of a theology that is based on the Word of God, manifests its power in the church-community and must concretely shape the world that

---

[15] *DBWE* 1, 271, note 430.
[16] *DBWE* 1, 272, note 430.

suffers. Programmatic for his reflection is the acclamation: "No apotheosis of the proletariat! It is neither the bourgeois nor the proletarian who is right, but the gospel alone. Here is neither Jew nor Greek."[17]

The fundamental insight "the gospel alone" is one of the structural pillars of Bonhoeffer's theological work. The criterion that applies to all his theological decisions is the Word of God. A few years later, in his lecture on the history of systematic theology at the University of Berlin in the winter semester 1931–1932, he expresses the same insight most succinctly: "*Deus dixit* – to accept this is the beginning of all genuine theological thinking, to allow space for the freedom of the living God."[18] Because God has spoken and revealed himself in his word, therefore the Word of God stands between what he calls the bourgeois and the proletariat. Bonhoeffer's usage of these two terms is rather interesting. Given his own bourgeois heritage, Bonhoeffer seems hesitant to transgress boundaries that would betray certain sympathies for the proletariat. Yet, intuitively he knows that if theology and the church are any good, they must precisely be able to speak to the conditions that divide the masses into bourgeois and the proletariat. He never defines these terms, but it seems that the economic realities and their "class background"[19] attached to either of them would not have escaped his usually lucid perception of reality. He notes that the gospel's proclamation confronts his times with "the problem of the proletariat" in a church that is bourgeois. "The best proof," he argues, "remains that the proletariat has turned its back on the church, while the bourgeois (civil servant, skilled worker, merchant) stayed."[20] For this reason, "sermons are thus aimed at people who live relatively securely and comfortably, in orderly family circumstances who are relatively 'educated', and relatively stable morally."[21] While Bonhoeffer laments the bourgeois nature of the church, he also thinks that "the coming church will not be 'bourgeois'. How it will look is today still unclear."[22]

Curiously, in that discussion Bonhoeffer also invokes terms such as "working-class people" and "socialist doctrine."[23] It is obvious that while

---

[17] *DBWE* 1, 272, note 430.
[18] *DBWE* 11, 231.
[19] *DBWE* 1, 272, note 430.
[20] *DBWE* 1, 273, note 430.
[21] *DBWE* 1, 273, note 430.
[22] *DBWE* 1, 273, note 430.
[23] *DBWE* 1, 273, note 430. On a historical note, however, Bonhoeffer understands why socialism emerged. He is in agreement with Ludwig Feuerbach who questioned whether religious claims actually correspond to the reality of life. While Feuerbach denies such a correspondence, Bonhoeffer thinks that because theology did not address

he welcomes the demise of a bourgeois church he is also reticent about a church with socialist characteristics. "It is incorrect," he remarks, "to think that the idea of socialism as such would sociologically correspond to the Christian concept of community ... or God's Realm on earth."[24] Bonhoeffer argues that "the socialist idea of equality is theologically and sociologically untenable ... The Christian community is based on the dissimilarity and inequality of persons."[25] Here then is one of the reasons why Bonhoeffer rejects socialism, at least when it is predicated on equality and placed on the same level as the church. Socialism, he thinks, brushes over human inequality, over each person's uniqueness – in theological language, it does not see that each person bears the unique impression of God's image.

The Value of the Human Being

In accordance with Bonhoeffer's view that there is only one reality in Jesus Christ, he contends: "Jesus Christ the human being – that means that God enters into created reality, that we may be and should be human beings before God."[26] In other words, Bonhoeffer's assumption of the unity of reality is not an abstract theological datum, but points to a concrete structure of being for and in the world. "The entire new humanity," says Bonhoeffer, "is established in reality in Jesus Christ, *he represents the whole history of humanity in his historical life.*"[27] As the context of Bonhoeffer's discussion indicates, this statement must not be interpreted as a quantitative claim, namely that the life of Jesus Christ universally subsumes all historical events. Rather, it is a theological statement to the effect that because of the earthly Jesus of Nazareth and the resurrected Christ, there is now for humanity as a whole, in the here and now, a new way of being in the world, the new path toward life.

Given that the Christ-reality encompasses all aspects of the world's reality, human life in particular has a unique locus in the world. In Bonhoeffer's own words: "Life created and preserved by God possesses an inherent right, completely independent of its social utility. The right to life inheres

---

the matter of correspondence, therefore socialism filled the void and emerged as a social force (cf. *DBWE* 11, 185–186).

[24] *DBWE* 1, 274, note 430.
[25] *DBWE* 1, 274, note 430.
[26] *DBWE* 6, 157.
[27] *DBWE* 1, 147; original emphasis.

in what exists [*im Seienden*] and not is some value or other. There is no worthless life before God, because God holds life itself to be valuable."[28]

Just as God pronounced creation itself as good, so likewise is the creation of the human being in itself good. Because all life comes from God, the human being has, as Bonhoeffer says, "an inherent right." This right is completely autonomous. In other words, while Bonhoeffer grants the autonomy of the value of life independent from "social utility" or any other qualifier, he rejects, as we saw above, the existence of any other autonomous sphere. Concretely, only the human being as such has an inherent and autonomous value. This value is a given, a fact that is grounded in the unity of the Christ-reality; it is, one of the inviolable human rights. For this reason, Bonhoeffer boldly but correctly asserts: "The destruction of humaneness [*Menschsein*] is sin."[29] As an autonomous value embedded as it were in the very existence of a person, the inherent worth of the human being cannot be constructed, or deconstructed as such. Human worth and dignity may be violated or enhanced, but it cannot be taken from a person. Nevertheless, when Bonhoeffer says that "the destruction of *Menschsein*" is the work of sin, in my view he cannot thereby mean the destruction of the inherent and inviolable value and dignity of a person, but only refer to the attacks on a person's dignity. Nonetheless, as we shall see below, such attacks have far-reaching implications on a person's life, not least of which may be the economic one.

At any rate, long after Bonhoeffer had joined the conspiracy circle and had come to understand the full measure of Nazi atrocities did he once again reflect on the value of human life. In *After Ten Years*, his new year's reflection of 1943 addressed to his co-conspirators, he includes a warning under the title, "Contempt for Humanity?" "The danger of allowing ourselves to be driven to contempt for humanity is very real. We know very well that we have no right to let this happen and that it would lead us into the most unfruitful relation to human beings ... The only fruitful relation to human beings – particularly to the weak among them – is love, that is, the will to enter into and keep community [*Gemeinschaft*] with them. God did not hold human beings in contempt but became human for their sake."[30]

In terms of the history of theology in the twentieth century, it is the movement known as the "Theology of Liberation" that has most clearly analyzed and articulated what is at stake in a world that has contempt for

---

[28] *DBWE* 6, 193.
[29] *DBWE* 6, 157.
[30] *DBWE* 8, 44–45.

humanity and a theology that does not refute the dehumanizing effects of economic structures. Many of the founding fathers, such as Gustavo Gutiérrez,[31] Jon Sobrino[32] and Leonardo Boff,[33] have taken some of Bonhoeffer's ideas – most of all his call to see history "from below" – and have constructed a theology that addresses as a central concern the humanizing of the poor person in the midst of economic oppression. Gutiérrez has more than anyone else painted a disturbing picture of what happens to the dehumanized person: those "below," the economically exploited, oppressed and marginalized in effect become *"nonpersons."*[34] Their identity as a *human* being is nearly eradicated by economic structures. In this regard, Jon Sobrino very succinctly illuminates the nexus between economics and humanity. He comments on the fact that the economic development of the rich counties has had an almost exclusively negative impact on the humanization of poor peoples. "The civilization of wealth," he laments, *"has failed as a way of guaranteeing the life* of the majorities because its 'quality' of life cannot be universalized, given the universal correlation between resources and population; even if it could be universalized *it would not be desirable* to do so, because it has also failed as a *way of humanizing people and peoples."*[35]

In other words, what Sobrino unmasks as the wide gap between poverty and wealth is not a mere neutral phenomenon or a natural part of our world order. This gap is horrendous not primarily because there are rich and poor persons, but because the existence of wealth implies an inescapable structural consequence, namely the dehumanization of the poor persons. Poverty is a sin not because money and wealth are evil, but because they can potentially destroy the humanity and dignity of human beings. In the words of Sobrino, wealth has "failed as a *way of humanizing people and peoples."*

---

[31] Cf. Gustavo Gutiérrez, *A Theology of Liberation: History, Politics, and Salvation*, translated by Sister Caridad Inda and John Eaglson. Maryknoll: Orbis Books, revised edition, 1988, 24, 42, 119, 227, 253.

[32] For example, cf. his *Christology at the Crossroads*, translated by John Drury. Maryknoll: Orbis Books 1976, 197, 221, 262–263, 274, 308; *Jesus the Liberator*, translated by Paul Burns and Francis McDonagh. Maryknoll: Orbis Books 1993, 2, 56, 232, 250–251 and many of his other works.

[33] For example, *Jesus Christ Liberator. A Critical Christology for our Time*, translated by Patrick Hughes. Maryknoll: Orbis Books 1972, 245, 320.

[34] Gustavo Gutiérrez, "Theology from the Underside of History," in idem, *The Power of the Poor in History*. Maryknoll: Orbis Books 1983, 169–221, here 193. For a constructive interpretation of Gutiérrez and Bonhoeffer, see Clifford Green, "Bonhoeffer, Modernity and Liberation Theology," in Wayne Whitson Floyd, Jr. and Charles Marsch (eds), *Theology and the Practice of Responsibility. Essays on Dietrich Bonhoeffer*. Valley Forge: Trinity Press International 1994, 117–131.

[35] Jon Sobrino, *Where is God? Earthquakes, Terrorism, Barbarity, and Hope*. Maryknoll: Orbis Books 2004, 99.

Economic Systems and Humanity

We are now at a position to examine Bonhoeffer's more concrete statements on economics in relation to the assumptions of this theology in general, but also as articulated above in a more particular sense. In order to
frame our discussion, we will begin with one of the few passages in which
Bonhoeffer addresses the question of economic structures directly. In *Ethics*, he comments that: "There are, for example, certain economic or social
attitudes and conditions that hinder faith in Jesus Christ, which means that
they also destroy the essence of human beings and the world. It can be
asked, for example, whether capitalism, or socialism, or collectivism are
such economic systems that hinder faith. The church has a twofold approach here: on the one hand, it must declare as reprehensible, by the authority of the Word of God, such economic attitudes or systems that clearly hinder faith in Christ, thereby drawing a negative boundary. On the
other hand, it will not be able to make positive contributions to a new order
on the authority of the Word of God, but merely on the authority of responsible counsel by Christian experts."[36]

The issues raised by these lines that we will now address in more detail
are the questions of faith vis-à-vis economics and the broad question of the
role of the church in acting as an agent of economic critique.

Faith and Economics

First. Bonheoffer's words provide an unambiguous indication of the inexorable nexus between economics, sociality and human life. Economic systems and structures have an inescapable force on "the essence of human
beings and the world." Bonhoeffer's view on this matter fits squarely with
the theological movement seen from the beginning to the end of his theological oeuvre, namely to shift the emphasis from the individual (believer)
to the (church) community, and by extension, to the world.

In *Act and Being*, for example, Bonhoeffer attempted to demonstrate
that the "transcendental attempt of pure actualism" as also the attempt of
ontology "to establish the continuity of the I" failed because of its reference to the individual human being. "In searching for 'reality' it [transcen-
dental, ontological approach] overlooked the fact that in reality human
beings are never individuals only, not even those 'addressed by the You'.
Human beings, rather, are always part of a community, in 'Adam' or in

---

[36] *DBWE* 6, 361.

'Christ'."[37] Even though in this context Bonhoeffer speaks of philosophical and theological baselines, it is one of the bedrocks of his theology that all theoretical notions of these disciplines must find their relevance in sociality. In this sense, the questions of economic systems are also not a primary individualistic matter, but one that is centrally located in sociality. It is noteworthy that the term "economics" etymologically derives from the Greek compound οἶκος and νόμος, thus suggesting the governance (law) of the family (house), and by extension the governance of a community, society, nation and the world. The point is that the very definition of "economy" is social and communal. No one person is a law to her/himself, but in the Greek sense, law governs the house, hence the family, that is to say in relation to other people.

Second. Twice in the above citation, Bonheoffer mentions that economic and social conditions may "hinder faith in Jesus Christ." At first glance, this may come as an unexpected utterance from the very thinker who receives almost iconic esteem for his statements on "religionless Christianity." Is he not the man who championed some sort of secular Christianity? Suffice it to say here, that not only is there – even still today – an undue and therefore imbalanced weight placed on the raw intuitions penned down in his prison letters, there is likewise in my view an underestimation of Bonhoeffer's deep rootedness in orthodox theological thinking. Even though our pluralistic age prefers a (post)modern Bonhoeffer over a dogmatic one, there is every indication that he espoused a traditional conception of salvation and redemption. Bonhoeffer himself expresses it in this way: "The kind of thinking that starts out with human problems, and then looks for solutions from that vantage point, has to be overcome – it is unbiblical. The way of Jesus Christ, and thus the way of all Christian thought, is not the way from the world to God but from God to the world. This means that the essence of the gospel does not consist in solving worldly problems, and also that this cannot be the essential task of the church. However, it does not follow from this that the church would have no task at all in this regard. *But we will not recognize its legitimate task unless we first find the correct starting point.*"[38]

In a similar vein, and perhaps even more startling, Bonhoeffer seems very convinced of his position: "The problem of the poor and rich can never be solved in any other way than leaving it unsolved."[39] Whatever

---

[37] *DBWE* 2, 113.
[38] *DBWE* 6, 356.
[39] *DBWE* 6, 355.

Bonhoeffer may have intended with this last citation, it is more important to return to the end of the previous statement. Even though the solving of social issues, including that of poverty, is not the primary task of the church, it does not mean that "the church would have no task" in the sociality of the world. What matters in this regard is that the church understands her correct starting point. *In nuce*, the starting point for Bonhoeffer is that "in Jesus Christ God comes down into the very depths of the human fall, of guilt, and of need," and offers "the justice and grace of God." The endpoint is also clear: God's coming "is especially close to the very people who are deprived of rights, humiliated, and exploited."[40]

The context of Bonhoeffer's words is that of the discussion of the ultimate and penultimate dialectic in *Ethics*. The coming of the grace of God in the proclamation of his word has an almost irreversible sequence for Bonhoeffer. Coming is preparing; preparing is responsible action. "Preparing the way is indeed a matter of concrete intervention in the visible world, as concrete and visible as hunger and nourishment."[41] Since the Word of God always addresses the concrete human being who has her/his value independent of any social utility, as we saw above, it follows for Bonhoeffer that "it is hard for those thrust into extreme disgrace, desolation, poverty, and helplessness to believe in God's justice and goodness."[42] "If the hungry do not come to faith, the guilt falls on those who denied them bread. To bring bread to the hungry is preparing the way for the coming of grace."[43]

Bonhoeffer does not address the question of economic systems in this context. His reflections seem to be more on the micro-economic rather than macro-economic level. Yet, just as the theological starting point for social transformation is rooted in the coming of God's grace in the person Jesus Christ, so likewise, the economic starting point for social transformation lies on the micro-economic level of responsible Christian action. For Bonhoeffer such action is not an option of the person who claims to walk in the *Nachfolge* of Jesus Christ. "It is, instead, a commission of immeasurable responsibility given to all who know about the coming of Jesus Christ. The hungry person needs bread, the homeless person needs shelter, the one deprived of rights needs justice, the lonely person needs community, the undisciplined one needs order, and the slave needs freedom. It would

---

[40] *DBWE* 6, 163.
[41] *DBWE* 6, 164.
[42] *DBWE* 6, 162. Conversely, "it is hard for the well-fed and the powerful to comprehend God's judgment and God's grace."
[43] *DBWE* 6, 163.

be blasphemy against God and our neighbor to leave the hungry unfed while saying that God is closest to those in deepest need."[44] To repeat, for Bonhoeffer, the proclamation of the coming grace of God goes hand in hand with the social activism for those in need. The two belong together – irrevocably and undivided. They are the micro-economic preparation for the Word of God to bear fruit and not "hinder faith in Christ."

The Church and Economic Critique

The question of the macro-economic task of the church vis-à-vis contemporary economic structures is a far more difficult subject in Bonhoeffer, least of which because he rarely touches on this matter. There are, nonetheless, several principles we can discern in his statements.

First. In the quotation above, Bonhoeffer specifically mentions capitalism, socialism and collectivism (seemingly his way of referring to Marxism) and characterizes them once as "economic systems" and once as "economic or social attitudes." As we noted, Bonhoeffer's primary interest lies in whether they hinder or facilitate a person's coming to faith. Nonetheless, the main point here is that he clearly recognizes that economic structures are systems that play themselves out in the arena of sociality. This is true of all three economic systems mentioned by Bonhoeffer. Be it capitalism, socialism or Marxism – all of them are more or less rigid structures that prescribe for peoples how they must accomplish their work, be compensated for it and how they are free or repressed to spend those earnings. In other words, there is hardly any person anywhere who is not in one way or another tied to an economic structure. Conversely, every economic system vies to impose its structures on all the people who live within its confines. Bonhoeffer is prudent, however, in that he does not forthrightly declare one system superior over another. For him – and this is decisive – the question he brings to all three of these systems in not in terms of industrial productivity or economic profitability. For example, he does not assume that capitalism is the best and Marxism (collectivism) the worst economic structure. His interest in these economic systems does not lie in the economic realm as such, but on the impact any economic system has on sociality.

Second. Given the above, the task of the church is therefore precisely not in assessing an economic system vis-à-vis its impact on market, industry, finances and wealth of a county. Quite to the contrary, the church must be

---

[44] *DBWE* 6, 163.

keenly aware of the underside of economic malpractice and draw the "negative boundary." In Bonhoeffer's words, the church has the responsibility to "declare reprehensible" those acts within economic systems that "destroy the essence of human beings and the world." So this is the benchmark by which Bonhoeffer assesses economic systems: it is the question of whether they enhance or destroy the human being. Given Bonhoeffer's theological perspectives, he is not interested in the orthodox economic methods of assessment. The performance of an economic system is for him secondary to its ability to enhance life for the people who live and work within its structures.

As we mentioned at the beginning of this essay, Bonhoeffer's experience of the structures of economics moved more and more on a downward spiral. For him this downward economic spiral was, of course, yoked for ill to the ideology that drove economics forward. Nazi ideology had the unintentional effect that it "destroyed the essence of human beings and the world." The fact that every economic system is predicated on an underlying ideology needs no accounting. This is the case with industrial war economics and Nazism, with Stalinism and Marxist ideology, capitalism and Friedmanian unrestricted-market ideology and with socialism and its own various ideologies. Bonhoeffer looks at all of these economic structures from the single vantage point of whether they destroy of enhance life.

Suffice to mention here, that by current assessments, the world as a whole has not done well. A quick look at the statistics of worldwide poverty will preclude any triumphalism in an instant;[45] over 1 trillion dollars has not helped to improve the overall quality of life in the entire continent of Africa.[46] Similarly, the unrestraint, greedy post-World War II capitalism of the wealthiest countries has ruined more nations in the last century than the ordinary person can imagine.[47] The reality for the masses of this world is staggering: millions of refugees, migrant workers, hundreds of millions of malnourished people, scores of underemployed and unemployed.[48] To be sure, all of these evils are not exclusively the result of an economic struc-

---

[45] Cf. Christine Schliesser, "Verantwortung nach Bonhoeffer: Armut als Fallbeispiel," in John W. Gruchy, Stephen Plant and Christiane Tietz (eds), *Dietrich Bonhoeffers Theologie heute. Dietrich Bonhoeffer's Theology Today. Ein Weg zwischen Fundamentalismus und Säkularismus? A Way between Fundamentalism and Secularism?* Gütersloh: Gütersloher Verlagshaus, 2009, 292–304.

[46] Cf. Dambisa Moyo, *Dead Aid. Why Aid is Not Working and How there is a Better Way for Africa.* New York: Farrar, Straus and Giroux 2009.

[47] Cf. Naomi Klein, *The Shock Doctrine. The Rise of Disaster Capitalism.* Toronto: Knopf 2008.

[48] For a proven approach to reduce poverty on the micro-economic scale, see Paul

ture as such; for indeed, there is much misuse and corruption among those who are in control of these structures. Nonetheless, it is undeniable that certain forms of capitalistic structures do bring about oppression and – to repeat – contribute to "destroy the essence of human beings and the world."

Conclusion:
Towards A Theological "Critical Theory" – And More

Today, it seems to me, one of the most urgent needs for theology is to engage proactively in what Bonhoeffer termed the "positive contribution" with respect to dominant economic systems and structures. How can contemporary theology dare to contribute positively to matters of economics? Are theologians entitled to transgress into the field of other experts? In this regard, Bonhoeffer calls for "Christian experts." Presumably, what he means is not theologians, but Christians who are trained as experts in the fields of economics. As contemporary theologians, we concede that economic issues are the prerogative of economic experts. Yet, any successful dialogue on economic systems must not only be inter-disciplinary and multi-disciplinary, it must also include the voice of theologians who will never get tired of promoting humanizing economic systems.

But what may be the contributions of theologians? In his essay on Bonhoeffer, for example, Gutiérrez cites the famous text from "After Ten Years" that we cited above. "It would be unwarranted," he comments, "to attempt to deduce from Bonhoeffer's use of terms such as 'poor' and 'oppressed' that we are in the presence of a critical analysis of modern society on grounds of that society's injustice and oppression."[49] Even so, Gutiérrez recognizes that "there are weighty indications that Bonhoeffer had begun to move forward in the perspective of 'those beneath' – those on the 'underside of history'."[50]

As the father of Liberation Theology, Gutiérrez proposes a kind of theology that critically looks at the interplay between theology and economic structures vis-à-vis the very essence of humanity. Even before him, the Frankfurt School of Critical Theory had addressed very similar questions, albeit from a philosophical, Marxist oriented perspective. One of its chief

---

Polak, *Out of Poverty. What Works when Traditional Approaches Fail*. San Francisco: Berret-Koehler 2008.

[49] "The Limitations of Modern Theology: On a Letter of Dietrich Bonhoeffer," in idem, *The Power of the Poor in History*, 231.

[50] "The Limitations of Modern Theology: On a Letter of Dietrich Bonhoeffer," 231.

architects, Max Horkheimer, unmistakably understood that all "cultural forms which are based on struggle and oppression are not evidence of a homogeneous self-conscious will; this world is not theirs, but belongs to capital."[51] Whatever one may make of the success or failure of the Frankfurt School, one fact remains: the members of the school understood far more clearly than their theological counterparts (there are, of course exceptions, such as Moltmann, Metz and others) that culture is largely constructed by economic ideology which has the potential to destroy humanity at its essence. In the face of contemporary economic crises, post-modern theology must have the courage to articulate a kind of critical theological theory. What kind of shape, what specific tasks, what objectives and desired outcomes such a venture will entail is a matter for this generation of theologians to determine. This is the easy part.

The real question lies completely elsewhere. Even if theologians succeed in articulating a powerful "critical theology" – who will subscribe to this kind of theology? Will economists, will the corporate world, will shareholders and politicians – in short, the privileged and powerful – really care about a theology that could facilitate a more economically equitable and globally more sustainable world? As long as critical theology is just "public theology" for the sake of theology, it has no sting. A true public, critical theology must aim squarely at real life transformations of those who experience the world "from below." Theology always begins in reflection, but it must end in praxis.

Both Bonhoeffer and Horkheimer experienced the events of world history "from below", as does Gutiérrez in his life with the Quechan people of Peru. Their own *Sitz im Leben* and commitment to the plight of those "below" undoubtedly shaped the contours of their thought and the ways in which they lived. They all understood that "a purely spiritual resistance becomes just a wheel in the machine of the totalitarian state. True discipleship, to which many Christians may once again be called, does not lead men back to religion."[52] These words seem as if they could be the prose of Bonhoeffer, but in fact, Horkheimer uttered them. For Bonhoeffer, true

---

[51] Max Horkheimer, *Critical Theory: Selected Essays*. New York: Herder and Herder 1972, 207–208. One of the problems today is as follows: the revolutionary working class – or, to use Bonhoeffer's term: the now outdated expression "the proletariat" – exists no longer in a post-Berlin-Wall world and so there is no longer a dialectical lever to activate the whole or large portions of society. Consumption for the sake of consumption has numbed the social consciousness of the masses, other than giving to charity and superficial sympathy with "the less fortunate."

[52] Max Horkheimer, "Thoughts on Religion," in idem, *Critical Theory: Selected Essays*, 130–131.

discipleship leads to the following of Jesus Christ and, by extension, true critical theology must lead to the equitable economic life of those "below." Not a single person in this world is excluded from what Bonhoeffer declared:

God
wants us to be wholly
what we are.
Be men and women,
both wholly
and in their essence
as created by God.
Be human beings
with your own wills, with your own passions
and your own concerns,
your happiness and your distress,
your seriousness and your frivolity,
your jubilation and your misery.[53]

Such wholeness of humanity is not merely a matter of an inner strength or fundamental disposition toward life. A person's wholeness is critically shaped by the structures of economic systems within which he and she lives. As such it is the task of every good theology to work with other disciplines toward economic structures that make possible a life of human dignity by providing work, education, health, food, clothing and whatever else is necessary for the livelihood of every people in our world. This journey is a long one, and possibly a rocky one, but theology has to become a leader on that path – and not miss this obvious challenge. The goal is nothing less than humanity's life and experience of genuine economic sociality.

---

[53] *DBWE* 10, 530.

12. Bonhoeffer, Theology and Religion: What do they Teach us for a South-North Dialogue?[*]

El lema es ahora *otro mundo es posible*,
aunque no haya una palabra para designar este otro mundo,
ni se hayan formulado estrategias de transformación:
Todo es búsqueda.
Franz Hinkelammert[1]

Introduction

In July 1979, the Nicaraguan dictator Somoza was defeated in Managua by the Sandinistas. Ten years later in 1989, taking the world by surprise, the Berlin Wall crumbled unexpectedly and almost overnight. In the first half of the 1990s, the long awaited demise of Apartheid in South Africa became reality while in Eastern Europe one country after the other broke off the chains of decades of communism. In 2006, the peoples of Bolivia welcomed Evo Morales, the first indigenous president since the Spanish inquisition. In 2008, the American people voted for the African-American Democrat Barak Obama, thus effectively turning their backs on the capitalist terror of the Bush-Rumsfeld administration. Hand in hand, at about the same time, unfettered capitalism, Friedmanian style, showed its real face and cast the entire world into a near economic and financial apocalypse.[2]

What does all of this have to do with theology? Everything – and more, as I will argue. For in these historic transformations we have precedents that large-scale political, social and economic changes are possible – both positive and negative. At the bottom of historic transformations lies always

---

[*] This essay was first presented at Universidade Presbiteriana Mackenzie in São Paulo, Brazil, in May 2009.
[1] Franz Hinkelammert, "Pensar en alternativas: capitalismo, socialismo y la posibilidad de otro mundo," in Jorge Pixley (ed), *Por un mundo otro. Alternativas al Mercado global.* Quito: Consejo Latinoamericano de Iglesias 2003, 11.
[2] For a devastating critique of American imperialist capitalism, see Naomi Klein, *The Shock Doctrine. The Rise of Disaster Capitalism.* Toronto: Knopf 2008.

the deeply anchored hope, rendered here in the words that can often be heard in Latin America, that "otro mundo es posible."[3]

As the title of this essay indicates, this study engages four distinct themes, namely, Dietrich Bonhoeffer, theology, religion and dialogue. Our task is not so much to examine each of these themes in detail, but to work out a matrix that allows each of the themes to have a specific and important place in a genuine conversation. Our main objective is thus the question of how Bonhoeffer, theology and religion fit together in a coherent and integrative dialogue among theologians of the south and north and by extension between east and west. Since the chief objective is that of articulating a framework for such a dialogue, our discussion of Bonhoeffer, theology and religion focuses on the particular promise each of them brings to such a forum. Nonetheless, this study is a tentative endeavour predicated on the working hypothesis that Bonhoeffer, theology and religion each have a specific contribution to make to the south-north dialogue, a dialogue that is not only important but also necessary and possible. The key question addressed in this essay is why and to what extent these four aspects yield a promising basis for global theological dialogue aimed, ultimately, at the transformation of local and global communities.

Dietrich Bonhoeffer

Why is Bonhoeffer – among the host of theologians – the one who can contribute the most in defining the contours of a wide-ranging theological dialogue? The answer, in short, is two-fold. One the one hand, there is Bonhoeffer's biography, namely the journey from the height of Berlin's aristocracy into the heart of Leviathan's hell on the gallows of a concentration camp. On the other hand, there is the promise of his theology that sought to articulate a synthesis between the good news of Jesus Christ and the concrete reality of a secular and religionless life in Nazi Germany. In both instances – in biography and theology – the path began "from above" and ended up "below."

---

[3] Cf. as a representative view, Pablo Richard, *Fuerza ética y espiritual de la teología de la liberación. En el context actual de la globilización.* San José: Departamento Ecuménico de Investigaciones 2004. Richard asks that "si otro mundo es posible, ¿por qué no sera possible construir otro modelo de Iglesia?," 81.

The Beginning: From Above

Bonhoeffer's biography is one of the best-known aspects of his life, in particular the fact that he resisted the Nazi regime, participated in the conspiracy on Hitler's life and was hanged in the concentration camp Flossenbürg shortly before the end of the Second World War. As important as such an abbreviated sketch of his life may be, it masks the fact that his life has deep roots in the kind of theology he espoused.

Bonhoeffer's life began in Berlin, where his father was a famous neurologist and the head of the university hospital Charité. Bonhoeffer lived in the Grunewald district of Berlin, a neighbourhood that included the homes and villas of the intellectual and economic elite of Berlin. Like himself, his brothers and brothers-in-law had received doctorates at a young age. For example, the doctoral supervisor of his brother Karl Friedrich at the University of Berlin was Walther Nernst, who was honoured as a Nobel laureate in chemistry while Karl Friedrich was his student. As a post-doctoral researcher, Karl Friedrich worked with Fritz Haber, Nobel Prize recipient in Chemistry in 1918 and one of the friends of Albert Einstein, Nobel Prize laureate in Physics in 1921. Intellectual elitism, cultural bourgeoisie and economic affluence were characteristic of the life of the Bonhoeffer family. Given this kind of a social context, the life of Dietrich Bonhoeffer was undoubtedly one of privilege and status. When the young Bonhoeffer finished his doctoral dissertation at the age of 21, he had achieved much, even by the standards of Berlin. The prism through which he looked at the world in 1928 was "from above." Nevertheless, from now on, slowly but surely, his vantage point of the world was about to change and Bonhoeffer was drawn into these changes, not as a spectator, but progressively more as one of the actors.

The Middle: Falling Deeper

Bonhoeffer's descent from his life "from above" to the suffering world "below" happened in various stages. Two such crucial stages in this journey were the experiences in Barcelona and New York City. In 1928, Bonhoeffer went a year to Barcelona in order to be an assistant pastor to a German Lutheran congregation. On his way there, he visited a high mass in Paris that was attended by many prostitutes. Of that mass, these are the impressions of the freshly baked pastor: "it was an enormously impressive picture, and once again one could see quite clearly how close, precisely through their fate and guilt, these most heavily burdened people are to the heart of the gospel."[4] Here we have one of the earliest utterances of Bonhoeffer's emerging social conscience. He speaks of the "most heavily burdened people," burdens often brought about by "fate and guilt." The number of burdened people in his life was to grow steadily. During the year in Barcelona, Bonhoeffer's eyes were opened to a reality of what he termed the "social question."[5]

Interestingly, Bonhoeffer's biographical encounter with the underside of social realities had as its correlative a re-conception of his theology. In an entry in his diary, he notes: "My theology is beginning to become humanistic; what does that mean? I wonder whether Barth ever lived abroad?"[6] Here Bonhoeffer gives us a glimpse into his theological formation. Prompted by his personal experiences of the "social question" he is thinking about theology in a new key. It is taking shape in a more "humanistic" fashion even though he does not quite know what that means. A first answer is given in one of his sermons. "Christians," he proclaims, "serve *their own time*, and that means they step into the midst of it with all its problems and difficulties, with it seriousness and distress, and there they serve. Christians are people of the present in the most profound sense. Be it *political* and *economic* problems, *moral* and *religious* decline, concern for the present generation of young people – everywhere the point is to enter into the problems of the present."[7] Bonhoeffer's admonition leaves no doubt: theology is not a mere abstract academic undertaking but must relate in a most concrete manner to the social realities of life.

In New York, we observe a subtle yet important terminological change in Bonhoeffer's characterization of social realities. Whereas in Barcelona he spoke in general terms of the "social question," now in New York, he speaks of the "social problem."[8] Why this adaptation in expression? Without making too much of it, it is likely that Bonhoeffer's exposure to the social realities in Barcelona were still more coloured from his life "from above." While not denying that social issues did exist, the young Bonhoeffer still judged those somewhat disinterestedly, hence the expression "social ques-

---

[4] *DBWE* 10, 59.

[5] *DBWE* 10, 62, 69. The social question emerged as Bonhoeffer witnessed both the extravagance of the German business community (cf. *DBWE* 10, 69, 78), human hardship (cf. *DBWE* 10, 78: financial difficulties) and social marginality (cf. *DBWE* 10, 110). He encountered globetrotters, vagrants, escaped criminals, hired killers, legionnaires, circus people, dancers.

[6] *DBWE* 10, 64.

[7] *DBWE* 10, 529.

[8] *DBWE* 10, 307.

tion." A question does not per se imply an issue. In New York, however, Bonhoeffer took his sermon from Barcelona to heart, especially in his confrontation with racism in Harlem and the economic crisis in the United States. Racism and economics were not mere academic issues or neutral social realities. They were concrete social evils and problems. Now Bonhoeffer understood unmistakably: social realities imply tremendous issues, suffering, imbalances, dysfunction and destruction. What was at stake was not theology, but human lives; hence, theology must address these social issues in a manner that it supports and facilitates social transformations.

The Conclusion: Here Below

Bonhoeffer's return to the continent brought him eventually back to Berlin, via London and Finkenwalde. As the grip of Nazi evil became stronger and the atrocities against the Jews revealed themselves as a crime against humanity, Bonhoeffer's life "from above" became irrevocably shattered. His existence was now on a descent "from above" to the "below." The details of that downward spiral are well known and the stations need only be mentioned: involved in the conspiracy on Hitler's life, the arrest, various imprisonments, mock trial and murder at Flossenbürg concentration camp in April 1945, shortly before the end of the war.

In the middle of this journey "from above to below," Bonhoeffer penned down the now famous recollection for his fellow-conspirators at New Year's Eve 1943, entitled "After Ten Years." Even though he had still not arrived at the bottom himself, Bonhoeffer ponders: "It remains an experience of incomparable value that we have for once learnt to see the great events of world history from below, from the perspective of the outcast, the suspects, the maltreated, the powerless, the oppressed and the reviled, in short from the perspective of the suffering."[9]

Theology

Theology in the South

As you well know, many theologians of the South knew the theology of Dietrich Bonhoeffer from the time his works began to appear in print. Gustavo Gutiérrez, for example, engaged Bonhoeffer as early as his *A*

---

[9] *DBWE* 8, 52.

Theology of Liberation[10] and subsequently in his essay "The Limitations of Modern Theology: On a Letter of Dietrich Bonhoeffer."[11] The same substantial engagement with Bonhoeffer we find in Jon Sobrino,[12] Leonardo Boff[13] and many others to this very day. In his essay on Bonhoeffer, for example, Gutiérrez cites the same text from "After Ten Years" that we just cited above. "It would be unwarranted," he comments, "to attempt to deduce from Bonhoeffer's use of terms such as 'poor' and 'oppressed' that we are in the presence of a critical analysis of modern society on grounds of that society's injustice and oppression."[14] It seems to me that Gutiérrez is right in cautioning against using Bonhoeffer as model to construct a theology of social critique predicated on a person's participation in an unjust and oppressive society. Even so, Gutiérrez is also correct in recognizing that "there are weighty indications that Bonhoeffer had begun to move forward in the perspective of 'those beneath' – those on the 'underside of history'."[15]

As we noted already, the young Bonhoeffer was on a journey to discover the formation of his "humanistic" theology. Bonhoeffer was fortunate to discover early in his career that any theology must be humanistic to some degree. For a theology that does not focus on the human condition in a substantial manner forfeits its relevance and may end up becoming a mere philosophy of life. In God's story with the cosmos, human beings matter the most. Perhaps this is the reason why Gutiérrez maintains that "we meet God in our encounter with others."[16] The other – or in biblical terminology, the neighbour – is the one who in our encounter receives agapeic love. But to give our agapeic love freely to the neighbour is neither an automatic nor an inevitable Christian act; it must be practiced – intentionally. In this regard, Gutiérrez provides one of the most profound understanding of neighbour in his comments on the Good Samaritan. "The neighbour," he

---

[10] Cf. Gustavo Gutiérrez, *A Theology of Liberation: History, Politics, and Salvation*, translated by Sister Caridad Inda and John Eagleson. Maryknoll: Orbis Books, revised edition, 1988, 24, 42, 119, 227, 253.

[11] Gustavo Gutiérrez, *The Power of the Poor in History*, translated by Robert R. Barr. Maryknoll: Orbis Books 1983, 222–234.

[12] For example, cf. his *Christology at the Crossroads*, translated by John Drury. Maryknoll: Orbis Books 1976, 197, 221, 262–3, 274, 308; *Jesus the Liberator* translated by Paul Burns and Francis McDonagh. Maryknoll: Orbis Books 1993, 2, 56, 232, 250–251 and many of his other works.

[13] For example, *Jesus Christ Liberator. A Critical Christology for our Time*, translated by Patrick Hughes. Maryknoll: Orbis Books 1972, 245, 320.

[14] "The Limitations of Modern Theology: On a Letter of Dietrich Bonhoeffer," 231.

[15] "The Limitations of Modern Theology: On a Letter of Dietrich Bonhoeffer," 231.

[16] *A Theology of Liberation*, 110.

remarks, "was the Samaritan who *approached* the wounded man and *made him his neighbour*. The neighbour, as has been said, is not the one whom I find in my path, but rather the one in whose path I place myself."[17]

What does "the neighbour" mean with reference to a global theological dialogue? The answer, in short, is that theology must strive to articulate its doctrines in terms of the concreteness of the other, the neighbour. The difficulty lies not so much in incorporating the neighbour into a theological system as one of the various elements that together make up the cohesive structure of a particular theology. The difficulty, rather, lies in making the neighbour a crucial focal point of an entire theology. Again, the neighbour becomes not merely a focal point *in abstracto*, as the object or climax of theological thinking, but is central *in concreto* as the person created in the image of God. The other is not the content of my theology, but the recipient of my love.[18] In Pauline language, theology must prompt the follower of Jesus Christ to carry the burdens of others (Galatians 6:2). Alternatively, in the classical expression of liberation theology: Christian theology needs to push towards a preferential option for the poor, the neighbour, the other. However, what concretely does it mean to carry the neighbour's burdens?

Theology in the North

When it comes to the theological understanding of the neighbour, I think that for the most part theologies that work within a framework of redemption and liberation are a good step ahead of theologies that – although mindful of, to use Bonhoeffer's expression, the "the social problem" – do not make social issues their starting point. This is the case for most theologies in European and North American contexts. What is at stake in this approach?

Although theologians of the North Atlantic have mostly focused on theology as a system of thought, as doctrine and as academic discipline, a few understood from the beginning that theology at its core has to play the role of social and political critique. One may think of the theological proposals of Johann Baptist Metz and Jürgen Moltmann.[19] However, exceptions not-

---

[17] *A Theology of Liberation*, 113.

[18] In *DBWE* 1, 169, Bonhoeffer remarks: Christian love "*loves the real neighbor* ... I do not love God in the 'neighbor', but I love the concrete You."

[19] In his now famous open letter to Bonino, Moltmann initially challenged some of the assumptions of liberation theology, cf. his "An Open Letter to José Miguez Bonino", in *Christianity and Crisis* 29 (1976), 57. As the dialogue between continental and libera-

withstanding, theologies in the northern hemisphere have failed in a major and irreconcilable way. As difficult as it may be for theologians of the north to admit this, their theologies have fallen short in addressing the economic implications of the vast gap between wealth and poverty. In other words, northern theologies failed to delineate a critique of structural wealth; not the wealth of the wealthy, but in particular the wealth of Christians. Such an appraisal is not simply a lofty disavowal of theology. It is, on the contrary, a timely wakeup call to correct what Jon Sobrino describes with utmost clarity. "The civilization of wealth *has failed as a way of guaranteeing the life* of the majorities because its 'quality' of life cannot be universalized, given the universal correlation between resources and population; even if it could be universalized *it would not be desirable* to do so, because it has also failed as a *way of humanizing people and peoples.*"[20]

In other words, what Sobrino asserts in general terms about the inequalities of a civilization controlled by wealth must be of prime concern for theologians of all stripes. The wide gap between poverty and wealth is not a mere neutral phenomenon or a natural part of our world order. This gap is horrendous not primarily because there are rich and poor persons, but because the existence of wealth implies an inescapable structural consequence, namely the dehumanization of the poor persons. Poverty is a sin not because money is evil, but because it destroys the humanity and dignity of human beings. In the words of Sobrino, wealth has "failed as a *way of humanizing people and peoples.*"

Let us return to Bonhoeffer for a moment. In one of the fragments in *Ethics* he writes: "There are, for example, certain economic or social attitudes and conditions that hinder faith in Jesus Christ, which means that they also destroy the essence of human beings and the world [*das Wesen des Menschen und der Welt*]. It can be asked, for example, whether capitalism, or socialism, or collectivism are such economic systems that hinder faith."[21] Like Sobrino, Bonhoeffer connects the economic structures of the world with humanity. Aside from the fact that economic conditions play a role in preparing the way of faith, the decisive point for both Sobrino and Bonhoeffer is the correlation between economics and the essence of what it means to be a human being. While Bonhoeffer wonders in a more neutral tone whether capitalism, socialism or collectivism (communism) are most

---

tion theologians matured, Moltmann became favourably disposed toward the objectives of liberation theology.

[20] Jon Sobrino, *Where is God? Earthquakes, Terrorism, Barbarity, and Hope.* Maryknoll: Orbis Books 2004, 99.

[21] *DBWE* 6, 361.

appropriate for human well-being, Sobrino judges quite correctly that the social injustice brought about by the unequal distribution of wealth dehumanizes people. In other words, for Sobrino the economic issue is not primarily a question of what system fits the market, but what system brings about the greatest possible humanizing of the peoples of our planet. Sobrino has thus opened a very crucial window for theology: theological reflection on questions of economics must be predicated not on the questions of the market and profits but on the humanizing effect of the market on the greatest good of human beings. Perhaps at the risk of oversimplification, the framing of the issue in these terms does not seem to favour an economic structure of unregulated market-capitalism. We will return to this issue below.

Religion

Religion, as distinct from theology, must play a part in the humanizing processes of the world. Yet Bonhoeffer, like Barth, was not very fond of religion and both, as is well known, critiqued religion frequently and rigorously. In a recent essay, Christiane Tietz examined Bonhoeffer's assessment of religion anew and offers the following succinct insights. She maintains that Bonhoeffer's arguments for the end of religion – and correspondingly, the arrival of a "religionless" Christianity – are not based on socio-religious reasons, but on *theological* ones. Fundamentally, Bonhoeffer asserts that the concept [Tietz calls it *die Sache*] of religion is juxtaposed to the core of the Christian faith and Bonhoeffer therefore decouples religion and Christianity. He directs his critique against religion *within* Christianity in order to lay bare the potential *of* Christianity.[22]

Important as Bonhoeffer's theological critique of religion vis-à-vis religion may be, for the moment we are not concerned with religion from a theological perspective but from the socio-economic one. Because the phenomenon of religion is universal across all peoples, nations, languages and cultures, it follows that any global dialogue focussed on the transformation of an economically imbalanced and unjust society must reckon with the transformative power embedded in every religion. At the core, just as Bonhoeffer was discovering a "humanistic theology" religion must likewise

---

22 Cf. Christiane Tietz, "Unzeitgemäße Aktualität. Religionskritik in Zeiten der 'Wiederkehr der Religion'," in Ingolf U. Dalferth and Hans-Peter Grosshans (eds), *Kritik der Religion*, Religion in Philosophy and Theology 23. Tübingen: Mohr Siebeck 2006, 243–258.

seek to be a "humanistic religion." This is easier said than done. As Juan Luis Segundo has argued already in the 1970, the problem with popular religion, in other words, with the religious mass, is more of a psychological than a theological matter. The question at hand is how the religious masses are motivated for transformative social changes. Since it is the inscribed habit of the masses to follow without critical judgement, it is difficult to create an impulse for social transformation that is fully embraced within popular religion. Moreover, even when the mass of popular religion does embrace change, it is questionable whether the change stems from a deep religious conviction or is a mere reflection of the current *Zeitgeist*. Given these realities, Segundo's insights are still valid: "So we are left with a major issue that must still be explored. On the one hand we find *majority* lines of conduct that are quantitatively supreme; on the other hand we find *minority* lines of conduct that are qualitatively critical and decisive."[23]

Dialogue and Transformation

Let us attempt to bring together Bonhoeffer, theology and religion in view of a fruitful dialogue that aims at a transformation of the human condition. In this section, I will very briefly sketch some ideas on the nature of dialogue and then, in the final section, delineate some of the prospects and limitations.

Dialogue

The essence of the human being is the ability to speak, to engage in rational conversation, to be in dialogue. In the dialectic of speaking and listening, a person participates in his/her own reality, namely the reality of "humanity." Without conversation, the very essence of humanity is limited and hindered to unfold its potential. Conversely, participation in dialogue is one form by which humanity comes to itself. If dialogue is indeed one of the defining characteristics of humanity, what, then, is unique about a dialogue between Bonhoeffer, theology and religion? What does this conversation offer, what are its underlying assumptions, promises and limitations?

The Need for Dialogue. Even though every conversation implies the risk of emptiness and meaninglessness, there is no potential for change, trans-

---

[23] Juan Luis Segundo, *The Liberation of Theology*, translated by John Drury. Maryknoll: Orbis Books 1976, 205.

formation and humanity's coming of age apart from the actuality of conversation. At the surface, this may seem trivial, but it is the beginning of transformation. Only when people, groups and nations enter into genuine dialogue does the possibility for change arise – not before. In other words, the starting point for transformation is genuine dialogue. But dialogue always involves at least two partners. As the opportunities arose, both Bonhoeffer and a host of Latin American theologians engaged in dialogue with ecumenical groups, ecclesiastical authorities, the academy, local congregations, base communities and social action groups.

The Partners in Dialogue. Dialogue is typically not straightforward. The more complicated the subject matter, the higher the stakes and the higher the risk for failure. The success of dialogue is thus from the beginning tied to the partners in dialogue, their expectations regarding the outcome and their willingness to negotiate compromise solutions. In our context of attempting to establish a global theological dialogue, the structures of such a dialogue are notoriously complicated. The complexity lies in several, interdependent facts: theological dialogue aimed at social-economic transformation, frequently unequal partners in dialogue, conflicting analyses and understanding of the questions, issues and objectives. Theological dialogue that aims at economic issues – in particular the global imbalance between wealth and poverty – will inevitably encounter enormous resistance, critique and attempts to end such a dialogue.

On the practical level, theological dialogue must start as a local dialogue before it can grow into a global endeavour. The beginning of dialogue rests with each theological group. Theologians of the south must first engage in dialogue at the horizontal level; the same is true of North Atlantic theologies and theological dialogue in Africa, Asia and Oceania. Each of the local theological partners much first engage in work with each other. These sub-dialogues are critical in that they not only provide for the unique context, needs and promises of each region, but that they also set the stage for discerning larger patterns, similarities, differences etc. within the worldwide Christian communities and beyond.

Transformation

Dialogue for the sake of conversation may have an intellectual, academic and even an enlightening side to it, but it does not automatically yield social transformations. The theological dialogue envisioned here is precisely, however, about social change.

Social Transformation. As any act of communication, theological dialogue is predicated on two assumptions. One, the state of the world with regard to economic justice is unacceptably wide, and two, the gap between wealthy and poor can be overcome and must be reduced. In other words, it is possible to create another world based on a more equitable distribution of the world's goods and resources. Precisely at this point lies a key factor in theological dialogue. It is decisive for the effectiveness of such dialogue to demonstrate that the global structures that undergird the reality of poverty and injustice are contingent upon economic, financial and political interests that can be changed and adapted; otherwise, the expression *un otro mundo es posible* becomes a mere mockery and illusionary thinking.

From What to What? If it is the case that structures of injustice can be modified, then the process of transformation requires comprehensive expert analysis, insights, tools and objectives. For example, the point of departure and the desired outcome in the process of transformation must be fully explicated, both on the micro and macro level. Since this analytic and constructive process lies at the heart of transformation and determines its success and failures, much energy and long-term efforts must be invested into the process.

Humanity

The goal of all transformative dialogue is the enhancement and well-being of humanity. All discussions, analyses, conferences, strategy and actions must ultimately demonstrate their intrinsic value vis-à-vis the good of the human race. As we briefly mentioned above, this key aspect has been emphasized by Bonhoeffer, Sobrino and Gutiérrez in their reflections on the interplay between economic realities and humanity.

Theology's principal task is to articulate compellingly the intrinsic value of every person. That every person is created in the image of God entails, correspondingly to its inherent value, the basic provisions for life, such as food, water, decent housing, work and so on. In the context of his distinction between the ultimate and penultimate realities, Bonhoeffer connected the dignity of being human, life's conditions and the way of grace. Bonhoeffer asserts that if "human life is deprived of the conditions that are part of being human, the justification of such a life by grace and faith is at least hindered." Therefore, Christian activism must be a "visible, creative activity on the greatest scale" that seeks to alleviate "human misery … human bondage [and] human poverty."[24]

---

[24] *DBWE* 6, 161.

Conclusion: Prospects and Limitations

If what I have said so far gives the impression as if theological dialogue is a simple and easy undertaking that will logically lead to the desired outcome, then let me now put into broader perspective the challenges that will predictably curtail the process of social transformation. Indeed, there are many ensuing issues, prospects and limitations, but I will only touch on some of them now. Any success in social transformation hinges on understanding the questions before anything else. The quality of the questions will determine the quality of the final answers. What are the questions?

Resistance to Dialogue and Transformation

It is all too human to resist change. This is a psychological phenomenon based on anxiety, perceived inability and the fear of failure and can be found in both individuals and groups. However, when the result of social transformation is considered, the resistance to change from psychological reasons can conceivably be overcome. More significant to the process of social transformation is the resistance that comes from those who have created the structures of oppression and who continue to hold the power over these structures. In real terms, these power holders (corporations, politicians, national elites) are the ones who will resist change to the greatest degree because they will be implicated in the transformed reality. They will have to give up and share power and this means the benefits that come with power monopolies.

Resistance to dialogue may also stem from hard-line theological and denominational positions. For example, it is often difficult enough as it is to engage diverse groups within Christianity to participate in dialogue. The reasons are typically theological and of such a nature that one group feels it cannot compromise their surely correct doctrinal or ethical positions. However, in the context of the dialogue envisioned here, the focus is not on a theological dialogue that challenges the theology of a particular group, church or denomination. It is, rather, on working together for the common good of all peoples. In this regard, there is a striking recollection in Moltmann's recent autobiography. He recounts a meeting in Lima with his "old friend" Gustavo Gutiérrez. "From Gustavo I heard the astonishing comment," says Moltmann, "that his people work on the outskirts of the slums, the evangelical Pentecostal preachers go into the slums themselves. After that, the need to bring liberation theology and Pentecostal theology together in Latin America became increasingly important for me."[25] Moltmann's comments clearly suggest that theological dialogue must bridge the spectrum of theological positions, no matter how wide they should be. "Liberals" must listen to "conservatives" and vice-versa, Catholics to Protestants and so on.[26]

The Role of Theology

Arguably, as an academic discipline, theology is by nature more existential than many other disciplines in the humanities and the social sciences. It is "more existential" to the degree that it seeks to bring about a specific and concrete change via the faith and conduct of Christians in the church. In that sense, to recall Barth's dictum, theology must always be in the service of the church.

But in addition to theology's task of coherent expression of the doctrines of the church, there must also be another vital function of theology. It is the responsibility of social critique, both within the Christian communities and outside of them within the larger, local and global social environment. In this regard, most theology has been rather timid. What is at stake? In short, it is the critique, in the words of Horkheimer, of "the present economic forms and the total culture based on them as the product of human labour" in a world controlled by capital.[27] What Marx, the Frankfurt School and countless others have long argued is still the case today: the basic structure of our world is so trenchantly economic that all parts of life are inextricably in its grip. Moreover, the basic economic structures are such that the majority of the peoples of the world are disadvantaged by it while a minority is the beneficiary. In other words, the economic framework, the flow of capital and the practices of labour are the underlying issues that theology must address critically and existentially.

No doubt, many of the theological proposals of the south have clearly perceived this nexus between economics and the quality of life for the masses. But since the fall of the Berlin Wall, theologies of the south are faced with the challenge of re-conceiving the premises, processes and po-

---

[25] Jürgen Moltmann, *A Broad Place. An Autobiography*, translated by Margaret Kohl. Minneapolis: Fortress Press 2008, 366.

[26] A good example to bring radical evangelicalism to the table of theological dialogue is Carlos Caldas, *Orlando Costas. Sua contribuição na historia da teologia latino-americana*. São Paulo: Editora Vida 2007.

[27] Max Horkheimer, "Traditionelle und kritische Theorie," in idem, *Kritische Theorie*. Frankfurt 1968, vol. 2, 162.

tential of their theological conceptions. Holding on to the *status quo* of a bygone era will no longer be enough. It is neither my right nor my task to enter into this discussion. There is already an enormous effort made in Latin America to sort out the issues being faced by virtually all theological proposals today. One such effort, among many others is that of Ivan Petrella.[28] As is evident in the studies edited by Petrella, there are indeed new issues that must be addressed within a re-conception of theology, such as the issues of diversity, sexism, machismo, racism, migration etc.

But if we are genuinely interested in transformative dialogue, then we must go beyond a re-conception of a theology of the south on its own terms. I am suggesting that the effectiveness, and perhaps even the survival, of theologies of the south is not a matter of only re-conceiving new theologies on their own contextual terms any more than the effectiveness of North Atlantic theologies is a matter for only North Atlantic theological proposals on their own terms. The South needs the North and the North needs the South. Why?

As Petrella's concluding essay of his edited work demonstrates, he is working on the assumption that the project of theologies of the south are "different from those produced in affluent Western Europe and the United States."[29] The crux of this statement and similar ones is not that the theologies in the North are different from those in the South; this is so by virtue of the fact that every theology is contextual and historical. The issue at stake here is much more fundamental, namely the supposition that the theologies from the North and South are juxtaposed to one another and perceived as either entirely or partly incompatible. In other words, if the re-conception of the emerging identity of theologies of the South amounts to a flat rejection of European and American theologies, then the very attempt to engage diverse theologies in fruitful dialogue amounts to little more than empty rhetoric. This is not an issue peculiar to theologies of the South. The same applies to North Atlantic theologies and their rejection of any theology outside of their immediate contexts. Various theologies' rejection of each other raises of course a very serious issue: the question is whether distinct theologies must not, at some level, still be able to enter into dialogue with each other because of a unifying factor that makes them a theology – and not merely a world-view – in the first place. If so, what is the aspect that underlies all theologies without emptying their distinctive

---

[28] Cf. Ivan Patrella (ed), *Latin American Liberation Theology. The Next Generation.* Maryknoll: Orbis Books 2005.

[29] Cf. Ivan Patrella, "Liberation Theology – A Programmatic Statement" in idem. *Latin American Liberation Theology*, 147.

and contextual features and without imposing disguised new theologies of colonialism?

How can theologies of the South cooperate with European and American theologies? For an answer, let us return to Bonhoeffer. Although he was a rare exception, he modelled what must become more commonplace within theologies embedded in societies of privilege and wealth. More than any of his contemporaries Bonhoeffer modeled a kind of kenotic theology, a theology that moved from above to below. In concrete terms and in our postmodern context, the adaptation of this movement means the deliberate shifting of the wealth of the communities above to the neighbour below. This shifting must not be, however, the mere transfer of money and resources; if it is only that, then it amounts to no more than an economic act of goodwill. However valid such an act is in itself, the initiative must grow out of a theological raison d'être which becomes deeply entrenched in the soul of wealthy Christian communities. Put differently, Christian charity must be more than a church program. How can this happen in the North? Here we must once more come back to Gutiérrez and his insistence that as Christians we place ourselves deliberately in the paths of our neighbours. Northern theologies must learn from Southern theologies to articulate their own kind of redemptive theology, namely a theology that unshackles from the ensnarement of wealth and the hording of material securities. For better or worse, it is a fact that North Atlantic churches have colossal wealth that is directed toward its own programs. A genuine love of the neighbour – the one far away as much as the close by – implies a radical redistribution of the wealth of privileged Christians and communities. To be sure, any "anti-prosperity theology" aimed at wealthy Christians will not be popular and surely be resisted; it is nonetheless the hallmark of genuine discipleship. Such a path will unquestionably be a long and stony one, but one that theologians from the North and South need to embark on together. Here is one of the moments of genuine global theological dialogue.

Comprehensive Dialogue

How is it possible to accomplish genuine and long-lasting transformation because of theological dialogue? In short, the answer is that theological dialogue must be embedded in the larger global dialogue. With very few exceptions, theologians are not trained in economics, sociology, political science and related disciplines. Above we referred to Bonhoeffer's questioning of capitalism, socialism and collectivism and whether such economic systems hinder faith. However, Bonhoeffer is sufficiently rooted in reality that he also realized theology's limitations. He continues: "The church has a twofold approach here: on the one hand, it must declare as reprehensible, by the authority of the Word of God, such economic attitudes or systems that clearly hinder faith in Christ, thereby drawing a negative boundary. On the other hand, it will not be able to make positive contributions to a new order on the authority of the Word of God, but merely on the authority of responsible counsel by Christian experts."[30] The point is clear: the church and theologians are not universal experts trained to solve all the economic issues of the world. Whereas Bonhoeffer speaks of "Christian experts," in the context of theological dialogue, it is advisable to draw also on the professional expertise of person irrespective of whether they are Christian or not.

For example, since the fall of the Berlin Wall, there is a sustained discussion of the question of the best global economic framework.[31] After the collapse of communism, is socialism the best possible alternative. What about the thesis that globalization is economically inevitable and in the long-term the best possible. Where did this assumption originate, what are its premises, strength, weaknesses and alternatives? It will not so much be theologians who will address these and related questions in the fields of sociology, religious studies, philosophy, ethics, ecology, green energy, sexuality, psychology and so on, but they will need to be present to shape the questions, contexts and processes of this multidisciplinary undertaking.

Immediate Beginnings

Finally, let me conclude by saying that every person interested in theological dialogue can become an agent of change – immediately. To work for the good of humanity does not require waiting for the right moment, important conferences, skilful diplomacy, the best possible education, effective church programs and so on. Every man and woman who confesses to be a

---

[30] *DBWE* 6, 361.

[31] Cf. Francis Fukuyama, *The End of History and the Last Man*. New York: Free Press 1992. Fukuyama has since revised his view of "the end of history," most notably in *America at the Crossroads: Democracy, Power, and the Neoconservative Legacy*. New Haven: Yale University Press 2006 and *After the Neocons: America at the Crossroads*. London: Profile 2006. For a discussion of Fukuyama and Bonhoeffer, see Steven Schroeder, "The End of History and the New World Order," in Wayne Whitson Floyd, Jr. and Charles Marsh (eds), *Theology and the Practice of Responsibility*. Valley Forge: Trinity Press International 21–38.

follower of Jesus Christ can live out the immediate placing of oneself in the path of one's neighbour. Global transformation of the social conditions are indeed the utopia we will have to envision, but the reign of God begins here on earth by giving water to the thirsty, food to the hungry, hope to the hopeless and a word of grace and love to every person with whom we cross our paths.

13. Bonhoeffer on the Social-Political Dimension of Grace[*]

Dort, wo Gnade verkündet wird,
[ist] der Mensch zur Frage nach dem Tun aufgerufen,
weil ihm sonst die Gnade zum Gericht wird
DBW 14, 428.

μὴ εἰς κενὸν
τὴν χάριν τοῦ θεοῦ δέξασθαι ὑμᾶς
2 Corinthians 6:1

Introduction

The thesis of this short essay is that Bonhoeffer's theology of grace has a decidedly social-political dimension. This is to claim that we do not fully comprehend Bonhoeffer's teaching on grace if we focus only or predominantly on its theological aspects. In other words, even if we were able to articulate with unparalleled clarity his doctrine of cheap grace against its Lutheran background in the historical context of Nazi Germany, we would, no doubt, say something significant – but we would not tell the entire story. It is not enough to uphold *Discipleship* as if it contained all of Bonhoeffer's teaching on grace. The objective of this study is to begin with *Discipleship*, but then to concentrate on how Bonhoeffer extends grace from a theological doctrine to the social-political realm without creating an artificial dichotomy between theology and praxis. I will set up my argument in three steps: first I will briefly comment on Bonhoeffer's now classic insights on cheap grace in *Discipleship*; second, I will reflect on Bonhoeffer's other theological notes on grace during the Finkenwalde period and, third, I will examine how his theology of grace comes to fruition in *Ethics*.

---

[*] This essay was first presented at the International Bonhoeffer Congress, Sigtuna, Sweden, in July 2012

The Cheap Doctrine on Grace

It is perhaps no overstatement to say that *Discipleship* is Bonhoeffer's most known and read work. And if a reader remembers anything of that book, it is usually the lines from the opening chapter where Bonhoeffer unleashes his attack on cheap grace like unexpected lightning illuminates a dark sky.[1] Indeed, the very first sentence still stands like a landmark: "Cheap grace is the mortal enemy of our church. Our struggle today is for costly grace."[2]

Let us briefly review what precisely Bonhoeffer sees as the issue that makes grace cheap. Out of the "inexhaustible pantry" of grace, he laments, the church provides free grace that comes with no price and no cost; it is there for everyone to have, at all time and for all occasions. This careless doling out of grace, however, makes grace into a principle and a system. The upshot of the gala of cheap grace – and this is the main point for Bonhoeffer – is that "everything can stay in its old ways." Consequently, in the first chapter of *Discipleship*, Bonhoeffer rails rather sarcastically against the Christian who hides behind cheap grace and justifies everything with it. "The world is justified by grace" and this then means that "in all things the Christian should go along with the world and not venture ... to live a different life under grace from that of sin! ... The Christian has to let grace truly be grace enough so that the world does not lose faith in this cheap grace."[3] Ultimately, the issue with cheap grace is straightforward: "the Christian need not follow Christ."[4] In other words, the more grace covers everything freely and cheaply in the entire world, the less is there any need for change in the life of the church and its members. Cheap grace has no real impact on either the church or the world. Even though, in the strictest

---

[1] It is certain that Bonhoeffer's understanding of cheap grace was influenced by a reading of Kierkegaard and his critique of Lutheran Christendom in Denmark. Cf. Geffrey B. Kelly, "Kierkegaard as 'Antidote' and as Impact on Dietrich Bonhoeffer's Concept of Christian Discipleship," in Peter Frick (ed), *Bonhoeffer's Intellectual Formation. Theology and Philosophy in his Thought*. Religion in Philosophy and Theology 29. Tübingen: Mohr Siebeck 2008, 148–150. According to Ralph Garlin Clingan, "Against Cheap Grace in a World Come of Age. A Study in the Hermeneutics of Adam Clayton Powell, 1865–1953, in His Intellectual Context," Drew University Ph.D. dissertation, 1997, Powell apparently used the expression "cheap grace" and may have influenced Bonhoeffer in his adoption of the expression in *Discipleship*. Bonhoeffer employed the expression as early as December 1932 in a lecture to the German Christian Student Association; cf. *DBWE* 12, 258. Cf. also his 1935–1936 summative comments on costly versus cheap grace in *DBWE* 14, 624 and 748.

[2] *DBWE* 4, 43.
[3] *DBWE* 4, 44.
[4] *DBWE* 4, 44.

theological sense, there is in actuality no such thing as cheap grace, but only a (false) doctrine of cheap grace – hence the title of this section. That is to say, a doctrine of grace that overlooks that cheap grace is not grace at all misses the point entirely.

It is theologically nearly self-evident that for Bonhoeffer an understanding of grace as cheap grace has absolutely nothing to do with the core of the Christian faith, namely with following Jesus Christ. In the first few chapters of *Discipleship*, Bonhoeffer works out the theological importance of the notions of discipleship and faith. This is obvious. But there are also two other concepts that cannot be severed from discipleship and faith: obedience and works. We can provisionally say that the transition from cheap grace to costly grace is the transition from discipleship as mere faith to discipleship as obedient works. Indeed, in the second chapter in *Discipleship*, Bonhoeffer claims that in genuine discipleship "external works have to take place; we have to get into the situation of being able to believe;"[5] there is "the significance of the first step [of faith] as an external deed."[6]

Being mindful of the history of (mis)interpretation of the Lutheran doctrine of grace, Bonhoeffer is careful to avoid the pitfall of a theology of works-righteousness. By claiming that costly grace requires the "necessity of our works,"[7] Bonhoeffer is not advocating a "switch from grace to law as the basic idiom of Christianity."[8] In other words, he is not advocating a Christian form of Torah-obedience, where grace and corresponding works take the place of Torah. To be sure, grace and works must precisely correspond, but in a manner that is distinct from Torah obedience, at least as this obedience was (mis)understood in the Lutheran circles of Bonhoeffer's day. The full dynamic of faith and works is later commented on in Bonhoeffer's discussion of "The Saints" in his exposition of the Sermon on the Mount. "Grace and deeds belong together," he insists. "There is no faith without good work, just as there is no good work without faith."[9] How then does a Christian do external works properly? "We take this step in the right way only," Bonhoeffer remarks, "when we do not look at our works, but solely with a view to the word of Jesus Christ, which calls us to take the first step ... This call is his grace, which calls us out of death into the new

---

[5] *DBWE* 4, 66.
[6] *DBWE* 4, 65.
[7] *DBWE* 4, 66.
[8] H. Wilmer, "Costly Discipleship," in *CCDB*, 177.
[9] *DBWE* 4, 278. In note 21 Bonhoeffer briefly comments on the Paul versus James debate and concludes that it is "the concern of both Paul and James that we truly live by grace and not by our own faculties."

life of obedience ... So it is, indeed, the case that the first step of obedience is itself an act of faith in Christ's word."[10]

In other words, "it is not the works that create faith" but we find ourselves in a situation in which we "can have faith."[11] In the language of cheap and costly grace, we may say that for Bonhoeffer, the power of discipleship rests on the obedient response in an external work to the call of Christ's word. This is discipleship, this is faith, this is costly grace.[12]

Grace as Boundary and Judgment

In *Discipleship*, Bonhoeffer explains what costly grace means in terms of the following of Jesus Christ and why there is no such thing as costly grace apart from "external works," works that simply become the obedient response to the call of Jesus Christ. In that classic book he does not, however, address the question of what happens when the word and call of grace goes unheeded. That this question was in fact on his mind during the Finkenwalde years is evident in how he examines it sporadically in several lectures.

The Boundaries of God's Grace

During the second semester at Finkenwalde, in 1935–1936, Bonhoeffer gave a lecture on the doctrine of the Holy Spirit. In one of the sections of the lecture, he discussed the possibility of a Christian sinning against the Holy Spirit. In this context, he makes two remarks, both times in reference to verses from the book of Hebrews. In his interpretation of the difficult passage Hebrews 6:4–6, Bonhoeffer detects an "irrevocability of lost grace ... There are boundaries at which God's grace can [no longer] be [experienced]."[13] Those who are filled with the Holy Spirit and then willfully sin – even though it is impossible to determine the content of such a sin – crucify the Son of God again.[14] That there is a boundary of grace does not mean that grace itself is limited; rather, it means that willful sinners cut themselves off from that grace.

---

[10] *DBWE* 4, 66.

[11] *DBWE* 4, 67.

[12] Cf. Bonhoeffer's statement in 1932: "This *discipleship of Christ* arises [from] and is based entirely on simple *faith*, and inversely, faith is only true in discipleship" (*DBWE* 12, 259).

[13] *DBWE* 14, 485; translation slightly altered.

[14] Cf. *DBWE* 14, 485.

The notion that grace has a limit is explicated a second time in Bonhoeffer's short exegesis of Hebrews 12:14–17. The story of Esau, who sold his birthright and then sought repentance in vain, teaches us that we should "not miss the chance for grace."[15] If, however, we fail to obtain divine grace, we come to the boundary of grace: the time of grace is itself limited. Obedience is required today; tomorrow the grace of time may be over.[16] For Bonhoeffer, it seems, God's grace is not an eternal guarantee for salvation, at least in the sense that a person can forfeit the grace once received. Such forfeiting may happen either by committing an act of sin against God's spirit or by not responding to the claim of grace within the time of grace.

In a lecture on pastoral theology in the same semester, Bonhoeffer returns once more to a discussion of the predicament of unforgiven sins. He emphasizes: "*There are countless Christians who are able to hear the proclamation of grace only as temporarily calming opium, not realizing that this is stubbornness (Verstockung)!*"[17] The upshot is that the good news of grace cannot be heard where a Christian lives in sin and has hardened his/her heart. In such a situation, grace constitutes again a limit.

Grace as Judgment

Anticipating what he will expound in *Discipleship*, Bonhoeffer criticizes in 1935–1936 that Protestantism has made grace into a principle and thereby untrue. But "as soon as the proclamation of grace blocks the way to Christ, it is apostasy and lies (*Abfall und Lüge*)."[18] As if the degrading of grace into *Abfall und Lüge* was not enough, Bonhoeffer explicates another, perhaps the most disquieting boundary of grace. If the word of grace goes unheeded, he asserts, it may become the word of judgment. These thoughts are the results of Bonhoeffer's theological interpretation of the Apostle Peter's speech in Acts 2. He focuses on verse 2, and in particular on the question: "brothers and sisters, what shall we do?" Bonhoeffer remarks: "They have heard about the grace to which Peter is witnessing, but they know this grace does not belong to them. Initially it is merely proclaimed grace. That is judgment: to hear and know about grace and yet to know that it does not yet belong to me. This tension leads immediately to the question: What

---

15 *DBWE* 14, 485.
16 *DBWE* 14, 486.
17 *DBWE* 14, 562; original emphasis.
18 *DBWE* 14, 431.

should we do? Act – such that this grace does not become judgment, but rather might belong to us. The listeners' response is not: That was a good sermon, this resolves the problem of the Old Testament promise, this proclaimed grace puts everything in good order, and we can continue to live as before. They know that wherever grace is proclaimed, people are summoned to question what they should do, since otherwise grace becomes judgment. A proclamation of grace that does not raise this question is [drug intoxication; *Giftrausch*]. Grace must be repeatedly seized anew."[19]

Two brief comments are in order. First, even though the biblical text does not mention the word "grace," Bonhoeffer puts the theological emphasis of Peter's speech on exactly that notion. For Bonhoeffer, those who heard Peter's speech were confronted by grace proclaimed. More precisely, the hearers were confronted by the claim of grace and they realized this because they asked: What should we do? They realized that the claim of grace calls for action and not – as Bonhoeffer sarcastically points out – for the affirmation "that was a good sermon ... and we can continue to live as before." The point that Bonhoeffer wishes to drive home is foundational to his theology of grace: when confronted by grace, the call is for action and not reflection; the call is for active obedience and not for sophisticated excuses. Unless the call of grace becomes an obedient act, it remains cheap grace. Bonhoeffer is so sure about his position that he reminds his students: "a proclamation of grace that does not raise this question is [drug intoxication; *Giftrausch*]." In other words, if the proclamation of grace fails to call for action, it is mere intoxication, spiritual wishful thinking.

Second, and related to the first point, even when grace is proclaimed as the call to action it is, as Bonhoeffer says: "initially ... merely proclaimed grace. That is judgment: to hear and know about grace and yet to know that it does not yet belong to me." As long as grace is only heard and known, it remains an idea, a system, theology, cheap grace and judgment.[20] The call of grace that goes unanswered is not simply a mere neutral hearing. If so, the word of grace inevitably becomes the word of judgement. In the context of the church and its Christian members, if the word of grace is not acted upon, it is judgment. Put differently, grace only exists when it is acted upon by those who heard its claims. There is no other grace than grace in action and, therefore, the church becomes visible to the extent that grace becomes visible. This leads to my final third point.

---

[19] *DBWE* 14, 440.
[20] Cf. *DBW* 14, 740: "'billige' Gnade ist eine Gnade, die genommen und gesehen wird losgelöst vom Gericht und von Heiligung und Zucht'."

The Costly Doctrine on Grace: Socio-Political

Bonhoeffer's achievement in *Discipleship* was his ability to articulate with utmost clarity what it means to follow the call of Jesus Christ in such a way that it is neither simplistic nor unrealistic. The substance of his theology is straightforward: either the following of Christ is genuine, costly grace and therefore has an impact on how Christians live in the world or it is useless. As we noted above, this idea was articulated – with less detail but with equal vigor and insight – in some of the lectures during the Finkenwalde period. In those lectures, Bonhoeffer asserted with clarity that grace requires action and when that action does not come forth, the word of grace becomes the word of judgment. The link between the Finkenwalde reflections and the argument of *Discipleship* come fruitfully together in one of the fragments of his unfinished *Ethics*. Perhaps surprisingly, in the section "Ultimate and Penultimate Things,"[21] the notion of grace plays the central role and completes Bonhoeffer's theology of grace.

Grace as the Ultimate Word

Above we noted that there is no grace other than grace that responds to the claim of grace, or grace in action. This claim needs further clarification, in particular the theological correlation between the word of grace and the act of grace. Regarding the word of grace, Bonhoeffer maintains: "The word of God's justifying grace never leaves its place as the ultimate word ... The word remains irreversibly the ultimate; otherwise it would be degraded to something calculable, a commodity, and would be robbed of its essential divinity. Grace would become cheap."[22]

The last and final divine word is the word of grace. Bonhoeffer puts it in these terms: "There is no word of God that goes beyond God's grace."[23] Concretely, this word is "the justification of the sinner by grace alone"[24] received in faith, hope and love. For Bonhoeffer, the sovereignty of God's

---

[21] For an excellent and critical review of Bonhoeffer understanding of the ultimate and penultimate realities see Thomas Tseng, "Christologie und Eschatologie. Das Letzte und Vorletzte bei Dietrich Bonhoeffer," in Clifford Green and Thomas Tseng (eds), *Dietrich Bonhoeffer und Sino-Theologie/Dietrich Bonhoeffer and Sino-Theology*, Sino-Christian Studies Supplement Series 1. Taipei: Chung Yuan Christian University 2008, 319–359.

[22] *DBWE* 6, 151.

[23] *DBWE* 6, 149.

[24] *DBWE* 6, 146.

word of grace is absolute. The mystery of this divine word is beyond all insight. The power of this divine word is beyond all human manipulation. God alone addresses the human being in the word of grace as the ultimate claim.[25] In the ultimacy of that word of justifying grace Bonhoeffer locates the alpha and omega of the Christian life: the preparing of the entry of grace.

Grace as Penultimate Action

Since the justifying word of grace is the temporally ultimate word, it follows that "something always precedes it, some action, suffering, movement, intention, defeat, recovery, pleading, hoping – in short, quite literally a span of time at which end it stands."[26] Another way of saying this is that since justification is the ultimate thing, that which precedes it is the justifying, the penultimate thing; *justification* is complete, *justifying* is not yet complete, it is still ongoing. Although he does not make it explicit, it seems to me that Bonhoeffer's theo-logic would locate the justifying word of grace in the penultimate realm.[27] This seems evident when he comments that "not all time is a time of grace; but now – precisely now and finally now – is the 'day of salvation' (2 Corinthians 6:2)."[28] For Bonhoeffer, there is a certain urgency not to miss the time of grace because every offer of grace may not repeat itself. As he puts it: "The time of grace is the final time in the sense that one can never reckon with a further, future word beyond the word of God that confronts me now."[29] The emphasis is clearly on the now; now is the time to act on the claim of the word of grace. For "there is a time of God's permission, waiting, and preparation; and there is an ultimate time that judges and breaks off the penultimate."[30]

But how precisely is the penultimate and ultimate related with respect to grace? Although the following words are well known and often rehearsed among Bonhoeffer scholars, they assume a new tone when read through the lens of Bonhoeffer's theology of grace: "The penultimate does not de-

---

[25] Paul Tillich, "Die Frage nach dem Unbedingten," in *Gesammelte Werke* 5, Stuttgart 1964, 180, speaks of God's word as "event" and an element "der letzten Wirklichkeit; es ist die Macht des Seins." Peter Zimmerling, *Bonhoeffer als praktischer Theologe*, Göttingen: Vandenhoeck & Ruprecht 2006, characterizes Bonhoeffer's understanding of God's word with the terms "Selbstmächtigkeit" and "Selbstwirksamkeit."

[26] Zimmerling, *Bonhoeffer als praktischer Theologe*, 150–151.

[27] Cf. *DBWE* 6, 163.

[28] *DBWE* 6, 151.

[29] *DBWE* 6, 151.

[30] *DBWE* 6, 151.

termine the ultimate; the ultimate determines the penultimate. The penultimate is not a condition in itself; it is a judgment by the ultimate on what has gone before. It is therefore never something present, but always something in the past. Concretely, from the perspective of the justification of the sinner through grace two things are addressed as penultimate: *being human [Menschsein] and being good [Gutsein]*. It would be false, and a violation of the ultimate, for example, to call being human a precondition for justification by grace. Instead, only from the perspective of the ultimate can we recognize what being human is, and therefore how being human is based on and determined by being justified. Still, it is the case that being human precedes being justified, and seen from the perspective of the ultimate must precede it. The penultimate therefore does not negate the freedom of the ultimate; instead, the freedom of the ultimate empowers the penultimate. So, for example, being human may – with all necessary reservations – be addressed as penultimate to justification by grace. Only the human being can be justified, simply because only the one who is justified becomes a 'human being'."[31]

Here then lies the crux for our argument: being human – or as he says elsewhere: becoming human again[32] – is played out in the sphere of penultimate reality. Even though Bonhoeffer never loses sight of the finality of grace as the ultimate thing, he clearly sees that "being human may ... be addressed as penultimate to justification by grace." Elsewhere he puts it in the clearest of terms: "the destruction of humanness is sin, and as such it hinders God's work of redeeming humanity."[33] In other words, the overarching dynamic between penultimate and ultimate realities is mirrored in the dynamic between being human and justifying grace.

"From this follows now something of decisive importance" for Bonhoeffer, namely, "that the penultimate must be preserved for the sake of the ultimate."[34] Expressed in different terms, the penultimate sphere, that is to say, our earthly life as we encounter it all around us, does matter both in view of the ultimate but also in view of the fact that God created all life and gave it to us as a gift. Later in prison Bonhoeffer speaks of the essential this-worldliness (*Diesseitigkeit*) of human life.[35] Because of the sanctity of all earthly life, any "arbitrary destruction of the penultimate seriously harms the ultimate. When, for example, a human life is deprived of the

---

[31] *DBWE* 6, 159–160.
[32] *DBWE* 6, 166.
[33] *DBWE* 6, 157.
[34] *DBWE* 6, 160.
[35] Cf. *DBWE* 8, 485–486.

conditions that are part of being human, the justification of such life by grace and faith is at least seriously hindered, if not made impossible."[36]

The transition from understanding grace principally as a theological doctrine to making it visible and concrete in the life of human beings and their world becomes Bonhoeffer's central focus. Now emerges what we may characterize as the social-political dimension of grace. When I speak of grace as belonging to the political sphere, I do not mean the limited understanding of politics as office or government. Rather, for our purposes, political means the matrix of social interaction that creates and challenges structures of power and shapes the conditions for human existence, both in a positive and negative manner. It is clear from the larger context of the section on "Ultimate and Penultimate Things" that Bonhoeffer has in mind the social, economic, and political dimensions of human life.[37] In this sense, the political dimension of grace operates in the penultimate realm. Or, in different words, one of the crucial dimensions of our this-worldly existence is the degree to which we are able to make grace visible.

How does Bonhoeffer suggest this grace becomes visible? Repeatedly, he speaks of "the coming of grace" or "the receiving of grace" or "the entry of grace."[38] The grace of Christ is free to come as it wishes, but Bonhoeffer warns that "we can oppose that coming in grace."[39] How do we oppose the coming of grace? By overlooking that "there are conditions of the heart, of life, and in the world that especially hinder the receiving of grace, that is, which make it infinitely difficult to believe." And although "grace must finally clear and smooth its own way ... all this does not release us from preparing the way for the coming of grace, from doing away with whatever hinders and makes it more difficult."[40] Juan Segundo put it succinctly when he says that grace is not "exclusively a liberative dynamism"[41] although it has its own "broad, incalculable pathways."[42]

Bonhoeffer's argument can be summed up in this way: because the conditions of life are not irrelevant vis-à-vis the coming and receiving of grace, a Christian cannot be neutral toward these conditions. Or, to put it differ-

---

[36] *DBWE* 6, 160.

[37] On this theme see my essay in this volume: "Bonhoeffer's Theology and Economic Humanism. An Exploration in Interdisciplinary Sociality."

[38] Cf. *DBWE* 6, 161–165.

[39] *DBWE* 6, 162.

[40] *DBWE* 6, 162; cf. 151: "there is a depth of human bondage, of human poverty, and of human ignorance that hinders the gracious coming of Christ."

[41] Juan Luis Segundo, *Grace and the Human Condition. A Theology for Artisans of a New Humanity*, Vol. 2. Maryknoll: Orbis 1973, 37.

[42] Juan Luis Segundo, *Grace and the Human Condition*, 117.

ently: those men and women in Christ who have received the grace of God in their lives are called to responsible action in making possible conditions in which the grace of God may be received by others. Bonhoeffer designates a Christian's working in the penultimate realm "a commission of immeasurable responsibility" and provides the following examples: "The hungry person needs bread, the homeless person needs shelter, the one deprived of rights needs justice, the lonely person needs community, the undisciplined needs order, and the slave needs freedom. It would be blasphemy against God and the neighbor to leave the hungry unfed while saying that God is closest to those in deepest need ... If the hungry do not come to faith, the guilt falls on those who denied them bread."[43] Similarly, he cautions, "it is hard for those thrust into extreme disgrace, desolation, poverty, and helplessness to believe in God's justice and goodness" as it is equally as "hard for the well-fed and the powerful to comprehend God's judgment and God's grace."[44]

Conclusion

As these last words indicate, and as Bonhoeffer has emphasized in his Finkenwalde lectures, grace and judgement belong very closely together. Most of us, I take it, prefer the Bonhoeffer who speaks of the positive side of grace. We mold Bonhoeffer according to our own theological image, and may become guilty in the process of cheapening grace a little. Or – this is always safe – we see cheap grace operate in other Christians and other churches. Even if we read *Discipleship* with the sentimentality that costly grace is bitterly needed in others, the lectures during the Finkenwalde period should make us sufficiently uncomfortable in that Bonhoeffer correlates grace and the call to action. Grace is not merely a static doctrine, but a call to demonstrate with one's deeds the tangibility of following Christ in this world. Unless grace is acted upon, it becomes God's word of judgment over us. But finally, in *Ethics*, Bonhoeffer cuts through the last remnant of our excuse not to act on the claim of faith by saying that for a Christian the work of grace must be "a visible, creative activity on the greatest scale."[45] No occasional, half-hearted tinkering with grace allowed. Indifference, apathy and sophistry must give rise to a joyful – and, if nec-

---

[43] *DBWE* 6, 163.
[44] *DBWE* 6, 162.
[45] *DBWE* 6, 161.

essary, suffering – discipleship. If grace is not social-political in its out-working, it ceases to be grace.

Bonhoeffer's clearest and most challenging word on grace is that the external works of grace must be done. Grace entails both God's good news to the sinner and a person's existential transformation. Yet doing good works for the sake of grace is neither a new form of Christian legalism nor merely a social reform in the guise of Christian activism.[46] "Everything depends on this action being a spiritual reality, since what is finally at stake is not the reform of worldly conditions but the coming of Christ."[47] Our participation in the work of grace in the penultimate sphere of life is thus nothing other than our own obedient response to the claims of grace, so that "the entry of grace is the ultimate."[48]

---

[46] Cf. *DBWE* 6, 164.
[47] *DBWE* 6, 164.
[48] *DBWE* 6, 163.

14. What does Hiroshima have to do with Berlin? Dietrich Bonhoeffer on Theology, Peace and Social Responsibility*

> There is no way to peace along the way of safety.
> For peace must be dared. It is the great venture.[1]

Introduction

By February 1945, Berlin was utterly bombed out. The city looked more like a barren, lifeless moonscape than a place that was once inhabited by human beings. The same is true for Hiroshima. In August 1945, the A-bomb wiped out the city in an instant and turned a once populated place into a deserted ghost town. This then, is at the end of war: the total destruction and self-destruction[2] of human life.

Almost 80 years ago, in August 1934, a young and unknown pastor and theologian gave an address to the Ecumenical Council of Christian Churches, a forerunner of the World Council of Churches. As the International Youth Secretary, Dietrich Bonhoeffer warned the Christian leaders of the world of the impending danger of war and the need to speak out for peace without delay. The church leaders were mostly bewildered by the clarion call of this young theologian and had little inkling that indeed, five years later, Hitler would force the world into a diabolic war that was contrived in Berlin and ended in Hiroshima.

---

* This paper was first presented at the tri-annual meeting of the International Association for Methodist Schools, Colleges and Universities (IAMSCU) in Hiroshima, Japan, in May 2014.

[1] *DBWE* 13, 308–309.

[2] In a lecture on "The Theological Foundation of the Work of the World Alliance," in July 1932, Bonhoeffer says explicitly that war is "certain self-destruction" and that it is "absolutely destructive... of the inner life and the external life. Today's war destroys soul and body;" cf. *DBWE* 11, 366–367.

Given the fact that we, too, are gathered from around the world as a group of church leaders in reflection on the theme of peace, right here in Hiroshima, I trust that our discourse with Bonhoeffer will contribute to clarifying our theology and practice of peace. In what follows, we will take Bonhoeffer's Fanø address as a starting point and examine it from the perspective of three questions: First, how is Bonhoeffer's peace theology anchored in his theology as a whole; second, what is the role of the church within peace theology; and third, what distinct action toward peace must the Christian church practice?

The Context for Bonhoeffer's Fanø Speech

In August 1934, the Ecumenical Council of Christian Churches met in Fanø, Denmark. Dietrich Bonhoeffer addressed the assembly as one of the International Youth Secretaries. Even though he was only 28 years old at the time, he had already achieved much. He came from a prominent and wealthy Berlin family. His father held the most prestigious appointment in psychology and neurology at the University of Berlin. All of the eight Bonhoeffer children were educated at the university and it was a given for the men in the family that they would complete their studies with a doctorate. So at age 21, the young Bonhoeffer finished a doctorate in theology,[3] a work that he wrote on the side of his regular studies. Then he entered his first pastoral work, as a vicar of the Lutheran church in Barcelona, Spain. When he returned to Berlin, now 24 years of age, he completed a second dissertation,[4] a prerequisite for a professorial appointment in a German university. His next step was a year at Union Theological Seminary in New York City. By his own account, this year was decisive for both his spiritual and intellectual-theological developments.[5] For our purposes, it must suffice to mention two things: his encounter with American racism and his friendship with the Frenchman Jean Lasserre, a committed pacifist. While his encounter with racism in the New York of the early 1930s primed him for unmasking the anti-Semitism in Germany that was unleashed immedi-

---

[3] *DBWE* 1 (*Sanctorum Communio. A Theological Study of the Sociology of the Church*).

[4] *DBWE* 2 (*Act and Being: Transcendental Philosophy and Ontology in Systematic Theology*).

[5] Cf. Bonhoeffer's letter to Elisabeth Zinn, *DBWE* 14, 134–135 and Clifford Green, "Bonhoeffer at Union. Critical Turning Points: 1931 and 1939," in *Union Seminary Quarterly Review* 62 (2010), 1–16.

ately with Hitler's rise to power in 1933, the newly gained pacifist position isolated him within the church[6] and led him into a serious predicament, since being a conscientious objector in place of military service was not an option under Nazi law. In order to clarify his thinking on peace and his role in the church struggle, Bonhoeffer accept a call to serve a German congregation in London, in the fall of 1933.

While in London, Bonhoeffer worked actively as one of the youth secretaries for the World Alliance for International Friendship Through the Churches, whose stated goal was working toward peace among nations.[7] It was in that capacity that Bonhoeffer presented his address to the delegates in Fanø in 1934. In other words, when we examine Bonhoeffer's call for peace, we must bear in mind that he has already witnessed and theologically analyzed a vast spectrum of topics and experiences: racism, pacifism and the social gospel in New York; anti-Semitism, tyranny and the church struggle in Berlin; pastoral work and social-economic dysfunction in Barcelona and ecumenism in London. By the summer of 1934 there was one additional element and urgency: Bonhoeffer's prophetic conviction that Hitler would soon start a war.

Bonhoeffer's Theology of Peace

Bonhoeffer's discourse on peace clearly distinguishes the theological from the political sphere. Although the two overlap, they are not identical; while the theological debate desires to impact the political sphere; the political is hardly ever interested in the theological. For now we are only interested in Bonhoeffer's theology of peace, which rests on two basic considerations: God's commandment and the overcoming of the grip of fear.

Peace as Commandment

Bonhoeffer opens his Fanø address with Psalm 85:9: "I will hear what God the Lord will speak; for he will speak peace unto his people, and to his saints." Bonhoeffer then implicitly connects these words of the Psalmist with the angelic choir of Luke 2:14 and boldly declares: "peace on earth is

---

6 Eberhard Bethge, *Dietrich Bonhoeffer. Theologian, Christian, Man of his Time. A Biography*, translated and revised by Victoria Barnett. Minneapolis: Fortress Press 2000, 325, notes that "no one shared his pacifist leanings toward pacifism."

7 Cf. *DBWE* 11, 364; *DBWE* 13, 305, thesis 2.

not a problem, but a commandment given at Christ's coming."[8] Moreover, Bonhoeffer invokes the commandment "you shall not kill"[9] and thus establishes his theology of peace on the two biblical injunctions that Christ desires peace on earth and that human beings are commanded not to kill. In a lecture in 1932 to the German Christian Student Association, entitled "Christ and Peace," Bonhoeffer also emphasized Jesus' commandment "love your enemies" in the Sermon on the Mount (Matthew 5:44).[10]

Crucial for our purposes is that Bonhoeffer understands these commandments in a literal sense. "God does not exempt us from obeying his commandments,"[11] he warns and then repeats his conviction in even stronger terms: "he who questions the commandment of God before obeying has already denied him."[12] In all practical terms this means that Christians "cannot take up arms against Christ himself – yet this is what they do if they take up arms against one another."[13] What Bonhoeffer suggests here, in effect, is that Christians are excluded from active military service by virtue of being a follower of Christ. Or to put it differently: by not taking up arms against Christ, Christians are essentially not permitted to participate in military combat. In Bonhoeffer's own words: "Pure love, in obedience to the fifth commandment,[14] gives up its life for a brother, whether he is on this side or on the other side. Pure love quite simply cannot lift up a sword against a Christian, because that would mean to lift it against Christ."[15]

The biblical commandments not to kill, to love one's neighbour and enemy and to proclaim the word of peace on earth are thus the hermeneutical foundations of Bonhoeffer's theology of peace. If a theology of peace is an answer to a problem, then the question arises to what, precisely, peace is the answer. This brings us to the second consideration.

---

[8] *DBWE* 13, 307.

[9] At a second meeting in Fanø, Bonhoeffer presented several thesis on "The Fundamental Principles of the World Alliance," in which he thought to clarify the work of the Church for peace. In that presentation he invoked the commandment not to kill; cf. *DBWE* 13, 305.

[10] Cf. *DBWE* 12, 260.

[11] *DBWE* 13, 305.

[12] *DBWE* 13, 308.

[13] *DBWE* 13, 308.

[14] "You shall not kill."

[15] *DBWE* 12, 262.

Fear: the Opposite of Peace

A second theological position that informs Bonhoeffer's theology of peace is that of overcoming fear. In the Fanø address, he mentions both "mistrust" and "distrust" as realities that propagate war.[16] Although, from a psychological point of view mistrust and fear are not identical, for our purposes I will subsume distrust under the category of fear. Shortly before Hitler came to power in January 1933, Bonhoeffer preached a gripping sermon on fear, based on Matthew 8:23–27 (Jesus' calming of the storm). Right at the outset, he says: "The Bible, the gospel, Christ, the church, the faith – all are one great battle cry against fear in the lives of human beings. Fear is, somehow or other, the archenemy itself... It hollows out their inside... Fear secretly gnaws and eats away at all ties that bind a person to God and to others."[17]

Since the very beginning of human existence, fear is eating away at our humanity. In the Hebrew Bible, not surprisingly, the first human conversation after the fall mentions fear: Adam says to God: "I heard the sound of you in the garden, and I was afraid, because I was naked; and I hid myself" (Genesis 3:10). In the New Testament, Jesus repeatedly links fear and the absence of peace. In the Gospel of John, Jesus announces "peace I leave with you; my peace I give to you. I do not give to you as the world gives. Do not let your hearts be troubled, and do not let them be afraid" (John 14:27; cf. 16:33). After the resurrection, when the disciples had locked themselves in a room because they were afraid of the religious leaders, Jesus enters in their midst and says "Peace be with you" (John 20:19). Even these few references are enough to establish that theologically fear is a result of sin while psychologically "fear is evil's net, spread to catch us. Once evil has made us afraid, confused us, we are in its clutches."[18] Bonhoeffer says elsewhere that "fear takes away a person's humanity."[19] And this is precisely the reason, then, why fear is in such stark contrast to peace: while peace brings life, fear destroys life. Bonhoeffer could witness first-hand what happens when the fear of the other literally destroys the life of human beings; racism in the United States and anti-Semitism in Germany were two chapters in the life of the young theologian that opened up his heart and mind for the harsh realities of violence against humanity.

---

[16] Cf. *DBWE* 13, 309.

[17] *DBWE* 12, 455.

[18] *DBWE* 12, 459.

[19] *DBWE* 12, 455.

Indeed, we may even say that in one sense fear is the opposite of peace. Theologically fear is one of the markers of our sin and separation from God as the source of life and peace; psychologically fear destructs life and therefore the peace we desire and need in our lives. Without going into details here, I understand peace in the Hebrew sense of shalom (שָׁלוֹם), that is to so as a peace understood as overall well-being, wholeness and blessing in a profound sense.[20]

But there is another dimension to fear: in its opposition to peace, fear is always a lack of trust. In his Fanø presentation, to repeat, Bonhoeffer speaks of mistrust and distrust. Mistrust, he suggests "brings forth war" and "dreadful is the distrust that looks out of all peoples' eyes."[21] Mistrust and distrust may theologically be characterized as a lack of faith or unbelief. And since a lack of trust in God leaves a void that human beings want to fill, they are left to themselves to find peace. Bonhoeffer comments that apart from God's love, however, the human path toward peace is the political path of safety and security. But precisely here lies the predicament of political peace. Bonhoeffer argues that "there is no way to peace along the way of safety. For peace must be dared. It is the great venture. It cannot be made safe. Peace is the opposite of security."[22] If peace must be dared, if peace itself is the way to peace, if it is indeed a venture that we must dare, then it follows that peace can only come about by trust. In the absence of security, we will need to trust others. And by trusting others, we must also somehow let go of the fear of the other. We have come thus full circle: we said that fear is the opposite of peace and leads to distrust and, in its most violent form, to war. But as trust makes gains, fear is proportionately diminished.

The Question for Us Today

What do we make of Bonhoeffer's position that peace is a divine commandment that must be spoken in and to a world that is gripped by fear? We come from all over the world and many of us have a national history of that is stained by distrust, violence and war. Bonhoeffer's time and circumstance are not ours and therefore we need to be mindful not commit the error of anachronism. But we must also keep away a certain naïveté.

---

[20] Cf. Joseph P. Healey, "Peace. Old Testament," and William Klassen, "Peace. New Testament," in in David Noel Freedman (ed), *Anchor Bible Dictionary*. New York: Doubleday 1992, vol. 5, 206–212.

[21] *DBWE* 13, 309; translation slightly altered.

[22] *DBWE* 13, 309.

Is it not the case that too many nations are gripped by fear? Many governments are driven by fear and mistrust – or they use fear mongering and other propaganda to create an enemy. It is a fact that we are the most surveillance-controlled human population that ever lived. This is a very sad state of affairs because surveillance is always predicated on fear and mistrust, notwithstanding that its apparent necessity is sold to us as a measure of national security or war against terrorism. Should we be concerned because far too many governments and corporate ventures seek total control over all our human activities? How far away, or how close, are we today to war?

The Church and Peace

The answer that we give to the question just posed above depends to a significant degree on the answer to another question, namely that of the relation between the Church and her work for peace.

The Church is neither Political Body nor Society

At Fanø, Bonhoeffer clarifies at the outset that the poles of "nationalism" and "internationalism" exist as political categories, but he rejects them as not suitable for the work of the Church. These categories have to do with "political necessities and possibilities" while the Church is not involved in these matters but announces "the commandments of God"[23] to the world in need of peace. In other words, the Church is not a political organization.

But the Church is also not a society or an association [*Gesellschaft*] that exists because it has a common objective or purpose. Should the Church identify itself a society, then "it stands without authority"[24] and is merely on the level of other societies of its kind. Indeed, the differentiation of the Church from a society is decisive for Bonhoeffer. He claims that the destiny of the World Alliance is "determined by the following: whether it regards itself as a Church or as a society with a definite purpose."[25] And this is the reason: "It is only as a Church that the World Alliance can preach the Word of Christ in full authority to the Churches and the nations."[26] Only as the Church does the Church have to offer something distinct to the

---

[23] *DBWE* 13, 307.
[24] *DBWE* 13, 305.
[25] *DBWE* 13, 304.
[26] *DBWE* 13, 304–5.

work for peace, only as the Church can the Church sound forth a voice that would otherwise not be sounded. Only the Church proclaims the Word of the living God, only the Church offers Christ's words for peace. This is the unique contribution of the Church for peace.

The Church is Not a Pacifist Body

Before Bonhoeffer says in positive terms what the Church is, he adds one more negative qualification. While the church is not a political organization, it is also not simply a religious group that has as its ideal what he termed "secular pacifism"[27] or "pacifist humanitarianism."[28] And most important, in spite of the fact that the good news of God is at core a message of peace, the Church herself must not make the mistake of making peace a "final order of fulfillment that has value in itself."[29] In Bonhoeffer' own words: "International peace is therefore also not an absolutely ideal condition but rather an order that is aimed at something else and that is not valuable in and of itself. Naturally, the establishment of such an order of preservation can have absolute urgency, although never for its own sake, but rather for the sake of its goal, namely, for the sake of the hearing of revelation."[30]

Here we have reached a decisive point in Bonhoeffer's argument. We may summarize it as follows: even though the Christian message is one of peace, and even though Bonhoeffer considered himself a pacifist,[31] the message of peace or the condition of peace cannot be the main identity and responsibility of the Church. Why not? For Bonhoeffer, the reason is the-

---

[27] *DBWE* 13, 305.

[28] *DBWE* 11. 365.

[29] *DBWE* 11, 365.

[30] *DBWE* 11, 365.

[31] We know from Bonhoeffer himself that he underwent a radical shift in his own views on pacifism. In a letter to a friend he reflects back on the days in New York. "Christian pacifism," he writes, "which I had previously fought against with passion, all at once seemed perfectly obvious," cf. Letter to Elisabeth Zinn, *DBWE* 14, 134; cf. also *DBWE* 11, 367. In Nazi Germany, to hold a pacifist position, even within the Confessing Church, was a rare instance. But Bonhoeffer was gradually so completely convinced by it, that he taught it to the students at the underground seminary. Hand in hand with pacifism he also advocated for a corollary position: the rejection of military service, cf. *DBWE* 12, 260: "For Christians, any military service except in the ambulance corps, and any preparation for war, is forbidden." For a recent discussion of Bonhoeffer's position on pacifism that challenges his involvement in the conspiracy on Hitler, see Mark Thiessen Nation, Anthony G. Siegrist and Daniel P. Umbel, *Bonhoeffer the Assassin? Challenging the Myth, Recovering His Call to Peacemaking*. Grand Rapids: Baker Academic 2013.

ological: "It is not pacifism that is the victory which overcomes the world (1 John 5:4) but faith, which expects everything from God and hopes in the coming of Christ and His kingdom."[32]

It is clear that Bonhoeffer rejects pacifism as an end or goal for the Church on the basis of his uncompromising Christological theology.[33] "True peace," he explains, "can only be in God and come from God."[34] This implies that peace is not so much a foundation or core responsibility of the Church as it is the result of her proclamation. Christians, by following after Christ and by proclaiming his word, "can only dare to make peace through faith."[35] This, then, is what Bonhoeffer means by peace making when he says that it is "for the sake of the hearing of revelation," namely that peace allows the hearing of revelation, the hearing of the gospel of Christ, in whose name and power peace is possible. And this means concretely that "peace can never consist in reconciling the gospel with religious worldviews,"[36] and for that matter we may add also with political and ideological worldviews. The Christian message of peace does not need to be reconciled to the world, but the world needs to be healed by the power of God's peace. If this is so, then what precisely does the Church announce in its message to the world?

The Church Proclaims the Word of Peace

Bonhoeffer says the Church *is* "the presence of God in the world; truly in the world, truly a present God."[37] Thus the Church "is to some extent qualified world, qualified by God's own entry into it and for it." In other words, the incarnation, God's love for the sinful world, gives the Church a double identify as it has at the same time "visible form" and "hidden divinity."[38] Paradoxically, the church exists in the world but she is not from the world. As part of this paradox, the Church *does* something, namely she proclaims the Word of God as the good news to the world. By proclaiming God's good news to the world, the Christian message is *the peace message par excellence*. This is important. Bonhoeffer says that for the "ecumenical

---

[32] *DBWE* 13, 306.

[33] The pinnacle of his Christological reflection during the Finkenwalde Seminary period is his most famous book (*The Cost of*) *Discipleship*, *DBWE* 4.

[34] *DBWE* 12, 261.

[35] *DBWE* 12, 260.

[36] *DBWE* 12, 261.

[37] *DBWE* 12, 263.

[38] *DBWE* 12, 264.

Church," Christ's "commandment is more holy, more inviolable than the most revered words"[39] of human beings. He comes from a theological tradition in which the Word of God is understood to be self-effective.[40] Romans 1:16, that the gospel is the power for salvation, is taken in a sense that God himself effects that which he announces in his word. In that sense, the proclamation of the God's word – in Bonhoeffer's terms: the proclamation of the commandments not to kill, to love our neighbours and enemies – is thus the content of the Church's proclamation. It is, of course, embedded in the full narrative of salvation, that is to say, it is God's story of love for the world through his son Jesus, the Messiah. On the question of peace, therefore, says Bonhoeffer, "there is only one *authority* that has spoken definitively on this question, and that is *Jesus* Christ."[41]

The Question for Us Today

Bonhoeffer's reflections at the Fanø conference addressed a group of church leaders not unlike ours today. Some of the questions he posed then are still valid for us today. For example, are we here as the representatives of the church, and if so, of the local church or of the one universal Church of Jesus Christ? Or are we here because of a political or social-activist interest? In whose name do we speak words of peace, and whose words do we speak? Do we speak our own words of peace, or do we proclaim the words of peace of the resurrected Christ?

The Church and Social Responsibility for Peace

We are now in a position to connect Bonhoeffer's understanding of a theological foundation of peace and his understanding of the Church more concretely in terms of what the Church actually does in its effort to bring about peace on earth. Bonhoeffer programmatically declares: "The church stands against war in favor of peace among all the peoples, between nations, classes and races."[42] But what, exactly, does the Church *do* in her stand for peace?

---

[39] *DBWE* 13, 308.

[40] See further my essay in this volume: "Bonhoeffer the Preacher: Philosophy and Theology in the Service of the Sermon."

[41] *DBWE* 12, 259.

[42] *DBWE* 11, 380.

No Peace without Justice and Truth

We noted above that Bonhoeffer rejects the view that the Church pursues peace as a value or end in itself. For him, peace cannot be attained unless it is in a "vivid relationship to the concept of truth and justice."[43] What is that relation? In short, the foundation of peace is justice, just as the foundation of justice is truth; or more exactly, truth is the unmasking of injustice. That the foundation of peace is justice is theologically expressed by the Apostle Paul. In Rom. 5:1 he says: "because we are justified by faith, we have peace with God through our Lord Jesus Christ." This sequence is irreversible: first is justification, and then comes peace as a result, and not the other way round. The peace of God, as the forgiveness of our sins, "is the reality of the gospel in which truth and peace are preserved together."[44]

The upshot of this for our deliberations is rather obvious. As the Church that proclaims peace to the world we cannot simply speak of peace as a kind of optimism the world needs, as a positive religious world view or as some kind of Christian sentimental message. Every time we proclaim peace, we need to be mindful that "a community of peace can exist only when it does not rest on *a lie* or on *injustice*;" or to express it positively: "the peace demanded by God has two boundaries: first, the truth; second, justice."[45] Hence, when the Church speaks of peace to an individual or to a small group of people, she declares peace possible only because of Christ. When she proclaims peace to peoples or nations, she does so as the commandment of God and because she herself has peace. "If we do not have this personal peace," Bonhoeffer remarks, "we cannot preach peace to the nations."[46]

But in addition the proclamation of the commandment to peace, there is also the necessary dimension to address the issues of injustice. The Church cannot speak of peace and be silent on matters of injustice. The way to peace is the way from injustice to justice. This is no small matter. Bonhoeffer experienced the injustices against humanity more than enough in his own life. As the grip of Nazi atrocities escalated into a crime against humanity, Bonhoeffer's existence was equally on a descent "from above" to the "below." In the middle of that downward spiral Bonhoeffer penned down the now famous recollection for his fellow-conspirators on New Year's Eve 1943, entitled "After Ten Years." Even though he had still not arrived at the bottom himself, Bonhoeffer ponders: "It remains an experi-

---

[43] *DBWE* 11, 361.
[44] *DBWE* 11, 366.
[45] *DBWE* 11, 365; original emphasis.
[46] *DBWE* 12, 260.

ence of incomparable value that we have for once learned to see the great events of world history from below, from the perspective of the outcast, the suspects, the maltreated, the powerless, the oppressed, the reviled, in short from the perspective of the suffering."[47]

Bonhoeffer's words are a necessary reminder: as long as the Church merely talks of peace without also addressing issues of justice with concrete action, her words will be a mere noise of clinging cymbals. If we Christians desire peace on earth, then we must also speak and act for those who are the victims of unjust, corrupt and evil systems and ideologies.

The Church and Peace Action

What does the Church add that is otherwise missing from the peace discourse? What is the distinctly Christian element that the Church brings to the table of peace discourse? I suspect that some of us would call for action and stand as activists and reformers in solidarity with those who desire peace, denounce military rearmament, violence etc. No doubt, these things do have their place in the lives of Christians, but Bonhoeffer points also to a completely different plan of action. "We can be Christians today in only two ways, through prayer and in doing justice among human beings. All Christian thinking, talking, and organizing must be born anew, out of that prayer and action."[48]

Bonhoeffer affirms the need for "doing justice among human beings" but he also urges us to engage in a different kind of action: prayer – a Christian action par excellence. At Fanø, Bonhoeffer asserted that "the powers of evil will not be broken by means of organisations, but by prayer and fasting (Mark 9:29)... Prayer is stronger than organisation."[49] Let us pause here for a moment. In the face of evil and powerful systems at the brink of war Bonhoeffer actually calls for prayer as a means of overcoming politically corrupt organisations. We may wonder whether he has any sense of reality or whether he has just become a religious dreamer or simply desires a happy end to an otherwise depressive situation in Nazi Germany. No, none of these things are true. Bonhoeffer was incredibly tuned in to the realities of life, wherever he lived.[50]

---

[47] DBWE 8, 52. As far as I know, Bonhoeffer was the first theologian to employ the expression "from below;" later it was adopted by Gustavo Gutiérrez and liberation theology and from there by many other liberation theologies.

[48] *DBWE* 8, 389.

[49] *DBWE* 13, 306.

[50] On Bonhoeffer's view of reality, see *DBWE* 6, 58: "There are not two realities, but

"The Christian cause lives or dies – and yet this is impossible – with prayer; prayer is the heart of Christian life."[51] In clear, unadorned words he reminds us that prayer is the heartbeat of our lives and actions as Christians. Prayer is powerful – indeed more powerful than any other power – because it is rooted in the power of God. "There is nothing that is impossible for us anymore," writes Bonhoeffer from prison, "because there is nothing that is impossible for God; that no earthly power can touch us without God's will."[52] Bonhoeffer does not say that as long as we pray, God will hear us and make sure that the world will live in perpetual peace. The power of prayer, rather, lies precisely in the mystery of God's unfathomable will and power and our trust that God both can and may intervene precisely in world history, if he so deems it necessary.

The Question for Us Today?

As church leaders from around the world gathered under the umbrella of the Methodist Church, how are we resolving the tension between 1. appropriate social responsibility and action, in other words, actions visibly directed towards the world, and 2. action that is internal to the Church but no less powerful, action such as prayer and meditation?

A Constructive Conclusion

By way of conclusion, let us articulate three distinct ways in which we as individuals but also and especially as a Church may embrace tangible steps forward in becoming concrete agents toward peace.

Renewal of Faith

At the beginning of the Church's call for peace stands her own renewal of faith. This is necessary both personally and collectively. As persons, we leave our own fear at the feet of the resurrected Christ. As a Church, we do so likewise. By leaving our fear with Christ, we take hold at the same time

---

only one reality, and that is God's reality revealed in Christ in the reality of the world." See now also Barry Harvey, *Taking Hold of the Real. Dietrich Bonhoeffer and the Profound Worldliness of Christianity.* Eugene: Cascade Books 2015.

51 *DBWE* 10, 577.
52 *DBWE* 8, 515.

of trust, or faith, in the power and wisdom of God. "Only the faith that leaves behind all false confidence, letting it fall and break down, can overcome fear. This is faith: it does not rely on itself or on favorable seas, favorable conditions; it does not rely on its own strength or on other people's strength, but believes only and alone in God, whether or not there is a storm. It is the only faith that is not superstition and does not let us slip back into fear, but makes us free of fear. Lord, make this faith strong in us who have little faith!"[53]

Righteous Action

In a poem written from prison, entitled "Stations of the Way to Freedom," Bonhoeffer writes the following on action: "Not always doing and daring what's random, but seeking the right thing, Hover not over the possible, but boldly reach for the real. Not in escaping to thought, in action alone is found freedom."[54] The poem points to what Bonhoeffer called elsewhere "responsible action."[55] For Bonhoeffer this implies that our action must be measured in relation to reality and the action of Jesus Christ. "Neither a servile attitude toward the status quo, nor a protest based on principle against the status quo in the name of some ideal reality, leads to genuine accordance with reality, the hallmark of responsible action." True responsible action is related to the reality of Christ: He notes, for example: "All human responsibility is rooted in the real vicarious representative action of Jesus Christ on behalf of all human beings. Responsible action is vicarious action."[56]

In our context, then, we must not shy away from the effort to situate ourselves in our own contemporary reality, with respect to two key questions: 1. Do we have a theology, a foundation upon which we base our reflection and action. For example, do we share a peace theology, are we united on the questions of national and international armament, on the rejection of military service etc. 2. The answer we give to the above question will then determine our concrete action. We may act in word and in deed, but it has to be reflective of the action of Jesus Christ himself, be responsible, timely and in accordance with our realities. To determine such action is of utmost difficulty. Even Jesus' assurance "Blessed are the peacemakers,

---

[53] *DBWE* 12, 460.
[54] *DBWE* 8, 513.
[55] *DBWE* 6, 232.
[56] *DBWE* 6, 223.

for they will be called children of God" (Matthew 5:9) is not crystal clear. It will remain our Christian task to make concrete Jesus' words.

Berlin and Hiroshima

I would like to conclude with returning to the beginning of the essay. We saw pictures of Berlin and Hiroshima after their total destruction in 1945. Both cities are rebuilt and the marks of war and destruction are hardly visible any more. Both cities have deliberate sites to remember the dark events of their histories: here we have the Hiroshima Peace Memorial Museum and Berlin has a host of memorial sites, including the Holocaust Museum right next to the Brandenburg Gate. Even though both cities are rebuilt and very vibrant, we must never forget that peace is volatile. Peace is there one day, but the next it can be lost. As Christians we must be a "peace memorial," a signpost so to speak, to the world. The world needs daily reminders that peace is a costly privilege. But how can we as Christians best be a memorial unto peace?

I would like to end with the words of Bonhoeffer. After the failed attempt on Hitler's life on 20 July 1944, the next day Bonhoeffer wrote a letter to his best friend. "Later on I discovered, and am still discovering to this day, that one only learns to have faith by living in the full this-worldliness of life... one throws oneself completely into the arms of God, and this is what I call this-worldliness [*Diesseitigkeit*]: living fully in the midst of life's tasks, questions, successes and failures, experiences and perplexities – then one takes seriously no longer one's own sufferings but rather the sufferings of God in the world. Then one stays awake with Christ in Gethsemane. And I think this is faith; this is μετάνοια [repentance]. And this is how one becomes a human being, a Christian."[57]

For us Christians, speaking up and making peace will never become absolute and independent activities. They are deeply embedded in our lives. And our lives are, just like Bonhoeffer's life, often pressured from all sides. May God give us the grace to live also "unreservedly in life's duties, problems, successes and failures, experiences and perplexities. In so doing, we throw ourselves completely into the arms of God" and hope that he will grant peace to ourselves and the world.

---

[57] *DBWE* 8, 486.

15. Bonhoeffer as Preacher:
Philosophy and Theology in the Service of the Sermon[*]

Introduction

Given the recent centennial commemoration of Dietrich Bonhoeffer's birth (1906–1945) and the fact that among the theologians of the twentieth century he enjoys great respect and admiration and is somewhat of a "phenomenon,"[1] this study is an attempt to examine anew one of the most fundamental questions that interpreters must raise in view of Bonhoeffer's legacy. It is the deceptively simple question: "Who was Bonhoeffer?" The question, however, is neither merely abstract nor simple just because the answer is obviously tied to his biography. Indeed, it is deceptive, because the question is neither a biographical surface issue nor a matter that Bonhoeffer himself explicitly worked out. For this reason, we are justified to look at the question afresh, precisely because it spans the intellectual framework of Bonhoeffer's life. To find an entry point that leads us on the road to discover a viable answer to our guiding question let us begin with an exchange of letters between Bonhoeffer and Bethge.

Bonhoeffer writes in a letter to Eberhard Bethge from the Benedictine monastery in Ettal that his aunt "has inoperable liver cancer and that the doc- tor gives her only four to six weeks [to live] ... What would I do if I knew that in four to six weeks it would all be over? That is running through my head. I believe that I would try to teach *theology* again as before and to *preach often*."[2] Faced with the immediacy of death, Bonhoeffer is lucid about what matters most to him: teaching theology and preaching as often as possible. Theology and preaching are central to his mission, he says – or,

---

[*] This essay was first presented to the International Bonhoeffer Society, Annual Meeting of the American Academy of Religion, San Diego, November 2007.
[1] See the recent study by Stephen R. Haynes, *The Bonhoeffer Phenomenon: Portraits of a Protestant Saint*. Minneapolis: Fortress 2004, which examines Bonhoeffer's reception in a broad context.
[2] *DBWE* 16, 161, emphasis added. The aunt, Countess Hanna von der Goltz, died 21 March 1941, cf. *DBWE* 16, 182 note 8.

we might say, theology in the service of preaching. For, I will argue, all of the main professional roles Bonhoeffer assumed over his lifetime – such as theologian, philosopher, exegete, and pastor – may well be understood as undertaken in the service of preaching. How do these roles relate to what Bethge suggested in the subtitle of his biography, that Bonhoeffer was a "Christian and a Man of His Times"?[3] Was he primarily one of these roles, or did his life bear witness to a multiplicity and simultaneity of these roles? In short, I will argue that Bonhoeffer was first and foremost a preacher. But since a preacher is typically also a pastor, and since every pastor must necessarily also be a theologian, and since a good theologian must also be a skilled exegete and ideally also a philosopher, it follows that these four roles are mutually correlated in such a manner that they culminate in the role of preacher.

Before we proceed, one caveat and one point of clarification are in order. First, the caveat. My argument that Bonhoeffer was foremost a preacher entails an unavoidable overlap between chronological development and the maturation of theological concepts. That said, it is, however, not a main objective to retrace a line in Bonhoeffer's life that allows us to correlate chronology with theological or philosophical insights in a simplistic manner. The nature of the correlation is more like a piece of a woven fabric that is held together by all kinds of threads, both visible and invisible. Second, given our limited space, in order to illustrate the nexus of the multiplicity of roles, chronological development, and proliferation of intellectual formation in Bonhoeffer, I will use the concept of sin in the following sections to substantiate my thesis. Because of its succinctness, the notion of sin lends itself quite readily to demonstrate how in Bonhoeffer a theological idea encompasses a spectrum of fields and precisely in its diversity amounts to cohesive concept.

Bonhoeffer the Theologian

When Bonhoeffer was a mere fourteen years old he announced that he was going to become "a minister and theologian," and apparently "he never seems to have wavered in this ambition."[4] It is well known that the teenage Bonhoeffer received mostly curious if not outright contemptuous comments from his older brothers when he announced this decision. Arguably,

---

[3] Eberhard Bethge, *Dietrich Bonhoeffer. Theologian, Christian, Man for His Time*, translated and revised by Victoria J. Barnett. Minneapolis: Fortress 2000.

[4] Bethge, *Dietrich Bonhoeffer*, 36.

at this young age, this was merely a *professional* decision; just as his siblings studied physics, law, and biology, so he decided to study theology. Whether his aim was to become an academic theologian as a professor in a theological faculty or a minister in a pastorate is difficult to ascertain from these youthful comments. Bethge makes an interesting remark regarding Bonhoeffer's resolution: "The impulse to become a theologian for the sake of the real church belonged to a later period."[5] In Bethge's view, Bonhoeffer initially separated theology for its own sake and a theology "for the sake of the church." Indeed, for Bonhoeffer to become an academic theologian did not, strictly speaking, imply the confessing of faith in or the following of Jesus Christ,[6] as he later wrote in *Discipleship*. He admitted retrospectively that much himself, as three letters written in the mid-1930s indicate. In a letter to Elisabeth Zinn in 1936, Bonhoeffer made a rare confession about his own path from theology to discipleship. Looking back at the years 1929–1931, Bonhoeffer wrote, "Something happened, something that has changed and transformed my life to the present day. For the first time I discovered the Bible ... I had often preached, I had seen a great deal of the church, spoken and preached about it – but I had not yet become a Christian."[7] In fact, he had written a doctoral dissertation as a theologian and started on the path from theologian to Christian, without abandoning the former, at the time he was writing *Act and Being*.

At any rate, here was a crucial juncture in Bonhoeffer's biography. In simple terms, the academic theologian became a Christian. This was a decisive moment for the young man's spiritual development and for his theological formation. Theology and faith became the two sides of the one coin and the formerly peripheral existence of the Church became tied to how "he did theology." More and more, his theology became the backbone for his piety. Chronologically speaking, when he returned from his first visit to the United States in 1932, Bonhoeffer was for the first time both a theologian and a Christian. From that period onwards, the two were no longer independent but interdependent. All his work as a theologian was deliberately carried out as a Christian theologian and increasingly in view of the Church. Therefore, when Bonhoeffer began his short teaching career in Berlin he was a Christian theologian. Nevertheless, while it is relatively straightforward to assert that Bonhoeffer was a theologian, two ensuing

---

questions are more difficult to answer: What kind of theologian was he – biblical, systematic one? And what kind of theological method did he employ?

What Kind of Theologian?

Regarding the question of what kind of theologian he was, an answer is not as lucid as it may appear at first glance. Some scholars emphasize that Bonhoeffer was not a systematic theologian. Their assertion is correct to the extent that Bonhoeffer hardly composed works that fall within the discipline and scope of systematic theology. We have really no essays that treat the major themes of theology methodologically and systematically. Bonhoeffer did not present, for example, his concept of God in a systematic treatise, nor, unlike Barth, did he work on a magnum opus comparable to the *Church Dogmatics* or write a multi-volume *Systematic Theology* like Tillich and his former Finkenwalde student Gerhard Ebeling.[8] Why is there a lack of systematic presentation of his theology? As Wayne Floyd suggests, "Bonhoeffer's non-systematic style is not so much a symptom of its incompleteness as it is an affirmation of incompletion in theological method." Moreover, the lack of "a systematic, exhaustive accounting of his theology is not to be had – not because he did not live long enough – or have adequately systematic a mind – to bring together a theological compendium."[9] I agree with Floyd that the lack of Bonhoeffer's systematic theology is not a matter of his intellectual acumen, but I am inclined to think that it is less due to an "incompletion in theological method" than to the ever-changing circumstances of his life and his idiosyncratic notion of theological method.

Indeed, I am suggesting that the assertion that Bonhoeffer was not a systematic theologian is inaccurate in a more substantial manner. The absence of a written legacy of systematic works should not mislead us to judge that he did not *think of* and *conceptualize* theology in a systematic mode. Granted, when systematic theology is measured in a modern aca-

---

[8] See Karl Barth, *Church Dogmatics*, 4 vols. New York: Scribner 1956–1977; Paul Tillich, *Systematic Theology*, 3 vols. Chicago: University of Chicago Press 1951–1963; Gerhard Ebeling, *Dogmatik des christlichen Glaubens*, 3 vols. Tübingen: Mohr Siebeck, fourth edition 2012.

[9] Wayne Whitson Floyd, "Encounter with an Other: Immanuel Kant and G. W. F. Hegel in the Theology of Dietrich Bonhoeffer," in Peter Frick (ed), *Bonhoeffer's Intellectual Formation: Theology and Philosophy in His Thought*, Religion in Philosophy and Theology 29. Tübingen: Mohr Siebeck 2008, 111–112.

demic context, concretely as the list of published works, then Bonhoeffer does not perform well. But in my view, such a standard of assessment has its own limits, and it is certainly misleading in Bonhoeffer's context. It is noteworthy in this regard that Bonhoeffer himself thought of *Act and Being* as a work that belongs to the discipline of systematic theology, as the subtitle – *Transcendental Philosophy and Ontology in Systematic Theology* – indicates. Moreover, we should not forget that during the winter semester 1931–1932 in Berlin, Bonhoeffer presented a lecture on "The History of Twentieth-Century Systematic Theology."[10] A quick perusal of the table of contents indicates something extremely important about Bonhoeffer's conception of systematic theology. In short, the array of topics is mind-boggling. The young lecturer discusses subjects such as society, Church, and theology in the context of the early twentieth century, the theory of religion, the philosophy of neo-Kantianism, epistemology and religion, the nature of Christianity, the absoluteness of Christianity, the biblical Christ, justification and sanctification, ethics and culture, God, the Word of God and theology, proclamation, the problem of ethics, and obedience. This list leaves no doubt that Bonhoeffer freely transgresses the boundaries of the subjects that were customarily reckoned to fall within the discipline of systematic theology. A good test case, so to speak, is Karl Barth's *Church Dogmatics* that appeared in its first volume shortly after Bonhoeffer had finished this lecture. Barth conceptualized his work in a standard mode, beginning with a section on Prolegomena, followed by sections on the Word of God, Revelation, God, and so on. Why did Bonhoeffer conceive of systematic theology in so completely different a manner? Was he too young, theologically immature, or too careless in his presentation of theology?

In my view, there is really only one explanation, details of which Bonhoeffer himself hinted at in a letter written before he visited the United States for the first time. In a letter to the German Academic Exchange Program in January 1930, Bonhoeffer explains that he wishes to study at an American university. Then he identifies "systematic theology" as his "academic discipline" (*meine Wissenschaftsdisziplin*) and notes further that his interest lies in studying "dogmatics" and the two related fields (*Grenzgebiete*) of "sociology" and "philosophy." And finally he adds that in his dissertation he worked out "the systematic foundation of the sociology of the church."[11]

---

[10] Cf. *DBWE* 11, 177–244.
[11] *DBWE* 10, 162.

Bonhoeffer's classification of these academic fields is crucial for understanding his view of theology. It seems to me that this conception of theology was intentionally integrative in that he attempted to work out a genuine coherence of the various fields and sub-fields within the discipline of theology. Bonhoeffer subsumed these various aspects of theology enumerated in his lecture under the umbrella of "systematic theology," not because they all belong technically to that rubric or are "systematic" in a unique sense. Quite to the contrary, I think that he understood theology to be "systematic" precisely by going *beyond* the confines of "systematic theology." Indeed, his lecture wanted to demonstrate how all the theological topoi must be related to and cohere with the questions of theology in both a narrow and a wider sense. In other words, for Bonhoeffer, systematic theology comes to full bloom only when it is a matter of comprehensive integration and methodological correlation of questions that belong, technically speaking, to the fields of philosophy, biblical studies, sociology, and pastoral theology. In this broad understanding of "systematic" theology, the sermon, for example, is then not relegated to a seminar on homiletics, but is the fruit of a long process that began with the questions of revelation and epistemology and was refined in exegetical interpretation. Seen in this light, Bonhoeffer's sermons are more or less examples that indicate the systematic structure and backbone of his "systematic" theological reflections.[12]

Theological Method

If, for the sake of our argument, we accept the proposition that Bonhoeffer was a "systematic" even though methodologically unorthodox theologian, the question arises what kind of theological method he employed in his theologizing. Bonhoeffer hardly discusses "theological method," but there are several scattered sayings that indicate what he had in mind. Toward the end of his lecture on "The History of Systematic Theology in the Twentieth Century," he proclaims, *"Deus dixit* – to accept this is the beginning of all genuine theological thinking, to allow space for freedom of the living God."[13] The expression *deus dixit* (God has spoken) is shorthand here for

---

[12] Good examples are the sermons delivered in London; see *DBWE* 13, 313–408.

[13] *DBWE* 11, 231. The original reads (*DBW* 11, 199), "Deus dixit – das hinzunehmen, das ist Anfang alles echten theologischen Denkens, Raum geben der Freiheit, [der] Lebendigkeit Gottes."

what he elsewhere articulates quite well. That God has spoken means nothing else but a reference to divine revelation.

For example, describing his theological project in *Sanctorum Communio* "methodologically," the young doctoral student explains that his argument "is possible only on the basis of our understanding of the church, i.e. from the revelation we have heard.[14] Thus social-philosophical and sociological problems can be dealt with in the context of theology not because they can be proved generally necessary on the basis of creation, but because they are presupposed and included in revelation. Only in this perspective can they be fully understood."[15] These comments give a first indication of Bonhoeffer's methodological trajectory: theology begins with the given of revelation, given in the reality of faith, recorded in God's Word, and interpreted in the social networks of the Church. *Deus dixit* entails the understanding that God has spoken and that God's speech, understood as revelation, as the "we have heard," is the formal starting point for theology. More precisely, Bonhoeffer claims that any social, philosophical, or sociological understanding of the concept of the church is "presupposed and included in revelation." His justi- fication for this presupposition of revelation is that "the basis for all theology is the fact of faith," which in turn is predicated on the fact that "theology ...starts with the statement of the reality of God and that is its particular right."[16] Hence, it is not surprising that Bonhoeffer can make a statement that for the contemporary academic theologian must have sounded like an oxymoron: "Theology as a science (*Wissenschaft*) has to focus on faith as a reality."[17] In a most concise way we may summarize that, for Bonhoeffer, theological method starts from the premise of God's revealed reality, a fact received in faith.

Furthermore, Bonhoeffer argues, as long as theology does not see its essential difference from all philosophical thinking, it does not begin with a statement concerning God's reality but tries rather to build a support for such a statement. Indeed, this is the main fault with theology, which in our days no longer knows its particular province and its limits. It is not only a methodological fault but, likewise, a misunderstanding of the Christian idea of God from the very beginning.[18]

---

[14] Cf. *DBWE* 1, 65 and 134: "Only the concept of revelation can lead to the Christian concept of the church."

[15] *DBWE* 1, 65.

[16] *DBWE* 10, 454.

[17] *DBWE* 13, 190.

[18] *DBWE* 10, 452.

Here Bonhoeffer uses the term *methodological*. He criticizes theology for trying to make a case for the reality of God, hence also for revelation, rather than accepting it as a given. The reality of God does not need to be proven, since in theology "truth itself is the object."[19] This truth cannot be obtained by means of human insight; it is simply a matter that legitimates itself by virtue of God's Word that proclaims this divine reality. Hence, at the beginning of theology stands "an act of recognition (*Anerkennung*)"[20] of that given reality.[21]

In order to make intelligible how the roles of theologian, philosopher, exegete, and pastor/preacher cohere in Bonhoeffer's thought as a whole, let us use the example of the notion of sin. As we just saw, Bonhoeffer's basic premise is that theology needs to have as its starting point the concept of revelation. Congruent with this premise is Bonhoeffer's understanding of sin, in a two-fold manner. On the one hand, he accepts the Augustinian view of humanity's original sin.[22] "'Being in Adam'," notes Bonhoeffer, "is a more pointed ontological, and a more biblically based ... designation for *esse peccator*. Were it really a human possibility for persons themselves to know that they are sinners apart from revelation, neither 'being in Adam' nor 'being in Christ' would be existential designations of their being."[23] In other words, Bonhoeffer affirms Augustine's dictum *non posse non peccare* (that it is not possible not to sin) and assigns to that understanding onto-logical significance. In plain language, every person is a sinner. On the other hand, Bonhoeffer is quick to explain that a person's knowledge of sin

---

[19] *DBWE* 11, 231.

[20] *DBWE* 11, 232.

[21] See also Bonhoeffer's explanation earlier in the same context: "Theology may not, at any price, be confused with the philosophy of religion or with the doctrine of faith [Glaubenslehre]. In the philosophy of religion, reasons must be given for that which theology takes as its object, because this means giving evidence for the truth. But the object of theology [may] only be the *logos theou*, the act of God, which is its own reason for being. Human beings cannot go back behind this beginning. Theology no longer has to ground its truth outside itself in another discipline, but must proceed from its own basis, its own presuppositions" (*DBWE* 11, 231).

[22] For a recent discussion of this question, see Barry Harvey, "Augustine and Thomas Aquinas in the Theology of Dietrich Bonhoeffer," in Peter Frick, *Bonhoeffer's Intellectual Formation*, 14–17.

[23] *DBWE* 2, 136, cf. 97. Already in *Sanctorum Communio*, Bonhoeffer had rejected Heidegger's category of "possibility" as belonging to theological discourse. See *DBWE* 1, 143: If "one regarded revelation only as beginning (potentiality), and not at the same time also as completion (reality), this would take away what is decisive about the revelation of God, namely that God's word became history." See also note 40, where Bultmann is mentioned. See Ernst Feil, *The Theology of Dietrich Bonhoeffer*, translated by Martin Rumscheidt. Philadelphia: Fortress 1985, 29–32, 37–39.

is a matter of revelation and not the result of a logical reductionism or human experience. He leaves no doubt: "The knowledge of what sin is comes solely through the mediation of the Word of God in Christ ... *Sola fide credendum est nos esse peccatores* (only by faith we believe that we are sinner)."[24] What is significant for our argument in this context is that Bonhoeffer's understanding of sin is predicated on the notion of revelation. In faith, Bonhoeffer simply accepts as a theological axiom that God revealed to us that we are sinners. But even the knowledge of sin itself is a matter of revealed faith.

Bonhoeffer the Philosopher

For good reasons, hardly anyone would disagree that Bonhoeffer was among the most important theologians of the last century. I am proposing, however, that any adequate understanding of Bonhoeffer's oeuvre must also take into account the philosophical assumptions that undergird and stabilize the theological structures built on them.

Philosophical and Theological Premises

"Philosophical thinking," says Bonhoeffer, "attempts to be free from premises (if that is possible at all); Christian thinking has to be conscious of its particular premise, that is, of the premise of the reality of God, before and beyond all thinking. In the protection of this presupposition, theological thinking convicts philosophical thinking of being bound also to a presupposition, namely, that thinking in itself can give truth. But philosophical truth always remains truth which is given only within the category of possibility. Philosophical thinking never can extend beyond this category – it can never be a thinking in reality. It can form a conception of reality, but conceived reality is not reality any longer. The reason for this is that thinking is in itself a closed circle, with the ego as the center."[25]

Here Bonhoeffer makes an important distinction with reference to the basic philosophical and theological presuppositions. Theology assumes, as he says, "the reality of God, before and beyond all thinking." But philosophy is stuck in the error "that thinking in itself can give truth." Put differently, theology takes truth for granted in an unconditioned ontological

---

[24] *DBWE* 1, 145.
[25] *DBWE* 10, 452.

sense. But philosophy is trying to establish, if not truth itself, then at least the parameter within which truth can manifest itself. This very attempt is futile, however, in Bonhoeffer's judgment, because philosophical truth is self-limiting. "Godless thought – even when it is ethical – remains self-enclosed. Even a critical philosophy cannot place one into the truth, because its crisis emerges from within itself, and its apparent reality is still subservient to the claims of the *cor curvum in se* that have lost the power to claim anyone. Revelation gives itself without precondition and is alone able to place one into reality. Theological thought goes from God to reality, not from reality to God."[26]

Here, then, lies the *crux interpretum* for Bonhoeffer vis-à-vis philosophy's claim: it is self-limiting because of sin. In his own words, "Although theology accepts these results of philosophical inquiry, it interprets them in its own fashion as the thinking of the *cor curvum in se*. The I does indeed remain self-enclosed; this, however, is not its credit but is its guilt."[27]

Theological Epistemology

What are the implications of Bonhoeffer's view that there is really no genuine philosophical epistemology because of sin, because of the human heart turned upon itself? The consequences are immense for all of Bonhoeffer's theologizing. As one of the overarching conclusions Bonhoeffer drew from philosophy, as *Act and Being* amply demonstrates – and equally important, as a datum that is the invisible spine of all his later writings and sermons – is the idea that the I, the human self, can never come to itself because of its *curvum in se*. For Bonhoeffer – and this is absolutely decisive – this insight is drawn from philosophy but becomes concrete in theology. His philosophical position that the I cannot come to itself – because of its self-confining *ratio* – is the tip of the iceberg that is predicated on the subterranean mass of the heart turned upon itself because of sin.[28] Congruent with his premises, Bonhoeffer therefore argues that if it were really a philosophical "possibility for persons themselves to know that they are sinners apart from revelation, neither 'being in Adam' nor 'being in Christ' would be existential designations of their being. For it would mean that human beings could place themselves into the truth."[29]

---

[26] *DBWE* 2, 89.

[27] *DBWE* 10, 399–400.

[28] See *DBWE* 10, 461: "No religion, no ethics, no metaphysical knowledge may serve man to approach God"; and *DBWE* 1, 45: "There is no purely cognitive way to know God."

[29] *DBWE* 2, 136.

In what ways is this rejection of philosophical epistemology important for Bonhoeffer's concept of sin? Above we concluded that Bonhoeffer takes the datum of human sinfulness as a matter of reality, a reality that is given to humanity by means of God's revelation and appropriated in faith. To repeat the Lutheran saying *sola fide credendum est nos esse peccatores* once more, the gist of that dictum is simply that the first statement of faith is that we are sinners. Indeed, this confession is possible only as a statement of faith. Philosophy cannot ever arrive at that same insight because it can never place a person into the reality and truth of sin. The very essence of sin is such that it cannot be known by a self that is itself corrupted by sin. Sin cannot be seen in its own darkness, but only in the light of revelation.

Bonhoeffer the Exegete

If sin prefers darkness, revelation is the light of Holy Scripture. Since, as we saw above, self-enclosed and self-limited thinking cannot arrive at an adequate knowledge of either self or humanity as a whole, such knowledge must come from the "outside," from revelation. For Bonhoeffer, revelation is God's Word recorded in Holy Scripture. Hence, revelation and God's Word require the work of exegesis. In the context of Christian theology, exegesis presupposes Holy Scripture in the forms of the Old Testament/ Hebrew Bible and the New Testament. In Bonhoeffer's case, the task of exegesis was to provide a textual analysis that would lead to a decidedly theological interpretation of the biblical text. Contrary to much of current biblical scholarship, Bonhoeffer did not engage in exegesis for the sake of academic analysis of the philological, social, or historical details. Not surprisingly, Bonhoeffer took the Greek term ἐξήγησις (exegesis) quite literally in its meaning as "leading out," hence "explanation." For Bonhoeffer the biblical text is leading outward, is leading away from itself to the higher plane of theological interpretation, or in even more precise terms, into the truth of human existence revealed in the biblical texts.[30]

In almost all of his work on biblical texts it is evident that Bonhoeffer predicates his exegetical work on the assumption that biblical interpretation must be *theological*. A case in point is his lecture on *Creation and Fall*. The subtitle leaves no doubt as to Bonhoeffer's intention: *A Theological*

---

[30] Philo, *De Vita Contemplativa* 78, employs the phrase ἐξηγήσεις τῶν γραμμάτων in this way. Unlike Philo, however, Bonhoeffer did not engage in allegorical but in theological interpretation.

Exposition of Genesis 1–3.[31] Anyone who reads this work will immediately detect that Bonhoeffer – following Barth's approach in his *Epistle to the Romans* – married exegesis and theology in such a manner that the first must be made fruitful for the latter.

On Bonhoeffer's handling of biblical texts we have an interesting remark by Wilhelm Rott, who belonged to the inner circle of Finkenwaldians. In one of his autobiographical reflections he says of Bonhoeffer, "Historico-critical research was a matter of course for him, but it had 'got in his way,' and he said: 'The professors accuse me of being unscholarly, because of my biblical work on the Old Testament' … Like Karl Barth whose 'every word' he had read, Bonhoeffer approached the texts as a dogmatist and a preacher; the question of method hardly arose at that time. All the same, he was acquainted with the idea and matter of hermeneutics – not every theologian of those times knew the word – he was reading Hofmann's *Hermeneutics*. Bonhoeffer was determined to make the texts speak to our time."[32]

Rott's observations point to two important aspects of Bonhoeffer's methodological approach to biblical texts. First, we are told that "Bonhoeffer approached the texts as a dogmatist and a preacher." That he explained texts as a "dogmatist," that is to say as a "theologian," is simply evidence of Bonhoeffer's predilection to interpret texts theologically. But that he approached the text also as a "preacher" points to the most decisive aspect of his biblical exegesis: the attempt to relate even his theological interpretation to the proclamation of the gospel in the sermon. In other words, as important as theological interpretation is in and of itself, it is not its own end. The end of that task lies in the sermon. Second, Rott claims that Bonhoeffer "was acquainted with the idea and matter of hermeneutics" at a time when "not every theologian" even knew the word *hermeneutic* or was interested in matters of method. This observation is important yet difficult to comprehend. Perhaps these claims applied to the reality of the Finkenwaldian students more than they did to professional theologians. It seems curious to downplay the interest in hermeneutics since Schleiermacher in German theological circles and to deny the attention given to theological method at a time when Barth and Harnack fiercely debated some of these questions. At any rate, Rott's comment is significant in that it suggests that Bonhoeffer was aware of the questions posed by hermeneutics, the so-called historical-critical method and his own theo-

---

[31] See *DBWE* 1.
[32] Wilhelm Rott, "Something Always Occurred to Him," in Wolf-Dieter Zimmerman and Ronald Gregor Smith (eds), *I Knew Dietrich Bonhoeffer*, translated by Käthe Gregor Smith. London: Collins 1966, 133.

logical interpretation of biblical texts; how these matters correlate in Bonhoeffer's work requires further research and examination. He not only read a work on hermeneutics during the Finkenwalde period, but he also intended to write a book on the subject himself. In other words, for Bonhoeffer the question of exegesis was embedded in the task of hermeneutics. He was cognizant of the importance of hermeneutics. In a letter to Erwin Sutz, his Swiss friend he met at Union Theological Seminary, he writes in October 1936 from Finkenwalde, "I am hoping to finish my book [*Discipleship*] during the course of this semester, after which I would really like to try my hand at a book on hermeneutics. There seems to me to be a very great gap here. But first things first."[33] Unfortunately, this book was never written and we can only suspect that he would have made the case for a hermeneutics adequate to both theological interpretation and preaching.

Let us now demonstrate Bonhoeffer's exegetical approach by returning to the concept of sin. It was beyond any question for Bonhoeffer and his students that exegetical work must be done in Greek and Hebrew. That a preacher would not be able to base the sermon on the Greek text was simply unimaginable for him. In Finkenwalde, Bonhoeffer thus offered several exegetical exercises on various New Testament terms and concepts.[34] One of these exercises focused on the concept of "sin." At the very beginning of this study, Bonhoeffer listed several Greek expressions denoting the semantic domain of "sin," such as ἁμαρτία, ἁμαρτίαι and ἄφεσιν ἁμαρτιῶν. Regarding the last expression, Bethge recorded a somewhat truncated comment that Bonhoeffer had apparently included in his introductory remarks. He refers to "the difference between singular and plural. Usage of the concept – never ἄφεσιν ἁμαρτίας (forgiveness of sin)."[35] On the surface, this rather terse remark may seem to be nothing more than a hair-splitting exegetical detail. Quite to the contrary, here we have evidence for a key biblical and theological distinction that undergirds all of Bonhoeffer's theology, from beginning to end, from theological discourse to sermon. What is Bethge referring to, and what is at stake in his comment? Bethge simply recorded in a few words what amounts to one of the most crucial distinctions in all of Christian theology: the distinction be-

---

[33] *DBWE* 14:273. See Bethge, *Dietrich Bonhoeffer*, 567–568, on the question of hermeneutics during the Finkenwalde courses.

[34] During the five semesters at Finkenwalde, Bonhoeffer offered an incredible array of exegetical exercises (see the list of course offerings, seminars, and exercises in *DBWE* 14, 1027–1036), and later in the collective pastorates he engaged the young pastors in exegetical work on topics such as sin, temptation, patience, perseverance, joy, peace, abstinence, death, and thanksgiving (see *DBWE* 15, 322–437).

[35] *DBWE* 15, 344 note 3.

tween sin (singular) and sins (plural). As far as I know, Bonhoeffer never explicitly discussed the significance of this distinction in any of his published works. And yet, there is no doubt that he understood that distinction in its full theological weight. Given his theological premise that sin is a matter of revealed faith, combined with his philosophical premise that the self cannot come to itself, is now added the further theological interpretation, based on an exegetical insight of the Greek text, that the power of sin (singular) cannot be forgiven. In other words, Bonhoeffer assumed as another theological baseline the Pauline teaching that we are under the unforgivable power of sin (see Romans 7:14; Galatians 3:22). For Bonhoeffer, sin as a deathly power cannot be forgiven but only broken and overcome; only the deeds resulting from the power of sin, the daily sins, can be forgiven, hence the plural expression ἄφεσιν ἁμαρτίων, the forgiveness of "sins."

Bonhoeffer the Pastor and Preacher

As we mentioned above, the fourteen-year-old Bonhoeffer wanted to become "a minister and theologian" and at around the age of thirty he confessed to a friend that for the "first time I discovered the Bible." Retrospectively it seems rather self-evident that the role of preacher implicates the roles of the minister and theologian and the focus on the Bible. In terms of the chronology of Bonhoeffer's life, however, these elements had their own unique moments of development and subsequent conceptual correlations. Before he was a minister, he had become an academic theologian, and only after he had worked as both minister and theologian did he discover the Bible. It suffices for our purposes to remember that around age thirty, Bonhoeffer had so much matured in his understanding of the roles of theology and the pastorate that there was no undoing of that new insight. For him there was only one feasible way of being a minister: trained as a (philosophical and exegetical) theologian, for him the heart of the pastorate is the sermon.[36] Ultimately, everything in Christian ministry hinges on the sermon. Why is this so?

Bonhoeffer's overarching hermeneutical presupposition is that the Chris- tian message, concretely the sermon, should not be "a justification of

---

[36] See *DBWE* 14, 489 and 15, 429–430. where Bonhoeffer makes the distinction between being called to a *Pfarramt* and a *Predigtamt*. For a good recent discussion, see Peter Zimmerling, *Bonhoeffer als praktischer Theologe*. Goettingen: Vandenhoeck & Ruprecht 2006.

Christianity to the present, but a *justification of the present to the Christian message.*[37] How can this be achieved? Any justification of the Christian message cannot be accomplished by the rhetorical giftedness of the preacher or a special technique of preaching; indeed, in the strictest theological sense, we may even say that any justification of the Christian message as such is impossible. What Bonhoeffer asserts is that the relevance of the Christian message is anchored in an absolute and unique fact: God's Word in the New Testament is itself its own effective and relevant power. "Wherever God is present in the divine word, there one has the present; there God posits the present. The *subject of the present* is the Holy Spirit, not we ourselves, and that is also why the subject of *contemporization* is the Holy Spirit itself... [For this reason,] Christ speaks to us through Christ's Holy Spirit, and . . . this takes place not outside or alongside but only and exclusively *through the word* of Scripture itself."[38] In short, Bonhoeffer argues that "the *concretissimum of the Christian message* and textual exposition is not a human act of contemporizing but rather always God, the Holy Spirit."[39] Put differently, in the words of the young theology student Bonhoeffer, "I will never be able to convert through the power of *my* sermon unless the Spirit comes and makes *my* word into *the Spirit's* word."[40]

Why does the Word of God – revealed in Scripture and proclaimed in the sermon – occupy such a fundamental place in Bonhoeffer's hermeneutic? What is it about God's Word that allows Bonhoeffer to make such absolute claims? The answer, in short, is that God's Word[41] is self-effective (*selbstwirksam*).[42] Bonhoeffer's conviction that God's Word is its own power can be seen from the time of his teenage years until the end of his life. Probably the first conscious reflection on the idea that God's Word is its own power goes back to Bonhoeffer's confirmation. As was and still is customary in the Lutheran Church, every confirmand receives a Bible verse on the day of confirmation. This is the verse that was given to Bonhoeffer: Οὐ γὰρ ἐπαισχύνομαι τὸ εὐαγγέλιον, δύναμις γὰρ θεοῦ ἐστιν εἰς σωτηρίαν παντὶ τῷ

---

[37] *DBWE* 14, 416; emphasis in original.

[38] *DBWE*, 417.

[39] *DBWE*, 417.

[40] *DBWE* 9, 363. See *DBW* 14, 409: "Das concretissimum der Predigt ist nicht die von *mir gegebene Anwendung*, sondern der durch den Text der Bibel redende Heilige Geist selbst."

[41] On God's Word in Bonhoeffer, see Wolf Krötke, "Dietrich Bonhoeffer and Martin Luther," in Peter Frick (ed), *Bonhoeffer's Intellectual Formation*, 57–60.

[42] Zimmerling, *Bonhoeffer als praktischer Theologe*, 87: "Bonhoeffer geht von der Selbstwirksamkeit des Wortes Gottes, seiner Eigenbewegung aus." See also 89, where he speaks of the "Selbstmächtigkeit" and "Selbstwirksamkeit" of God's Word.

πιστεύοντι. Yes, the verse chosen for him was Romans 1:16 – in Greek! This verse, more than any other in the New Testament, expresses what for Bonhoeffer undergirds the non-negotiable hermeneutic of his preaching: τὸ εὐαγγέλιον, δύναμις γὰρ θεοῦ, that the gospel is the *power* (δύναμις) of God for salvation. The "Word of God is power, victory, overcoming. It still works and bears fruit; it creates new life out of nothing,"[43] he says. In his first sermon in London, Bonhoeffer summarizes all of these thoughts very well: "Not our word, but God's Word: yet even so, God's Word speaking through ours. This is what makes a sermon something unique in all the world, so completely different from any kind of speech. When a preacher opens his Bible and interprets the Word of God, a mystery takes place, a miracle."[44]

Such an understanding of the Word of God has far-reaching implications for the preacher. (1) The basis for the sermon must be a biblical text and not an aphorism of Nietzsche or Goethe[45] or a poem or anything else. In Bonhoeffer's words, "Because the sermon carries God's revelation in Christ further, it is necessarily a sermon on a biblical text" and thus "the preaching of God's revelation in Christ is God's Word to the present."[46] This also means that topical sermons should be used rather sparingly. (2) The origin of the sermon is not the pastor's personal and pious experiences, or the contemporary situation, or the pastor's knowledge of Greek or other forms of learning.[47] Likewise, the goal of the sermon is not to influence the hearers, to impart wisdom or the desire to make the hearers better people. Another way of saying this is that Bonhoeffer would be most cautious with what we now call narrative sermons because only God's Word is self-effective and not personal narratives, irrespective of how interesting or awe-inspiring they may be. The preacher proclaims God's revealed Word, simply because it is his or her divine calling in the Church. The existence of the Church legitimates both the sermon itself and the content of the sermon: God's interest and work for humanity.[48] (3) The preacher preaches without any method, pathos, rhetoric, imploring and inflated intonations,

---

[43] *DBWE* 16, 498; see also *DBWE* 15, 517 and *DBWE* 16, 501, where Bonhoeffer speaks of the power of God's Word (*Macht des Wortes Gottes*).

[44] *DBWE* 13, 323.

[45] Cf. *DBWE* 10, 382.

[46] *DBWE* 10, 382.

[47] See Zimmerling, *Bonhoeffer als praktischer Theologe*, 81, who notes that Bonhoeffer's sermon in Barcelona on the topic of the Church contains no academic pompous statements, even though he had just finished his dissertation on that very topic. Nor does he give an example of his own life to illustrate a point.

[48] See *DBWE* 14, 488–490.

artificial constructions, obtrusiveness, and so on. None of these techniques works, because each masks the self-effective power of God's Word. (4) Bonhoeffer makes a distinction between being called to the pastorate (*Pfarramt*) and preaching (*Predigtamt*). While the former may be temporal and dependent on particular places and contexts, the latter is irreversible. "One is called to the *preaching office of preaching*. This call is irrevocable; we cannot out from under God's command."[49]

These four observations illustrate what has in fact been the argument of this whole essay, that Bonhoeffer's homiletics stand at the centre of his life's mission and that they were decisively shaped by theological, philosophical, and exegetical presuppositions. It is no overstatement to claim that the backbone of Bonhoeffer's sermons is indeed his theology, understood in an encyclopedic sense;[50] the same can be said about his philosophical and exegetical work as well.

Bonhoeffer's presentation of the concept of sin is an excellent example of just this point. By the time the topic of sin emerges in a sermon, it has already gone through the requisite stages of theological and exegetical scrutiny. When sin comes up in the sermon, it is addressed to the hearer as the pronouncement of God, via the biblical text, and not as a matter of invoking psychological guilt. The preacher knows that from a pastoral point of view sins are part of the reality of the disruption of life.[51] That is enough. It is up to the power of God's Word to effect repentance, confession, and a breakthrough to genuine spiritual community.

Conclusion

In terms of the history of philosophy, Aristotle was the first to employ the term θεολογία in a technical sense as the science of "theology." For him, theology was defined as the first philosophy (πρώτη φιλοσοφία) by virtue of its reflecting on the first causes and principles of what truly exists and the cause thereof: God.[52] Congruent with this understanding, the bounda-

---

[49] *DBWE* 14, 489.

[50] See Zimmeling, *Bonhoeffer als praktischer Theologe*, 79: "So lassen sich an Bonhoeffers Predigten theologische Grundanschauungen nachweisen, die in allen Perioden durchgehalten werden."

[51] Two fitting examples of how Bonhoeffer deals with sin theologically and pastorally are his meditation on "The Best Physician" in *DBWE* 16, 500–501 and his attempt to instruct children in Barcelona in understanding what sin is in *DBWE* 10, 558–559.

[52] See *Metaphysics* 983a, 1026a, and Jan Rohls, *Philosophie und Theologie in Geschichte und Gegenwart*. Tübingen: Mohr Siebeck 2002, 59–60.

ries between theology and philosophy are rather fluid, perhaps even super-fluous. Arguably, in an Aristotelian sense there is no substantial difference whether one approaches the question of God from a theological or philo-sophical point of view. For Bonhoeffer, however, the methodological movement between the two disciplines is such that philosophy is the hand-maid of theology. As we saw, Bonhoeffer attempts to integrate the two disciplines, ever being mindful of their limits and strengths. Philosophical and theological reflection shaped his sense of the limitation of philosophy, the inadequacy of Heidegger's cate- gory of "possibility," the need for rev-elation and God's Word, the contours of theological exegesis, the centrality of Scripture, and the conviction that all of these insights bear on the proc-lamation of God's Word in the sermon. To be sure, philosophy and theol-ogy are important to Bonhoeffer's thought, but mainly in the way that scaffolding is important for the construction of a building. When the building is complete, no one thinks of the scaffolding any longer. Some-where positioned between Barth's theology of the Word of God and Tillich's methodological correlation, Bonhoeffer integrated various disci-plines and fields of study in his own construction of a framework within which he could articulate the meaning of life. But the concretion and tangibility of that meaning was found principally in God's revealed Word and expressed foremost in the sermon. For ultimately only here, in the preaching of God's Word, was for Bonhoeffer the locus where philosophy, theology, and exegesis became the backbone for a life imbued with mean-ing.

Conclusion

16. The Way of Dietrich Bonhoeffer: Fragmentary Wholeness

Introduction

Sometimes our intellectual formation takes shape in ways we cannot anticipate. My encounter with Dietrich Bonhoeffer was one such moment on the path of my own intellectual and spiritual journey. When I was a student at the University of Tübingen, Bonhoeffer's name was a standard household item, so to speak. But for whatever reason I had read hardly any of his writings and his life was known to me in the familiar cliché of the pastor who resisted the Nazis and was murdered for it in a concentration camp at the end of the war.

The Beginning of the Journey

The first substantial step of the journey with Bonhoeffer came about in this way. My doctoral studies all finished, I finally put in practice what I had purposed in my mind for many years: to read Bonhoeffer's own writings. So in 1998 I purchased my first Bonhoeffer book: *Gemeinsames Leben* (*Life Together*). The reason I bought this book was not so much that it was one of the classic Bonhoeffer works, but simply because it was the cheapest in the new critical 17-volume hardcover series *Dietrich Bonhoeffer Werke (DBW)*. At that time, I had no intention to read all of these volumes as they amount to about 10.000 pages. And yet, as I started reading Bonhoeffer I was drawn irresistibly into his way of thinking and writing. Like many before me, I became fascinated with the freshness of his ideas, the brilliance of his theological insights and the personal courage of his life. It was a very long way, exactly one decade, but I did persevere and read all 10.000 pages. So without intention, more and more I was drawn into his writings and before I knew it, I had published essays and books, joined the International Bonhoeffer Society, became an elected Board member and joined the teams of editors and translators who produced the Dietrich Bonhoeffer Works English (*DBWE*).

The First Station on the Way

Bonhoeffer's *Life Together* – written at the request of his former students in a four week period after the closing of the Underground Seminary by the Gestapo – is a reflection on Christian community life as practiced at the seminary. As such it is not simply a manual for Christian community that can be used anachronistically in our contemporary context. Nonetheless, on almost every page I discovered golden nuggets that made me pause and reflect on them. Bonhoeffer writes about the dynamics between silence and speech, the importance of meditation and service, the need for genuine confession as the breakthrough to cross and community and so on. And yet, there was one topic that gripped me perhaps more profoundly than the others: Bonhoeffer's discussion of the characteristics between a genuine and an illusionary Christian community.

In a nutshell, this is what inspired me: Bonhoeffer argues that in genuine Christian community the foundation for human relationships and interaction is the fact that Christ is the mediator. In this context, Bonhoeffer is not speaking of Christ being the mediator of the divine-human relationship, but of the person-to-person relationship. For him, to claim that Christ is mediator implies that there is no direct human to human, soul to soul relationship.[1] Such an understanding, Bonhoeffer claims, is "of immeasurable significance."[2] As a theological statement, hardly any Christian would disagree that Christ is the mediator between human beings. This is not the difficulty. The real challenge of the claim has to with its psychological and sociological implications. In our postmodern age when human beings are drawn to each other for mostly emotional reasons, it is worth our while to listen to the fresh voice of Bonhoeffer's claim. This is at least how I encountered his words. As fallen beings, it is our nature to like those who like us. Often rather unconsciously, we want the other to be like us, we prefer the other to be "in our image." It is precisely this attempt to mold and sculpt the other according to our liking that is an illusion and ultimately destroys human relationships and community. For this reason, the theological statement that Christ is the sole mediator flows into the psychological release of

---

[1] Cf. *DBWE* 5, 32–33.
[2] *DBWE* 5, 34.

the other. What does this mean? In Bonhoeffer's own words, "this means that I must release others from all attempts to control, coerce, and dominate them with my love. In their freedom from me, other persons want to be loved for who they are, as those for whom Christ became a human being, died, and rose again... This is the meaning of the claim that we can encounter others only through the mediation of Christ. Self-centered love constructs its own image of other persons, about what they are and what they should become."[3] When I first read these lines, Bonhoeffer's words (in substantial ways I see parallels with Emmanuel Levinas' ideas on alterity and the face-to-face encounter) had a tremendously powerful and fresh impact on me. The way he phrased his conviction that human relations must be unconditional to the core struck me as being far more than a sophisticated manner to express theology. That Christ stands between people is tremendously freeing. It frees the Christian community from a false and cheap idealism about human bonding and protects it from becoming a club of privileged like-minded friends at the exclusion of the other. Bonhoeffer's claim that all human relationships are mediated through Christ still strikes me as the strongest possible foundation of human relations in general and also the church. The church, however, is also under the further demand to exemplify a life of costly grace.

As is well known, Bonhoeffer insists in his classic book *Discipleship* that the Lutheran discovery of grace – as important a corrective as it was during the Reformation – had by the beginning of the twentieth century been so radically misunderstood and misrepresented among Lutherans that the entire integrity of the Christian faith was at stake. In the vein of Kierkegaard's critique of Christendom and Karl Barth's deconstruction (curiously a term first used by Luther in theological debate and not the invention of postmodernism) of cultural Protestantism, Bonhoeffer attempted to redraw the map of grace to such an extent that its cheap abuse would once more yield a firm foundation for Christian life. The very first sentence of *Discipleship* leaves no doubt as to Bonhoeffer's intentions: "Cheap grace is the mortal enemy of our church. Our struggle today is for costly grace... Cheap grace means grace as doctrine, as principle, as system. It means forgiveness of sins as a general truth; it means God's love as merely a Christian idea of God."[4]

Bonhoeffer's achievement in *Discipleship* for me was his ability to articulate with utmost clarity what it means to follow the call of Jesus Christ in

---

[3] *DBWE* 5, 44.
[4] *DBWE* 4, 43.

such a way that it is neither simplistic nor unrealistic. The gist of his theology is straightforward: either the following of Christ is genuine, costly grace and therefore has an impact on how Christians live in the world or it is useless. It is therefore in accordance with his ideas in *Discipleship* when he later wrote in his unfinished *Ethics* that there is a political dimension of grace. Repeatedly he speaks of the way or the coming of grace. Since costly grace is not merely God's love as an idea, for Bonhoeffer it follows that "there is a depth of human bondage, of human poverty, and of human ignorance that hinders the gracious coming of Christ."[5] While firmly holding on the teaching that justification of the sinner comes solely by the grace of and faith in God, Bonhoeffer nonetheless argues that "there are conditions of the heart, of life, and in the world that especially hinder the receiving of grace."[6] Concretely, "the hungry person needs bread, the homeless person needs shelter, the one deprived of rights needs justice, the lonely person needs community, the undisciplined needs order, and the slave needs freedom. It would be blasphemy against God and the neighbor to leave the hungry unfed while saying that God is closest to those in deepest need… If the hungry do not come to faith, the guilt falls on those who denied them bread."[7]

Bonhoeffer's idea on grace – the unity of his theological articulation and the social political implications – was another decisive milestone for me when I first encountered it in his writings. He himself often used the expression "to stand on solid ground;" his teaching on grace has become such a solid ground in my own spiritual formation. I can go as far as saying that reading Bonhoeffer at the time I did was an experience that shaped my spiritual life to such an extent that without this encounter I may conceivably not be the same person. The insights I gained from his understanding of unconditional human relations mediated through the risen Christ coupled to his teaching on the power of grace have shaped my spiritual formation in immeasurable ways. And yet – this is only half the story. The other side, equally as important to me, is the manner in which reading Bonhoeffer had a significant influence on my intellectual formation.

---

[5] *DBWE* 6.
[6] *DBWE* 6, 162.
[7] *DBWE* 6, 163.

The Second Station on the Way

My first encounter with Bonhoeffer as a kind of spiritual mentor was very soon enhanced by my reading of his second academic dissertation, entitled *Act and Being. Transcendental Philosophy and Ontology in Systematic Theology*. As the subtitle of this book suggests, its theme is about theology and philosophy. This work is by far the most dense and demanding of all his works. It is a tightly argued engagement with the epistemological tradition since Kant and idealistic philosophy since Hegel. The key attempt of the young Bonhoeffer – he was only 24 years old, after he had finished his doctoral dissertation at age 21 – was to articulate a theologically and philosophically viable concept of revelation that neither does violence to the absolute being of God (Barth's influence on his thought) nor the contingency and concreteness of revelation in human life (the act character of revelation). On my first reading of *Act and Being* I was only partially able to understand the intricacies of his argument. At any rate, what did grab my attention immediately was his position that the human self cannot come to an adequate self-understanding (because of its fallenness) apart from revelation.

As I understand it, Bonhoeffer's argument unfolds in this way: He starts with an essentially epistemological presupposition by referring to Luther's dictum *sola fide credendum est nos esse peccatores* (we know by faith alone that we are sinners). In language often resembling Heidegger, he argues that as human beings we cannot know that we are sinners, for we have in us no organ that can arrive at such a conclusion. "Were it really a human possibility," he notes, "for persons themselves to know that they are sinners apart from revelation, neither 'being in Adam' nor 'being in Christ' would be existential designations for their being. For it would mean that human beings could place themselves into the truth, that they could somehow withdraw to a deeper being of their own, apart from their being sinners, their 'not being in the truth'."[8] In other words, Bonhoeffer understands being in Adam/Christ as possessing ontological reality. But, and this is crucial, the ontological category of being in Adam/sin is such that it is epistemologically impossible for a person to conclude that s/he belongs to such a category – apart from revelation.

Elsewhere Bonhoeffer explains the epistemological impasse in these terms. Everything comes down to "the decisive question that must be put to transcendentalism and idealism alike: Can the I understand itself out of

---

[8] *DBWE 2.*

itself?"[9] For Bonhoeffer, the answer is an emphatic negation. "The attempt to understand oneself purely from oneself must come to nothing because Dasein"[10] is never independent but in reference to the ontological reality of the fallen person. Put differently, the fallen self is always ontologically and epistemologically limited to the extent that it cannot know its own state of not being in the truth. The self as a starting point for self-knowledge is always limited by its own incapacity to see itself precisely in its own limit in the same way as the eye cannot see itself.[11]

More than I can explain in these terse lines here, I constructed from Bonhoeffer's reflections my own "solid ground" to stand on as far as ontology, epistemology and existence (*Dasein*) are concerned. More than any other thinker (Paul Tillich is important here as well) Bonhoeffer has helped me in staking out the intellectual matrix of my own human existence, the being of the world, the fallenness and finitude of all things, the existence of evil, my faith in God as the Triune One, the search for meaning and the freedom to be myself. I find in Bonhoeffer the genius to articulate a theology that upholds both a high view of Christology and at the same time a high view of the human being. I am not claiming that Bonhoeffer has helped me solve all of these questions in my life; I am merely saying that he has like no other thinker shaped the visible and invisible threads of my thinking.

The Third Station on the Way

After I had completed my doctoral dissertation on the concept of divine providence in Philo of Alexandria, it dawned on me one day (I cannot recall any details of that "revelation") that the structure of my thinking is interested in "system." By that I mean that I am interested in the larger, systemic questions and issues in life and not in the details. For example, I am interested in Pauline theology, that is to say the overarching questions, challenges and contexts of his life and teaching, and not in the exegetical details of a particular verse. I should clarify that these details are also important, but for my way of thinking they are subordinate to the larger whole.

---

[9] *DBWE* 2, 46.
[10] *DBWE* 2, 38.
[11] Cf. *DBWE* 2, 46.

With regards to Bonhoeffer's influence on my thinking: he opened up the spiritual and intellectual dimensions of my thinking on my journey to discover my own system (Bonhoeffer himself disliked the idea of system). Another way of putting these matters is to acknowledge that I discovered in him the attempt to articulate the important questions in life – before one attempts the answers. This sequence is crucial for me. Understanding the questions of *Dasein* is of primary hermeneutical significance; answers follow from the depth of our understanding of the questions. In some cases we may never arrive at a satisfying answer to a question.

In terms of my own intellectual (I use this term in deliberate distinction from "academic") journey, this is the path were I am on right now. Even though I have achieved a certain clarity and comprehensiveness in my theological thinking, I am still on this journey to clarify further and to ask the same questions over and over again in the hope to discover new insights. It may be an overstatement, but I do see life as an essentially hermeneutical endeavor. As human beings we are all engaged in this never-ending predicament of making sense of ourselves and the world around us. Bonhoeffer has helped me in establishing enough solid ground under my feet so that I could reach a certain maturity in my thinking. To say that I have gained a certain maturity in my thinking is not to say that I have adequately understood life's questions leave alone found viable answers. Indeed, to put it in the most precise terms, in spite of my penchant to think systematically and comprehensively, I have learned (to a large extent from Bonhoeffer) that life is in its very nature always incomplete and fragmentary. This brings me to my final point.

Fragmentary Wholeness

In spite of the fact that I am intensely preoccupied with theological and philosophical questions and that I am constantly engaged in the hermeneutical circle to make intelligible my own *Dasein* and that of the world, there is something beyond and above the intellectual life. It is, in short, life fully lived. While Bonhoeffer lived in unusual historical times – when Nazi crimes despised humanity and the church failed to speak out and resist in action – he somehow was able to make sense of his own life. What is so inspiring about his life is not that he has become a saint, or phenomenon or some kind of icon. What inspires me is the way in which he evaluates what he terms "the polyphony of life." On 21 July 1944, the day after the failed conspiracy on Hitler's life, he writes from prison to his best friend: I "am

still discovering right up to this moment, that it is only by living completely in this world that one learns to have faith. One must completely abandon
any attempt to make something of oneself, whether it be a saint, or a converted sinner, or a churchman (a so-called priestly type!), a righteous man
or an unrighteous one, a sick man or a healthy one. By this-worldliness
[*Diesseitigkeit*] I mean living unreservedly in life's duties, problems, successes and failures, experiences and perplexities. In so doing, we throw
ourselves completely into the arms of God, taking seriously, not our own
sufferings, but those of God in the world—watching with Christ in Gethsemane. That, I think, is faith; that is μετάνοια; and that is how one becomes a human and a Christian."[12]

What I learned from Bonhoeffer is this: although we take great pains in
thinking through the intricacies of our lives, the purpose of life is to live
every day in the knowledge that the power of God's love for ourselves and
for all of the world is sufficient to give it meaning, even if this meaning
must remain fragmentary in the whole of our lives.

---

[12] *DBWE* 8, 486.

Bibliography

Primary Sources

DBW 1   *Sanctorum Communio: Eine dogmatische Untersuchung zur Sozio-logie der Kirche.* Edited by Joachim von Soosten. Munich: Chr. Kaiser 1986.

DBWE 1   *Sanctorum Communio: A Theological Study of the Sociology of the Church.* Edited by Clifford J. Green. Translated by Reinhard Krauss and Nancy Lukens. Minneapolis: Fortress Press 1998.

DBW 2   *Akt und Sein: Transzendentalphilosophie und Ontologie in der systematischen Theologie.* Edited by Hans-Richard Reuter. Munich: Chr. Kaiser 1988.

DBWE 2   *Act and Being: Transcendental Philosophy and Ontology in Systematic Theology.* Edited by Wayne Whitson Floyd Jr. Translated by Martin Rumscheidt. Minneapolis: Fortress Press 1996.

DBW 3   *Schöpfung und Fall. Theologische Auslegung von Genesis 1–3.* Edited by Martin Rüter and Ilse Tödt. Munich: Chr. Kaiser 1989.

DBWE 3   *Creation and Fall: A Theological Exposition of Genesis 1–3.* Edited by John W. de Gruchy. Translated by Douglas Stephen Bax. Minneapolis: Fortress Press 1996.

DBW 4   *Nachfolge.* Edited by Martin Kuske and Ilse Tödt. Munich: Chr. Kaiser, 1989/Gütersloh: Gütersloher Verlagshaus, second edition 1994.

DBWE 4   *Discipleship.* Edited by Geffrey B. Kelly and John D. Godsey. Translated by Barbara Green and Reinhard Krauss. Minneapolis: Fortress Press 2001.

DBW 5   *Gemeinsames Leben. Das Gebetbuch der Bibel.* Edited by Gerhard Ludwig Müller and Albrecht Schönherr. Munich: Chr. Kaiser 1987.

DBWE 5   *Life Together* and *Prayerbook of the Bible.* Edited by Geffrey B. Kelly. Translated by Daniel W. Bloesch and James H. Burtness. Minneapolis: Fortress Press 1996.

DBW 6   *Ethik.* Edited by Ilse Tödt, Heinz Eduard Tödt, Ernst Feil, and Clifford Green. Munich: Chr. Kaiser/Gütersloher Verlagshaus, second edition 1998.

DBWE 6   *Ethics.* Edited by Clifford J. Green. Translated by Reinhard Krauss, Charles C. West, and Douglas W. Stott. Minneapolis: Fortress Press 2005.

DBW 7   *Fragmente aus Tegel.* Edited by Renate Bethge and Ilse Tödt. Gütersloh: Chr. Kaiser/Gütersloher Verlagshaus 1994.

DBWE 7   *Fiction from Tegel Prison.* Edited by Clifford J. Green. Translated by Nancy Lukens. Minneapolis: Fortress Press 2000.

DBW 8   *Widerstand und Ergebung.* Edited by Christian Gremmels, Eberhard Bethge and Renate Bethge, with Ilse Tödt. Gütersloh: Chr. Kaiser/ Gütersloher Verlagshaus 1998.

DBWE 8   Letters and Papers from Prison. Edited by John W. de Gruchy. Translated by Isabel Best, Lisa E. Dahill, Reinhard Krauss, Nancy Lukens, Barbara and Martin Rumscheidt and Douglas W. Stott. Minneapolis: Fortress Press 2010.

DBW 9   *Jugend und Studium 1918–1927.* Edited by Hans Pfeifer, with Clifford Green and Carl-Jürgen Kaltenborn. Munich: Chr. Kaiser 1986.

DBWE 9   *The Young Bonhoeffer: 1918–1927.* Edited by Paul Matheny, Clifford J. Green, and Marshall Johnson. Translated by Mary Nebelsick, with the assistance of Douglas W. Stott. Minneapolis: Fortress Press 2001.

DBW 10   *Barcelona, Berlin, Amerika 1928–1931.* Edited by Reinhard Staats and Hans-Christoph von Hase, with Holger Roggelin and Matthias Wünsche. Munich: Chr. Kaiser 1991.

DBWE 10 *Barcelona, Berlin, New York 1928–1931.* Edited by Clifford J. Green. Translated by Douglas W. Stott. Minneapolis: Fortress Press 2008.

DBW 11   *Ökumene, Universität, Pfarramt 1931–1932.* Edited by Eberhard Amelung and Christoph Strohm. Gütersloh: Chr. Kaiser/Gütersloher Ver-lagshaus 1994.

DBWE 11 *Ecumenical, Academic, and Pastoral Work: 1931–1932.* Edited by Victoria J. Barnett, Mark S. Brocker and Michael B. Lukens. Translated by Anne Schmidt-Lange, Isabell Best, Nicolas Humphrey, Marion Pauck and Douglas W. Stott. Minneapolis: Fortress Press 2012.

DBW 12   *Berlin: 1932–1933.* Edited by Carsten Nicolaisen und Ernst-Albert Scharffenorth. Gütersloh: Chr. Kaiser/Gütersloher Verlagshaus 1997.

DBWE 12 *Berlin: 1932–1933.* Edited by Larry L. Rasmussen. Translated by Isabell Best, David Higgins and Douglas W. Stott. Minneapolis: Fortress Press 2009.

DBW 13   *London 1933–1935.* Edited by Hans Goedeking, Martin Heimbucher, and Hans-Walter Schleicher. Gütersloh: Chr. Kaiser/ Gütersloher Verlagshaus 1994.

DBWE 13 *London 1933–1935.* Edited by Keith Clements. Translated by Isabel Best and Douglas W. Stott. Minneapolis: Fortress Press 2007.

DBW 14   *Illegale Theologenausbildung: Finkenwalde 1935–1937.* Edited by Otto Dudzus und Jürgen Henkys with Sabine Bobert-Stützel, Dirk Schulz, and Ilse Tödt. Gütersloh: Chr. Kaiser/Gütersloher Verlagshaus 1996.

DBWE 14   *Theological Education at Finkenwalde: 1935–1937.* Edited by H.
            Gaylon Barker and Mark S. Brocker. Translated by Douglas W.
            Stott. Minneapolis: Fortress Press 2013.
DBW 15   *Illegale Theologenausbildung: Sammelvikariate 1937–1940.* Edited
            by Dirk Schulz. Gütersloh: Chr. Kaiser/Gütersloher Verlagshaus,
            1998.
DBWE 15   *Theological Education Underground: 1937–1940.* Edited by Victo-
            ria J Barnett. Translated by Victoria J. Barnett, Claudia D. Berg-
            mann, Peter Frick, Scott A. Moore and Douglas W. Stott. Min-
            neapolis: Fortress Press 2012.
DBW 16   *Konspiration und Haft 1940–1945.* Edited by Jørgen Glenthøj,
            Ulrich Kabitz and Wolf Krötke. Gütersloh: Chr. Kaiser/Güters-
            loher Ver-lagshaus 1996.
DBWE 16   *Conspiracy and Imprisonment 1940–1945.* Edited by Mark Brocker.
            Translated by Lisa Dahill. Minneapolis: Fortress Press 2006.
DBW 17   *Register und Ergänzungen.* Edited by Herbert Anzinger and Hans
            Pfeiffer. Gütersloh: Chr. Kaiser/Gütersloher Verlagshaus 1999.
DBWE 17   *Indexes and Supplementary Materials.* Edited by Victoria J. Varnett,
            Barbara Vojhoski and Mark S. Brocker. Minneapolis: Fortress
            Press 2014.

Secondary Sources

Ackermann, Josef. *Dietrich Bonhoeffer – Freiheit hat offene Augen. Eine Biografie.*
    Gütersloh: Gütersloher Verlag 2006.

Arnold, Hardy. "Bruderhof-Korrespondenz," in *Bonhoeffer Jahrbuch/Yearbook* 2
    (2005–2006), 75–109.

Badiou, Alain. *Saint Paul. The Foundation of Universalism.* Stanford: Stanford Uni-
    versity Press 2003.

Barnett, Victoria J. "Dietrich Bonhoeffer's Relevance for a Post-Holocaust Christian
    Theology" in Peter Frick (ed). *Bonhoeffer and Interpretive Theory. Essays on
    Methods and Understanding,* 213–237.

Barth, Karl. *Evangelical Theology: An Introduction.* Translated by Grover Foley.
    New York: Holt, Rinehart and Winston, 1963.

Barth, Karl. *Gespräche 1963.* Gesamtausgabe IV, 41. Zurich: TVZ 2005.

Barth, Karl. *Offene Briefe 1945–1968,* Gesamtausgabe V 15. Zurich: TVZ 1984.

Barthes, Roland. "The Death of the Author," in idem. *Image, Music Text.* Glasgow:
    Fontana 1977, 142–148.

Bernasconi, Robert and Sybol Cook (eds). *Race and Racism in Continental Philo-
    sophy.* Bloomington: Indiana University Press 2003.

Bethge, Eberhard. *Dietrich Bonhoeffer. Theologian, Christian, Man of his Time. A
    Biography.* Translated and revised by Victoria Barnett. Minnesota: Fortress Press
    2000.

Bethge, Eberhard (ed). *Letters and Papers from Prison.* Translated by Reginald Fuller.
    New York: Macmillan Publishing 1971.

Bethge, Eberhard. "The Challenge of Dietrich Bonhoeffer's Life and Theology," in *WCA*, 22–88.

Beutel, Albrecht. *Gerhard Ebeling. Eine Biographie.* Tübingen: Mohr Siebeck 2012.

Biddis, Michael D. *Father of Racist Ideology: The Social and Political Thought of Count Gobineau.* London: Weidenfeld and Nicholson 1970.

Boff, Leonardo. *Jesus Christ Liberator. A Critical Christology for our Time.* Translated by Patrick Hughes. Maryknoll: Orbis Books 1972.

Botman, H. Russel. "Is Bonhoeffer Still of Any Use in South Africa?" in John W. de Gruchy (ed). *Bonhoeffer for a New Day. Theology in a Time of Transition.* Grand Rapids/Cambridge: William B. Eerdmans 1997, 366–372.

Buenzod, Janine. *La formation de la pensée de Gobineau et l'essai sur l'inégalité des races humaines.* Paris: Librairie A.-G. Nizet 1967.

Bultmann, Rudolf. "Die Bedeutung der neuerschlossenen mandäischen und manichäischen Quellen für das Verständnis des Johannesevangeliums," in *ZNW* 24 (1925), 100–146.

Bultmann, Rudolf. *Existence and Faith.* Edited by Schubert M. Odgen. Cleveland/New York: World Publishing Co. 1960.

Bultmann, Rudolf. *Faith and Understanding*, volume 1. Edited by Robert W. Funk. London: Harper & Row 1969.

Bultmann, Rudolf. "Neues Testament und Mythologie. Das Problem der Entmythologisierung der neutestamentlichen Verkündigung," in idem. *Offenbarung und Heilsgeschehen.* Munich: Lempp 1941, 27–69.

Bultmann, Rudolf. *New Testament and Mythology.* Philadelphia: Fortress Press, 1984.

Bultmann, Rudolf. *Offenbarung und Heilsgeschehen.* Munich: Lempp 1941.

Bultmann, Rudolf. "On the Question of Christology" in idem. *Faith and Understanding*, 116–144.

Bultmann, Rudolf. *The Gospel of John. A Commentary.* Philadelphia: Westminster Press 1971.

Bultmann, Rudolf. "The Historicity of Man and Faith" in idem. *Existence and Faith*, 92–110.

Rudolf, Bultmann. "The Question of Dialectic Theology: A Discussion with Peterson" in James M. Robinson (ed). *The Beginnings of Dialectic Theology.* Richmond: John Know Press 1968, 257–274.

Bultmann, Rudolf. "The Significance of 'Dialectical Theology' for the Scientific Study of the New Testament" in idem. *Faith and Understanding*, 145–164.

Bultmann, Rudolf. "What does it Mean to Speak of God" in idem. *Faith and Understanding*, 53–65.

Burke, Seán. *The Death and Return of the Author. Criticism and Subjectivity in Barthes, Foucault and Derrida.* Edinburgh: Edinburgh University Press, third edition 2008.

Caldas, Carlos. *Orlando Costas. Sua contribuição na historia da teologia latino-americana.* São Paulo: Editora Vida 2007.

Capozza, Nicoletta. *Im Namen der Treue zur Erde: Versuch eines Vergleichs zwischen Bonhoeffers und Nietzsches Denken.* Münster: LIT Verlag 2003.

Caputo, John. "Heidegger and Theology," in *CCH*, 326–344.

Clements, Keith. *Bonhoeffer*. London: SPCK Publishing 2010.

Clingan, Ralph Garlin. "Against Cheap Grace in a World Come of Age. A Study in the Hermeneutics of Adam Clayton Powell, 1865–1953, in His Intellectual Context," Drew University, Ph.D. dissertation 1997.

Cone, James H. *A Black Theology of Liberation*. Philadelphia: J.B. Lippincott 1970.

Cone, James H. *Risks of Faith: The Emergence of a Black Theology of Liberation, 1968–1998*. Boston: Beacon Press 1999.

Dabrock, Peter. "Responding to 'Wirklichkeit.' Reclaiming Bonhoeffer's Approach to Theological Ethics between Mystery and the Formation of the World," in Kirsten Busch Nielsen, Ulrik Nissen and Christiane Tietz (eds). *Mysteries in the Theology of Dietrich Bonhoeffer: A Copenhagen Bonhoeffer Symposium*, Forschungen zur systematischen und ökumenischen Theologie 119. Göttingen: Vandenhoeck & Ruprecht 2007, 49–80.

Dahill, Lisa E. *Reading from the Underside of Selfhood. Bonhoeffer and Spiritual Formation*. PTMS. Eugene: Pickwick Publications 2009.

Dahill, Lisa E. "'There's Some Contradiction Here': Gender and the Relation of *Above* and *Below* in Bonhoeffer," in Peter Frick (ed). *Bonhoeffer and Interpretive Theory. Essays on Methods and Understanding*, 53–84.

Davies, Alan. "The Ideology of Racism," in *Concilium* 151 (1982), 11–16.

Dilthey, Wilhelm. *Einleitung in die Geisteswissenschaften*, Gesammelte Schriften 1. Stuttgart: B.G. Teubner Verlagsgesellschaft, ninth edition 1995.

Dinkler, Erich (ed). *Zeit und Geschichte*. Dankesgabe an Rudolf Bultmann zum 80. Geburtstag. Tübingen: J.C.B. Mohr (Paul Siebeck) 1964.

Dramm, Sabine. *Dietrich Bonhoeffer. An Introduction to His Thought*. Peabody: Hendrickson 2007.

Dramm, Sabine. *Dietrich Bonhoeffer. Eine Einführung in sein Denken*. Gütersloh: Gütersloher Verlag 2001.

Ebeling, Gerhard. "Die 'nicht-religiöse Interpretation biblischer Begriffe'," in idem. *Wort und Glaube*. Tübingen: J.C.B. Mohr (Paul Siebeck), third edition, 1967, 90–160.

Ebeling, Gerhard. *Dogmatik des christlichen Glaubens*, 3 volumes. Tübingen: Mohr Siebeck, fourth edition 2012.

Ebeling, Gerhard. *Evangelische Evangelienauslegung: eine Untersuchung zu Luthers Hermeneutik*. Darmstadt: Wissenschaftliche Buchgesellschaft 1962.

Ebeling, Gerhard. "Gespräch über Dietrich Bonhoeffer," in idem. *Wort und Glaube*, vol. 4. Tübingen: J.C.B. Mohr [Paul Siebeck] 1995, 647–657 .

Ebeling, Gerhard. "Hauptprobleme der protestantischen Theologie in der Gegenwart. Anfragen an die Theologie," in idem. *Wort und Glaube*, vol. 2. Tübingen: J.C.B. Mohr [Paul Siebeck] 1969, 56–71.

Ebeling, Gerhard. "Hermeneutik," in *Die Religion in Geschichte und Gegenwart*. Tübingen: J.C.B. Mohr [Paul Siebeck] third edition 1962, vol. 3, 242–262.

Ebeling, Gerhard. *Umgang mit Luther*. Tübingen: J.C.B. Mohr [Paul Siebeck] 1983.

Ebeling, Gerhard. *Word and Faith*. Philadelphia: Fortress Press 1963.

Ebeling, Gerhard. "Word of God and Hermeneutics," in idem. *Word and Faith*, 305–332.

Feil, Ernst. *The Theology of Dietrich Bonhoeffer.* Translated by Martin Rumscheidt. Philadelphia: Fortress Press 1985.

Feil, Ernst and Barbara E. Fink (eds). *International Bibliography on Dietrich Bonhoeffer/Internationale Bibliographie zu Dietrich Bonhoeffer.* Gütersloh: Chr. Kaiser/Gütersloher Verlagshaus 1998.

Fink, Eugen. *Nietzsche's Philosophy.* New York: Continuum, 2003.

Floyd, Wayne Whitson. "Encounter with an Other: Immanuel Kant and G. W. F. Hegel in the Theology of Dietrich Bonhoeffer," in Peter Frick (ed). *Bonhoeffer's Intellectual Formation: Theology and Philosophy in His Thought*, 83–119.

Floyd, Wayne Whitson and Charles Marsh (eds). *Theology and Practice of Responsibility. Essays on Dietrich Bonhoeffer. Valley Forge: Trinity Press International* 1994.

Franz, Markus. "Inside and Beyond the 'Bonhoeffer-Archive' – Foucaultian Reflections on the Discourse of Bonhoeffer's Life and Theology," in Peter Frick (ed). *Bonhoeffer and Interpretive Theory. Essays on Methods and Understanding*, 27–51.

Frick, Peter (ed). *Bonhoeffer and Interpretive Theory. Essays on Methods and Understanding.* International Bonhoeffer Interpretations 6. Frankfurt: Peter Lang 2013.

Frick, Peter (ed). *Bonhoeffer's Intellectual Formation. Theology and Philosophy in his Thought.* Religion in Philosophy and Theology 29. Tübingen: Mohr Siebeck 2008.

Fukuyama, Francis. *After the Neocons: America at the Crossroads.* London: Profile 2006.

Fukuyama, Francis. *America at the Crossroads: Democracy, Power, and the Neoconservative Legacy.* New Haven: Yale University Press 2006.

Fukuyama, Francis. *The End of History and the Last Man.* New York: Free Press 1992.

Gadamer, Hans-Georg. "Martin Heidegger und die Marburger Theologie" in Erich Dinkler (ed). *Zeit und Geschichte.* Dankesgabe an Rudolf Bultmann zum 80. Geburtstag. Tübingen: J. C. B. Mohr (Paul Siebeck) 1964, 479–490.

Gadamer, Hans-Georg. "Text und Interpretation," in *Wahrheit und Methode. Ergänzungen, Register.* Tübingen: J. C. B. Mohr (Paul Siebeck) 1986, 334–360.

Gadamer, Hans-Georg. *Wahrheit und Methode. Grundzüge einer philosophischen Hermeneutik.* Tübingen: Mohr Siebeck, seventh edition 2010.

Gerlach, Wolfgang. *And the Witnesses Were Silent: The Confessing Church and the Persecution of the Jews.* Translated and edited by Victoria J. Barnett. Lincoln: University of Nebraska Press 2000.

Goldhagen, Daniel Jonah. *Hitler's Willing Executioners: Ordinary Germans and the Holocaust.* New York: Knopf 1996.

Goleano, Eduardo. *Open Veins of Latin America. Five Centuries of the Pillage of a Continent.* New York: Monthly Review Press 1973.

Green, Clifford. *Bonhoeffer. A Theology of Sociality.* Grand Rapids: Eerdmans, revised edition 1999.

Green, Clifford. "Bonhoeffer at Union. Critical Turning Points: 1931 and 1939," in *Union Seminary Quarterly Review* 62 (2010), 1–16.

Green, Clifford. "Bonhoeffer, Modernity and Liberation Theology," in Wayne Whitson Floyd, Jr. and Charles Marsch (eds). *Theology and the Practice of Responsibility. Essays on Dietrich Bonhoeffer*, 117–131.

Green Clifford and Thomas Tseng (eds). *Dietrich Bonhoeffer und Sino-Theologie/ Dietrich Bonhoeffer and Sino-Theology*, Sino-Christian Studies Supplement Series 1. Taipei: Chung Yuan Christian University 2008.

Gregor, Brian. "The Critique of Religion and Post-Metaphysical Faith: Bonhoeffer's Influence on Ricoeur's Hermeneutic of Religion," in Matthew D. Kirkpatrick (ed). *Engaging Bonhoeffer: The Impact and Influence of Bonhoeffer's Life and Thought*. Minneapolis: Fortress Press 2016, 259–282.

Gregor, Brian and Jens Zimmermann (eds). *Bonhoeffer and Continental Thought: Cruciform Philosophy*. Bloomington/Indianapolis: Indiana University Press 2009.

Grondin, Jean. *Einführung zu Gadamer*, UTB 2139. Tübingen: Mohr Siebeck 2000.

Gutiérrez, Gustavo. *A Theology of Liberation: History, Politics, and Salvation*. Translated by Sister Caridad Inda and John Eagleson. Maryknoll: Orbis Books, revised edition, 1988.

Gutiérrez, Gustavo. *Las Casas. In Search of the Poor of Jesus Christ*. Maryknoll: Orbis Books 1993.

Gutiérrez, Gustavo. "The Limitations of Modern Theology: On a Letter of Dietrich Bonhoeffer," in idem. *The Power of the Poor in History*, 222–234.

Gutiérrez, Gustavo. *The Power of the Poor in History: Selected Writings*. Maryknoll: Orbis Books 1983.

Gutiérrez, Gustavo. "Theology from the Underside of History," in idem. *The Power of the Poor in History*, 169–221.

Hall, Douglas John. "Ecclesia Crucis: The Disciple Community and the Future of the Church in North America," in Wayne Whitson Floyd, Jr. and Charles Marsh (eds). *Theology and Practice of Responsibility. Essays on Dietrich Bonhoeffer*, 70–73.

Harbsmeier, Götz. "Die 'nicht-religiöse Interpretation biblischer Begriffe' bei Bonhoeffer und die Entmythologisierung," in Ernst Wolf, Charlotte von Kirschbaum and Rudolf Frey (eds). *Antwort*. Karl Barth zum Siebzigsten Geburtstag am 10. Mai 1956. Zurich 1956, 544–561.

Hartwich, Wolf-Daniel, Aleida Assman and Jan Assman, afterword to Jacob Taubes. *The Political Theology of Paul*. Stanford: Stanford University Press 2004.

Harvey, Barry. "Augustine and Thomas Aquinas in the Theology of Dietrich Bonhoeffer," in Peter Frick, *Bonhoeffer's Intellectual Formation. Theology and Philosophy in his Thought*, 11–29.

Harvey, Barry. *Taking Hold of the Real. Dietrich Bonhoeffer and the Profound Worldliness of Christianity*. Eugene: Cascade Books 2015.

Hatab, Lawrence J. *Nietzsche's Life Sentence. Coming to Terms with Eternal Recurrence*. New York/London: Routledge 2005.

Havenstein, Martin. *Nietzsche als Erzieher*. Berlin: E. S. Mittler 1922.

Haynes, Stephen. *The Bonhoeffer Phenomenon: Portraits of a Protestant Saint*. Minneapolis: Fortress Press 2004.

Healey, Joseph P. "Peace. Old Testament," and William Klassen, "Peace. New Testament," in David Noel Freedman (ed). *Anchor Bible Dictionary*. New York: Doubleday 1992, vol. 5, 206–212.

Hegel, Georg W. F. *Lectures on the Philosophy of Religion*, vol. 3. Edited by Peter C. Hodgson. Berkeley and Los Angeles: University of California Press 1984.

Heidegger, Martin. *Being and Time*. Translated by John Macquarrie and Edward Robinson. New York: Harper and Row Publishers 1962.

Hinkelammert, Franz. "Pensar en alternativas: capitalismo, socialismo y la posibilidad de otro mundo," in Jorge Pixley (ed). *Por un mundo otro. Alternativas al Mercado global*. Quito: Consejo Latinoamericano de Iglesias 2003, 11–28.

Hopkins, Dwight N. *Being Human: Race, Culture and Religion*. Minneapolis: Fortress Press 2005.

Hopkins, Dwight N. *Introducing Black Theology of Liberation*. Maryknoll: Orbis Books 1999.

Horkheimer, Max. *Critical Theory: Selected Essays*. New York: Herder and Herder 1972.

Horkheimer, Max. "Traditionelle und kritische Theorie," in idem. *Kritische Theorie*. Frankfurt: Fischer 1968, vol. 2.

Horkheimer, Max. "Thoughts on Religion," in idem. *Critical Theory: Selected Essays*, 130–131.

Hübner, Hans. *Nietzsche und das Neue Testament*. Tübingen: Mohr Siebeck 2000.

Hübner, Hans. "'Existentiale' Interpretation bei Rudolf Bultmann und Martin Heidegger," in *ZThK* 103 (2006), 533–567.

Hunger, Margaret L. *Race, Gender, and the Politics of Skin Tone*. New York and London: Routledge 2005.

Ignatius of Loyola. *The Spiritual Exercises of St. Ignatius*. Translated by Louis J. Puhl, Vintage Spiritual Classic. New York: Vintage 2000.

Jaspers, Karl. *Nietzsche: Eine Einführung in das Verständnis seines Philosophierens*. Berlin: Walter de Gruyter 1936.

Kaufmann, Walter. *The Portable Nietzsche*. Selected and translated, with an Introduction, Preface and Notes. New York: Viking 1968.

Kelly, Geffrey B. "Kierkegaard as 'Antidote' and as Impact on Dietrich Bonhoeffer's Concept of Christian Discipleship," in Peter Frick (ed). *Bonhoeffer's Intellectual Formation. Theology and Philosophy in his Thought*, 145–165.

Kirkpatrick, Matthew D. (ed). *Engaging Bonhoeffer: The Impact and Influence of Bonhoeffer's Life and Thought*. Minneapolis: Fortress Press 2016.

Klein, Naomi. *The Shock Doctrine. The Rise of Disaster Capitalism*. Toronto: Knopf 2008.

Kolb, Robert and Timothy J. Wengert (eds). *Book of Concord: Confessions of the Evangelical Lutheran Church*. Minneapolis: Fortress Press 2000.

Knox, Robert. *Races of Man: A Fragment*. Philadelphia: Lea and Blanchard 1850.

Köpf, Ulrich. "Thomas von Kempen," in *TRE* 33, 480–483.

Köster, Peter. "Nietzsche als verborgener Antipode in Bonhoeffers 'Ethik'," in *Nietzsche Studien* 19 (1990), 367–419.

Krause, Gerhard. "Dietrich Bonhoeffer (1906–1945)," in *TRE* 7, 55–66.

Krause, Gerhard. "Dietrich Bonhoeffer und Rudolf Bultmann," in Erich Dinkler (ed). *Zeit und Geschichte*, 439–460.

Kreis, Rudolf. *Antisemitismus und Kirche: In den Gedächtnislücken deutscher Geschichte mit Heine, Freud, Kafka und Goldhagen*. Hamburg: Rowohlt 1999.

Krötke, Wolf. "Dietrich Bonhoeffer and Martin Luther," in Peter Frick (ed). *Bonhoeffer's Intellectual Formation. Theology and Philosophy in his Thought*, 57–60.

Levinas, Emmanuel. *God, Death and Time*. Translated by Bettina Bergo. Stanford: Stanford University Press 2000.

Levinas, Emmanuel. *Of God Who Comes to Mind*. Translated by Bettina Bergo. Stanford: Stanford University Press 1998.

Marsh, Charles. *Reclaiming Dietrich Bonhoeffer. The Promise of his Theology*. New York: Oxford University Press 1994.

Marty, Martin E. *Dietrich Bonhoeffer's Letters and Papers from Prison. A Biography*. Princeton: Princeton University Press 2011.

Metaxas, Eric. *Bonhoeffer: Pastor, Martyr, Prophet, Spy*. Nashville: Thomas Nelson 2010.

Moltmann, Jürgen. *A Broad Place. An Autobiography*. Translated by Margaret Kohl. Minneapolis: Fortress Press 2008.

Moltmann, Jürgen. "An Open Letter to José Miguez Bonino," in *Christianity and Crisis* 29 (1976), 57.

Moltmann, Jürgen. "Dietrich Bonhoeffer und die Theologie. Eine persönliche Würdigung," in Clifford Green and Thomas Tseng (eds). *Dietrich Bonhoeffer and Sino-Theology*, 15–33.

Moltmann, Jürgen. *Herrschaft Christi und soziale Wirklichkeit nach Dietrich Bonhoeffer*. Munich: Chr. Kaiser 1959.

Morino, Zen-emon. "Zur Logik und Ethik der Nachfolge [Thomas a Kempis und Luther, Kierkegaard und Bonhoeffer]," in *Fukujû no Roni to Roni (Evangelium und Welt)* 3 (1965), 26–31.

Moyo, Dambisa. *Dead Aid. Why Aid is Not Working and How there is a Better Way for Africa*. New York: Farrar, Straus and Giroux 2009.

Patrella, Ivan (ed). "Liberation Theology – A Programmatic Statement," in *Latin American Liberation Theology. The Next Generation*. Maryknoll: Orbis Books 2005, 147–172.

Plant, Stephen. *Bonhoeffer*. London/New York: Continuum 2004.

Plant, Stephen. "'In the Sphere of the Familiar.' Heidegger and Bonhoeffer," in Peter Frick (ed). *Bonhoeffer's Intellectual Formation. Theology and Philosophy in his Thought*, 301–327.

Polak, Paul. *Out of Poverty. What Works when Traditional Approaches Fail*. San Francisco: Berret-Koehler 2008.

Rasmussen, Larry. "Interview mit Herbert Jehle (1.3.1968)," in *Bonhoeffer Jahrbuch/Yearbook* 2 (2005–2006), 110–121.

Richard, Pablo. *Fuerza ética y espiritual de la teología de la liberación. En el context actual de la globilización*. San José: Departamento Ecuménico de Investigaciones 2004.

Ricoeur, Paul. "The Hermeneutics of Testimony," in *Essays on Biblical Interpretation*, edited by Lewis S. Mudge. Philadelphia: Fortress Press 1980, 119–154.

Roberts, J. Deotis. *Bonhoeffer and King: Speaking Truth to Power*. Louisville: Westminster John Knox Press 2005.

Roberts, J. Deotis. *Liberation and Reconciliation: A Black Theology*. Philadelphia: The Westminster Press 1971.

Robinson, James M. (ed). *The Beginnings of Dialectic Theology*. Richmond 1968.

Rott, Wilhelm. "Something Always Occurred to Him," in Wolf-Dieter Zimmerman and Ronald Gregor Smith (eds). *I Knew Dietrich Bonhoeffer*, 130–137.

Salaquarda, Jörg. "Dionysus versus the Crucified One: Nietzsche's Understanding of the Apostle Paul," in James C. O'Flaherty, Timothy F. Sellner and Robert M. Helm (eds). *Studies in Nietzsche and the Judeo-Christian Tradition*. Chapel Hill/London: The University of North Carolina Press 1985, 100–129.

Scharlemann, Robert P. "Authenticity and Encounter: Bonhoeffer's Appropriation of Ontology," in Wayne Floyd and Charles Marsh (eds). *Theology and the Practice of Responsibility. Essays on Dietrich Bonhoeffer*, 253–265.

Schleiermacher, Friedrich. *On Religion. Speeches to its Cultural Despisers*. Translated by John Oman. New York: Harper Torchbooks 1958.

Schliesser, Christine. "Verantwortung nach Bonhoeffer: Armut als Fallbeispiel," in John W. Gruchy, Stephen Plant and Christiane Tietz (eds). *Dietrich Bonhoeffers Theologie heute. Dietrich Bonhoeffer's Theology Today. Ein Weg zwischen Fundamentalismus und Säkularismus? A Way between Fundamentalism and Secularism?* Gütersloh: Gütersloher Verlagshaus 2009, 292–304.

Schlingensiepen, Ferdinand. *Dietrich Bonhoeffer 1906–1945. Martyr, Thinker, Man of Resistance*. Translated by Isabel Best. London/New York: T & T Clark 2010.

Schmithals, Walter. "Rudolf Bultmann," in *TRE* 7, 387–396.

Schroeder, Steven. "The End of History and the New World Order," in Wayne Whitson Floyd, Jr. and Charles Marsh (eds). *Theology and the Practice of Responsibility*, 21–38.

Scully, Vincent. "Thomas à Kempis," in *Catholic Encyclopedia*. New York: Robert Appleton Company 1912, volume 15.

Segundo, Juan Luis. *Grace and the Human Condition. A Theology for Artisans of a New Humanity*, Vol. 2. Maryknoll: Orbis 1973.

Segundo, Juan Luis. *The Liberation of Theology*. Translated by John Drury. Maryknoll: Orbis Books 1976.

Smith, Ronald Gregor (ed). *World Come of Age. A Symposium on Dietrich Bonhoeffer*. London: Colins 1967.

Sobrino, Jon. *Christology at the Crossroads*. Translated by John Drury. Maryknoll: Orbis Books 1976.

Sobrino, Jon. "Five Hundred Years. Structural Sin and Structural Grace," in idem. *The Principle of Mercy. Taking the Crucified People from the Cross*. Maryknoll: Orbis Books 1994.

Sobrino, Jon. *Jesus the Liberator*. Translated by Paul Burns and Francis McDonagh. Maryknoll: Orbis Books 1993.

Sobrino, Jon. *Where is God? Earthquakes, Terrorism, Barbarity, and Hope*. Maryknoll: Orbis Books 2004.

Staubach, Nikolaus. "Thomas von Kempen," *RGG*[4] 8, 377.

Taubes, Jacob. *The Political Theology of Paul.* Stanford: Stanford University Press 2004.

Thiessen Nation, Mark and G. Siegrist and Daniel P. Umbel, *Bonhoeffer the Assassin? Challenging the Myth, Recovering His Call to Peacemaking.* Grand Rapids: Baker Academic 2013.

Thomas à Kempis. Werke, vol. 2, *Imitatio Christi.* Freiburg: Herder 1904.

Tietz, Christiane. "Friedrich Schleiermacher and Dietrich Bonhoeffer," in Frick (ed). *Bonhoeffer's Intellectual Formation. Theology and Philosophy in his Thought,* 121–143.

Tietz, Christiane. "Unzeitgemäße Aktualität. Religionskritik in Zeiten der 'Wiederkehr der Religion'," in Ingolf U. Dalferth and Hans-Peter Grosshans (eds). *Kritik der Religion,* Religion in Philosophy and Theology 23. Tübingen: Mohr Siebeck 2006, 243–258.

Tietz-Steiding, Christiane. *Bonhoeffers Kritik der verkrümmten Vernunft.* Beiträge zur historischen Theologie 112. Tübingen: Mohr Siebeck 1999.

Tillich, Paul. *A History of Christian Thought.* New York: Harper & Row 1968.

Tillich, Paul. *Die Frage nach dem Unbedingten. Schriften zur Religionsphilosophie. Gesammelte Werke* 5, Stuttgart: Evangelisches Verlagswerk 1964.

Tillich, Paul. "Die Idee der Offenbarung" (1927) in *Main Works/Hauptwerke,* vol. 6, Gert Hummel (ed). Berlin/NewYork: Walter de Gruyter 1992, 99–106.

Tillich, Paul. *Die religiöse Lage der Gegenwart* (Berlin: Ullstein 1926) in *Main Works/ Hauptwerke,* vol. 5, Robert P. Scharlemann (ed). Berlin/NewYork: Walter de Gruyter 1988.

Tillich, Paul. *Masse und Geist. Studien zur Philosophie der Masse.* Berlin: Verlag der Arbeitsgemeinschaft 1922.

Tillich, Paul. "Offenbarung: Religionsphilosopisch" (1930) in *Main Works/ Hauptwerke,* vol. 4, John Clayton (ed). Berlin/NewYork: Walter de Gruyter 1987, 237–242.

Tillich, Paul. *Offenbarung und Glaube,* Gesammelte Werke 8. Stuttgart: Evangelisches Verlagswerk 1970.

Tillich, Paul. *Systematic Theology,* 3 volumes. Chicago: Chicago University Press 1951, 1957, 1963.

Tödt, Ilse (ed). *Dietrich Bonhoeffers Hegel-Seminar 1933. Nach Aufzeichnungen von Ferenc Lehel.* Munich: Chr. Kaiser 1988.

Trowitzsch, Michael. "Jesus Christus: Wahrheit der Kirche, Einheit der Wirklichkeit – oder: Bonhoeffer und die Postmoderne," in Michael Trowitzsch (ed). *Über die Moderne hinaus: Theologie im Übergang.* Tübingen: Mohr Siebeck 1999, 159–173.

Tseng, Thomas. "Christologie und Eschatologie. Das Letzte und Vorletzte bei Dietrich Bonhoeffer," in Clifford Green and Thomas Tseng (eds). *Dietrich Bonhoeffer und Sino-Theologie/Dietrich Bonhoeffer and Sino-Theology,* 319–359.

Tylenda, Joseph N. *The Imitation of Christ.* New York: Vintage, revised edition 1998.

Weischedel, Wilhelm (ed). *Immanuel Kant. Werke in sechs Bänden.* Wiesbaden/ Darmstadt: Insel 1956–1964.

Williams, Reggie L. *Bonhoeffer's Black Jesus. Harlem Renaissance Theology and an Ethic of Resistance.* Waco: Baylor University Press, 2014.

Williams, Stephen N. *The Shadow of the Antichrist. Nietzsche's Critique of Christianity*. Grand Rapids: Baker Academic, 2006.

Wilmer, Haddon. "Costly Discipleship," in *CCDB*, 173–189.

Woltersdorff, Nicholas. "Resuscitating the Author," in Kevin J. Vanhoozer, James K. A. Smith and Bruce Ellis Benson (eds). *Hermeneutics at the Crossroads*. Bloomington: Indiana University Press 2006, 35–50.

Wüstenberg, Ralf. *A Theology of Life: Dietrich Bonhoeffer's Religionless Christianity*. Grand Rapids: Eerdmans 1998.

Young, Josiah Ulysses. "Dietrich Bonhoeffer and Three Black Writers: James W. Johnson, Langston Hughes and Countee Cullen," in Peter Frick (ed). *Bonhoeffer and Interpretive Theory. Essays on Methods and Understanding*, 85–98.

Young, Josiah Ulysses. *No Difference in the Fare: Dietrich Bonhoeffer and the Problem of Racism*. Grand Rapids: Eerdmans 1998.

Zerner, Ruth. "Church, State and the 'Jewish Question,'" in *CCDB*, 190–205.

Zimmerling, Peter. *Bonhoeffer als praktischer Theologe*. Göttingen: Vandenhoeck & Ruprecht 2006.

Zimmermann, Jens. *Recovering Theological Hermeneutics. An Incarnational-Trinitarian Theory of Interpretation*. Grand Rapids: Baker Academics 2004.

Zimmermann, Wolf-Dieter and Ronald Gregor Smith (eds). *I Knew Dietrich Bonhoeffer: Reminiscences by his Friends*. Translated by Ka̎the Gregor Smith. New York: Harper and Row Publishers 1966.

Index of Subjects

Note: a page reference in italics indicates that a subject entry is only mentioned in the footnotes.

Index of Names

Note: a page reference in italics indicates that a person is only mentioned in the footnotes.

Acknowledgements

1. "Dietrich Bonhoeffer: Engaging Intellect – Legendary Life," in *Religion Compass* 6/6 (2012), 309–322. Used by permission, John Wiley and Sons.

2. "Understanding Bonhoeffer: from Default to Hermeneutic Reading," in Peter Frick (ed). *Bonhoeffer and Interpretive Theory: Essays on Methods and Understanding*, International Bonhoeffer Interpretations 6, Frankfurt: Peter Lang 2013, 9–26. Used by permission, Peter Lang Verlag.

3. "*Interpretatio quaerens intellectum* – 'Translation Seeking Understanding': The Hermeneutics of Translating Bonhoeffer," in *Theology* 115 (2012), 330–338. Used by permission, SPCK Publishing.

4. "The *Imitatio Christi* of Thomas à Kempis and Dietrich Bonhoeffer," in Peter Frick (ed). *Bonhoeffer's Intellectual Formation. Theology and Philosophy in His Thought*, RPT 29. Tübingen: Mohr Siebeck 2008, 31–52. Used by permission, Mohr Siebeck Verlag.

5. "Friedrich Nietzsche's Aphorisms and Dietrich Bonhoeffer's Theology," in Peter Frick (ed). *Bonhoeffer's Intellectual Formation. Theology and Philosophy in His Thought*, RPT 29. Tübingen: Mohr Siebeck 2008, 175–199. Used by permission, Mohr Siebeck Verlag.

6. "Nietzsche's *Übermensch* and Bonhoeffer's *mündiger Mensch*: Are They of Any Use for a Contemporary Christian Anthropology?," in *Sino-Christian Studies. An International Journal of Bible, Theology and Philosophy* 7 (2009), 9–42. Used by permission.

7. "Rudolf Bultmann, Paul Tillich and Dietrich Bonhoeffer," in Peter Frick (ed). *Bonhoeffer's Intellectual Formation. Theology and Philosophy in His Thought*, RPT 29. Tübingen: Mohr Siebeck 2008, 225–244. Used by permission, Mohr Siebeck Verlag.

8. "Dietrich Bonhoeffer and Gerhard Ebeling: An Encounter of Theological Minds," in Matthew D. Kirkpatrick (ed). *Engaging Bonhoeffer. The Impact and Influence of Bonhoeffer's Life and Thought*. Minneapolis: Fortress Press 2016, 239–258. Used by permission, Fortress Press.

9. "Bonhoeffer and Philosophy," translation of "Bonhoeffers philosophische Gesprächspartner," forthcoming in Christiane Tietz (ed). *Bonhoeffer Handbuch*. Tübingen: Mohr Siebeck 2016. Used by permission, Mohr Siebeck Verlag.

10. "Notes on Bonhoeffer's Theological Anthropology: The Case of Racism," in Jeremy M. Bergen, Paul G. Doerksen and Paul Koop (eds). *Creed and Conscience. Essays in Honour of A. James Reimer.* Kitchener: Pandora Press 2007, 135–151. Used by permission, Pandora Press.

11. "Bonhoeffer's Theology and Economic Humanism: an Exploration in Interdisciplinary Sociality," in Brian Gregor and Jens Zimmermann (eds). *Being Human, Becoming Human: Dietrich Bonhoeffer and Social Thought.* Eugene, OR: Pickwick Publications 2010, 49–68.

12. "Bonhoeffer, Theology and Religion: What do they Teach us for a South-North Dialogue?," in *Ciências da Religião - História e Sociedade,* 8 (2009), 168–191. Used by Permission.

13. "Bonhoeffer on the Social-Political Dimension of Grace," in Kirsten Busch Nielsen, Ralf K. Wüstenberg and Jens Zimmermann (eds). *Dem Rad in die Speichen fallen. Das Politische in der Theologie Dietrich Bonhoeffers/A Spoke in the Wheel. The Political in the Theology of Dietrich Bonhoeffer.* Gütersloh: Gütersloher Verlagshaus 2013, 137–149. Used by permission, Gütersloher Verlagshaus.

14. "What does Hiroshima have to do with Berlin? Dietrich Bonhoeffer on Theology, Peace and Social Responsibility," previously unpublished.

15. "Bonhoeffer the Preacher: Philosophy and Theology in the Service of the Sermon," in *Toronto Journal of Theology* 25 (2009), 77–93. Used by permission, University of Toronto Press.

16. "The Way of Bonhoeffer: Fragmentary Wholeness," in Darrol Bryant (ed). *Ways of the Spirit. Celebrating Dialogue, Diversity & Spirituality,* vol. 3. Kitchener: Pandora Press 2015, 234–242. Used by permission, Pandora Press.